D1596490

INNOCENT VICTIMS

Author's Note

All of the stories related in this book are true and represent a small fraction of the rescues carried out by Meryl Harrison and her SPCA colleagues during Zimbabwe's land invasions.
Some names have been changed for security reasons.

Catherine Buckle

INNOCENT VICTIMS

Rescuing the stranded animals of
Zimbabwe's farm invasions

Meryl Harrison's extraordinary story
by Catherine Buckle

MERLIN UNWIN BOOKS

First published in Great Britain by Merlin Unwin Books, 2009

Published by:
Merlin Unwin Books
Palmers House
7 Corve Street
Ludlow
Shropshire SY8 1DB
U.K.

www.merlinunwin.co.uk

Designed and set in Bembo by Merlin Unwin
Printed in England by TJ International, Padstow, England

ISBN 978-1-906122-07-2

For Colin and Roly – the past,
for Nick and Tim – the present,
for the Animals of Zimbabwe – our future.

And in memory of all the animals who died in
Zimbabwe's farm invasions.

Contents

Acknowledgements

Firstly, and most importantly, respect and gratitude go to Meryl's co-workers. Their courage and teamwork were exemplary, their bravery, dedication and determination saved the lives of so many.

Thank you: Simon Chikadaya, John Chikomo, Addmore Chinhembe, Steven Mabvuta, Mark Manhuwa, Justin Samakande, Mathias Tengaruwa, Jimmy Zuze.

Thank you to the farmers who agreed to have the stories of their animals included in this book. Men and women who lost everything, often in the most violent and terrifying circumstances, and yet agreed to relive the memories and revisit the horrors. Men, women and children who will forever cherish the memories of the animals that Meryl and her team rescued.

Thank you: Tommy Bayley, Roy and Heather Bennett, Roger Birdwood, Vicky and Peter Bowen, Guy and Rosalind Cartwright, Ian and Jo Cochrane, Ed and Pat Cumming, Debbie du Toit (now Tingle), Mark Ford, Andy and Elva Fraser, Fred and Denise Gaisford, Charl and Tertia Geldenhuys, Rob Gordon, Guy Hilton Barber, Paul and Jenny Hill, Liena Hoffman, Paul and Di Hopcroft, Kerry and Iain Kay, Ann and Sandy Murray, Alan and Jenny Parsons, Stuart and Peepes Reid, Chris and Eleanor Shepard, Alastair and Fiona Smith, Sandie and Chalkie van Schalkwyk, Rachel and Shannon Wheeler, Lesley and Alan Windrum.

To Meryl's colleagues and friends who gave advice, practical help, financial and moral assistance, friendship and sometimes a shoulder to cry on.

Thank you: Linda Ainsworth, Rob and Belinda Bowie, Fred Bridgland, Sue Burr, Mike Clarke, Pippa Cory, Juanita Crawford, Jimmy and Mignon Dodds, Dr Ant Donohoe, Claire and Mark Evans, Dr Chris Foggin, Patricia Glyn, Dr Rob Gordon, Cherry Grobler, Dr Astrid Huelin, Dr Stuart Hargreaves, Grettl Hughes, Gerry Jackson, Maryanne Jacobs, Ann Kempen, Stella Killick, Richard Maasdorp, Nadia Marabini, Rose Nurse, Tim Paulet, Mandy Retzlaff, Liz and Duncan Rixom, Johnny Rodrigues, Dr Richard Russell, John Robbie, Lynn Santer, Ken Scott, Sheila Siddle, Angus Shaw, Gill Stenning, Joy Stevens, Esme Smithwhite, Linda Townsend, Estelle Walters, Kelvin Weare, Pat Webb, Ann and Freddie Wilkinson, Nigel Wilson, Vicky Windsor, John Worsley-Worswick, Val Zangel. Thanks also to the many others, too numerous to mention, whose generosity, compassion and support of Meryl and her team will never be forgotten.

To the organisations, locally, regionally and internationally whose invaluable support was a vital lifeline for Meryl and her team during the farm animal rescues: Golfing and Giving (Zimbabwe); HSUS (Humane Society of the United States), IFAW (International Fund for Animal Welfare), Motor Sport - South Africa, The North Shore Animal League (USA), NSPCA (South Africa), The Rhodesian Ridgeback Club (Netherlands), RSPCA (UK), SPANA (UK) (Society for the Protection of Animals Abroad), WSPA (World Society for the Protection of Animals), ZNSPCA (The Zimbabwe National Society for the Prevention of Cruelty to Animals), The Zimbabwe Pet Project (South Africa); and many of the Breed Dog Clubs in the UK, particularly The Staffordshire Bull Terrier Club.

To the people who gave permission for the use of their photographs in the book.

Thank you: Tommy Bayley, Roy and Heather Bennett, Belinda Bowey, Guy and Ros Cartwright, Ian and Jo Cochrane, Ed and Pat Cumming, Nick Dean, Lenie de Jager, Mark Evans, Mark Ford, Linnette Frewin, FJ Gaisford, Rob Gordon, Kewpie Hawkins, Guy Hilton-Barber, Lisa Hywood, Kerry Kay, Chris Milligan, Alan and Jenny Parsons, Deidre Reichard, Reuters, Liz Rixom, Joy Stevens, Brent Stirton/Getty Images (courtesy of Readers Digest), Chalkie and Sandie van Schalkwyk, Gary and Theresa Warth. Also to Emma Haigh for proof reading the book.

And, to Roger Catterall whose battery powered light kept me working night after night; to Erin Ellison whose food parcels kept me going; to Pauline Henson and Barry McCartney for assistance with research and to Steve, for listening, again and again.

Glossary

ARDA: Agricultural Rural Development Authority.

Biltong: Marinaded, air-dried lean meat, made from beef or game.

Boma: Sturdy enclosure for animals, usually made from poles or branches.

BSAP: British South Africa Police.

Chef: Colloquialism meaning senior politician, chief or boss.

CFU: Commercial Farmers Union.

Chibuku: Very popular and low priced, thick, traditional opaque beer.

Chimurenga: Shona word meaning revolt or rebellion.

First Chimurenga: The first uprisings against white settlers in the 1890s.

Second Chimurenga: The full scale armed struggle for liberation which began in the 1960s and culminated in Independence in 1980.

Third Chimurenga: Phrase adopted by Zanu PF and President Mugabe referring to farm invasions from 2000-2008.

CIO: Central Intelligence Organisation (Secret Police).

Combi: Minibus used for public transport; V.W. Campervan.

DA: District Administrator.

DISPOL: District Police Officer.

DDF: District Development Fund.

Duiker: Small African antelope.

EPZ: Export Processing Zone.

GAPWUZ: General Agricultural and Plantation Workers Union.

Gum tree: Eucalyptus tree.

Highveld: Areas with an average altitude of between 1,200 and 1,500 metres.

I/C: In Charge.

JAG: Justice For Agriculture – agricultural lobby group formed during the land invasions fighting for legal rights of farmers and their employees.

Jambanja: Violent struggle or fight, not necessarily physical, which may involve the use of extortion or intimidation to achieve one's aim.

Kopje: A rocky outcrop or hill.

Kraal: A small enclosure for cattle or other animals.

Knobkerrie: Cudgel; stout stick with a knob on top.

Lowveld: Areas with an average altitude of between 600 and 1,200 metres.

MDC: Movement for Democratic Change – the biggest opposition party in Zimbabwe, born out of the Trade Union movement in 1997 and headed by Morgan Tsvangirai.

MIC: Member in Charge.

O/C: Officer Commanding.

PA: Provincial Administrator .

Panga: Large bladed cane-cutting knife.

Povo: Colloquialism: peasants, masses.

PROPOL: Provinical Police.

Pungwe: A meeting or gathering at night with a political purpose when liberation songs are sung and slogans are repeated. The term originated in the 2nd Chimurenga where it was used to politicise the rural population.

Putzi: A fly which lays its eggs in damp, shady places where animals lie. Body warmth hatches the eggs and larvae burrow into the skin and grow. A boil-like lesion forms and bursts after a fortnight.

Sadza: Thick maize meal porridge.

Scud: The popular name for the brown plastic bottle containing traditional opaque beer; so called because of the bottle's resemblance to a missile.

Shebeen: Illicit beer hall where alcohol is sold without a licence.

Shumba: Shona for 'lion'.

Simbi: Iron pipe.

SITREP: (abb) Situation Report.

Sjambok: Animal hide whip.

SPCA: Society for the Prevention of Cruelty to Animals.

Toyi Toyi: A high stepping dance/march commonly performed at political events with decided political overtones.

UZ: University of Zimbabwe.

Veld: Open grassland.

Vets: War Veterans (pro-Mugabe supporters involved in the eviction of Zimbabwean farmers from the land).

Vlei: Low lying ground where a shallow lake forms in the wet season.

WWF: World Wide Fund for Nature (Formerly World Wildlife Fund)

ZANU (PF): Zimbabwe African National Party (Patriotic Front). The ruling party in Zimbabwe, formed in the struggle for Independence in the 1960s and headed by Robert Mugabe.

ZDF: Zimbabwe Defence Forces.

ZDI: Zimbabwe Defence Industries.

ZESA: Zimbabwe Electricity Supply Authority.

ZNA: Zimbabwe National Army.

ZNSPCA: Zimbabwe National Society for the Prevention of Cruelty to Animals.

ZRP: Zimbabwe Republic Police.

Foreword by David Shepherd

'The greatness of a nation and its moral progress can be judged by the way its animals are treated.'– Mahatma Gandhi, 1869-1948

I felt extremely privileged to be invited to write a foreword to this book and let me tell you why it is so special.

Every day in our lives now in this troubled world, we are fed unremittingly with stories of human tragedy, as we seem to set about destroying ourselves and everything around us. But how often do we hear of the donkeys of Baghdad being blown apart by suicide bombers? Never. Nor, until now, have we been made aware of the plight of domestic animals in war-torn Zimbabwe. The cattle, donkeys, cats and dogs not only witness the horror of seeing their homes ravaged by criminal thugs but then face their own eventual horrifying end. The story in this book redresses the balance, and that is why it is so special, speaking up for animals which don't have a voice. Meryl Harrison has opened a door to what is happening in Zimbabwe in an emotive and dramatic way which will, although disturbing in its details, delight the reader as Meryl tells of her many rescue successes.

In my long involvement over many years with animals, I have so often wept in despair at the way we treat our fellow creatures. On an evening in London in December 2002, I certainly shed many tears and these were shared with the huge audience at the BBC Animals Award ceremony. Meryl had flown over especially from Zimbabwe to receive her award and as the story unfolded on the screen, we watched in awe and horror.

The focus of attention was an ordinary little dog called Nandi. She never asked to be involved in the orgy of destruction around her. But she had no choice. The family in question, like many others, had been forced to flee their home with only the clothes they stood up in as they faced a gang of drug-crazed thugs who were destroying everything on the farm that represented the white man. Meryl found the terrified dog in the bathroom of the house awaiting whatever might befall her. Was this little dog to be hacked to pieces like so many others had been as she watched the horror of unremitting bloodlust? No, she was rescued by Meryl. This brave lady, supported by Addmore Chinhembe and many others, drove into the black night in answer to appeals for immediate help not knowing what carnage she might encounter and she has rescued countless other pets who now once again have secure and loving homes. So I pay tribute to Meryl and her wonderful support team. Thank you Meryl.

David Shepherd, OBE, CBE, October 2008

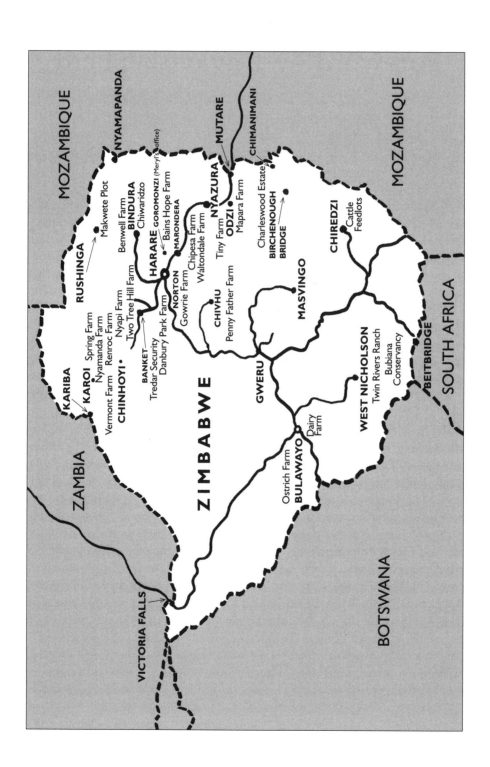

CHAPTER ONE

Black Jacques

Courage and resolution are the spirit and soul of virtue.
— Proverb

Harare, March 2000

Black Jacques was one of 10 puppies in his mother's first ever litter. Her name was Princess Annika (Annie for short) and his father was called Hooch. They were pure-bred Great Danes owned by Liz and Duncan Rixom, and Black Jacques was the biggest puppy and undoubtedly the pick of the litter. It was thanks to this one dog, with his exotic and intriguing name, that many thousands of animals of all shapes, sizes, colours and species were rescued in Zimbabwe in the first five years of the twenty-first century.

Meryl Harrison was the Chief Inspector of the Society for the Prevention of Cruelty to Animals and her first sighting of Black Jacques was on television over the Easter weekend in April 2000. She was at home in Bulawayo, the TV news was on and she watched in horror as a black Great Dane was beaten repeatedly by thugs armed with sticks, stones and bricks. It was a Zimbabwean farm invasion and the images were so shocking that Meryl could hardly bear to watch. Finally the dog was left, his black body unmoving, in the hot sun. Meryl could not tell if the animal had survived, if he was still alive. Further film footage showed other dogs being beaten and stoned, some even attacked as they cowered in their kennels. A Rhodesian Ridgeback lay on the steps outside the house – also beaten and now unmoving. The video footage was so shocking that in less than 24 hours it had been removed from all international news reports – too shocking to show, too distressing for viewers to watch. For Meryl these brief glimpses had been enough. She couldn't get the pictures of the black Great Dane out of her head. She didn't know the dog's name or who his owner was but he was about to change her life.

When the mob of men had gone, Black Jacques and two other dogs that had survived the beating were rescued and rushed to a veterinary surgery in Harare. Two days later Meryl left Bulawayo and drove to the capital, Harare.

She was already determined that the SPCA should do whatever they could to help the animals on the farms and when Meryl put her mind to something concerning animal welfare there was little that would stop her! Meryl had already phoned Bryan Nel, the National Chairman of the Zimbabwean National Society for the Prevention of Cruelty to Animals and he must have known that this was a dangerous situation, but he was immediately supportive.

He suggested that the first thing was for Meryl to see what help could be given to the beaten and brutalised dogs whose horrific treatment had been seen on world television. Bryan had already contacted the Commissioner of Police requesting their full support for SPCA Inspectors to go on to invaded farms. Meryl had made countless phone calls, left messages on answering machines and contacted everyone she thought should know about what was happening.

When Meryl tracked down the dog whose image had both haunted and motivated her, Black Jacques was barely alive. He was attached to a drip and had a large plaster cast covering his right hind leg where his tibia had been fractured in several places. Black Jacques' head was swollen and misshapen as a result of the multiple blows he had received. He had a 12-inch gash on his head – a slash from a cane-cutting knife known as a 'panga'. Black Jacques had a perforated eye and ear drum and had been made both blind and deaf as a result of the beatings. Meryl stroked his large, silky black head as he lay there, hovering between life and death, and she wept. She promised, to herself and to Black Jacques, that she would do everything in her power to help the animals, the silent victims who were trapped in the middle of land invasions.

While Black Jacques' life hung in the balance and as vets and nurses ministered to the dog, Meryl's work was just beginning. A letter had come from Police Headquarters stating that the SPCA would receive police support to visit invaded farms and a memo reinforcing the fact had apparently been copied to police stations around the country. Meryl soon discovered that letters and memos were all very well but they held little sway on the ground. On the very first rescue that Meryl attempted, the police insisted that an escort was unnecessary but advised that it would not be safe for Meryl herself to go onto the farm.

For two hours Meryl sat under a tree at a police station while two SPCA Inspectors went onto an invaded farm alone to try and rescue five dogs, two puppies and two cats who were stranded. Those two hours dragged past interminably and Meryl resolved that from then on either the small team of SPCA rescuers went onto the invaded farms together or no one went at all. Meryl quickly realised that the only way the farm rescues would succeed was if the SPCA had the co-operation of the war veterans. But farmers, members of the public, businessmen, lawyers, union leaders and sometimes even police couldn't get onto seized and invaded farms – so why should the SPCA be any different?

At the time it seemed the only person in charge when it came to land invasions was the Chairman of the war veterans. His name was Chenjerai Hunzvi, a man who had laughingly, boastfully, announced that his middle name was 'Hitler'. Hunzvi was spearheading the land invasions and Meryl knew that the only way there would be a chance of saving the animals left behind on the farms when the owners were forcibly evicted, was with the co-operation of the new occupiers, the self-styled 'war veterans'. It would mean explaining to them that the SPCA was totally non-political and impartial and that their only agenda was the welfare of the animals that had been left behind on the farms. It took some days but finally the news came. The Commercial Farmers Union (CFU) had held discussions with Hunzvi and he had agreed that the SPCA could go on to invaded farms. Hunzvi laid down a strict protocol: the SPCA Inspectors must be in uniform; they must be in marked vehicles; they must inform the Base Commander (war veteran in charge) of an area of their presence; they must only take animals that they specified on arrival and nothing else, and that there was to be no publicity.

As the preliminary guidelines were laid down, Meryl began going onto invaded farms with one or sometimes two SPCA Inspectors; any more than that, she soon found out, was far too confrontational. The Inspector most often accompanying her was Addmore, a young man in his early twenties who cared enormously about the welfare of animals. When the farm rescues began Addmore was only a kennel hand based at Kadoma SPCA but because he was already showing that he had an exceptional way with animals, he was invited to join the rescue team.

Addmore was married with two little boys whom he absolutely adored and, even though he was nearly forty years younger than her, Meryl said:

'With Addmore by my side I knew we would succeed, however tough things got.'

Two other SPCA Inspectors involved from the beginning were ex-policemen and both proved to be extremely helpful – particularly when it came to dealing with unco-operative members of the police. Misheck, married with children, was one of the longest-serving SPCA Inspectors in the country and he and Meryl had worked together for many years. Augustine a man in his fifties who had risen to the rank of Inspector in the police force was described by Meryl as the intellectual of the group.

'He didn't suffer fools gladly – as many accused found to their cost!'

Meryl and her colleagues had very little to work with. Meryl did all the driving in a one-tonne, blue SPCA pick-up truck with a canopy. They had cages for small animals, buckets and containers for holding and carrying water and four large plastic boxes. In these were all the tools of the trade: First Aid equipment for animals; educational material including pamphlets in English and the vernacular; ropes; bolt cutters; blankets; animal food for domestic pets and livestock; a humane killer/stun gun; collars, leads and head collars for horses.

Meryl tried to be prepared for any eventuality but rescuing animals from invaded farms was uncharted territory: it had never been done before, by anyone, anywhere in the world. Meryl had one cell phone for communication – that was all! She did not have satellite tracking, a GPS, a laptop computer, internet access, or even two-way radios. The cell phone, when it was in range of a tower and had a signal, was her only means of communication.

As the rescues began Meryl made up the rule book. She developed a system, and it worked:

'There had to be trust on both sides – SPCA Inspectors and war veterans – and we were careful not to abuse that trust, even when tearful farmers' wives asked us if we could bring precious photos of weddings or graduations back from the farms. When farmers indicated to me where we could find their passports or other documents – we reluctantly had to turn down their requests.
'Nothing was worth jeopardising the work we had to do. We always adhered to our objective – simply the rescue of the animal.'

Meryl did not ever forget that first dog that had started her on what would become an incredible saga. Black Jacques had amazing courage and strength and thanks to this and the most dedicated and expert veterinary care, he survived. When Meryl next saw him a few weeks after his brutal beating, Black Jacques was at home with his devoted mistress.

At one stage the veterinary experts had felt that they would have to give up on him but once back home and with continuous love and attention, Black Jacques had turned the corner. Lying on a large foam mattress in front of a roaring fire, Black Jacques was having his legs massaged with aromatherapy oils when Meryl saw him. An aluminium plate had been inserted into his leg to hold the broken bone together.

The splint had been designed for a calf but was the only thing that had been big enough to support the bones of the Great Dane! His front legs had grown tremendously in strength from supporting the rest of his body and he had even come to terms with his loss of sight and had learnt to find his way around his new territory.

As the months passed Black Jacques went from strength to strength and made an almost complete recovery. His owner wrote to Meryl:

'The most courageous part of him was when he heard the lead chain rustle. Even in the most extreme pain he would manage to get to his feet to come out for a walk so that he did not soil his bed, the house, or even his own back yard! Whenever I moved from one room to another he would look up at me sideways to see where I was off to and, again, enduring incredible pain and straining to get up, he would follow me wherever I went. He later even regained partial sight and most of his hearing. How could any of us give up with this Great Heart giving his all to life?'

Black Jacques showed such courage and unconditional love that his example drove Meryl Harrison and a small team to rescue many thousands of animals in the next five years, a rescue unheard-of in modern times, an achievement of immense proportions – for Zimbabwe and for the world community of animal welfare workers.

Extracts from Meryl's Diary:

'We hit the ground running. There were no handbooks. There was no protocol. I literally had to make the rules up as we went along.'
– Meryl Harrison, March 2000

March 2000
Kwekwe:
4th March. The very first rescue of animals stranded on an invaded farm in Kwekwe is carried out by Bryan Nel (Chairman of the ZNSPCA and Chairman of the Kwekwe branch of the SPCA.) He is accompanied by one kennel hand and two police Constables. 'Heidi', a Saint Bernard, and 'Lucy', a Bull Terrier cross are rescued from a farm which has been taken over by 40 war veterans.

Arcturus:
Seven dogs and one cat are uplifted from an invaded farm by the owner.

Bulawayo:
Farmer reports that cattle are being killed on his farm when war veterans are hungry.

April 2000
Schalk van Zydam, a journalist with Associated Press phones wanting a statement on

the work that the SPCA is doing on invaded farms – the first journalist who realises that we have an important role to play.

4 April. My son Nick's birthday. Can hardly believe that he was almost an 11 pound baby and that I nearly died having him and that now he's a Dad himself and I'm a grandmother to his children – Michaela and Travers.

Arcturus:
Police advise me to wait at Juru growth point while SPCA Inspector Misheck and kennel hand Tawanda go to a farm in Arcturus. They rescue three dogs and a cat. The farm manager says that of a herd of 170 sheep, only 50 are alive – the rest have been slaughtered – presumably by war veterans and farm invaders.

Arcturus:
Five dogs, two puppies and two cats are rescued. One dog accidentally shut in the car when the owners fled from the invaders is found dead.

May 2000
Over the first weekend in May the situation deteriorated rapidly in farming areas right across the country. Farmers began bringing their domestic pets to the SPCA centres for safe-keeping. In that first weekend we at Bulawayo SPCA took in 37 dogs, three cats and a baby bush pig and we had to quickly make some old disused kennels habitable for the many animals that were coming in. Chegutu SPCA took in 16 dogs, two cats, two birds and a hamster. Chiredzi SPCA took in 19 dogs. Kwekwe SPCA took in 18 dogs and seven cats. No information yet on the other Zimbabwean SPCA centres: Harare, Mutare, Masvingo, Mashava, Gweru, Hwange, Kadoma, Marondera, Chinhoyi and Zvishavane.

ZNSPCA Chairman Bryan Nel sends out a circular to all SPCA centres in Zimbabwe, requesting them to ensure that they all had adequate supplies of Euthapent (euthanasing drug) in stock.

June 2000
Parliamentary elections – kennel staff given time off to go and vote. Continuing calls from farmers about war veterans confining cattle to small paddocks as they claim the land for themselves. Often a phone call reminding people about The Prevention of Cruelty to Animals Act has the desired effect.

CHAPTER TWO

All Aboard!

'Late on the third day, at the very moment when, at sunset, we were making our way through a herd of hippopotamuses, there flashed upon my mind, unforeseen and unsought, the phrase: "Reverence for Life".'
– Albert Schweitzer, 1875-1965

Bulawayo, July 2000

Meryl was driving back to Bulawayo a month after the 2000 elections. Like almost everyone else in the country she could not believe that farm invasions were still going on. Already well over a hundred animals had been rescued from farms in just three months and still there seemed no end in sight. It was hard to accept and even harder to understand. Meryl wondered if her life, her job or anything in Zimbabwe would ever be the same again. On the other side of Gweru, as she got near Shangani, a pick-up truck overtook Meryl and began slowing down in front of her, the two male occupants signalling to her to stop. Recognising one of the men as 'Mac' – a well-known farmer and CFU leader in Bulawayo, Meryl pulled in behind them and saw that they had a baby baboon in a cage. Mac and his colleague had been asked to drop the little primate off at Chipangali – a wildlife orphanage outside Bulawayo but when they saw Meryl they decided to put their charge into her hands and she, of course, didn't say no! It didn't take long for mayhem to unfold:

'With the baby baboon ensconced in her cage in the back of my pick-up truck, I set off again for Bulawayo. Whilst I was driving I was aware through my rear view mirror that there was quite a lot of activity going on in the back. Before I'd left Harare a friend had given me several boxes of seedlings and also some Canna plants. To pass the time the little baboon was pulling all the seedlings up and shredding the Canna plants – having a lovely time! I kept seeing a skinny little arm come through the bars and snatch handfuls of greenery! I stopped to see if I could move things around out of her way but as usual the truck was pretty full with all the usual equipment we carried for rescues. I did manage to put the remains of the seedlings on the passenger seat in

7

the front of the truck and gave the baboon some dog biscuits to chew on!

'Nearer Bulawayo I saw a goat lying at the side of the road that looked as if it had been hit by a car. I stopped and on checking, I could see that it had a bad cut on its side and a broken and bleeding horn. The goat couldn't stand up and obviously needed veterinary attention. There was no way I could put the goat in the back of the truck with the plant wrecker so I moved the seedlings onto the floor and lifted the goat onto the passenger seat of the truck – quite a job as it was a big goat and very heavy.

'I phoned the Bulawayo SPCA and asked them to meet me at the vets so that they could collect the baby baboon from me and deliver it to Chipangali who have a very successful programme of releasing troops of baboons back into the bush. By the time I reached the vets late in the afternoon, the back of my truck looked like a bomb had hit it. The little primate had, with her very long arms and inquisitive fingers, dragged just about everything she could next to the cage and some of it into her cage. This included cotton wool, dogs' leads, dog biscuits, ropes, education pamphlets and of course the remaining stumps of my precious Canna plants. Berry Oosthuizen from the Bulawayo SPCA just burst out laughing when she saw the goat in the front and the baboon and utter chaos in the back – she remarked that only I could arrive like that!'

A baboon wrecking the back of the truck, a bleeding goat on the front passenger seat – these were the things that made up a normal day for Meryl – if there is such a thing in the world of animal welfare! Zimbabwe seemed to have become engulfed in a time of madness and Meryl held on to memories of 'normal' – it helped her to cope with the horrors she was witnessing in the ongoing farm rescues.

Meryl had turned 61 in February 2000 and hers had been an unusual life by most people's standards! Meryl was a twin: she and her brother Colin were born in London in 1939 and were illegitimate, put up for adoption by their single mother when they were six weeks old. The twins spent the first few months of their life in an orphanage before both being adopted by Pam and Leslie Anderson. The Andersons always told Meryl and Colin that their mother had died in childbirth and that their father had been killed in the war. 60 years later, at the start of Zimbabwe's land invasions, Meryl had still not learned the truth about her biological parents.

Meryl remembered growing up as an Anderson with mixed feelings. She thought it strange that a couple who wanted children badly enough to adopt, would then put them into boarding school for all of their schooling, starting when the twins were just five years old. Meryl and Colin wanted for very little when they were growing up, first in England and then Rhodesia. The twins were sent to the best schools and given anything that money could buy but Meryl said she would have given it all up to have love, affection and a feeling that she belonged. The Andersons were extremely strict and undemonstrative parents. Meryl recently found a letter that she wrote when at boarding school in South Africa, asking her mother to write more letters as all the other girls received far more letters from their parents than she did! The end of school terms also held painful memories for Meryl and she clearly remembered her feelings as the school train pulled into Salisbury station.

'All of us would lean out of the windows to try and catch a glimpse of our parents whom we hadn't seen for three months. Our parents would stand motionless with a faint smile on their faces at the far end of the station, whilst our friends' parents would run down the platform, arms outstretched, to hug and greet their sons and daughters.'

Meryl didn't excel academically at school but it didn't stop her from putting her heart and soul into her future working life. From a young child she had always been passionate about animals, not really appreciating until she was much older the unconditional love that an animal gives. Living in South Africa in 1983 Meryl started a Rescue Scheme for Staffordshire Bull Terriers and she owned, bred and judged these dogs which she particularly admired. Later she began helping at the Sandton SPCA as a volunteer and that started her on the path of animal welfare.

When she returned to Zimbabwe Meryl became involved in fund raising, sat on committees and went on to become the Vice Chairman of the Harare SPCA. Such was her love of dogs that in 1996 Meryl started an annual dog show for mongrels which she called Scruffs and the money raised from it went to help SPCA's around the country. Well-known local people would be invited to come and judge and included the Rhino Girls, Henry Olonga, Cara Black and Minister David Karamanzira.

When she was offered the position of General Manager of the SPCA, Meryl soon realised that the Inspectors had no formal training and were therefore unable to tell her what to do! Meryl contacted the NSPCA in South Africa and attended one of their training courses and was later appointed an Inspector by the Zimbabwean Government in 1994. Later that same year Meryl began to leave her own indelible mark on Zimbabwe and was noticed and recognised for her achievements. Meryl won the Rothmans Communicator of the Year Award for 1994/95, joining Ministers, doctors and other leaders in Zimbabwean society. Three years later, in 1997 Meryl moved to the Bulawayo

SPCA and shortly after the land invasions started, she was promoted to Chief Inspector of the Zimbabwe National SPCA.

Meryl liked to get to work before everyone else so that she could walk around the kennels checking on all the animals. She liked to see which animals had been bought in during the night, check with the security guards for urgent messages and then prepare for the day ahead. Once the Inspectors arrived, Meryl headed the daily meeting. They would talk about problems that had arisen and cases that had been dealt with on the previous day and then new cases would be allocated. The options, possibilities and most desirable ways to handle each case were discussed and Meryl always reminded the Inspectors that any decision made must be in the best interest of the animals and not necessarily people.

Meryl admitted that she was a perfectionist and said that there was only one way to do something – the right way and to the very best of your ability. Meryl wasn't sure if being a perfectionist was a good point or a bad one but she suspected that people who worked under her probably thought it was a bad point! Hopefully people who worked alongside her thought the opposite!

After the daily meeting and allocation of cases, the SPCA vet would usually drop in to Meryl's office before he started operating. Meryl liked to have this opportunity to ask him for advice about animals she was worried about – either in the SPCA kennels or in ongoing cases that she and the other Inspectors were dealing with. Meryl's office was like a railway station for the first couple of hours in the morning with staff members coming in and out and constant phone calls and interruptions.

Any urgent cruelty reports would be dealt with immediately and Inspectors sent out to the scene. These could involve any number of things such as broken-down cattle trucks, road traffic accidents involving animals, horses, livestock or dogs running loose on a main road. Then there were the big issues to deal with: the welfare of animals at research institutions, pet shops and abattoirs; security company guard dogs and spot checks on trucks transporting live animals.

Every time there was a spare half hour, Meryl would turn to the great piles of paperwork that never seemed to end. Statements for court cases had to be prepared, reports and records had to be kept up to date and Meryl also wrote a Junior and Adult newsletter every month which was sent out to SPCA members and donors. Meryl firmly believed that anyone who sent a donation, no matter how small, should get a personal letter of thanks sent to them – rather than an impersonal standard letter which she hated.

Throughout the day Meryl interviewed people who came to the kennels wanting to adopt a dog or cat. She would go through the responsibilities of having a pet in the home and the numerous issues associated with owning a pet. Meryl liked to meet the whole family:

'Often the husband would be looking for a macho-type dog to guard the property but when I talked to the wife I'd discover that she and the children were terrified of that type of dog and were looking for something smaller and gentler – the dog finally chosen had to be one that the whole family was comfortable with.'

By midday Meryl liked to leave her desk and office and investigate cruelty reports that had come in over the past 24 hours. These might include reports on dogs that were very thin or had untreated wounds; dogs that had been seen confined or tied up or reports of bitches in season that were roaming the streets. Difficult cases were those that involved neighbours who reported hearing dogs yelping in pain for several minutes at a time and who they suspected were being beaten. Any number of reasons could be involved including dogs that jumped up at children, dug holes in the garden or stole food but they were always hard to investigate as owners denied allegations. The SPCA Inspectors would check the dog for injuries, give severe warnings and hope that that would be an end to it.

Many reports about cats came in too, especially the many feral cats that were often seen at the back of restaurants and hotels. The SPCA staff would set traps for the cats and then collect them as soon as they were informed that a cat had been caught. Once back at the SPCA kennels the vets sterilised and vaccinated the cats and snipped a small piece off the top of one ear while the cat was under anaesthetic. This enabled SPCA Inspectors to easily identify cats that had already been treated if they happened to be caught again. The cats were always returned to the same area they had been found – a standard procedure in many large cities.

Less domestic cases came from reports of goats being transported tied to the tops of buses, overcrowded cattle trucks, chickens being sold in market places with no shade, food or water. Complaints from the public would come in about conditions at pet shops and riding schools, about puppies being sold in cardboard boxes on the roadside or rabbits being sold in car parks. Whenever it was possible the SPCA Inspectors preferred to give a warning first, approaching the owner in a firm but friendly manner. From years of experience Meryl knew that nothing was gained, least of all for the animal involved, if the situation became hostile or if there was a breakdown of communication. Often just a little education was needed to resolve a problem but in some cases more intervention became necessary. When an animal was found abandoned on a property or in cases where an owner had been warned before, the animal would be removed and taken to the SPCA kennels. Verbal and written warnings would be given when necessary and prosecution decided on when all else failed and in cases of extreme cruelty.

It didn't matter what sort of day she'd had, the end of the day, like the beginning, was Meryl's favourite time.

'The best part of the day was when everyone had gone home! I would wander around the kennels checking on all the different animals in our care. It was always so quiet and peaceful after the noise associated with a large and busy SPCA kennel in the daytime. Everyone was bedded down for the night – their tummies full. In the cat house all the occupants would be curled up in their baskets although there might still be a couple of kittens rolling around together. Most of the puppies would be sleeping and out in the bigger kennels it was all quiet except for the odd dog who heard me walking past and came out to give my hand a lick through the wire fence. In the paddock the goats (confiscated from the tops of buses) would be having a last munch of their vegetables before the sun went down and it was just the best time of the day.'

Meryl didn't know in July 2000 that, for the next five years, virtually every day of her life and every aspect of her job would concentrate almost entirely on rescuing animals from seized and invaded farms. Her family, friends and personal life would all take second place as she worked tirelessly to do the right thing for the animals who had become helpless and innocent victims stranded in the midst of the mayhem. Meryl was compassionate, fair and responded well to a challenge and for the animals of Zimbabwe these qualities were to be their saving grace because abnormal had become normal in Zimbabwe, and would stay that way for some years.

Extracts from Meryl's Diary:

May the Irish hills caress you,
May her lakes and rivers bless you,
May the luck of the Irish enfold you,
May the blessings of Saint Patrick behold you.
– traditional Irish blessing

July 2000
Bulawayo:
I've been appointed as the National Co-ordinator of the ZNSPCA! It involves a lot more work and responsibility and is going to mean a lot of travelling. I'll be liaising with the 14 SPCA centres, trying to make sure we are all singing from the same sheet, giving

advice and helping source drugs, equipment and educational information. Because of this new role I've got, the Bulawayo SPCA have taken on a Committee member to take over my job of running the kennels – it's becoming impossible for me to juggle the two jobs. I moved into a tiny little office above a hardware store in Bulawayo and had hardly got my office sorted out when first 'Peter', a very determined freelance reporter, and then Carte Blanche [South African current affairs television programme] want interviews. The news is getting out.

Gwanda:
After a frantic call I drive out to Gwanda with a young trainee Inspector where there has been a horrific accident – a truck and trailer full of goats has overturned. It was a scene of total carnage: dead and dying goats trapped inside the truck and many others strewn all over the road. The occupants of the police camp which was directly opposite the scene of the crash had been very quick on the scene – but not to help. They had lost no time in taking some of the dead goats – their carcasses already skinned and hanging from trees. Bernard and I worked quickly, destroying those animals that were too badly injured, giving first aid to many others and finally transporting the walking wounded back to the kennels. It was a long and harrowing day.

Concession:
Addmore and I travel to Concession and rescue four Border Collies, one old cat and three owls. The farmer had been physically beaten by war veterans and the son was not allowed back to the farm to feed the dogs.

August 2000
Matabeleland:
Farmer reports that 11 head of cattle (Brahman) have been killed by snares. War vets pulling down fencing and telephone wires to make snares. 5 sheep slaughtered and 1 ostrich has its legs chopped off – left fluttering on the ground.

Chipinge:
Farmer asks for help as war veterans confine 321 cows and 64 calves into a five-hectare paddock and will not allow them to be moved.

Chinhoyi:
Rose Logan, Chairman of Chinhoyi SPCA contacts me to say she is deeply concerned about the plight of animals on invaded farms – particularly in her area and generally in Mashonaland West. Rose is such a gentle, lovely person – one of the nicest people involved in animal welfare. Rose sends a fax to the CFU asking them to inform all farmers that the SPCA are available to help take domestic animals off invaded farms to a place of safe keeping. Farmers are given my contact details.

September 2000
Bulawayo:
Box number 25 arrives from Vicky Windsor in Baltimore, USA. Contents include: 30 leads, 24 Puppy Drops; 24 Nylabones, 10 calendars, nine combs, one manual can opener, three toys, 10 pens, cable.

Vicky says: 'Call me the neurotic donor!' – she keeps meticulous records of the lists of items she donates. What an amazing lady. She is a retired foreign language teacher. She always had a dog when she was growing up and later volunteered at an animal rescue group; she says that now she donates to people who do 'hands-on rescues that do the most to relieve animal suffering'.

Vicky tells me she's got two dogs: 'Jake', a Bischon Frise (pretty little white dog a bit like a Maltese) and 'Angel', a cross-breed she took over from a homeless man who couldn't look after her. She has also got four cats: Spot, Rambo, Noel and Charlie.

Vicky's donations have made such a huge difference to our efficiency and to improve the welfare of thousands of animals in Zimbabwe. She sends a huge variety of things from antiseptic lotions and fly repellents to clippers and tweezers and everything in-between. She says: 'If I don't, who will!' She often sends reflectors – either stick on or screw on – the same as the ones used on cars. There must be literally hundreds of donkey-drawn scotch carts in Zim with Vicky's reflectors on the back of them.

October 2000
28 October. Tim's [Meryl's son] birthday. Phoned him at the Salon and told him present's in the post.

Bulawayo:
Am getting increasing media enquiries, and media attention beginning to build up. Will undoubtedly play a big role in bringing this work to the attention of the public. Donations are already starting to come in – in cash and kind, from individuals and from big organisations like WSPA, the RSPCA, NSPCA and IFAW.

November 2000
Masvingo:
In the Devure area four donkeys had paraffin poured on them and were then set alight – all perished and were buried. A fifth donkey endured the same treatment and was still alive – shot by police. The owner of the donkeys said three war veterans were the perpetrators.

Bulawayo:
I am getting really worried about how we are all going to cope – especially the smaller centres which are just not equipped financially or logistically in terms of staff, etc. to

deal with these ongoing problems. Our manpower, small as it is, is stretched to the limits.

December 2000

Rusape:

11 December. Got a desperate call from Rosemary in Rusape. War veterans are threatening to kill two hippos on a farm there because the animals are eating the maize crop that they have planted on the seized farm. The war veterans say the farm is now theirs, the hippos belong to the State and must be destroyed. The pair of hippo, a male and female, have been on the farm, living in the dam for 38 years. A game capture team from National Parks has arrived on the farm to remove the hippos and Rosemary desperately asks for help. Unable to get hold of National Parks, I phone wildlife vet Chris Foggin who says that Rosemary and her husband definitely own the hippos – not the war veterans or the State! He says that hippos are notoriously difficult to translocate as once they have been darted they run into the water and drown. Chris advises that the hippo should be destroyed.

22 December. Rosemary phones to say that National Parks have come to the farm and built a boma [small, secure enclosure made of poles, branches or thorn bushes to contain animals] *for the hippo. There are doubts if it will be strong enough.*

Vumba:

Roly [Meryl's partner] *has not been well and so we decide to get away for a couple of days over Christmas. We go to stay at the White Horse Inn in Vumba – a place he loves. We had three lovely days, went for walks, consumed much good food and wine but as always work intruded and it was the problems with the hippos on the farm dam in Rusape.*

Rusape:

27 December. Rosemary phones to say the female hippo has been caught but she has broken out of the boma. Roly and I drop in at the farm on our way back from the Vumba. The hippo were visible on the far side of the dam. National Parks suggest that Rosemary and her husband provide guards to protect the war veterans' maize crop from the hippo!

28 December. Rosemary phones to say that National Parks want to pull out of the capture and translocation of the hippos because the war veterans are pressuring them too much. Rosemary has been told that a doctor in Rusape town is giving the war veterans their instructions. I phone the most senior man in National Parks and ask him to intervene – the National Parks men must be given time to catch the hippos and the war veterans must not take the matter into their own hands.

Bulawayo:
I don't think I realised before now that this situation was going to go on and on. Roly never ever puts any sort of pressure on me and I never receive anything but his constant support and encouragement. He is very protective of our evenings together – when I am officially off duty! If members of the public phone while I'm having dinner (which he has lovingly prepared!) Roly tells them in no uncertain terms to phone a little later! Unless of course it's farmers with problems and then everything stops. Our time together is getting less and less with the ongoing farm rescues.

Chapter Three

The Wildlife Conservancy: a story of death and of life
(Part One: 2000)

'Animals are the great voteless and voiceless majority
who can only survive with our help.'
− Gerald Durrell

December 2000, Bubiana

Towards the end of 2000 and ten months into farm invasions and animal rescues, Meryl received news of the early effects that land seizures were having on wildlife on private farms in Zimbabwe. The information came from Guy Hilton-Barber, the owner of Barberton Ranch, one of ten properties that made up the Bubiana Conservancy. Guy had compiled a poaching report which covered the period from May to December 2000. It detailed 84 wild animals, from twelve species, which had been found dead in snares on Barberton Ranch in the past eight months.

Guy had no way of knowing how many other animals had been killed and not found but he said that 1,452 snares had been collected by his staff and that these were made of fencing wire and cable loops. Guy also reported on the killing of a black rhino bull. The rhino had been snared and then tracked by a gang of 15 poachers and their dogs who had run the wounded animal down and then killed him. At the top of the report to Meryl, Guy had written:

'Monthly reports have been circularised to thirteen bodies including National Parks Warden of Matabeleland South who has never reacted.'

Meryl was deeply saddened to hear of the inaction by officials; she had suspected this may be the case in such chaotic times when lawlessness was widespread and now here was the evidence in black and white.

'Guy's report made grim and heartbreaking reading – and made me cognisant of the fact that in the current political mayhem, it would not only be the domestic pets and livestock that were going to be affected, but Zimbabwe's precious wildlife too. I just knew that the SPCA would be powerless to stop the suffering of these innocent victims. Prior to the land invasions I had had little or no involvement with wildlife or poaching, this tended to be left to the real custodians – the Department of National Parks & Wildlife Management. The Prevention of Cruelty to Animals Act [Chapter 19:09 – Section 2b] states that our jurisdiction covers amongst others "any kind of wild animal in captivity", so the SPCA was really only called in when it involved animals literally in captivity.'

Meryl did the only thing she could at the time: she followed the reports coming out of the area and informed people she thought needed to know about events on the ground.

Barberton Ranch, south-east of West Nicholson, was registered as the first Wildlife Conservancy in Zimbabwe in 1991. Together with nine other ranches there was a combined total of 136,000 hectares of land named the Bubiana Conservancy. Seven landowners were involved in this project of great vision which would benefit both farmers and local communities. The Bubiana Conservancy was split by the upper reaches of the Bubye river. Land to the east of the river fell in the Masvingo Province and land on the west of the river was in Matabeleland South Province.

The joint policy of the neighbouring landowners was to replace conventional cattle ranching with wildlife which was far more suited to the fragile ecosystem of the area. In 1992 Zimbabwe was crippled by drought and this natural disaster accelerated the disposal of cattle from Barberton Ranch. At the same time 16 hippo were introduced, rescued from drying rivers in the lowveld and translocated into the abundant dams in the Bubiana.

The following year the Department of National Parks embarked on a black rhino relocation project with the World Wildlife Fund. 76 black rhinos were relocated from National Parks land into private Conservancies to protect them from poaching which had become rampant and was decimating the species. Bubiana and Save Conservancies, registered as 'Extensive Breeding Areas', each received 38 of the black rhino – these were the 'foundation stock'. There were also 'Intensive Breeding Areas' where National Parks allowed existing rhinos to remain and the occasional bull or cow rhino was introduced to make the numbers viable where necessary. In 1994 a family group of 40 elephants were translocated into Bubiana and a herd of another 40 moved into the Conservancy on their own accord, thought to have walked 200 kilometres from the south east lowveld. Wildlife populations within Bubiana were further increased as the landowners made purchases at various game sales of 23 foot and mouth disease-free buffalo, 60 sable as well as eland, wildebeest and zebra.

By the year 2000, at the start of the land invasions, Bubiana had viable populations of all game species, apart from lion. Black rhino had increased by natural breeding to 105 animals; there were 160 foot and mouth disease-free buffalo and over 300 sable antelope. After just nine years of being in operation, 60 people were employed and there were chalets, luxury lodges and a bush camp on Barberton, which had become an important tourist destination in the country. The neighbouring Mberengwa Communal land was a beneficiary of the vision of the Conservancy. Fortified with funds from overseas donors, Bubiana had established a programme which would see communal land neighbours benefiting from the Conservancy. It was a policy which would uplift an entire community and district and not just single farms or ranches.

The benefits to Mberengwa included a sewing factory and garden irrigation project which had already been established. Improvements to rural schools, clinics, roads and bridges had begun and communal neighbours were benefiting from supplies of game meat which were anticipated to increase along with tourism as the Conservancy developed further.

Meetings between the Conservancy landowners, District Councils and communal leaders were ongoing and priorities had been identified. The Maranda Communal land was also involved in what Conservancy owners called the 'good neighbourly ethos' and for all concerned, the future looked very bright. Prosperity and development seemed guaranteed – until March 2000 and the onset of land invasions.

When Guy faxed Meryl the first poaching report for the Bubiana Conservancy at the end of 2000, the mammoth enterprise was already collapsing. In a letter telling of the history of Barberton Ranch and the Bubiana Conservancy, Guy wrote:

'*May 2000 saw the start of the invasions of squatters from the Mberengwa Communal Lands (orchestrated by their MPs) and within one year four ranches were abandoned (64,000 hectares). Only two properties are fully operational at this time.*'

Meryl knew this was out of her jurisdiction and was frustrated at her powerlessness. Poaching and snaring came under the Wildlife Act and this gave powers of intervention, apprehension and prosecution to the Department of National Parks and to the police. Meryl had been involved in wildlife issues in the past and had dealt with security personnel and government departments but only where cruelty to animals being held in captivity was involved. She'd never forget one case of alleged cruelty that she went to investigate that concerned the Zimbabwe National Army. It hadn't involved a wild animal but rather the Regimental Army goat in Bulawayo.

'Someone had written to The Chronicle [newspaper] *voicing their concern about the welfare of the regimental goat at Brady Barracks – the headquarters of I Brigade in Bulawayo. I decided to go and have a look for myself. I found that 'Nduna' was in fact living the life of luxury, if anything he was a bit overweight – brushed every day and bathed once a week which included having his hooves polished! Nduna was regularly taken for walks round the barracks and daily taken up to the local store so that he got used to mingling in crowded places. Here he was apparently often fed popcorn on these outings which may have explained his extra weight. I learnt that the Regimental goats are carefully selected – they must be male, pure white and are always called 'Nduna' (which means Chief in Ndebele). When they die they are given a funeral with full military honours.*

'After my visit, I wrote to the paper to assure the writer that in fact his concerns were unfounded, adding that Nduna must be the luckiest goat in Zimbabwe! A few months later I was invited by the Commander of I Brigade to a Lunch at Brady Barracks. It was part of the celebrations for Defence Forces Day; apart from a local commercial farmer who had supplied a mombe [Shona for cow or bull] for the celebrations, I was the only white person there.'*

Meryl had also successfully fought for the release of baboons being held for research purposes at the University of Zimbabwe; she'd worked on prosecuting safari operators who used live bait to attract carnivores for trophy hunters and she was passionate about the welfare of leopards in the country. Meryl had even been involved with cold-blooded wildlife too and had worked to close down a snake park outside Harare. It had been a long and complex struggle, not made any easier by the fact that it involved a deceased estate and the second-most senior politician in the country.

'The snake park was on land owned by the late Joshua Nkomo and when he died, Viv Bristow opened a new snake park further out of town. This was not generally known and the public still continued to drop off snakes at the old place. One of the former employees kept the original snake park going and charged the public entrance fees – as if nothing had changed! Conditions were very poor, the snakes were thin and undernourished and not being fed sufficiently. The heaters were not working, the snakes had nowhere to hide and the cages didn't even have secure locks.'*

Finally Meryl had got permission from the Nkomo family and the snake park was closed down. Meryl had called on Steve Durrant for assistance; he was the Chairman of the Herpetological Society and always helpful, knowledgeable and ready to assist. Steve and Meryl had then released the snakes onto a farm some distance away from Harare.

Regardless of her previous successes and experience involving warm- and cold-blooded wildlife, Meryl knew that there was nothing that could be done to stop the rampant poaching and snaring that was now out of control on invaded farms. Properties where anti-poaching patrols had regularly been conducted; ranchers who employed Game Scouts and farmers who treated wildlife with the same respect as their cattle – all were now under threat and unable to protect themselves and their families – let alone the animals around them. Meryl could do nothing to help Guy Hilton-Barber or the animals under attack in the Bubiana Conservancy – but she read the reports and followed the information whenever it was made public.

Extracts from Meryl's Diary:

> *'If slaughterhouses had glass walls, everyone would be vegetarian.'*
> *– Paul McCartney*

January 2001
Rusape:
Contacted Rosemary who said that the war vets had been told to give National Parks a chance to catch the hippos in the farm dam. Cabbages have been put out to entice the hippos towards the bomas but not hopeful of success.

Chiredzi:
Monitored the loading of cattle onto a train, they are destined for Maputo in Mozambique and then on to Mauritius by ship – the train journey will take four days providing there are no breakdowns, which with the Mozambican railways is almost inevitable. The cattle have been walked from the feedlots in Chiredzi. Looking at them arriving at the small siding, they are a credit to our cattle breeders. Whilst ZNSPCA is totally opposed to the export of live cattle, we will work with the exporters to find ways of improving the welfare of the cattle involved on this long trip – each stage must be monitored by us.

Maputo, Mozambique:
The cattle exporters invite the SPCA Chairman to accompany them to Maputo to see for himself the cattle being loaded onto the ship. He says he can't find his passport, so I am asked to go in spite of the fact that I had only the week before had an op on my leg which included a skin graft – I still have stitches in my leg and have to dress the wound every day.

Have just had a suspicious-looking mole removed – I don't take any chances with these since the malignant melanoma found on my arm all those years ago. The plastic surgeon (Owen-Smith) had cut out an enormous piece of my arm (a friend said it looked like a cannon ball had gone through my arm!) Then he did a large skin graft and later he told me he was pretty sure he'd removed all the tumour as he had gone right to the bone. Since then I haven't taken any chances.

Monitored the loading of the cattle onto the 'Dania' – the rust bucket of a ship that was headed for Mauritius. In spite of the long train trip the cattle looked stressed but their condition still good. The 'Dania' has 3 decks and was formerly a car ferry – now converted into a livestock carrier. The trip by sea to Mauritius can take anything up to 12 days.

Unfortunately there was a major power cut in Maputo that night and as I got out of the hired combi that the cattle transporters had arranged, I didn't see a low wrought iron decorative fence around the garden of the hotel. I walked straight into the metal fence – right where the stitches on my leg were. I didn't tell my hosts as they were all men and I didn't know them very well.

Mauritius:
Nothing prepared me for the sight that greeted me when I went below deck the day the 'Dania' docked in Port Louis in Mauritius. I was assailed by the very strong smell of ammonia from the urine and it was very humid and stuffy below deck. They do have fans but of course these are not used whilst they are in port. Many of the cattle were 'down' – too weak to stand any more and many of them had lacerations on their legs and bodies where they had been continuously trodden on by those cattle still standing – all of them covered in urine and dung.

All the cattle looked exhausted and some were panting – not sure if this was from stress or the heat; many of them appeared to have eye infections. Although they did not appear to have lost much weight, they looked nothing like the magnificent cattle that had left the Chiredzi feed lot some three weeks before. Of course the heat and the stench on the very bottom deck was the very worst – these unfortunate animals had been the first to be loaded and would therefore be the last off. I lent on the bars of the pen and wept – as I have done so many times at man's inhumanity to the animals that we eat. I prayed that they would have a swift end at the hands of the Mauritian butchers.

When I went back above deck I slipped on some oil from the crane and went crashing to the ground.

Bulawayo:
Flew back from Mauritius and went to Bulawayo, said a quick 'Hi' to Roly and then

headed back to Harare, stopping overnight in Kadoma. I woke during the night with excruciating pain in my side. Friends rushed me to hospital where it was found that as a result of the fall on the ship I had a haematoma (internal blood clot). Was kept in hospital for four days before driving on to Harare and getting back to farm rescues. Chatsworth:

Farmer reports two cows axed; one cow with an axe in its back is nursed back to recovery.

Save Conservancy, Masvingo:
Report of 59 cattle lost to snares. Two cows hamstrung (cut just above their hooves and left to die).

February 2001
Bulawayo:
Roly's birthday on the 19th. Took him to lunch a day early at Nesbitt Castle in Bulawayo (his favourite place).

Masvingo:
Farmer reports 12 newborn calves have disappeared and one cow had her eye gouged out.

Harare:
As the weeks and months go by I feel more and more like I'm on a treadmill and I know I just can't get off. As we finish with one farm, we get called in for help on another. So it goes on, day after day. We work with so little back-up and there are many days when Addmore and I don't even get to have a proper meal – buns and cokes have to suffice. It is just unthinkable for me that we wouldn't be there for the farmers when they ask for our help and so we go on.

Bulawayo:
27 February. My birthday! Roly makes his special fantastic home-made ice cream. I have never tasted anything better – and this from someone who couldn't cook at all when I first met him. It's such a treat after we've eaten our evening meal to be able to sit down with a helping of his ice cream and chat about my day. He always says it is the best part of the day.

March 2001
Vumba:
My truck landed in a ditch in a raging storm at about 8pm as I was going up an horrendous road in the Vumba where I was to stay the night with friends John and Yvonne, having completed SPCA business in Marondera and Mutare. I had great difficulty in getting out of the truck because of the angle that it was at but eventually

scrambled out. It was bucketing down with rain and I could see the lights of a house some distance away on my right but thought I had better stick to the road ahead which by now was a sea of mud. Thank goodness I did because if I had set off towards the lights I would have been walking towards a sheer drop! It was very dark, but I did have a torch with me and started walking in the driving rain up the hill. Suddenly coming towards me I saw a torch light and through the noise of the rain heard John calling out to me. He and Yvonne had watched from the verandah as my headlights came up the hill and got worried when they disappeared! It wasn't long before I was in their warm, pretty lounge. The first thing Yvonne did was to put a Scotch and soda in my hand, before she packed me off to have a hot bath, followed by an excellent meal. The next day John took me back to the truck and together with some workers from the next-door farm, we soon dug the truck out of the mud, with no damage done.

April 2001
Epworth:
Rescue two dogs, two cats, seven horses and one parrot in a cage and check on turkeys, geese and chickens.

4 April. Nick's birthday. Time seems to have gone by so fast: seems like yesterday when I was bursting with pride when he won the Beit Trust award to do post-grad study in the UK but in fact it was way back in 1987 – happier times for us all.

Gweru:
A very dear friend passed away; very worried that I would not make it back to her funeral as I was in Gweru on SPCA business but I got there just in time.

Chipinge:
War vets have settled on a farm and chased off the owner. 168 cattle and 216 sheep now grazing in a 6-hectare paddock, most of which is planted to coffee.

May 2001
Mutare:
Judging at the Mutare dog show over one weekend and Roly and I are able to have some time together.

Harare:
Can hardly say that things are streamlined but beginning to accept that each rescue needs an interminable amount of time. Because we always have to inform the police and request an escort, we have to deal with the 'system'. This can take hours if the OIC [Officer in Charge] is 'in a meeting' or in a court or even just 'gone to town'! The junior officers just aren't prepared to take any sort of responsibility in decision-making and so we wait! I've lost count of how many hours I've sat waiting at rural police stations, staring at fly-stained 'Wanted' posters, reading two-week-old copies of The

Herald and wondering what dejected-looking men and women sitting handcuffed on the floor of the Charge Office have done.

After we've seen the OIC things do speed up but even then we have more obstacles as Support Unit officers go for tea or haven't got transport. The police don't like being seen in the ZNSPCA vehicles apparently in case they are seen by the war vets and settlers and then accused of helping the white farmers. Sometimes we are sent miles out of our way to pick up police officers who will help us and then of course they have to be delivered back again. It all means that even though we start off very early in the morning, it is usually dark by the time we get back to Harare and then we still have to deliver animals to kennels or distraught owners.

June 2001
Harare:
The South African current affairs TV programme 'Special Assignment' comes to Zimbabwe to film a programme about our fight to stop the illegal hunting of leopards using packs of dogs.

I had worked with a member of National Parks on many occasions to push for leopard hunting with dogs to be made illegal – to our great joy it was – as an amendment to The Wildlife Act. I remember him sending me a copy of the amendment with 'Victory is Ours' handwritten across the page. Our euphoria was short-lived – a few months later, after pressure from the Safari Club in the United States, and in order to please the professional hunters – a 'special' permit was issued by Parks, which would allow hunters to use packs of imported hounds for leopard hunts – the attraction of US dollars is behind it all.

Maybe this TV coverage will help a little – sadly it's not going to stop the hunting but at least it may raise awareness in South Africa and even further afield about what is happening to the diminishing number of leopards. The Zimbabwe government is giving out quotas of 500 leopards a year to be hunted and shot when no scientific survey has ever been carried out on just how many leopards there are in the country.

July 2001
Australia:
Flew to Australia where I had been invited to attend the Africat Ball where I was to make a speech about leopard hunting.

Began the trip by staying with Nick and Laura and the two children in Melbourne. It was really lovely to have some time with the family as I had seen so little of my grandchildren, Michaela and Travers, over the last few years. Nick managed to take a few days off to take me to some super places. We went to a wildlife sanctuary where I saw magnificent wedge-tailed eagles, duck-billed platypus and of course koala bears (what serious expressions!). I also went to my grandchildren's schools for the morning when they had a sort of open day – watched Michaela in a play and later saw Travers doing a karate display. On my last night, he and Laura took me for dinner on a tram which travels round the city of Melbourne whilst you have your dinner – delightful and excellent food.

Flew to Broad Beach on the Gold Coast where Lynn Santer lives. Lynn is a well-known Australian conservationist and novelist and she had invited me and the film star Tippi Hedren (she was in many of the Alfred Hitchcock films) to Australia – all at her expense. Lynn was putting on a series of events to raise funds and awareness of big cat conservation and these were culminating in the Africat Ball held at the Jupiter Casino on the Gold Coast. Tippi is the founder and President of the ROAR Foundation in America and she is passionate about big cats and has saved many from zoos and circuses. Lynn had also laid on several interviews for me in order to give the leopard hunting in Zimbabwe maximum exposure and also to give me the chance to let Australians know what was happening to Zimbabwean farmers and their animals – there was great interest. No idea what a nightmare I was about to return to when I got home.

CHAPTER FOUR

Nandi

'You shall not covet your neighbour's house,
You shall not covet your neighbour's wife, or his manservant or
maidservant, his ox or donkey or anything that belongs
to your neighbour.' – Exodus 20 verse 17

Two Tree Hill Farm, Chinhoyi, August 2001
Eye witness and News Reports:

'War veterans and Zanu PF supporters have taken control of that area and are using it as a base – no one has been able to get near it since.'

'Aerial views show that furniture has been thrown in the swimming pool and lies scattered in the grounds of the homestead.'

'The mob then started a fire. The farm foreman was beaten.'

'The gang leaders and others are living in the main house. They have stolen three of the farmer's jeeps, one of which has since been rolled.'

'2,000 cattle were let out into 30 hectares of wheat, ruining it completely.'

'A cow was axed in the head.'

'Four dairy cows were slaughtered – their heads were axed off – and loaded on to seven stolen trailers.'

'It is estimated that in excess of 8,000 people – farmers, their workers and their families – will have no livelihood.'

'The police have at best been turning a blind eye.'

'*One farmer has been left without so much as a teaspoon.*'

'*On one of the roads in the area a farm worker was riding on a bicycle to the local police post several miles away... He had a broken arm in a cast and was so traumatised that he could hardly speak.*'

'*Nothing prepared me for what I saw. As a friend of mine said, this is the work of the anti-Christ... Absolutely everything has gone including the roof and window frames. I had a digital camera with me and as we took pictures of every room it was hard to believe that a warm wonderful family once lived here. We then drove to our old home and could not believe what we found: all that was left was the walls. Every photograph had disappeared. There was nothing left; the only thing lying on the floor was a serviette ring that my daughter Katie had used at Rydings School. Even our cat had not been spared – they shot her with a shotgun – there were cartridges all over the house.*'

These were just a few of the eye witness and news reports coming out of the farming district of Chinhoyi in the first week of August 2001. It was just as well that Meryl did not have access to email and had not read reports like these before she set out to rescue animals trapped on the looted farms. All over the country, computers were inundated with emails which described in graphic detail the horrifying events that took place when, for the first time ever in the land invasions, there was a direct confrontation between commercial farmers and war veterans. Following calls for help on the farm radio network, a group of farmers went to the assistance of a neighbour under threat.

The farmer had been barricaded into his home by a mob of 40 men who were armed with axes, fence posts and sticks. When the mob attempted to break down the farmhouse door to get inside, the farmer called the police and neighbouring farmers – only the farmers came. Radio contact with the besieged farmer was suddenly lost and then the situation deteriorated very rapidly. Repeated calls to the police yielded nothing and so farmers forced their way through a mob of war veterans in order to get to the door of the farmhouse. In the process of the confrontation the inevitable happened and people got hurt: there were several injuries – both to farmers and invaders.

In the aftermath of this one confrontation, all hell broke loose. War veterans and trespassers were not apprehended but farmers were. 17 commercial farmers were arrested by the local police who, despite repeated calls, took some hours to attend the scene and arrived at the farm long after the confrontation was over. Later that day a man in his seventies took blankets to his son who was being held in the police cells and was himself arrested. The following morning other farmers who arrived at the police station to visit their colleagues were also arrested until 21 farmers were in police custody. A doctor who went to the police station with three of the farmers' wives to offer blankets and medical support was attacked at the station gate by thugs wielding bicycle chains. The incident was watched by uniformed police officers who did nothing and then refused to accept a Report of Assault form. In the following days, war veterans and government supporters went on the rampage in an eruption of violence, arson and looting which was soon completely out of control and covered the farming areas of Doma, Chinhoyi, Mhangura, Banket and Lions Den.

The President of the Commercial Farmers Union, Colin Cloete said that farms were: 'being pillaged and looted openly and blatantly by lawless elements in marauding bands of up to 300'. Cloete said that 60 out of 107 farms in one outlying farming district had been evacuated as the situation of lawlessness was completely out of control.

As the politics heated up and first government ministers and then state-owned ZBC TV cameras arrived in the area, rather than reducing, the violence increased. There were a number of reports of people being attacked in Chinhoyi town and *The Farmer* magazine reported that anyone with a white skin was being targeted for racist attacks, particularly women:

'At least 10 people were beaten, some severely. Many were women going about their innocent business. One woman, beaten in the police station, had been there to organise vehicle clearance to go on holiday. A farmer's wife was beaten when she tried to deliver an inhaler to her asthmatic husband who was being held in the police cells. Another woman was beaten in the post office while yet another was beaten at a local farmer's shop.'

BBC correspondent Rageh Omar reported on international news bulletins that the Chinhoyi region had become so volatile and dangerous that both local and foreign journalists were finding it almost impossible to enter the area. In just a few days 53 farm homesteads were looted, four journalists reporting the news were arrested and charged with sedition and at least 8,000 farmers and farm workers were made homeless and destitute.

As literally hundreds of people were getting out of the Chinhoyi farming area as fast as they could, Meryl Harrison was doing the exact opposite and heading straight into the extremely volatile situation.

Meryl had been treating donkeys near Birchenough Bridge in the east of Zimbabwe when she heard that an entire district had come under attack by war veterans and government supporters. The phone call to Meryl came from Rose Logan, the Chairman of the Chinhoyi centre of the SPCA, who said that scores of farms were being systematically invaded, trashed, looted and burnt over a huge area. Farmers and farm workers were literally fleeing in the path of marauding mobs and there were many hundreds of animals that had been abandoned. Rose had been faxing Meryl details of events regularly but finally, when the situation was completely out of control, she phoned and had just one desperate request: 'Help, we need you here as quickly as possible!'

The request was simple and the urgency obvious but the logistics of getting from Birchenough Bridge to Chinhoyi entailed a journey of over a thousand kilometres – a massive undertaking under any circumstances. Meryl had no one who could share the driving with her, no time to stop and rest and just the company of Pavarotti on the tape player in the car. Meryl drove the first half of the journey immediately, arriving at her home in Bulawayo late in the afternoon.

She unpacked, loaded her dark blue SPCA uniforms into the washing machine and collapsed into a chair. That evening she had dinner at home with her son Tim and partner Roly. Such a simple event was now a rare treat for Meryl who was seldom at home with her family in the chaotic days of the land invasions. The urgent demands for animals to be rescued from farms continued unabated and occupied almost every waking minute of Meryl's time. The following morning, uniforms barely dry and clothes hastily repacked, Meryl hugged her family, said goodbye yet again and set out almost as soon as it was daylight at 5am. She had no idea when she would next see her son or partner or how long it would be before she would be able to sleep in her own bed again.

Meryl got messages to the SPCA team to meet her in Chinhoyi as soon as possible. Addmore came by bus from the SPCA in Kadoma, Tawanda and Misheck drove from Harare in the SPCA's Mobile Clinic truck. This vehicle had additional supplies and was also split into compartments which meant that several cats and dogs could be carried together.

Arriving in Chinhoyi, Meryl was taken in by Rob and Belinda Bowie. Rob had just taken over as the Chairman of the Chinhoyi centre of the SPCA and Belinda was an SPCA Inspector. The couple briefed Meryl as best they could about what was happening and they tried to work out which properties should be visited first. The area involved was enormous and the list of farms that had been evacuated with little or no notice was massive.

A rescue operation of epic proportions lay ahead. Anywhere else in the world, a huge team of people with a fleet of vehicles, crates of equipment and containers full of supplies would have been mobilised. In Chinhoyi in August 2001, Meryl and Belinda and three SPCA men embarked on the most monumental rescue. In the days that followed the Bowie family became a tower of strength to Meryl and an invaluable part of this largely unknown rescue.

Meryl later wrote:

'Belinda was a star as she had to leave her five young children every day – Belinda's parents Stuart and Sally rose to the occasion magnificently. Not only did they put me up for about two weeks but overnight their home became an animal sanctuary, with Stuart converting their old aviary into dog kennels, the back verandah was fenced off for small dogs and an old fish pond and surrounding fenced area became a temporary home for rescued geese. Sally coped with helping to feed many hungry mouths – all this whilst trying to run their own business in Chinhoyi. When I got back to their house late each night there was always a warm welcome and a meal – never has a Scotch and soda tasted so good! Much of the pet food that we used over those many days was donated by members of the public dropping off donations at the Bowie's house and at Harare SPCA.'

At the very forefront of the rescues Meryl enlisted the help and support of the local police. In view of the now very public experiences of a number of Chinhoyi residents with the local police over the past few days, Meryl was naturally very apprehensive. She had heard farmers talking on the radio and they likened the situation on the farms to 'a war zone' and she knew she would get nowhere without police help. Meryl gathered her courage and began at the Chinhoyi Police Station and later recorded the details:

'I asked to see the Officer Commanding Mash. West Province (Propol) who was Senior Asst. Commissioner C.M. He listened politely to what I had to say, as I explained that our only agenda was the plight of the animals left behind on the farms and that we were totally non-political. He then informed me that he would provide an armed escort (Support Unit) which we would collect from Mhanguru Police Station. As I stood up to go, I was still very worried about our safety and voiced my concern – he shook my hand and said, "Madam, I would never let any harm come to you." I believed him.'

The starting point for the rescues in Chinhoyi was Two Tree Hill Farm. This was the farm that had been visited by a delegation of top Zanu PF officials, the farm where the family had been publicly berated and humiliated on national television and the farm where the orgy of looting, destruction and arson had reached unprecedented levels.

Two Tree Hill Farm was being managed by Charl and Tertia Geldenhuys and was an intensively cropped farm, producing maize, tobacco, soya beans, hypericum flowers and winter wheat. Two Tree Hill Farm was also teeming with game animals including kudu, tsessebe, sable, reedbuck and impala. There were six baby elephants and six bottle-fed giraffe on the farm as well as eland and zebra that had been relocated to the farm during a bad drought in the lowveld area of Zimbabwe. There was a large dam which was stocked with bass and bream and had yielded two all-Africa records. Charl Geldenhuys was passionate about Two Tree Hill Farm and all life on the property was sacrosanct. He did not allow any shooting or hunting on the farm at all – not even birds of which 260 species had been recorded. Charl also had one special love on Two Tree Hill Farm and his wife Tertia wrote about it:

'We had a very tame eland, which we named Em. Em was in love with my husband and I think Charl was a little bit in love with her too. Every time he passed Em, whether it was on his motorbike or with the pick-up, he had to stop to greet her. She would put her head on his shoulders and he had to rub her forehead. Whenever I was with Charl, Em would push me aside, looking me straight in the eyes as if she wanted to say this was her special boyfriend and this was her time with him now.'

There was no chance to save Em or any of the wild, domestic or farm animals on Two Tree Hill when the war veterans and their supporters arrived on 9 August 2001. Tertia and Charl, their 12-year-old daughter Resje and new baby Charl-Emil, just nine months old, were in the house when ten men arrived at the gate. They shouted for Charl to go outside.

'We want you out!' they yelled. 'We want you out here! We want to see your blood flow! Come out! Come out here!'

For the next nine hours the Geldenhuys were trapped, helpless and alone and could do nothing but watch through the windows as their workshops and sheds were looted. The police were called but did not come. Tertia watched as young and old men, women and even children looted the outbuildings and carried off bags of fertiliser on their shoulders, loading it onto the farmers' trailers and carting it off with Charl's tractors. The looters would go away for half an hour at a time, returning with more people and the looting would continue with renewed vigour. Each time they came back the war veterans were drunker and louder, shouting triumphantly and becoming more aggressive and wild.

Wearing running shoes in case they had to run for their lives, cradling the baby who would not settle, Tertia phoned her pastor, friends and family and asked that they pray for the family. 'I realised that this was some evil force controlling the people and that God alone could save us,' she said. At 11am, five hours after the looting had begun, the situation deteriorated even further. A war veteran walked up to the gate and shot at one of the dogs with a catapult and a little later he came back carrying an axe, accompanied by another man. In one quick movement they swung the axe at the gate and the padlock broke open and dropped off. The gate swung wide open. The Boerboel dog that had earlier been pelted with stones from the catapult challenged the intruders. In one movement the war veteran discarded his axe, pulled out a pistol and shot the Boerboel. The dog fell dead instantly.

For the next three hours the dog lay in a pool of blood in front of the house. 70 war veterans patrolled up and down outside the open gate and the Geldenhuys family remained in the house, terrified and paralysed, just praying and waiting for the police to come. They had been called repeatedly during the past nine hours. When they did finally arrive it was with a ZBC Television crew, a very well-known Zanu PF Minister, Zanu PF Member of Parliament and Zanu PF Governor.

The cameras rolled and the Minister sat on bags of looted fertiliser. He said that Charl Geldenhuys had started the destruction of Two Tree Hill Farm. The Minister said Charl had shot his own dog, had shot at the war veterans, had burnt their houses and had chased their cattle into the farm crops. Shortly after the Minister and his entourage left, the police came to the house and confiscated Charl's firearms, leaving him unarmed and unable to protect himself, his wife, their two children or his possessions. With neither time nor options left, Tertia began to pack. Opening cupboards and drawers she was paralysed and did not know what to take and what to leave. 'Everything was important and nothing was important,' she later told Meryl. The Geldenhuys family packed what they could into a couple of suitcases and left. They had no choice but to leave their dogs behind, they simply had no room for the remaining Boerboel, two Australian Cattle Dogs and eight puppies. Shortly afterwards the mob of looters, war veterans and hangers-on swarmed into the homestead.

By the time Meryl arrived on Two Tree Hill farm the damage had been done but she hoped at least to find and rescue the dogs, sure that some would have been able to hide somewhere. Meryl had been told that the dogs had been abducted by the looters but that one may have escaped. She was looking for: Nandi, an Australian Cattle Dog, her daughter Khanya and eight puppies.

Arriving outside the security gates of Two Tree Hill farm, the scene that greeted Meryl was almost beyond belief. The farmhouse had been completely destroyed and was just a blackened empty shell. It had been looted, trashed and then burnt down. Meryl stood staring at the horror and trying to get her emotions under control before she went in. Lost in her thoughts and trying to make some sense of what she saw, Meryl jumped in fright and spun round when something touched her on the shoulder. Expecting to find herself face-to-face with an angry thug or hostile looter, Meryl could hardly believe it when she saw an eland standing right behind her. This was Em the tame and very gentle eland who was besotted with Charl. Clearly now the eland was lonely and bewildered at the sudden absence of love and attention. Meryl stroked and patted Em, luxuriating in the soft rich brown fur on the eland's neck and face, letting her fingers linger there, giving and receiving tranquillity and a sense of calm. This Meryl could deal with: what lay beyond the gates she knew would be the start of another series of memories and nightmares that would haunt her in the months and years ahead.

Meryl and Addmore walked towards the ruins of the house. A huge jacaranda tree, which by now should have been preparing to carpet the ground with purple flowers, had been chopped down and lay across the driveway, obviously to form a barricade. Bags of fertiliser lay scattered all over the lawn – the remnants, abandoned by the looters. The green bags lay spoiling in the weather, exposed to dew and sun, going to waste. Outside the back door of the house a washing machine stood as a testament to what had been a modern kitchen. Now the machine was useless and powerless, its pipes and hoses ripped out of the walls, its purpose and function destroyed by a mob. The kitchen had been completely gutted. The cupboards and fittings had been ripped off the walls. The doors and windows, together with frames and hinges had literally been chopped and smashed out of the brickwork.

In the living room there remained what was left of the family piano, chopped up and reduced to splinters and chunks of wood which lay on the floor amongst the remains of the piano keys. Books and papers lay in a big pile on the living room floor, partially burnt, completely useless. There was smashed glass and broken bricks everywhere and Meryl had to watch her footing as she went down the passageway towards what had once been the bedroom. The contents of all the cupboards had been smashed and strewn on the floor. Meryl checked each cupboard very carefully; she was looking for eight little puppies who could have been hiding anywhere but they were nowhere to be seen. There was nothing here at all now, just an eerie silence in a house that had been so violated. It was hard to believe that just a week ago this had been a family home filled with love and laughter and now it was a burnt-out derelict wreck, a deserted ruin.

As Meryl turned to leave, she noticed a shower stall which she had not checked. She moved towards it and there, lying in the corner of the shower amongst the fittings that had been ripped off the wall, Meryl saw a dog. Her heart raced in excitement and relief: she had almost missed it. This was Nandi. The dog was not moving at all and her pupils were in the back of her head. Meryl bent down to stroke the dog and Nandi flinched at even this gentlest of touches. Meryl and Addmore lifted Nandi as carefully as they could but every movement caused the dog to yelp. Nandi had a very bad wound near her mouth and was obviously in great pain. Without any further delay Meryl immediately headed back to Chinhoyi town to get Nandi to a vet. If she could save the life of just this one animal, it would help ease the anguish of what had gone on at Two Tree Hill Farm.

Nandi was checked over by vet Rob Gordon in Chinhoyi. Later Rob told Meryl that there was not an inch of Nandi's body that hadn't been beaten. Rob had to anaesthetise Nandi in order to suture the wounds around her mouth. It looked as if these wounds were from where she had been tied up with wire. Nandi had literally chewed her way free in order to escape. Nandi's breed undoubtedly contributed to her courage and determination when faced with such adversity. A brief description of the breed explains this behaviour exactly:

'[They] *are active, energetic, intelligent dogs that benefit from training enormously – it stops them having time to think up other ways of amusing themselves! They are an interesting mixture as they can turn to jelly at the mention of nail clipping, yet they will be determined to carry on business as usual with a potentially life-threatening health problem.'* ("Breed Notes", *Dog World*)

Meryl later found out that Nandi, her daughter Khanya and four of the puppies had been snatched by the invaders and looters and taken to a village 15 kilometres from the farm. Of course no one admitted to being responsible for taking the dogs or tying them up for days but some villagers said they had seen a grey dog running through the bush. This could only have been Nandi. Beaten, bleeding and hugely traumatised, the dog had run away as soon as she could escape; run back to the only home she had ever known.

Nandi had been born on Two Tree Hill farm and was absolutely devoted to her mistress. Nandi would shadow her owner, sleeping outside whichever window of the house Tertia Geldenhuys was in. Meryl offered a reward to the villagers for the return of Nandi's daughter Khanya or any of her babies and this resulted in the recovery of two puppies from a nearby village. A further tip-off led Meryl to Khanya, who was found tied to a tree while her new 'owner', the settler who had seized her, was cutting down more trees to build a house. In the days that followed and in-between other rescues, Meryl never gave up hope for the remaining puppies. There were rumours and whispers and false leads but some time later the remaining puppies were found dead. Em, the tame eland, was also a casualty in the days ahead. She was slaughtered and eaten.

When Tertia Geldenhuys paid one brief visit back to Two Tree Hill Farm, she was shattered by the devastation. Simply nothing was left of their lives – clothes, pictures, paintings, certificates, documents, bedding, furniture – everything was either gone or destroyed. She wrote:

'While I was walking from one empty room to another demolished room, this vast nothingness dawned on me – it is as if we no longer have a past. Maybe that is how Em, our eland, felt when they slaughtered her. Maybe she also felt that she never existed.'

Leaving Nandi in the safe hands of the vet, Meryl and her team moved on to other ravaged farms in the area. There were scores of them and Meryl drove day in and day out from morning till night visiting one farm after another looking for animals, saving as many as she could.

What Meryl saw on those farms could only be described as the face of evil. Everywhere there was destruction and the evidence of acts of pure barbarity. Everything of any financial value was gone – furniture, electrical equipment, tools, machines, vehicles, clothing, food. Immovable fittings had been smashed where they stood – windows, mirrors, tiles, baths, sinks, toilets, geysers, built-in cupboards. There was a sea of paper underfoot – torn books, files, magazines, decades of farm records, family photographs, children's school reports, old letters – everything laid to waste for no earthly purpose at all.

In the ruins of people's homes Meryl saw things she would never be able to forget, things she would not even be able to tell the owners. Her feet crunched on shattered Christmas decorations, occasionally a child's toy, a piece of a family photograph, the cover of a book. In amongst these ruins of people's homes and lives Meryl looked for their beloved dogs and cats. She searched amongst the rubble and paper and broken glass in houses and outbuildings, she scoured gardens, checking under bushes, in hedges, and she called and called the names of the lost animals, again and again until there was no hope.

In the evenings and when it was too dark to continue, Meryl returned to the home of Rob and Belinda Bowie. She was always exhausted, filthy and drained but every night Meryl recorded in her diaries what she had seen on those looted and devastated farms. She faithfully wrote down the names of pets and recorded details of those she had been able to find and rescue. Meryl's diary entries were all that would be left in the years ahead for those who cared to know the truth of what went on under the guise of 'land redistribution'. The fragments and images that Meryl recorded would stand as testament to the massive destruction that had swept through the whole area. It had been a thriving community with thousands of people of all ages, colours and beliefs whose lives were ravaged in a fortnight of mayhem. To do justice to the events of that August 2001 would require thousands of pages. Just a small selection of

Meryl's diary entries were representative of the horror and devastation:

'Addmore and I just worked from dawn to dusk – driving from one farm to the next, day after day. Every single rescue in the area was undertaken with an escort of Support Unit or Army – very often both – all heavily armed. We couldn't have done it without them, they obviously knew how unsafe or dangerous our mission really was.'

'Winfield Farm: The house had been looted and trashed, the dogs fine – except a chocolate Labrador who had lost his voice from barking at the intruders in his house!'

'Cotswold Estates: After much searching we found Shauna, an old Border Collie bitch, hiding next to some pipes. She was very pleased to see us but kept running back to where she had been hiding. Eventually she started to trust me and then stuck to me like glue! I again walked right around the garden and spotted the large clump of banana trees. (I had been thinking: where would I hide if I were a dog?) I looked into the clump and called several times. As I turned away Tuff, a Ridgeback male, came out, appeared nervous but also stuck to me like glue. In spite of much calling and searching we could not find the other two dogs – which were Basil and Oscar. The gardener said he had seen Oscar being beaten with a knobkerrie.'

'Hunt's house (also on Cotswold Estate): Did not go into the property because Rocky – Bull Terrier – was very aggressive! With the maid's help he was put into the back of the truck, also Sisi, a young black-and-tan bitch. No sign of the cat which the maid said had hidden in the sofa which was then looted.'

'Kaukua: Uplifted dogs: Buster, Chaka, Marcus and Jock. Jock, a Labrador, had been beaten – he was holding his head on one side and dragging his hind legs due to the beating he had sustained.'

'Muir senior: The house had also been ransacked and looted. We uplifted Dinky, Spot and Titch. At this house I attempted to take photographs of the damage but a member of the Support Unit told me I was not a journalist and it would be "inappropriate".'

'Kyalami Farm: Found the house ransacked and totally burnt. In a cage near the back door we found a hutch with three rabbits.'

'Ozana Farm: Place also ransacked and looted. Looters had also taken all his tropical fish and the fish tank. What on earth the looters were going to do with tropical fish and a tank in a village with no electricity to run the heater and pump I could not imagine. We collected two Staffordshire Bull Terriers: Major, a brindle male – very lively; and Amber, a tan bitch – very nervous. As we left some 50 war vets/settlers could be seen waiting under the trees nearby to move on to the property.'

'Urume Farm: all grazing was burnt — cattle had very little to eat. At the Chinoyi SPCA we already had a Jack Russell called Pluto who was from this farm and had been found running down the road five days before — very thin and covered in ticks.'

Months after the horrors of the Chinhoyi farm lootings, Meryl knew the time had come for Nandi, the Australian Cattle Dog rescued from Two Tree Hill farm, to be permanently settled. Nandi had taken some time to recover from her wounds and get over the trauma of what had happened and in the process of her healing she made a lasting impression on everyone she came in contact with. For three months after the rescue, Nandi, Khanya and the pups stayed with Belinda Bowie's parents in the makeshift kennels erected in their back garden. It was a memorable time as Belinda recalled:

'It was my Mom and I that fed them and cleaned their "home" as "madam" Nandi hated all our staff and they equally hated her as she snuck up and bit them at every opportunity!'

Meryl had similar memories of how Nandi could be a right little 'toad' at times! On one occasion Meryl and the Bowies were invited to a big lunch party by the Lions Club of Mazowe that had been put on to raise money for the farm rescues. It was held at Zanadau farm in Mvurwi and was an idyllic setting next to a farm dam. Meryl had been asked to make a short speech and chose Nandi as her star guest:

'I asked Belinda to bring Nandi so I could tell her story of outstanding canine courage. We sat on the lawn of this beautiful garden, white uniformed waiters moving discreetly around re-filling our glasses with champagne. I, in the meantime, was trying to hold Nandi with a very firm grip as every now and again she would shoot out and grab a white trouser leg. After being severely admonished, she would sit there with a little smug expression on her face — the waiters I have to say, took it in very good spirit and found it very amusing! Nandi was a big hit with everyone — in spite of her anti-social behaviour.'

When Meryl was satisfied that Nandi was ready to move on, she and Addmore took her to her new home with relations of the Geldenhuys' family in South Africa. It was a very long and tiring journey to Johannesburg, extremely hot in the car, and Meryl heaved a great sigh of relief when they arrived at their night stop. Meryl, Addmore and Nandi were in South Africa at the invitation of the BBC who, unable to get into Zimbabwe, needed to film them for the pending BBC Animal Awards event.

The BBC had sponsored accommodation for Meryl and Addmore at a very smart bed and breakfast facility in Rosebank but the owners were not so happy when their guests arrived. Nandi jumped out of the truck and headed straight for a fountain in the courtyard. She plunged into the water, had a quick swim and a drink and then raced into the house shaking herself dry as she went, tearing through the immaculate rooms, spraying walls, splashing furniture and redecorating the floors and carpets of the beautiful house.

This was clearly a dog that was now completely healed; physically and mentally. Everything in her behaviour testified to this miracle. There was no doubt that because of Meryl, Addmore and the small SPCA team, Nandi would be able to go on to live a happy and fulfilled life with her new family – a fitting reward for a dog who had endured so much. In the years ahead when Meryl was plagued with nightmares of what she had witnessed on those looted and destroyed homes in the Chinhoyi district, it was thoughts of Nandi that kept her sane and helped her to cope. Meryl saved Nandi in August 2001: loving memories of the dog would save Meryl countless times in the years ahead.

Five years later, writing from England, Meryl said:

'They were days that I will never forget as long as I live. I still have nightmares about them. Somehow – I don't know why – Nandi came to mean so much to me. There was a very great bond between us and she would come to me when she wouldn't go to anyone else. Nandi's escape was one of extreme canine courage. Amongst the very few pictures I have here in my little flat, thousands of miles away from all the memories of those dark days – I have a photo of Nandi. For me she represents all the thousands of innocent animals of Zimbabwe that bore the brunt of the viciousness of the government's "land reform".'

Extracts from Meryl's Diary:

Honey is dug up by the honey-bear and left.
(When something desirable is obtained without effort.)
– Sindebele Proverb

August 2001
Harare:
After the trauma and exhaustion of the fortnight in Chinhoyi, I returned to Harare feeling as if I had been living on another planet. I remember realizing that life for folk in town had been proceeding as normal, the majority of my friends and even work colleagues really having no idea what hell the farming community – not that many miles from Harare – had been going through. The 'normality' of the life that I returned

to seemed surreal. But whilst I could not forget what I had seen and experienced, I knew that I just had to move on.

Nyamandlovu:
Farmer reports 950 cattle confined by war vets to a small kraal with no food or water.

Wedza:
Farmer reports 1,000 head of cattle confined to a small area on farm by war vets.

Ruwa:
Evicted farmer asks for help as war vets insist that three horses must be removed from farm.

Nyabira:
Nine dogs to be rescued from a farm. Owner informed me it was not safe for him to go to the farm and uplift the dogs himself. Dogs names are: Cider, Houginire, Sanesan, Asterix, Obelix, Delilah, Scamp, Ben and Barney.

Nyamandlovu:
Report of 172 heifers being kept in a kraal without access to food and water since yesterday. They had originally been kraaled to give foot and mouth vaccines but the war vets subsequently kept them impounded.

CHAPTER FIVE

Letters in the Sand

A bird does not sing because it has an answer.
It sings because it has a song.
– Chinese Proverb

Fynnland Farm, Chinhoyi, August 2001

At the end of August 2001, Meryl looked back on what had been the worst month since farm invasions and animal rescues had begun sixteen months before. The memories were still vivid, and the horrors raw, of a time that no one would want to remember. There was one farm among the scores in the Chinhoyi district, where Meryl found an imprint to a time nearly three quarters of a century before.

The owners of Fynnland farm in Chinhoyi had been evicted and the property had been looted and trashed some days before Meryl and her SPCA team arrived. They had been asked to look for Maxi, a much loved Stafford-shire bitch who belonged to farmers Andy and Elva Fraser. In the mayhem of the arrival of looters and invaders and the chaos of the evacuation that followed, Maxi must have taken fright and had been nowhere to be found. Andy and Elva were away at the time but their son Gary and his wife were on the farm and were distraught that they hadn't been able to find Maxi. Gary tried to go back to the farm but couldn't because of the continuing instability and so Meryl, Addmore and Misheck added Fynnland Farm to the list and went in search of the missing Staffie bitch.

Meryl stood in the garden of the farm and stared at the chaos all around her. There were 114 sheep grazing in the farm garden. Two sheep were dead in the swimming pool – they had obviously fallen in and drowned when they stooped to drink from the declining water level. Andy and Elva's house had been completely trashed and personal possessions were strewn everywhere. Meryl stared at the things that had made up the lives and home of the family, now scattered on the floor under her feet: crushed Christmas decorations, farm accounts, papers and books and signs that the invaders had tried to burn some things too.

'As I wandered around the garden feeling so saddened at the utter pointlessness of the destruction, I came across three pieces of paper, blowing about in the sand at the edge of the flower-beds. The wording in them referred to love and seemed all the more poignant given the reason for them being there.'

Meryl stooped and picked up the three scraps of paper. They were very old and handwritten in ink. They looked as if they had come from a small notebook and at the top of one discoloured page was the date: 10 December 1927. The pages were not in sequence, one written in blue ink and the other two in black. All were faded, pale and sepia-coloured with age. The handwriting was decisive and the words, those that were still legible and had not been torn or burnt away, were of love, nature and beauty. Meryl stood in the warmth of the August sun, surrounded by ruination and read some of the words from the fragments of paper in her hand:

10th December 1927

The Birth of Morn

An angel, robed in spotless white
Bent down and kissed the sleeping night
Night woke to blush. The sprite was gone
Men saw the blush and called it dawn

– Nan

Love can forgive all ....
Intentional and unintentional
The only unforgivable thing is a love which
Calls itself love, yet fails to forgive.

I have given you these things before but I want to write them here.
Flowers are lovely; Love is flower-like
Friendship is a sheltering tree
......The joys that come down flower-like
Of Friendship; Love and Liberty

– Nan

The Future

A wanderer is man from his birth
He was born in a ship
On the breast of the river of Time;
Brimming with wonder and joy
Rivets his gaze on the banks of the stream
And spreads out his arms to the night.

– Nan

A garden worker was hanging around. He looked dazed, shocked and disorientated and Meryl asked him if he knew who the papers may have belonged to.

'The madala Madam [the old lady]!' he replied, explaining that an old lady had lived there a long time ago.

Carefully Meryl picked up the three pages and put them away for safe-keeping. She asked the gardener if he knew where Maxi was but knew he was lying when he said that the farmer had taken the dog with him when he left. With thoughts of a missing dog and knowing that there were still horses and sheep on the farm that would need to be rescued, Meryl knew she had to keep the relations cordial and so she said: 'There will be a reward if you find Maxi!' Immediately the gardener changed his mind about the whereabouts of the dog and directed Meryl to a nearby village. 'Onias has him,' the gardener said, 'you ask people for Onias.'

Meryl drove to the village with Addmore and Misheck and they didn't have to ask for Onias or even look for his house. The dog found them instantly!

'As I stopped the truck, I saw a brindle streak coming from the direction of the huts. It was Maxi! She jumped straight into the back of the truck and I then had to go and ask permission from the Chairman of the war veterans to take the dog. He allowed us to take Maxi and I returned the next morning to dip the village dogs and also gave them cigarettes – the reward for Maxi!'

When Meryl re-established contact with the Frasers again, some years later, they were unable to shed any further light on the origin of the poems or who 'Nan' was, but they hadn't forgotten how Meryl had saved their dog. Elva spoke for many when she wrote to Meryl:

'Your rescue of our beloved pet Maxi was such a relief for Andy and myself and we can't tell you how much your courageous efforts meant, not only for us but for other farmers too.'

Meryl never found out who had written the poems on the three pages she had found lying in the sand that August morning in 2001 on a looted and abandoned Chinhoyi farm. She was sure that whoever it was must have been in love and wouldn't have minded her showing those poems to a world shocked and saddened by events in Zimbabwe 74 years later. One poem Meryl did manage to identify and in the years ahead she would never be able to read the famous lines of Byron again without remembering the Frasers, their beloved dog and a few letters she had found lying in the sand on a Zimbabwean farm.

There is a pleasure in the pathless woods,
There is a rapture on the lonely shore.
There is a society, where none intrudes,
By the deep sea, and music in its roar.
I love not man the less, but nature more.

– Byron

Extracts from Meryl's Diary:

What is behind is in front.
(One might someday have to return to what one has left,
so it is well to take farewell properly.)
– Sindebele proverb

September 2001
Rusape:
Speaking to National Parks about various issues I hear that the male hippo that was in the farm dam in Rusape had been shot. Parks thought the female hippo was still alive.

Bulawayo:
At 1pm approximately a fortnight ago while a farm owner was out, a vehicle arrived on the farm with two men and a woman. They said the farm was now theirs and they were 'going to burn it'. The herdsman drove the dairy cows away as the fires

were started. The cows were pinned against the barbed wire fence but the herdsman managed to get the fence down so the animals could get away.

Then another fire was started which drove the cattle towards the fence by the main road. A passing dairy farmer stopped and helped to get the fence down. By this time the herd had split into the three groups. 55 cows were together in one group – all burnt in varying degrees. The remaining 27 were found to be alright.

Of the burnt dairy cows, many were found to have had their eyes, ears and especially their udders burnt. The farmer said, 'Their udders looked like over-ripe tomatoes with vienna sausages hanging down.' Two vets tended to and treated all affected cows. Some will have to be dried off or slaughtered as it will be too painful to milk them. Their hooves have started to separate – the intense heat of the fire causing their feet to crack and split in several places.

Nyamandlovu:
On a farm in the Umguza district there was a fire during the night and 58 ostrich chicks were burnt to death. The farmer was forced off a fortnight before. The fire apparently started at 3am and the chicks, which were all just a week old, died in the pen where they were enclosed. It was believed that the fire had been started by war vets or invaders but a spokesperson for the war vets, Comrade Dube, said that the fire had been started deliberately to 'tarnish our image'.

Got permission from DISPOL Minor and went to the farm with a police Inspector and a Constable. The remains of the ostriches had been buried by the time we got there, but we could see how fierce the fire had been: all the surrounding plastic had melted; they wouldn't have stood a chance. With no proof of how it had happened, all I could do was threaten the surly crowd with prosecution under the Prevention of Cruelty to Animals Act. I was only too happy to leave the farm – there was a horrible atmosphere there. This is one of the few farms that we've been called to in the Matabeleland area.

Bulawayo:
More anonymous calls in the night. I've been receiving them since 1996 – must have been more than 200 calls by now. They are always in the early hours of the morning and no one ever speaks. I've always just put the phone down and then a few minutes later it rings again – this happens three or four times in a row. Have reported the calls to the police and they do seem to take it quite seriously – eventually handed it over to Fraud Squad. CID – Fraud Squad apparently deal with all cases of Threatening or Nuisance phone calls. They even put a trace on my phone but without success as the calls were made from outside Bulawayo. Eventually a pattern was noticed – the calls were rarely made over a weekend or public holiday and most were made on a Monday or Thursday. Police thought it might have been someone on night duty.

The calls came again tonight, at 2.13am, 2.16am, 2.25am, 2.30am and 3am. It has begun to dawn on me that it could well be either of the two guys who killed my twin brother Colin. I have often mentioned their names in the press and have been consistently outspoken about their crime.

October 2001
Bulawayo:
Roly's boss and dear friend passes away from cancer. Roly is devastated. They lived in the same road as us in Bulawayo.

28 October. Tim's birthday.

Mutare:
Invited to a meeting with various stakeholders from the timber industry with regard to the poisoning of baboons by the timber companies. ZNSPCA was totally opposed to this and had voiced our concerns on numerous occasions. We were eventually invited to sit on the stakeholders' committee that had been formed by the timber industry in an effort to address everyone's concerns – not just ourselves, but also WWF, local headmen, spirit mediums and workers' representatives, so that we could all work together.

All agreed that baboons do an enormous amount of damage to the trees. For some reason that no one can fathom, they love chewing the bark of the trees and in many cases ring bark them and then the tree dies. To make things worse, most of the time they don't even ingest the bark but just chew it like a form of chewing gum – and then spit it out! The damage caused by a big troop of baboons can be quite devastating – but they were there first in the area, long before timber plantations appeared.

It's become clear that every other method possible has been tried, ie: trapping, having guards drive them away, silver foil on the trees but nothing has worked. By the time we became involved the poisoning was already taking place as Zimbabwe had been given permission by the world body – the Forestry Stewardship Council (FSO) – to poison the baboons for a period of two years, obviously under strict controls. Legally we could not have stopped it, but we could monitor the entire process to minimise the trauma to the baboons.

As opposed as we were to the idea, I was always given every access to the sites where the poisoning was being carried out. When I found problems and made complaints, they were always dealt with and corrected. Notwithstanding the damage caused by the baboons, the future of the timber industry in Zimbabwe faces a bleak future as the timber estates are either taken over by Govt or burnt out by fires.

November 2001

Chegutu:

Ran a week-long course for Trainee SPCA Inspectors in Chegutu. It was attended by approx 15 trainee inspectors and by the end of the week there was an excellent sense of camaraderie amongst the candidates – many of whom had not met before.

December 2001

Mwenezi:

Farmer reports 200 cows together with calves have been kraaled by war vets. They have water but no food. Three head of cattle are paralysed after having been hit on their backs.

Harare:

10 December. Human Right's Day. Laid flowers for Colin at the Human Rights plaque in Harare Gardens. Feeling a bit bleak afterwards but went on to a meeting at National Parks regarding the exploitation of wildlife in Zim. After that I headed for the University to check on the rats, guinea pigs, monkeys, etc that are kept there for research purposes.

Glendale:

Farmer reports that a pack of 40 hunting dogs (with pups trying to keep up) are coming onto the farm from a neighbouring property. All dogs are in a pathetic condition.

Wedza:

Farmer reports that five cows and five calves are put in a small kraal by settlers who said that the cattle had eaten their paprika. The farmer says the fence had been cut enabling the cattle to get in. Settlers demanding damages – extortion.

Beatrice:

Requested to go to Beatrice farm (has been taken over by Vice President's husband) to uplift three rare black swans, two mandarin ducks and two purple crested Louries – the latter in an aviary. All are owned by farmer who has been violently evicted. It all looks weirdly peaceful when we get there – apart from a surly-looking war veteran seated in a lounge chair at the security gate. We released the Louries and took the swans (not easy to catch, wished we had the excellent custom-made 'swan carriers' that one sees the RSPCA using) and the duck out to a well-known farmer who special-ised in birds. The other mandarin duck, the female, was missing. The workers said she had been swallowed by a python! I later learnt that friends of the evicted farmer had shot the 14-year-old family dog, a Boerboel, and also a very old horse. I remember hoping that other farmers might also take the same responsible stance.

Masvingo:

After a fortnight of torrential rain in the Masvingo area and near Lake Kyle, ZTV reports rivers are in full flood and several families are cut off by flood water. Film footage shows a village surrounded on either side by swift flowing rivers. Water apparently coming out of Kyle at the rate of 190 cubic metres per second! Air Force helicopters are doing several trips a day to evacuate villagers.

Phoned Masvingo SPCA and ask for regular updates as there was obviously going to be quite a lot of livestock – poultry, dogs, etc – stranded on what was now an island. Inspector Happson phones to say he had driven as close as he could to the river bank and could see the cattle standing in the rain on the island – all their grazing now covered by the flooding.

Drive to Masvingo and call a meeting with as many stakeholders as possible – police, army, Air Force, local Water Board and Provincial Administrator all attend. The meeting is held at the Masvingo Police Station in one of their large rooms upstairs. The meeting went on into the evening and we were soon sitting in the dark, as the light bulb had broken and they didn't have a spare one! I requested the Air Force helicopter to take several bales of hay (which I had already sourced and which had been donated!) for the cattle, goats and donkeys and to uplift the dogs and chickens as their situation was now critical.

Everyone at the meeting agrees that the animals will die if there is no intervention but they all said there was nothing they could do to help. The Air Force told me they wanted $100,000 a trip – for a welfare organisation that was totally out of the question. I was furious but was banging my head against a brick wall. I told the meeting that in a disaster the Civil Service should rise to the occasion – they all nodded but said there was nothing they could do.

A week later the flooding receded and the villagers returned. Apparently some of their animals were still alive but only just. One hen had even hatched out some chicks but sadly many animals hadn't survived. When I later met some of the villagers and suggested they think of relocating their village to higher ground, my idea was met with absolute horror. They said it was traditional that they live there.

Chapter Six

Bindura Birds

'Life is mostly froth and bubble,
Two things stand like stone,
Kindness in another's trouble,
Courage in your own.'
– Adam Lindsay Gordon, 1860

Chiwaridzo suburb, Bindura, January 2002
Meryl headed to Bindura with SPCA Inspector Misheck after a call about chickens that needed to be rescued as soon as possible. The birds had been abandoned without food and water for a number of days and the call for help came from a neighbour in the Chiwadziro suburb of the town. Although Bindura was surrounded by highly productive maize and cotton farms, the call for help was not from a commercial farmer for a change but from a resident in the town itself. The owner of the house, Mr Masikela, was a supporter of the opposition MDC and was one of many who had fled their homes and the town after they had been beaten up in a frenzy of political violence. Bindura was one of three towns that had become the focus of extreme political tension in the first week of January 2002. The day before Meryl's visit the headlines in local newspapers were chilling: 'Bindura Sealed Off'; 'Bindura Epitomizes Civil War'. 88 kilometres north east of Harare the town had originally been called Kimberley Reefs and named after a gold mine. Known as Bindura since 1913 and usually famous for the Trojan Nickel Mine, it was the 2002 March Presidential elections and their shadow of violence which bought international media attention to the small mining town – the administrative capital of Mashonaland Central province.

The UK *Independent* newspaper reported that hundreds of youth militia had mounted illegal roadblocks and sealed off the town. Residents said the militant youths had gone door to door through the town demanding to see membership cards of Zanu PF. People unable to prove their membership to Zanu PF had been brutally beaten. Houses had been stoned, windows smashed and residents reported gangs of youths patrolling the town in the back of pick-up trucks which had government number plates.

Arriving at the Provincial Police Headquarters in Bindura to ask for an official escort, Meryl was told by the police that it wouldn't be safe for her to go into the suburb. The police said that SPCA Inspector Misheck should go alone into Chiwaridzo suburb and that Meryl should wait at the police station until he returned. Meryl immediately and without hesitation refused this instruction. She had made it a rule from the very start of the farm rescues almost two years before that no member of the SPCA team should ever be separated from the others and that no one should ever attempt a rescue alone. It was a rule that had worked until now and she had no intention of changing things just because an election was around the corner. Meryl told the police that under no circumstances would Misheck go alone and said that they would proceed to the suburb together, with the police escort she was trying to get!

Not wanting to accept responsibility for the decision, the police shunted Meryl from one office to the next, to the OC (Officer Commanding) of the Bindura Police Station and then to the Station Intelligence Officer. At last Meryl succeeded and was given the escort she'd requested and Sergeant Maswere accompanied the SPCA team to Chiwaridzo suburb. The Sergeant warned Meryl that they would most likely be stopped by Zanu PF youths but as it happened they were not and the journey was uneventful.

The suburb was not far out of Bindura town and had the appearance typical of high density suburbs all over the country: women vendors sitting at the side of the road with little pyramids of tomatoes and limp bunches of rape for sale; scraggy chickens scratching in the dust; barefoot children playing with plastic bag footballs and the road littered with the chewed waste of sugar cane and sweet sorghum stalks. Arriving at the desired house they saw immediately that there was a problem.

'When we got to Mr Masikela's house, the Sgt with us realised it was directly opposite one of the ZANU PF bases that had sprung up in the township recently, and therefore thought that it would be wise to have an armed escort with us. I turned round and drove him back to the police station where we collected a uniformed member of the force who was armed with a pistol.'

On the way back Sergeant Maswere pointed out another house that was a Zanu PF 'base'. All the windows had been smashed and there were ten to fifteen youths standing around. They stopped at the house and Sergeant Maswere asked the youths if the SPCA could remove the white broilers belonging to the owner of the house.

'The house was not on our list, but the Sgt happened to know that the occupants, Mr
and Mrs Midzi, had been violently evicted by ZANU PF youths. The Midzi's were the
parents of Trymore Midzi, the MDC vice-chairman for Mashonaland Central, who had
been killed by nine Zanu PF supporters the previous month.'

The youths agreed that the birds could be removed and soon 28 chickens
had been caught and loaded into the back of Meryl's truck. Some of the youths
even helped with the loading and put two half full sacks of chicken food into the
truck. Two of the youths then climbed into the back of the truck and accompanied the SPCA team to Mr Masikela's house – the venue of the original rescue.
The gates were padlocked and so Misheck and the police officer climbed over
the wall of a neighbour's house to gain access. While she waited Meryl looked
across at the building that had been taken over as a Zanu PF Base.

'It was an ordinary-looking little house – no curtains at the windows. It had a
Zimbabwean flag fluttering on the end of a crudely fashioned pole. Several youths
were lounging around on the lawn – they never took their eyes off us, but thankfully
did not attempt to stop us from removing the chickens. Many of them were wearing
the now-familiar green uniform of the infamous Border Gezi Youths.'

It didn't take long before Misheck and the policeman were handing
chickens over the top of the wall. Mr Masikela's 29 brown layers were loaded into
cages in the back of the SPCA truck and Meryl could see that the birds were very
thin and showing the effects of neglect. Throughout the operation the youths at
the Zanu PF Base across the road stood and stared but did and said nothing.

Encouraged by two successes and taking full advantage of Meryl,
Misheck and the SPCA vehicle, Sergeant Maswere said there was one more
Zanu PF Base in the neighbourhood. He said the youths had chased away
the owner who was an MDC Ward Chairman and there were chickens that
needing rescuing there too. Meryl drove to the third house and immediately
saw a group of about fifteen youths hanging around. Sergeant Maswere went
and asked their permission to remove the chickens (even though he was the
law!) and when they agreed, Misheck and the police went behind the house to
catch the birds.

Suddenly Meryl realised she was alone and her heart started to thump a
little as the Zanu PF youths started singing and drumming. One, who appeared
to be the leader, came a little closer and stood copying all the words written on
the door of Meryl's truck (ie ZNSPCA Chief Inspector) onto a piece of paper.
Meryl tried to appear cool and in control and even offered the youth her ID but
he wasn't interested and turned away.

Meryl breathed a sigh of relief when she saw Misheck and the policeman come back into view, both carrying chickens destined for the cages in the back to the truck. Soon all the birds had been caught and loaded and Meryl was glad to be leaving the township and the town where once, in happier times, her sons had been to junior school. At that time the Ministry of Education had thought it a good idea for children of single parents to attend boarding school – particularly if they were boys. Newly divorced and trying to find places for both the boys at the same school, Meryl enrolled Nick and Tim at Bindura School and so the area and surroundings were familiar. That seemed like a lifetime ago to Meryl and now the atmosphere was palpably tense and it was very hard to differentiate between friend and foe. All three houses that the SPCA team had removed poultry from had been used as 'safe houses' for MDC members who had been displaced from their own homes by political violence.

When the whereabouts of the safe houses had been discovered, the Zanu PF and Gezi youths had damaged the buildings, evicted the occupants and simply left the birds to their own fate. In her usual precise, cool and controlled manner, Meryl recorded the closing details in her diary:

'Nine small black chickens were uplifted: one adult black hen; one adult turkey tom; one adult female turkey; three small white turkeys and one small black turkey. We returned the two ZRP officers to the Police Post – the two youths accompanied us and we left them at the Police Post. Returned to Harare and off-loaded all poultry – fed and watered; both cages padlocked.'

The following morning Meryl made contact with the MDC Provincial Chairman. She gave him all the details of the 66 chickens and seven turkeys that had been rescued from three houses in Chiwadziro in Bindura. He was effusive in his thanks and Meryl smiled when he sounded taken aback when she told him: 'I would have done the same thing if the birds had belonged to a Zanu PF member you know!'

Extracts from Meryl's Diary:

> *Where drums beat, laws are silent.*
> *– Proverb*

January 2002
Bulawayo:
Able to spend the first week of the New Year in my Bulawayo office but back on the road to Harare by Sunday 6th as rescue work starting again.

Harare:
Attended the funeral of Fran Milbank who had been murdered by her gardener. She was a great supporter of the SPCA and had only recently handed over a donation she had collected in the bar one night at Reps Theatre. The donation was to go to helping farm rescues.

Raffingora:
Spend several days in the area on four farms which had been totally trashed and looted. Dogs, cats and guinea pigs missing. Police and SPCA Inspector even visit a spirit medium (Mondoro Queen) in the area. Many looted tractors and trucks seen surrounding her hut – she told them nothing about the missing dogs.. 'Jessica', a German shepherd bitch suddenly appears out of the bush.... Drove across muddy fields to Village Three where we were given the name of the settler who had stolen 'Professor', a German Shepherd dog belonging to the Sandys-Thomas family of Cornrise Farm... At Chiwe Farm saw farm workers sitting on the ground being indoctrinated. Was a very heavy presence of war veterans, the local war lord Akim told me that if I was a journalist he would not have given me my ID card back. 4 head of cattle and 30 goats had been slaughtered... Six goats had also died during the night – believed to be from stress due to all-night drumming as their pen was right next to where the 'pungwe' was held... Spirit medium has been arrested but later released... A one-year-old Boerboel has been hit on the head with a shovel but is OK... Irresponsibly, 36 young crocodiles had been let out of their pen by the settlers... Ridgeback bitch called 'Pepsi' had been beaten on the back with a knobkerrie...

Three out of four guinea pigs have been found.... Another dog, 'Blackie', an elderly Staffie X, also from Cornrise Farm, was stolen but had later been returned (from villagers)... Went to Chinix farm to look for 'Professor' but the man called Chena who has abducted him, had already left... Drove 40-50 kilometres to Berry's Post farm where Chena's brother lives. He's not there and we only get back to Chinhoyi at 8pm....

Increase the reward for 'Professor' to $5,000.... Went back to Chinix Farm and waited. At 6.40pm Chena walked towards us through the bush accompanied by two women. He had four dogs and 'Professor' with him. Chena handed over to the police by us, and Professor had a joyous reunion with his owner Mike Sandys-Thomas in the car park of Raffingora Police Station. We had covered over 400 kilometres on shocking roads over the past few days and estimated Professor had been made to walk 45-50 kilometres. Professor was fine, just very hungry and very tired... Went back to Raffingora Police Post to get a statement from Chena... war veteran arrives and starts harassing me, tells Chena not to sign and launches a lengthy tirade at me – all watched by police who turn their heads away and do nothing.... This war veteran is apparently the local base commander and afterwards, farmers told me he was a particularly unpleasant character.... War vet leaves and Chena signs his statement voluntarily. I complained to the Member in Charge about the lack of support I'd been given – he looked me full in the face and said he didn't know what I was talking about.... A landmark case as this was the first time we had charged a settler with cruelty to a farm animal – he pleaded guilty and paid an Admission of Guilt fine.

Beatrice:
Begin a series of visits to a large pig farm (800 head) where owners have been evicted. Situation extremely volatile and police provide armed members of Support Unit... Dogs, cats, tortoises, guinea pigs, rabbits and hens are the first to be rescued. ... Three months of work lie ahead... Over 800 pigs, some in a very bad way with mange. Piglets dying at a rate of 20 to 30 per day... Next visit arrange trucks for pigs to be moved... farm workers arrive and say they haven't been paid... Trucks don't arrive in time... Three Support Unit officers, three army officers, Augustine and me go to the farm, pigs have not been fed, workers refuse to load as they say they have not been paid... try and load ourselves but no success – too few of us.

Many dead piglets seen; one large sow dead in a trough, live pigs eating dead ones... was trying to remove some of the dead piglets from the sties – as I picked them up – their bodies disintegrated in my hands – it was horrifying... Offer the farm workers my own money if they will help to load, they agree. On two trucks they need to load 100 pigs... Farm workers very rough with the pigs carrying them by their tails, ears, legs. Workers also throwing piglets into the back of the truck; once they landed, they stood there wide-eyed, legs trembling... Only managed to load 84 pigs, followed them to Ruwa where they were off-loaded – many too weak to even walk... A week later manage to load another 191 pigs – workers very rough, beating the pigs with short lengths of hosepipe and when I complained the foreman said if I complained again they would stop loading.

As I left the foreman screamed at me, 'Go back to England – don't come back'. ... As it turned out we were never able to get back onto the farm, there were many barricades and the situation was just far too hostile. In total we had rescued about 250 pigs and would never know what happened to the rest of the animals... This has been one of the most harrowing of all the farm rescues – the situation at the farm was very hostile... the horrific sights I saw and then the very rough handling are images that will stay with me for ever.

Zvimba:
To a farm in Zvimba to uplift three terriers from an invaded farm. Domestic worker had been doing his best to feed them with crushed maize.

CHAPTER SEVEN

The Rushinga Pigs

By his deeds we know a man.
— African Proverb

Rushinga, February 2002

It took three days for Meryl to get to the bottom of what was going on at Mrs Makwete's plot in Rushinga and when the news came it was very distressing. A number of phone calls and messages, some relayed by radio, gave the news about pigs and dogs that had been stranded after a bout of political violence left the owner chased out of her home and forced out of the area. This case was nothing to do with land or commercial farming and animals were in distress as a direct result of politics. The police Assistant Inspector who spoke to Meryl told her that the situation on Mrs Makwete's plot was not good. He said the pigs were starving and that there were also eleven dogs in need of help – two others had apparently already been shot.

Initially Meryl had been alerted to the situation by Mr Chinyika, a friend of the owner. He said there were 18 pigs that urgently needed to be rescued from the plot. When Mrs Makwete was chased away, one of her employees had been taking care of the animals but now even he had been forced to leave and the animals were stranded.

When the arrangements had been made, Meryl phoned Mr Chinyika to let him know that she and SPCA Inspectors Addmore and Tawanda were going to Rushinga to remove the pigs and she was given a bit more information:

'Mr Chinyika said that the two dogs had been shot by police who said they had rabies but the owner said that was not the case as they had been vaccinated by the SPCA. Mr Chinyika said that there were a few "skirmishes" between Zanu PF and MDC over the latter putting up posters. I asked Mr Chinyika whether we would come across any roadblocks – he said there would be one at the farm turnoff from Mount Darwin to Rushinga. Mr Chinyika thought that if I was in my SPCA vehicle and uniform, they'd let us through.'

Meryl arrived in Bindura and collected a police Constable who was armed with an Ouzi (a sub-machine gun) and they proceeded to Rushinga. After turning off at Mount Darwin, Meryl seemed to drive for a long time and when she looked at a map later she was surprised to see how close Rushinga was to the border with Mozambique. Rushinga was so remote that it wasn't even on most general maps of Zimbabwe! It was an isolated, hot and dusty little growth point and Meryl met there with police Inspector Gamiza. He asked the SPCA team to wait for him, saying he wanted to go and 'make some arrangements'.

Meryl waited and made no comment when Gamiza came back, accompanied by his 'arrangements' which were in fact a truck full of Zanu PF men. Several of them were wearing '3rd Chimurenga' T-shirts, others wore shirts which had a picture of a ballot slip and a message reading 'Vote Zanu PF'. It was just a fortnight before the Presidential elections and Meryl knew that she was lucky to be in the area at all and that silence was the best and safest policy!

'We proceeded to the property and found nine dogs and seven pups. Only six pigs out of 18 were left; two small pigs were seen but they were already dead and the remainder were all very thin and weak. One had severe wounds on its head – treated it with betadine and antiseptic wound spray. Pigs were given water and fed greens and pig food that I had bought with me.'

After they had done what they could for the pigs, Meryl, Addmore and Tawanda turned their attention to the other animals on Mrs Makwete's plot. They found two adult turkeys and a younger one which had its head stuck in the fence. Once they had freed the struggling bird from the wire, all three turkeys were given food and water and returned to their run. A sense of normalcy was returning and Meryl was relieved that throughout the process their work had not been hindered by the gang of Zanu PF men; one had even got involved in the work and been very helpful. All the dogs were loaded into the SPCA truck and Meryl, Addmore and Tawanda set off on the long return trip to Harare.

Once there the dogs were put in kennels, fed and settled down for the night and Meryl breathed a sigh of relief that half of the job was done. It had been a long day and an even longer journey and Meryl was tired. As usual she had done all the driving [because Addmore did not have a driving licence] and had covered over 300 kilometres – some of it over very bad gravel roads.

This first trip to Rushinga had been undertaken to assess the situation and provide emergency relief and with so many dogs in the truck there was no way they could have carried the pigs too. Meryl had taken pig food with her in the hope that there may have been someone who could feed and look after the animals and let them stay where they were. That would have been preferable to subjecting the animals to a long, hot and stressful journey but after what she had seen today, Meryl knew they were going to have to go back for the pigs and turkeys if they were to survive.

The following morning Meryl, Addmore and Tawanda again headed north east towards the border between Zimbabwe and Mozambique. The three worked well together and Meryl found her thoughts turning to Tawanda who had always worked for the Harare SPCA and had made his way up the ladder to where he was now. Tawanda had started out as a kennel hand, graduated to a driver and then attended a training course to become an Inspector. Like most of the team, Tawanda was a family man, married with children. He was of medium height and build, had a moustache and almost always had a big smile on his face – which went with his great sense of humour. Tawanda was always very chatty and would use 30 words to make his point when anyone else would have got by with half a dozen! He wasn't the tidiest of men and to see him with his shirt hanging out was quite normal, almost expected. Tawanda had helped a lot with the farm rescues in Mashonaland West in those dark days of looting and burning and he drove backwards and forwards from Chinhoyi to Harare carrying rescued pets in the SPCA Mobile Clinic.

As on the previous day, Meryl stopped at the Bindura Police Station to collect a police escort and it was the same Constable that had accompanied them the day before. Meryl headed straight to Mrs Makwete's plot. One dog that they had been told about but hadn't managed to find the day before was still missing and so they left food and water for it and turned their attention straight to the turkeys. The big birds were hastily and noisily caught and loading into cages in the back of the SPCA truck.

There were some guinea fowl in a cage and after inspecting them and seeing that their wings had not been clipped, Meryl released them into the nearby bush and they took off immediately. Flying low and flapping prolifically, the guinea fowl called out in the familiar and repetitive chattering, clattering alarm. Meryl was glad to see them go! They were not domestic fowl and had no place in captivity and were soon lost from sight, free at last!

Finally the team were able to turn their attention to the pigs – what they had come for in the first place. All six pigs were loaded loose into the back of Meryl's truck which made for a tight squeeze with a strange mix of travelling companions! Meryl would never have been able to find enough fuel for two vehicles to come all the way to Rushinga and rather than come back for a third time, everything and everyone managed to fit in. It must have been an amazing sight! Turkeys in cages faced one large white sow, three medium-sized weaners, one small brown pig with very bad wounds on its neck and face and one small black pig. No one seemed to know what had happened to the other 12 pigs and Meryl thought they must have either been stolen or died of starvation. The same Zanu PF man who had helped them the previous day was again involved in the loading and when it was over Meryl expressed her gratitude and gave him a small bag of sugar by way of thanks. Sugar had been unavailable countrywide for some weeks and it was a much appreciated gift.

As Meryl drove from Mount Darwin through Bindura, the Zanu PF youths and supporters were out in force – waving their fists and shouting insults at Meryl and the SPCA team as they passed. Having just spent two days being helped voluntarily and willingly by a Zanu PF man, Meryl was struck by the irony of the roadside taunts and raised, clenched fists – so much seemed to be for show but you could never be sure. Just the day before Meryl has seen photographs in the *Daily News* of Border Gezi youths training for a rally in Rushinga which was to be addressed by President Mugabe. Meryl was very glad to be leaving the area and kept her face expressionless as she drove past the hostile youths.

Meryl closed her diary notes on the Rushinga pig rescue when she met Mrs Makwete for the first time:

'Mrs Makwete came to see me and thanked me for fetching her animals. She said she would like to take the turkeys tomorrow. She chose the white male and black-and-white male dogs to take to her home in Harare. She requested that all the other dogs and puppies be destroyed. Through no fault of her own, she had to move to Mbare township and there was insufficient room for all her dogs. Mrs Makwete also requested that the SPCA keep the six pigs until after the elections – I agreed.'

When the elections were over and the political violence had died down again Mrs Makwete collected her pigs from the SPCA to take back to Rushinga. She told Meryl that she hoped she was going to be able to live in her own home again. Meryl was touched when, in spite of everything she had been through, Mrs Makwete gave a donation to the SPCA towards the cost of feeding the pigs.

Extracts from Meryl's Diary:

'When I play with my cat, who knows whether she isn't amusing
herself with me more that I am with her.'
— Montaigne, 1850

February 2002

Harare:
Harare SPCA have given me the use of one of their offices so manage a few days to catch up with the never-ending paperwork. Working late at the kennels most nights. Driving down Kingsway one evening, it was very hot so I had the windows open. While stopped at the traffic lights my driver's door was yanked open and a man started yelling at me — something about a caravan.

When the lights changed I drove on and only when I got home I found that my brief case was missing. It was found the following morning in the municipal car park. All the paperwork was still intact and the only thing missing were several samples of rat poison that I had taken off a vendor in the industrial sites. Rat poison is now being openly sold on the streets in Harare — 'for cheeky dogs' — and I'm having meetings with the Municipal Licensing dept (excellent co-operation) to try and stop the sale of this deadly poison.

Featherstone:
Frantic call from a farmer — his cattle have been confined to the dip tank area by settlers.

Kwekwe:
Sybil Nel phones with the very sad news that her husband, Bryan Nel, has died — until recently he was the Chairman of the ZNSPCA. Apart from his work with animals, he was an accomplished sculptor.

27 February. My birthday! Spent most of the morning trying to entice 'Tigga', a delightful tabby cat, down from a beam high up in the roof of a kitchen on an invaded farm in Chegutu. Waving a rapidly defrosting fish around, the moisture from it running down my arm! Tigga meanwhile was absolutely delighted to see me, purring his head off, kneading away with his paws on the beam but just wouldn't come down — not even for the smelly fish!

I then got a chair and stood on it to get myself closer to Tigga, still waving the fish at him and I thought: what a way to spend my birthday! Decided on another tactic which was to just totally ignore him. Went and sat in the dining room with my back to Tigga who was obviously enjoying playing hard to get. It would be of no concern to him that there was a crowd of very hostile war veterans and settlers at the farm gate – the same ones who had given his owners 30 minutes to leave the farm or risk death. I put my head down on the dining room table and must have dozed off for a couple of minutes and woke to find Tigga weaving his little body round and round my legs – still purring his head off!

CHAPTER EIGHT

Bob

'There was a Dachshund, once so long
He hadn't any notion
How long it took to notify
His tail of his emotion;
And so it happened, while his eyes
Were filled with woe and sadness,
His little tail went wagging on
Because of previous gladness.'
– Anon. (Quoted in J.F. Kennedy: 'Profiles in Courage.')

Nyapi Farm, Chinhoyi, March 2002
Meryl made a quick list of the animals that needed to be rescued from the farm in Chinhoyi. They were:

'Blue' and 'Smoke' – two Weimaraner dogs, both male
'Splash' – Black Labrador, male
'Bob' – Daxie, tan male
'Camilla' – Boeboel, old brown bitch
'Miss Budzi' – goat, very large, brown and white
'Pedro' and 'Rugie' – two cats; one black and white and one tabby.

Rob Gordon was a private vet in Chinhoyi town and had a very busy surgery which was often visited by Meryl and her SPCA team during the land invasions. As Meryl went onto the hundreds of farms that had been invaded in and around the Chinhoyi area rescuing pets and livestock, she often ended up at Rob's surgery with cages filled with all manner of traumatised, beaten, scared and confused animals.

Sometimes Meryl arrived with just one assistant but more often she was accompanied by the SPCA Inspector for Chinhoyi, Belinda Bowie, or by police or even members of the Police Support Unit.

Rob was as passionate about treating the rescued animals as Meryl was about saving them and between them they gave comfort to many hundreds of animals throughout those dark days. Neither of them ever dreamt that the day would come when it was Rob's animals that Meryl would be going to rescue from Nyapi Farm in Chinhoyi.

It started when Meryl got a call from Belinda of the Chinhoyi SPCA to say that Dr Gordon had been involved in an 'incident' with Zanu PF youths who had apparently 'shoved his car' and left him unable to get back onto his farm. It was only later that Meryl learnt what had really happened. It had started at election time a few days before when Rob had gone to a farm to treat a patient – a horse with a very serious eye infection.

As luck and fate would have it, there was a polling station on the farm that Rob was visiting and he arrived at the same time as an opposition support group who were bringing meals and relief to election monitors. Zanu PF ruling party youths chased away the opposition support team, Rob tried to detour around the mayhem but had no chance and found himself caught right in the middle. The government youths stoned Rob's car and he said that from then on he became 'a marked man'. Rob didn't give in easily and said:

'I did give chase to about ten of the brave youths on foot after they stoned my windscreen and my word did those brave and fearless ten take off at a pace from the fat vet. At least I had some satisfaction!'

Rob's satisfaction at trying to defend his property from the marauding Zanu PF youth was short-lived. Just a couple of days later Nyapi Farm, which Rob leased, was seized. Like all the farmers and people living on farms in the area, Rob was always prepared and ready for the worst. He described that last morning on Nyapi Farm:

'The morning of my "escape" (the third ambush), I had my bags packed and I left the farm, closing the gate. Little Bob (the Dachshund) peered at me with those little beady but uncertain eyes. It was a gut wrench from hell to leave him and his mates behind.'

Rob wasn't able to go home again and so Meryl was called to help rescue the animals. Meryl drove the 115 kilometres to Chinhoyi with ease. It had become a very familiar route to her over the past eight months as she travelled it again and again to rescue animals from invaded farms all over the area. Despite the circumstances this was such a beautiful drive out along the Harare to Kariba road; twisting and climbing up into the Great Dyke and then the panorama that came with the descent; the plains below stretching to Banket; and then, before the farm invasions, the vast wheat farms on the roadsides leading to Chinhoyi.

Arriving in the town Meryl started with DISPOL (District Police: the most senior policeman in the district) in Chinhoyi where she was given an escort to accompany her to Nyapi farm so that she could rescue the five dogs, two cats and a goat. The police were very co-operative: Meryl's reputation obviously preceded her, and she soon had two riot squad details both equipped with radios and tear gas and they headed straight to Nyapi:

'On arrival at the farm, the settlers who now occupied the property unlocked the gate and let us in. Several settlers were inside – they told Addmore they were "guarding" the house in relays – it appeared they were going inside the house as well. We loaded up the five dogs. The cats were inside the house but there was a window open and with some tinned cat food we had with us, we were able to entice them out.

'Bob wanted to bite the goat, so he travelled in the front. The goat was very big, mostly white in colour and although very tame, she kept leaping about in the back of the truck – very excited about the whole thing! The two cats went together in one cage and they cried and miaowed their heads off all the way back to Chinhoyi – much to the chagrin of the police officers! It was a great squash in the back with four dogs, two cats, a very large goat, two Inspectors and two Riot Squad officers.'

All in all it was a fairly simple rescue for Meryl and her team and yet the impact of her work on Rob Gordon was profound. Writing to Meryl a few days after the rescue, he spoke for himself and for a huge community whose lives had been completely ravaged. He also spoke for the animals:

'I cannot even begin to find words appropriate enough to fully express my appreciation for what you and the Bowies did for myself and my precious pets.

'It is our animals that are the silent victims of this madness. Uninvolved and uncomprehending, stolen, starved, beaten and shot; these innocents of a man-made situation often bear the brunt of this senselessness.

'The courage that you and your team have shown is exemplary. If there was an SPCA 'courage under fire' citation or equivalent I am sure you would receive it. The situations that you found yourself in and the negotiations you had to go through to secure the release of someone's valuable pets were amazing, York, Geldenheuys and many, many others. Often a thankless job with friction coming from both sides and, amazingly, the very people you were helping turned on you.

> *'We, as the community of Chinhoyi and myself as an individual, owe you and the SPCA a huge thank-you.'*

At the time Meryl did not understand the reference Rob made in his letter to how the very people she was trying to help had turned on her. Her days were so unceasingly busy that this was one of the things that would only really became clear later, when she had time to contemplate the numerous complex issues that came out of Zimbabwe's land invasions. Meryl knew that her determined stance of assisting the animals only, and not the farmers, was the one thing that kept her safe and, more importantly, ensured that she could keep going onto invaded farms.

She also knew that sometimes this very stance caused disgruntled mutterings from some farmers who did not understand why Meryl would not grab an envelope, look for a file or search for some papers. Some didn't appreciate that it was because of her impartiality that Meryl and her small team were able to rescue the many thousands of animals that they did. To some farmers it was confusing, questionable even, to see Meryl having good communications with police, war veterans and settlers.

From the farmers' point of view it didn't make sense that Meryl, a white woman in her sixties, could go where farmers, lawyers, civil society and even the international press could not. Farmers were desperate to find ways to stop their farms from being seized: they clutched at straws, pointed fingers; apportioned blame and did whatever they thought it would take to stay on their farms and in their homes. Some thought that if Meryl was seen in their area it would attract the attention of settlers and government authorities and that they would then be purged in the next wave of seizures. As Rob Gordon said, however: 'As it turned out it made no difference because we all got hammered in the end.' Rob was right in another regard too because in 2002 Meryl received the RSPCA (UK) Overseas Gallantry Award.

Four years after the ravage and clearance of hundreds of farms in and around Chinhoyi, Rob Gordon was practising his trade in Australia but the memories were still vivid – of his beloved dog Bob, and of what he called the last chapter of his life in Zimbabwe:

> *'Bob now lives with my sister who is still in Zim. Finance and the fact that he was positive for Erlichia meant he could not come with me. I love the grouchy little bugger and miss him tremendously. He is old now and has bad arthritis. He at least is safe and loved. For many people from our area the story was not so good. There often was no option but to euthanase the beloved pets. The look in those people's eyes – the pain – I will never forget.'*

Bob

Extracts from Meryl's Diary:

'He thought he saw a Rattlesnake,
That questioned him in Greek;
He looked again and found it was
The Middle of Next Week.
"The one thing I regret," he said,
"Is that it cannot speak!"'
– Lewis Carroll

March 2002
Harare:

Working late at the kennels one evening I suddenly thought back to the days when I'd been the General Manager of the Harare SPCA in the late 1990s and those innocent times seemed a world away. Even then I often worked late in the evenings at the kennels trying and catch up on the paperwork – it never seems to come to an end! Those were the days when I'd been able to spoil myself a bit and every couple of months a beauty therapist would come out to the office and give me a pedicure while I ploughed through the paperwork.

On one of these occasions I had forgotten all about the snake that was in a bag in my office waiting to be collected. It was a very large python that had been found in the industrial sites of Harare and because it was a Protected Species, I'd phoned the Department of National Parks and asked them to come and collect the snake. They had promised to come but as the afternoon drew to a close I realised that no one been and so I phoned again. It was too late! The Parks offices were closed and no one was answering the phone and so I had no choice but to keep the snake till the following morning – still secured in the hessian sack it had arrived in.

A little while later Mercy arrived from the beauty clinic and began the pedicure. After a while she started painting my toenails and moved things around to give herself a bit more room. Mercy placed her handbag on top of the sack containing the python and when I saw this I leant over and moved the bag. I mentioned that there was actually a snake in the sack so it wasn't a good place for Mercy to put her handbag.

Mercy can't have heard much more than that one sentence! She let out one very loud and piercing scream and ran out of the office door and was out of the SPCA security gates before I could stop her. Then I noticed that I had only had two toes painted but it was too late! Once the nail polish was dry I went home with my two painted toes and left the snake safely in its sack locked in my office.

Later that night I lay in bed thinking about painted toes and snakes – and memories of the Egyptian Circus came flooding back.

The Egyptian circus had arrived in Harare in 1995 and stayed seven long months. It had been on the road from Egypt for five years and all that time the four lions and four Siberian tigers had been kept in their 'beast wagons'. El Sayed Hussein Akef was the owner and had a reputation for smuggling animals out of Africa and selling them in the Far East – many believed that the circus was just a front for Akef's illegal activities. The number of animals he entered a country with, always differed from the number he left with. When he arrived in Zimbabwe, Akef's CITES [Convention on International Trade in Endangered Species of Wild Fauna and Flora] papers for the movement of his animals were invalid.

He had no export/import papers from Zambia, where he had come from, and no Certificate of Country of Origin for the animals, but he got away with it, saying that the circus was part of a cultural visit. Akef arrived with four pythons, undoubtedly sourced from the wild from one of the many countries the circus had passed through. One of the women used them in her act – putting the snake's head in her mouth and we later found that the snake's mouth had been bound up during each performance as we noticed a ring round its mouth that was not covered in lipstick!

I called in snake experts, Dr Ev Cock and Steve Durrant, to examine the snakes and both reported that the snakes were very underweight. One python had canker round its mouth, the heating in their cage was not sufficient for winter time and the heater at the top of the cage was not protected. The snakes were winding themselves round the heater to get warm and in the process were getting burns on their skin. The professional opinion was that the snakes would not survive unless they were removed and given urgent treatment.

I went with Dr Cock and SPCA Inspectors Stella Killick and Misheck to the circus to remove the pythons. Two policemen accompanied us. There had been considerable interest and comments in the press concerning the circus, and a reporter and photographer from The Herald *arrived at the same time as us. Once we'd gained access, I explained to Akef's relatives that we had come to remove one of the pythons. The words were hardly out of my mouth when all hell broke loose.*

Several of the women in the circus went beserk when they saw the press and the SPCA there – they grabbed the camera, breaking off the flash which they then hit Stella with – they punched Misheck and the photographer several times, later smashing his camera.

The policemen looked on in utter amazement but eventually restrained the women. Later Akef said that it was because in their culture it was not right to take photos of women – obviously he'd forgotten, that every night these same women were being photographed by the public as they performed in their skimpy costumes and laddered tights!

Stella, Misheck and I went to the hospital to have the wounds seen to and arrived at Casualty to find the women responsible for the assault had been driven there in style in the police car that attended the scene. To our utter amazement, one of the women had quickly shrouded her head in bandages – applied copious amounts of blue and purple make-up to her face and staggered into Casualty holding her head. On seeing Stella and Misheck she started shouting that they had assaulted her. The staff in Casualty were obviously impressed with her performance as they quickly ushered her through to a bed, whilst Stella stood with a bleeding face and Misheck was doubled over in pain with cracked ribs.

A few days later, I was so angry that I went down to the main police Charge Office to register a complaint. I asked for senior police officers to accompany me back to the circus so that I could launch another effort to confiscate the one surviving python (all the rest of the snakes had died by then). The second visit was also a total fiasco. Two very senior members of the police had agreed to accompany me and when we arrived at the circus, Akef ushered us all into his caravan. Long discussions began on the fact that I wanted to see and remove the python and after this had been going on for about two hours, things reached absurd levels.

The two police officers were given tickets to bring their families to the circus and all I managed to confiscate were two boxes of day old chicks that the circus workers had been feeding to the snake. As it was winter, the python should not have been offered any food as its metabolism would have slowed right down during the cold weather – the chicks don't get digested properly and start to cause problems in the snake's stomach. A BBC cameraman had been waiting in the dark at the entrance to the circus for some time – hoping to get footage of the python being carried out in a pillowcase – instead all he could film was a few day old chicks.

A few days later, Stella and I appeared in Court as the SPCA had been charged with 'fighting in a public place'. Fortunately the Magistrate, having heard the evidence, smiled and said he didn't think we had a case to answer – the circus workers who were in court, were gutted! Akef himself continued to claim diplomatic immunity – saying that the circus was in Zimbabwe courtesy of the two governments and they took out a Court Order banning me from the circus grounds.

The SPCA, with the help of Harare lawyer Rusty Russell who did so much pro bono work for us, then got a Court Order to remove some of the animals, got a vet to treat one of the lionesses who had an abscess and uplifted all the dogs that were being kept in appalling conditions.

At the end of it all Meryl wasn't the most popular person when it came to the circus owners and performers, but they were in the minority. In 1996 she received the RSPCA (UK) International Certificate of Appreciation for her fight against the visiting Egyptian Circus.

Featherstone:
Was in the area for several days working on various farms rescuing dogs, cats and horses.

Chivhu:
6 March. Up at 4.30am and to Pennyfather Farm: To Chivhu, 8kms out on blind rise turn to right, sign says Ngezi National Park – tarred road – go 17-18kms. Go over Large Umniati River then over Small Umniati River, will see Pennyfather store then farmhouse.

Didn't get through after all because of big mob on road.

CHAPTER NINE

Buddy

'A truth that's told with bad intent
Beats all the lies you can invent.'
— William Blake, 1803

Pennyfather Farm, Chivhu, March 2002

Meryl was prepared for the worst when she set out for Pennyfather Farm in Chivhu on 6 March 2002. She was going to try and find a dog and a cat but things did not look good, as she noted at the start of her diary recordings on Pennyfather:

> *'Ms Hoffman was chased off the farm two weeks ago. Left behind at the house is an old Bull Mastiff cross Boerboel (12 years old) by the name of Buddy and a ginger cat called Tokolosh (19 years old). The government vet in the area had been approached for assistance but when he tried to get on the property, he was turned away by war veterans.'*

Twice the local government vet had been to the farm but on both occasions he'd been unable to get to the house and hadn't seen the dog or cat in the garden. Everyone feared the worst for Buddy and Tokolosh. It was possible that they were in the house but they had been alone for over two weeks without food or water and this was a very long time, even under the best of circumstances. Liena Hoffman had been forced off the farm on 18 February but had asked someone to look after and feed the animals, thinking she would be able to return herself after a few days when the situation calmed down a little.

The situation on Pennyfather Farm did not calm down though and it was only two weeks later that Liena discovered that the person she thought was caring for the animals had also been evicted from the farm – just one day after taking over responsibility for Buddy and Tokolosh. This meant the animals had been left completely alone, unfed and untended for 16 days. Liena thought it very unlikely that her pets would have been able to survive for so long and so she asked Meryl to arrange for their burial in the family graveyard on the farm.

Arriving at the police station Meryl was told she wouldn't need a police escort as everything was 'quiet' on Pennyfather Farm. Meryl had been warned that the Officer in Charge of Featherstone Police Station was himself an ex-combatant and would inevitably find it very difficult to be impartial in affairs relating to land invasions. Meryl, Addmore and Misheck set out for Pennyfather Farm with caution and more than a little apprehension. It was just three days before the Presidential elections and 'quiet' seemed highly unlikely in a country engulfed in political violence. Chivhu was 142 kilometres south of Harare and the small town had once been called Enkeldoorn. Apparently many of the early white pioneers settled in the area because the plains resembled those of the Orange Free State in South Africa – where they had come from. The name 'Enkeldoorn' meant 'Single Thorn' and was a reference to the single thorn tree which was found in the site where the small town was built.

Once on Pennyfather Farm and about a kilometre from the homestead, two Zanu PF youths stepped out into the road and waved clenched fists at the SPCA team. They were the advance warning of a road-block and Meryl drew in her breath when she saw the extent of the welcoming party. For a moment she wondered if the police Officer in Charge at Featherstone had known there were this many youths hanging around in the area and wondered why he hadn't warned her. There was no time to pursue the thought and Meryl stared out at the scene in which she had become the centre of attention. There were 70 or 80 youths and war veterans and they swarmed around the vehicle, peering inside the windows and firing questions at Meryl, asking who she was and what she wanted out here. Meryl, as always polite and patient, but with hands gripping the steering wheel, explained about the SPCA and the rescue of animals and said she had only just been treating donkeys on that same road.

'It's SPCA!' one youth said, 'it's alright, they can go!'

Others weren't so sure though and someone called out:

'Don't forget that we control the whole area now!'

Meryl knew that in such a tense situation it would be foolhardy to continue without a police escort and so she abandoned the attempt to get to Pennyfather and went instead to a farm nearby where two dogs needed to be rescued. Here too the atmosphere was tense as Meryl described:

'On arrival at the farm, the workers were at first reluctant to let us take the dogs saying, "First you take the dogs, then someone takes the furniture – what will happen to us?" As we were about to leave, a Toyota truck full of war veterans and Zanu PF youths arrived (in a vehicle they had confiscated from a farmer). They wanted to know

what we were doing and seemed satisfied with the answer. Then they demanded money from me to guarantee our safe passage off the farm. I explained that we could not give them any money as we were a charity organisation. I offered them reflectors for their scotch carts [donkey-drawn carts] instead – and these were accepted!'

The following day Meryl again headed out to Pennyfather Farm, this time escorted by two police Constables. Arriving at the farm, the police went and called the two leading war veterans and while she waited Meryl wandered over to the little cemetery. From the dates on the headstones Meryl could see that members of the family had been buried there over a period of many years. It seemed that Pennyfather Farm had belonged to the Hoffman family for numerous decades, going back to the pioneer days.

When the police returned with the war veterans and after suitable introductions had been made, they were friendly and obliging, unlocking the security gates immediately. Fears that she would be digging graves because the dog and cat wouldn't have survived alone for two weeks were soon dispelled. One of the war veterans said he had heard a dog barking from inside the house the previous morning. As they all walked across the garden and approached the bedroom they heard barking. It was almost too good to be true:

'Looking through the window we could see Buddy alive and well! Even the war vets were happy! I thought this is crazy: they are the ones who locked her in the house in the first place. On going round the side of the house, I found Tokolosh, the cat, lying on the back doorstep by the kitchen. He was very thin and very weak but purred loudly.'

The cat was immediately lifted into a cage and taken to the truck. One down and one to go, Meryl was buoyed at the resilience of the animals and the relative ease of the rescue. Using the key given to her by Liena, Meryl went into the house through the kitchen door. There was excreta everywhere and the smell was overpowering but it meant good news: the dog had used its initiative and survival instinct and was alive and well.

'In the kitchen Buddy had torn open a bag of dog meal. She barked at me a lot and kept going backwards into the bedroom. She was very frightened of the war vets and police so I asked them to keep out of sight. Once in the bedroom I shut the door. We could see that she had survived by drinking water from the leaking toilet – there were paw marks all over the floor! She jumped on the bed and it was obvious that was where she spent most of her time. I slipped the rope over her head and started out of the bedroom – she was very nervous and finally Addmore had to carry her to the car.'

Finding the cat and dog alive and well after such a long time made a tremendous impression on Meryl and lifted her spirits and those of the SPCA Inspector who wrote in his records: 'It was God's might that the female dog survived.'

The next day Meryl was delighted to return Buddy and Tokolosh to Liena. By then the animals had been checked out by the vet. Both were very thin and the cat had dozens of ticks removed from his ears but otherwise they seemed physically none the worse for their ordeal. Buddy was still very nervous and traumatised but overjoyed to see Liena.

Tokolosh, already a very elderly cat, was very set in his ways and his life style and so he went to a cousin's farm outside Harare where he lived out his remaining days in the country air.

Buddy stayed with her owner, devoted to the end, and Liena wrote about the dog's life after the rescue, in a letter to Meryl four years later:

'Buddy was with me, stayed at the office and would lie on my feet all day until I had to put her down in February 2005. I carried her into the vet at Avondale and she died in my arms. At that time she had become very weak, she could no longer walk and was in a lot of pain.

'I see I wrote in my diary "Buddy vrede!" meaning Buddy was at peace now. So she lived for another three years, almost to the day, since she was rescued from the farm.

'I visited Pennyfather for the first time in more than two years at the beginning of September this year. The homestead and farm buildings are now used for a Border Gezi training camp, so I had to ask permission from the commander to visit my mother's grave, which you might recall was right next to the road. I did not have the opportunity to go into the yard, but truly did not desire to – also had the opportunity to reflect several minutes at the graves of Scotty and Molla, other dogs, who are buried beside my mother in the cemetery. Scotty's wooden cross is still standing, albeit crookedly.

'I thank you again for all the brave and courageous work you did for the countless number and now probably nameless animals of Zimbabwe. In our case I had a wonderful three years with Buddy – we could comfort one another in our mutual loss.'

Buddy

Extracts from Meryl's Diary:

> *'I think I could turn and live with animals,*
> *they are so placid and self contained;*
> *I stand and look at them long and long,*
> *They do not sweat and whine about their condition;*
> *They do not lie awake in the dark and weep for their sins;*
> *They do not make me sick discussing their duty to God'*
> *— Walt Whitman, 1819-1892*

March 2002

Chinhoyi:
Visiting many invaded farms in the area uplifting stranded animals.

Marereka:
To ZRP Marereka — collect a Constable and proceed to Kapfundi Farm — uplifted male Ridgeback called 'Romeo' who had been stoned by looters, managed to run and hide, followed in hot pursuit by his buddy a little Jack Russell. The Tredar security guard had been chased away on March 11th.

Harare:
Attended the funeral of murdered farmer, Terry Ford, asked by Jenni Williams of CFU if I can go to his farm and rescue some dogs — ironically only one of the dogs belonged to the Ford family but the others belonged to the man who had been arrested for Terry's murder and who had moved into Terry's aunt's house bringing his own dogs with him. There was now no one at the house to look after the dogs and they had to be treated like any other abandoned farm animal.

CHAPTER TEN

Squeak

The Secretary bird dies with its feathers.
(A man's character dies with him)
– Sindebele proverb

Gowrie Farm, Norton, March 2002

At 6.30am on the morning of 18 March 2002 Debbie du Toit [now Tingle] got a phone call from Norton from a neighbour of her cousin Terry Ford.

'Hurry, can you come? Terry has been found dead!'

The du Toit/McChlery and Ford families had owned Gowrie Farm since the early 1900s and Terry Ford operated both Gowrie and the neighbouring Msasa Farm in Norton for his mother, his Aunt Paddy and himself. The farms are located in the rural area of Zvimba, the homeland of President Robert Mugabe and the area in which his sister, Sabina Mugabe, was the sitting Member of Parliament. Terry's cousin Debbie told how it came to be that war veterans were living in their aunt's house when Terry was murdered:

'Our aunt, Paddy, had died the July before Terry was killed, with us all sitting around her bedside as she passed away. She had been like a mum to Terry (never having had kids of her own) so Terry, in his mourning, had left her whole household intact until he was ready to dispense all her beautiful stuff. He lived in a house that he had built only about 500 metres away so he thought things were safe to leave like that. And then the war vets moved into our Aunt Paddy's house! And we couldn't do anything about it.'

Terry was a successful farmer of both livestock and crops and produced 800 metric tons of wheat annually – enough for one million loaves of bread a year. Terry also reared thoroughbred horses and Merino sheep. Bob McChlery, another cousin, described Terry as a:

'Quiet, ever-smiling man; a teetotaller, always friendly, always compassionate to his family, his workers and his animals. He often had a dog on his lap, an orphaned lamb under his arm or a horse between his knees.'

When war veterans stopped Terry from farming he got a job in a school in Harare and commuted backwards and forwards to Gowrie Farm. He was at the farm preparing for the return of his son Mark from New Zealand when tragedy struck. Debbie du Toit described what she saw when she arrived at the scene:

'From blood marks and spoor, we gathered that Terry had been asleep upstairs in his bedroom. The war vets had broken into the downstairs part of his house, stolen the keys to the school vehicle and threatened to drive away with it. Terry, trying to stop the vehicle from being stolen – had charged downstairs (dressed only in his boxer shorts and sandals) with his revolver – and jumped onto the side of the vehicle, trying to grab and turn the steering wheel. You could see in the yard where the vehicle had spun when Terry grabbed the wheel. Terry had fallen off the side of the vehicle, and the war vets had turned the vehicle right around and tried to run Terry over. Terry had been trying to run away, but had slipped and lost his shoe in a large puddle. The shoe was still there. He had got up and run towards the fence. The vehicle had rammed him straight into the fence. He managed to get up again, and was running to try and hide behind a tree. But the vehicle got to him first and rammed him straight into the tree. He was crushed and fell down, dropping his revolver. The war vet picked up the revolver and shot Terry at point blank range in the forehead. There was blood splattered all over the tree under which he was lying and all over the vehicle that had rammed into him.'

Six shots were fired.

Terry's dog, a Jack Russell named Squeak, lay next to his master, faithful to the last and refusing to move. Debbie said:

'It was very traumatic. Harry and I had to lift Squeak off Terry's body – kicking and snarling and even trying to bite us, until we managed to get him into our car. There were three other dogs in the yard. All were absolutely traumatised by the time we got there. The two Border Collies, Bwana and Collie, had run a path around the security fence trying to ward off the war vets breaking in. There was a thatched grass fence that was shredded to pieces where the Collies had been ripping it with their teeth – trying to get at the war vets. The other little Jack Russell, Bubbles, we found cowering inside.'

While they waited for the police to arrive, Debbie went across for one last look at her late Aunt Paddy's house. What she found there is something she will never forget, details that seldom, if ever, were known or revealed after farmers' homes had been invaded by war veterans.

'I managed to retrieve some photos and trinkets – all that I could fit into a couple of plastic bags. The war vets clothes and hats were hanging on a coat rail, over my Aunt's clothes. They had been sleeping in the bed where she had died. There were cigarette stompies and Chibuku [beer] containers all over her bedroom. I still remember the smell. It was like a dirty, smoke-filled pub – what I imagine a shebeen [bar] smelling like. All the cupboards and drawers throughout the house had been vandalised. To be honest I could have retrieved a lot more stuff – but I have never encountered such an intense feeling of evil in all my life. I took fright and ran out of there as fast I could. Just as well because they found the revolver that shot Terry in the house later that day. A war vet called Bowambi, who had been living in Aunt Paddy's house, had been the one who pulled the trigger. Unbeknown to us he had also been standing in the crowd who had gathered at the crime scene but had run off when the riot police arrived. He was picked up but released later. Mark visited the police station at a later stage but no docket was found.'

Meryl knew only a few of these details when she attended the funeral of Terry Ford on 22 March 2002. Later that same day she set out to Gowrie Farm in Norton. The two Jack Russells, Bubbles and Squeak, had by then been taken in by family friends and the two Border Collies were being cared for by the SPCA in Chegutu until they could be moved to Debbie's farm in Selous. Meryl had been asked to try and rescue dogs that had belonged to Terry Ford's step father, Dan Coetzee who had died the year before and also to check on the dogs that belonged to war veterans who had been taken into custody by police investigating the murder. Accompanied by SPCA Inspector Tawanda, Meryl went to the police station in Norton.

The Chief Superintendent remembered Meryl from his last posting, commenting that the SPCA had done 'a very good job' rescuing animals in what he called the 'debacle' of invaded farms in Mhangura and he immediately agreed Meryl could go and collect dogs from Gowrie Farm. When Meryl said that the dogs belonging to the arrested war veteran may have to be removed if there was no one who was able to look after them, the Superintendent changed his mind. Clearly unhappy with having to agree to something that concerned a war veteran, the Superintendent made a phone call and then said that Meryl could only deal with the late Mr Ford's dogs but not those belonging to the war veteran. Meryl was not happy and tried to argue for the welfare of the animals

– regardless of who owned them – but could only get the Superintendent to agree to her assessing the situation once on the farm. With two police officers Meryl and Tawanda set out for the scene of the murder. In her records Meryl wrote:

'On arrival at Terry Ford's farm, his cook, Peter, who had been employed there for eight years, met us at the gate together with the old gardener, Tobias. Tobias had been working for Terry for 10 years. They showed us the place where Terry Ford had been killed. The soil had been freshly turned and there was a handful of wilted flowers from the garden placed there – it was a very sad moment. I had of course already seen the photo of Squeak lying on the blood-stained blue bedspread covering Terry. This picture had gone right round the world and probably did more to highlight what was happening in Zimbabwe, than any written reports by journalists had done.'

There were four dogs in the garden of Terry's aunt's house. All were thin and nervous and one little black-and-white bitch approached Meryl, more friendly than the others. This little dog had apparently been taken from Dan Coetzee by the war veterans and Terry had tried but failed to get it back. Meryl put the little dog into the back of the SPCA truck immediately. Another dog had a lot of dried blood on its paws and had been bleeding a great deal from his nose. This was a clear sign of a tick-borne disease so Meryl took this dog too, explaining to the police officers that even if the animal did belong to a war veteran, it was sick and needed to be treated. There was no argument and so Meryl concluded her first visit to Gowrie farm, leaving dog cubes and pet mince with Peter for the remaining dogs – and enough for another dog which was running out on the farm somewhere. In the next couple of days Meryl and Tawanda returned to Gowrie Farm and removed another three dogs, taking them temporarily to the safety of the SPCA kennels while their owner was being held by police.

Two months after the death of Terry Ford, Meryl, Tawanda and Addmore were back at Gowrie Farm again, this time to try and catch Star, Mark Ford's pony. Star, the only non-thoroughbred, was 18 years old and the very last of the animals belonging to Terry Ford left on the farm. They arrived on the farm to find that Steel, the war veteran in control of the property, was not there. Meryl hoped this would be a quick rescue but before it could even start the dogs had to be seen to:

'We were disappointed to see that the four dogs we had returned a couple of weeks before belonging to Bowambi had all lost weight since they left the SPCA. Their ribs were showing and of even greater concern, was the fact that the young black dog *had blood and saliva continually dripping from its mouth. The settlers explained that the dog had a bone stuck in its mouth and it had been there for several days. The two SPCA Inspectors took the dog into the horse box and after a bit of a struggle managed to get the offending bone out.'*

Meryl asked the settlers where Star was and wasn't happy when she heard that the pony was on the far side of the farm. The settlers admitted they had chased her away, saying she was eating their wheat. Meryl could see the wheat which was barely quarter of an inch high and so short it would have been almost impossible to graze. She made no comment but left a halter at the farm and returned a week later. On this occasion it seemed that at last a rescue attempt of the pony was in sight and Meryl recorded what was to be her last visit to Gowrie Farm:

'On arrival at the farm, the first person we saw was Steel – he was not at all surly and hostile as we had found him on a previous visit. He walked with us to the paddock where Star was. We were shocked at her condition, she was very thin, her coat was dull and we could see dried sweat on her back from where they had obviously been riding her and she had a nasty saddle sore that required treatment.'

While they loaded the pony Steel was friendly and chatty, telling Meryl that he was learning to grow wheat and that there had been too many 'crooks' coming to the farm but that he wasn't like that. Steel was young, probably in his mid-thirties and too young to have been a war veteran but he called himself the Base Commander and said he was in control. Steel had dreadlocks and was well-dressed and well-spoken. He held himself very upright and did not fit any of the stereotypes of war veterans now so familiar to Meryl. Steel told Meryl that he was well-travelled, had been to the UK and to Libya and that he was a 'good guy'.

Returning Mark Ford's pony to him was the first piece of stability and sanity Meryl had been able to offer the young man who had lost his father, his home and everything that was safe and familiar. Star had been Mark's first horse and he had had her since he was in junior school.

'Star was off-loaded and it was quite an emotional moment for Mark. He kept saying: "I was so chuffed when I saw you had my horse; it's so great to have my horse back".

It was only a brief moment of sanity for the young man because within days Meryl had no choice but to push him to make a decision about his father's 20 thoroughbred horses which had just a week before been removed from

Gowrie Farm. Many were weak, wounded and undernourished.

One mare had a broken pelvis, most were very thin and had saddle sores from being ridden without adequate padding and protection by the war veterans and settlers. Two had wounds across their chests which looked as if the animals had been harnessed and used for ploughing. Meryl knew that tough decisions were going to have to be made and as soon as a good home had been found and agreed upon, she got to work.

The farm in Selous where the horses were being temporarily kept until their condition improved had also been invaded by war veterans and the grazing was rapidly running out. Meryl went to Selous with a vet and her last diary entries concerning the animals from Gowrie farm were a sad ending indeed.

'The vet examined each horse and decided that three horses needed to be destroyed. These were a dark bay mare that had a broken pelvis, a chestnut mare that was old and in very poor condition and another chestnut mare that was actually aborting. The foal was very tiny and premature. The vet, Dr Geoff Lay, was extremely caring and professional with the euthanasing and the end was immediate. It tore at my heart to see them lying there. I walked away with eyes full of tears and thought all this tragedy is because of one man.'

This was the end of Meryl's involvement with the animals from Gowrie Farm in Norton but not the end of the story. Meryl carefully recorded all the details of Squeak's love and loyalty to his master and asked the Chairman of the ZNSPCA to submit them to the American North Shore Animal League. Squeak was then awarded the Lewyt Award for Heroic and Compassionate Pets in August 2002. The citation read: 'The Lewyt Award has been presented to Squeak to honour the exceptional loyalty and compassion he showed to Terry Ford.' Mark received US$500 from the North Shore Animal League as part of the award.'

Meryl kept in touch with Mark Ford and with Debbie du Toit, as she did with hundreds of other farmers whose lives she had been involved in as she rescued their animals and pets. Just over four years after the murder of Terry Ford, Debbie told Meryl the final story concerning a man and his little dog:

'Squeak passed away on Tuesday morning, 9 May 2006 at the grand old age of 15. The loyal little Jack Russell had been living with Dirk, Janet and Louise Benade (friends of Mark's) in Chegutu since Terry's murder on 18 March 2002.

'Written permission had to be obtained from the Chegutu DA's office for the burial party to visit our family gravesite where we decided to lay Squeak to rest, alongside

his beloved master and friend. Getting this permission was a time-consuming affair, so Dirk had Squeak entombed in a small concrete coffin.

'*The gravesite is right at the top of a very large rocky kopje, a good 15-minute steep, hard climb, but well worth the effort once on top; the magnificent view is breathtaking. There is a customary tale believed by the resident black people that a very large baboon living on the kopje holds the spirit of our grandfather, 'Pop' du Toit. They call the baboon 'Patoit.' Whilst we were sitting on the top of the kopje by Squeak's concrete tomb, a troop of inquisitive baboons came right up to see what was happening. The troop was led by a very large male?!*

'*On Squeak's plaque, Dirk had inscribed:*

'Squeaky. RIP
To a better place with your mate Terry. Man amongst men.
Dog amongst dogs. Till we meet again. Cheers.'

'*With a prayer followed by cracking a bottle of champagne (in true Zimbabwean style!) we toasted to celebrate the joy and love that Squeak gave us all and bade him farewell as we laid him to rest by his beloved friend and master's side on 16 May 2006 at 4pm.*

'*As we sat by the graves reflecting on all the tragedies that have taken place in Zimbabwe over the last few years, Dirk told us that just before Squeaky died, his normally floppy little ears pricked right up, almost as if he were seeing his master again as he closed his eyes and took his last breath.*'

Extracts from Meryl's Diary:

Good friends are hard to find, harder to leave and impossible to forget.
– Source Unknown

March 2002
Mount Hampden:
Three dogs and three cats to be rescued – farmer has fled the country after death threats. The dogs are a Saint Bernard, a Jack Russell and an old Beagle.

Harare:
Friends rush me to the Trauma Centre – problems with my heart – was put on a drip

with morphine for the pain. Back to work the next day and drove to Chegutu as I was speaking at a farmer's meeting. Over the weekend my good friend Nadia Marabini treated me to a wonderful aromatherapy session. Nadia has always been a tremendously loyal friend who is as committed to animal welfare as I am.

Marondera:
19 March: At ZRP Marondera from 1.45pm until 4.15pm waiting for Support Unit to get transport to escort us to farm.

CHAPTER ELEVEN

'Love is home'

'Laws are like cobwebs, which may catch small flies,
but let wasps and hornets break through.'
– Jonathan Swift, 1709

Chipesa Farm, Marondera, March 2002
Kerry and Iain Kay left their Marondera farm, Chipesa on a Friday morning in mid-March 2002 to visit Jon, their adopted son, in hospital. He was the latest victim in an outbreak of political violence that had engulfed the country as soon as the results of the March 9 elections had been announced. The violence, a show of strength from the winning Zanu PF party, was merciless and anyone who had supported the opposition or assisted with the polling, came under attack. Jon had been accused of giving a cell phone to an MDC polling agent and for this he and a security guard were assaulted by settlers and war veterans.

The two men were interrogated, beaten, kicked and thrashed with wooden pick handles and Darlington Vhekeveka, the security guard died on the way to Marondera hospital. It had been a savage beating and one of a series of particularly brutal events that had occurred in the Marondera farming area and the neighbourhood of Chipesa farm.

These were frightening and lawless days and particularly dangerous for people like Iain and Kerry Kay who openly supported the opposition. Iain was an MDC opposition candidate in Marondera, and he, his family and the farm employees had been the victims of a sustained campaign of violence for the past two years.

In 2000 Iain had been brutally assaulted and left for dead by farm invaders. His bloodied face appeared on the front page of newspapers and left Zimbabweans deeply shocked at the obvious result of supporting and representing the opposition.

In 2001 Iain, his eldest son, David, two neighbours and many of their farm employees were held hostage in the Chipesa farmhouse for three days. A report in a local newspaper told how 20 farm employees were severely assaulted

82

by farm invaders and war veterans and how law enforcers behaved as if they were bystanders.

'Policemen from Marondera deployed to break the stand-off, watched as the workers were beaten up.'

The Farmer magazine described the atmosphere in the garden of the homestead. Invaders had cut the fence and surrounded the house and were singing:

"'Beat Kay's head so he understands," they chanted, "we're tired of you long-noses," they shouted.'

Returning from the hospital on that March Day in 2002, Iain and David found that Chipesa farm had been sealed off completely. War veterans, state agents and government youths, had watched the Kays leave the property and had then moved in. Kerry described what happened when her husband and son went back to Chipesa Farm:

'Iain and David were then held up, in their truck, at gun-point by police, army and self-styled war veterans and Zanu PF youth. They managed to escape and that was the last time they were to see their farm and home as it was. All the farm employees were evicted at gun-point that night, having to leave, like we did, with nothing but the clothes they were wearing. The farm then became a "No-Go Area".'

No one was allowed in, no exceptions were being made and as soon it became obvious the Kays weren't going to be able to get back into their home, Meryl was contacted. The initial request, which came from a neighbour and friend, was for Meryl to rescue cats and dogs and to also try and collect a file containing emails and passports.

Meryl agreed immediately to do her best to rescue the animals but said that there was no way at all that she would even try and get passports, papers or anything else from the house. Meryl knew that it would only take the slightest suspicion that she was trying to take anything other than animals and the entire rescue would be at risk. If Meryl wavered even once she would destroy the strange trust she had managed to build up with the war veterans and nothing was worth endangering lives or jeopardizing future animal rescues.

Meryl had SPCA Inspectors Addmore and Misheck with her when she arrived at the Marondera Police Station to collect a police escort soon after lunch. She knew this was going to be a very difficult rescue in a dangerous area and had to wait a long time before finally a police Land Rover, and three policemen were ready to accompany her to Chipesa Farm. The delays and stalling seemed deliberate and continued even after they had left the town. Instead of going straight to the farm Meryl had no choice but to follow the police to a tented police Support Unit camp where she sat in the pouring rain for another half an hour. Meryl had no idea what was going on but there was nothing she could do except be silent and patient. It was 5pm when the two vehicles finally got to Chipesa Farm, and Meryl knew that at most they had maybe an hour and a half of daylight left.

Meryl never talked about her own bravery when it came to farm rescues but she always gave credit to the SPCA Inspectors who were accompanying her.

'Whenever I thought that there was a chance a rescue might be particularly dangerous like Chipesa, I would let the team know beforehand and inform them that they didn't have to come if they didn't want to, that there would be no recriminations if they decided not to come. To their credit, they – without exception – were always up for the job ahead.'

From the first moment the farm came into sight, Meryl knew they were going to be in for a hard time. By the farm gate the invaders had planted a Zimbabwe flag in the ground in clear view – this was a sign that the property had been taken over and was under the control of war veterans. The flag hung miserably limp, saturated and bedraggled in the heavy rain that continued to pour down. Several war veterans and a man in army uniform stood on guard at the entrance gate.

Sitting just outside the gate on the side of the road, were the remnants of the Kay's farm workers and their families. They had also just been evicted from their homes on Chipesa and now they sat in the pouring rain, surrounded by all their possessions, exposed to the weather and with nowhere to go and clearly no idea of what to do next. The war veterans and settlers showed no sympathy to men, women or children and it was a pathetically cruel sight to take in.

Meryl clearly remembered the shocking photographs of the first evictions of Chipesa farm workers which had made the front page of newspapers in August 2001. In a series of vicious and often violent evictions, war veterans cleansed Chipesa Farm of men, women and children who had any connections with the property.

The Farmer magazine had published a double page of photographs showing adults and children, young and old, literally camping in the bush and on the side of the road. 'The terror and misery of farm workers' was the headline. What Meryl saw now, seven months later, was obviously the next, perhaps the last phase of evictions.

Following the police Land Rover, Meryl drove slowly towards the farmhouse, detouring around tree trunks and branches which were placed as barricades on all the farm roads. Near the house there was a particularly large road block of tree trunks which the police went around but when Meryl followed she was stopped by a group of war veterans.

'No! You go back to the main gate,' one of the men ordered.

'But that's too far away,' Meryl protested. 'We need to get closer. It will be too difficult to try and carry the dogs and cats all the way from the house to here, and in this rain too.'

'Do what you are told!' another one of the war veterans shouted furiously at Meryl. 'Just do what the Commandant tells you. You drive back to the main gate, now!'

The police Land Rover (her escort!) had disappeared from sight and so Meryl had no choice but to follow the orders being spat at her by the war veterans. She reversed to the bottom of the hill by the main gate and waited. A little while later the police obviously realised that Meryl was no longer following them, and they reappeared. Meryl, Addmore and Misheck waited and watched as the police and war veterans engaged in an animated conversation which resulted in the SPCA vehicle being allowed to drive back up the hill to the Kay's farmhouse.

Addmore and Misheck took the cat cages out of the truck and walked straight through a pedestrian gate and into the garden of the farmhouse without any trouble; it wasn't going to be so easy for Meryl though. It was clear that the man they called the 'Commandant' was in charge. He was in his 50s, fairly slight in build and he behaved in a very authoritative manner. He was wearing a camouflage uniform and carried an AK rifle. Meryl got out of the truck to help catch the dogs and cats but was rebuffed immediately.

'No,' he screamed at her, his face distorted with rage: 'you stay here.'

Meryl didn't argue and got back in the car and sat helplessly watching Addmore and Misheck trying to catch dogs which were running frantically around the garden. After a few minutes the police, who were supposed to be escorting the SPCA team and enabling the animal rescue, got into their vehicle and disappeared. Suddenly Meryl was alone and began to feel distinctly uncomfortable.

'I sat in the truck with the door open trying to look very nonchalant but meantime was getting very wet! The whole time I was in the car (some 10-15 minutes), I was guarded by two war vets, one in dark glasses (even in the pouring rain!) who never took their

eyes off me. I was very frightened, the police had disappeared and I was totally alone with these two guys.'

Minutes dragged past as if they were hours and Meryl felt as if Addmore and Misheck had been gone for a very long time but at last they returned. They were empty-handed and hadn't managed to catch any of the Kay's dogs or cats. The afternoon had been a disaster and Meryl immediately started the engine and drove back to Harare in silence. As her fear subsided it was replaced with anger. Addmore and Misheck had left her in a position where she was completely alone with the war veterans.

It had been the one cardinal rule of all their rescues that the three would work as a team and that no one should ever be left out of sight of the others or the police. Today something had gone very wrong and it was unacceptable. No one in the team should be left in a position where they were alone or frightened: fear was the most dangerous emotion that could surface in these situations. Meryl had no doubt at all that if fear got the better of any of them, that would be the end of the animal rescues.

The following morning Meryl still had the word 'Chipesa' written in her diary and with a sense of determination and urgency for the well-being of the animals, she planned a second rescue attempt. She phoned the Marondera police in advance and complained about events of the previous afternoon – the endless delays in setting out from the police station and then the almost non-existent support from the police when they were at the farm. The police assured Meryl there had just been a communication problem that would not happen again but she soon discovered that nothing had changed overnight.

Arriving in Marondera at 2pm with Addmore and Misheck, Meryl was shunted from one office to the next and from one person to another until finally four armed Support Unit men were allocated to accompany the SPCA team to Chipesa Farm. Then came the excuse that there was no vehicle available and that the police were not allowed to travel in private cars. Seething with rage after a hopelessly frustrating afternoon, Meryl had to abandon the rescue altogether and go back to Harare. There now seemed no doubt at all that something was going on at Chipesa Farm that neither police nor war veterans wanted Meryl to see.

For the third day in a row Meryl drove out to Marondera with Addmore and Misheck. By now the police, perhaps worn down by her tenacious determination, or just to get her out of their hair, seemed more ready to assist. Accompanied by a police Sergeant and an armed member of the Support Unit, Meryl, Addmore and Misheck finally got a good chance to attempt the rescue. They arrived at the farm, passed road-blocks, barricades and surly war veterans and went to the main farmhouse. Meryl did not know how the animals had been coping during these three days and was very concerned.

'I was not sure whether there were domestic workers – if they were there, they certainly didn't make themselves known. Every time we went near the house there were always various youths lounging around on the lawn, and one had no idea who was friend or foe. Obviously the animals would have been very bewildered to start with, and what with not being fed, missing the Kays, plus the place being over-run with intruders, the dogs must have been becoming increasingly stressed.'

Meryl saw paw prints everywhere in the garden but the fence was broken in many places and despite much calling and whistling, the dogs were nowhere to be seen. As the war veterans didn't seem to be bothered by their presence and were not being aggressive, Meryl and her colleagues moved out of the garden and into the nearby fields. They caught and treated a heifer they saw which had a wound teeming with screw worm maggots.

Every day injuries on the farm animals were going untended and turning into major problems – especially in the hot, wet and humid days of March. Meryl and Addmore came across a run of chickens which had been left untended for days. There was a strong smell of ammonia and they quickly changed the straw bedding, filled water troughs and feed tins and let the chickens out in the sun while they worked. There were spectators all the time – war veterans, government youths and settlers. One who caught Meryl's eye was armed with a toy plastic gun. It was an absurd sight which would have made Meryl smile under normal circumstances, but the message the gun portrayed and the situation at Chipesa Farm, were all too real.

'I need a pig, one pig,' the man with the plastic gun suddenly announced. 'I am hungry. Or even some chickens will do.'

'I can't make that decision,' Meryl answered. 'These aren't my animals, I am just here to treat and feed them.'

Amazingly Meryl's answer was accepted without rebuttal. The youngster was just trying his luck.

Driving back to the main farmhouse Meryl suddenly had an idea and she left the engine running in the driveway. There was a chance that the dogs might hear the vehicle and come running out, thinking that perhaps it was their owners. It worked! Within minutes a dog came crashing through the bush and undergrowth. Shumba, a brindle-coloured Staffordshire Bull Terrier, exploded out of the grass and shot straight into the front of the truck next to Meryl without hesitation or prompting. Meryl could hardly believe her luck and she made a great fuss of the Staffie, rubbing and stroking and patting the dog, delighted she would be able to take at least one dog to his owners. Shumba wagged his tail excitedly, licking and snuffling at Meryl, clearly delighted to be safe at last. For Shumba the ordeal was over and, encouraged by her success, Meryl parked the truck in the shade and got out. She wanted to try and do more.

'I think we should go in the house and try to catch the cats,' she said to Misheck.

'They won't like that,' he responded, almost as if he had already spoken to the war veterans.

Meryl didn't comment but soon discovered exactly how the war veterans would respond.

'I noticed that the room next to the garage had been looted. There was a lot of newspaper and packing material lying on the ground and several removals boxes had been unpacked and some of the contents left on the garage floor – presumably items that were of no use to them. I walked across the garden and one of the war vets stayed very close to me. A settler by the name of Owen was also close by – swinging a golf club – I presume one of Iain's.'

The threat was obvious and menacing.

'We are going into the house now to try and catch the cats,' Meryl announced but her words caused an instant and dramatic reaction.

Two men in army uniform, one of whom they called the Commandant, immediately started shouting at Meryl and Misheck, 'Why do you want to go in the house? You are not allowed in the house. No, you are not permitted to get into the house.'

Meryl turned to the police Sergeant, looking for intervention and support. He had been specifically tasked to escort and assist the SPCA with the animal rescue but now that it had come down to a confrontation, the Sergeant let her down. Instead of assistance and backing, Meryl was shocked when suddenly the police Sergeant turned on her, shouting and berating her in front of the war veterans. A string of angry questions and accusations were fired at Meryl by her police escort:

'You never said you wanted to get into the Kay's house,' he said. 'Why didn't you mention this at the police station? What do you think you are going to find in the house?'

It was an utterly absurd situation: the very man who was supposed to be protecting and helping Meryl had turned on her and there was nothing at all that she could do except stand there and listen. The police Sergeant continued to belittle and shout at Meryl and when he finally ran out of accusations he pointed at his watch and said it was time to go and that they had already been on the farm for long enough. Meryl was seething but controlled her temper and tongue.

'Come with me,' she said, speaking slowly and quietly and she waved her arm to include all the angry, shouting men that had now gathered all around.

'All of you can come inside the house with me. I just want to look for the cats. That's all, nothing else. If you come inside with me, you'll see that I will take nothing except the cats.'

Meryl's pleas were useless and neither police nor war veterans were going to give permission for her to go into the house. Eventually, when she realised she was fighting a losing battle, Meryl gave up. She was angry and disappointed by the lack of support offered by Addmore and Misheck who hadn't made a sound during the entire confrontation and distraught that yet again she had failed the animals.

She turned away and stood at the back of her truck trying to get her temper under control. The whole afternoon just one dog had been rescued. Addmore and Misheck were busy catching and loading two pigs. It was a dismal record and Meryl wasn't satisfied at all. Suddenly the police Sergeant, her supposed protector and supporter, turned accuser and attacker, said: 'Pssst!'

'My name is Harrison, not Psst!' Meryl said.

The Sergeant said another dog had been seen at the other side of the garden – out of sight of her truck and of Addmore and Misheck.

At first Meryl ignored the police Sergeant. She didn't have any faith in him after the way he'd berated her and sided with the war veterans and she didn't believe the information that he was suddenly volunteering. By this time the SPCA team had been at the farm for over three hours and had searched every inch of the garden and had checked the farmyard and the surrounding bush, even going as far as the farm dam in their hunt for the animals.

They had whistled and called for the dogs over and over again and Meryl thought it suspicious and extremely unlikely that suddenly a dog had appeared, and right under their noses in the garden. Meryl's silence and inaction angered the policeman.

'I thought you came to rescue dogs,' he said. 'Why aren't you interested now? I am telling you a dog has been seen and you are not interested.'

Meryl knew that, despite her mistrust, anger and feelings of betrayal, she must check the garden one last time. What if it was true, she thought, what if there was one of the Kay's dogs right there in the garden? She would never have been able to forgive herself if she didn't check one last time.

'Addmore was just loading the second pig and as I started to walk towards the bottom of the garden (which was totally out of sight from where my truck was). I saw the settler who was carrying the golf club detach himself from the rest of the group and move across the lawn in the direction I was going. At the same time I noticed that the war vet who had stayed very close to me near the house was also going in the same direction. I saw him take some stones out of his shirt and could see that he had a catapult in his other hand. I suddenly realised that I was possibly walking into a trap – so called for Addmore to join me and together we walked to the bottom of the garden to the area where the dog had apparently been seen. Of course, when we got there, there was no sign of any dog. We asked the war vets where the dog was but they both appeared very disinterested and said that "it must have run away".

'The war vet said something in Shona to Addmore and shook his fist at him. I asked Addmore what he had just said and he replied that the war vet had threatened us by saying that if we kept coming to the farm we must not be surprised if we were attacked.'

The situation had deteriorated steadily ever since Meryl had tried to get into the house and now it was clearly time to leave. Satisfied that there were no dogs around, Meryl left as soon as they got back to the vehicle. The two policemen got in the front of the vehicle with Meryl and as she drove away she told them about the threat issued by the war veterans. When the police Sergeant said he didn't believe her, Meryl's anger raged back to the surface. She slammed on the brakes and insisted that the Sergeant ask Addmore if a threat had been made. Despite Addmore's confirmation and Meryl pointing out the man who had made the threats, it was obviously pointless to pursue the issue. The war veteran denied making any threats and Meryl let it go. She knew without a doubt that this policeman was either scared or simply not impartial and that she was fighting a losing battle. Meryl drove on in silence. There was one last chance for a rescue and Meryl headed for the farm workers' village where she had been told a dog had been seen.

The farm workers' village was completely deserted: every man, woman and child had been forced out by the war veterans and their followers. Doors stood open everywhere and there was not a single sound to be heard in the village, not a voice or a footstep or even a breath. Meryl bent to pick up a small grass mat that was lying in the dust on a once well-trodden path. Obviously dropped in haste by a farm worker or his wife as they fled the village, the grass mat had a message woven into it. *'Love is Home,'* it said. What home do they have now? Meryl thought. She stood for a minute holding the mat, thinking about all the farm workers she had seen huddled on the roadside, homeless and frightened. It was all so tragic and senseless that everything was being unravelled like this. Black, white, young and old, no one had a home on Chipesa Farm any more and it was a bleak and empty thought that recurred so often during Meryl's rescues. Mentally shaking herself back to the present, Meryl turned her attention to looking for the dog that had been seen.

'We searched the compound area for a while but no sign of the dog. As we walked back to the truck two police officers called me to say that there was a dog on the road. It was a brown X breed male with a bad scar on its back. We recognised it as being the same dog that the army guy had told us was one of the Kays' dogs on the first day we had visited. After some resistance, Addmore managed to get him into my truck. Shumba the Staffie was not at all happy about his and kept growling at him – we were only to discover why later!

'Iain and Kerry came in to the SPCA kennels the next morning and there was a joyous reunion between them and Shumba. However, when we brought the other dog out, to my embarrassment they said it was not their dog and must belong to one of the settlers on the farm!'

Meryl had rescued an invaders dog! This was a first but the dog, regardless of the identity or political persuasion of its owner, was also an innocent victim and would be taken back to the settler on the next visit to Chipesa.

For the next few days Meryl could do nothing about the remaining animals still stranded on Chipesa Farm. She knew it had become too dangerous to try and push her luck and get into the house again so soon. But Meryl was determined to attempt another rescue. Before she had a chance, she was called away on another urgent rescue and asked Addmore and Misheck to have one more try at Chipesa.

The men left early in the morning, the vehicle loaded with cages, meat for the dogs, bedding for the pigs and the usual assortment of veterinary first aid equipment. Meryl saw them off before she went in the opposite direction and was thrilled to hear the wonderful news from Chipesa later in the afternoon. The SPCA Inspectors had done well.

They rescued eight pigs, seven turkeys and a dog. In desperation Meryl had offered a one thousand dollar reward to the war veterans and settlers on Chipesa for whoever found a dog and, as always, money talked. Sasha, an enormous Great Dane cross Boxer had been found and kept by one of the settlers.

This giant of a dog with a soft velvety white and grey coat and a matching gentle nature had been saved at last. Sasha was taken back to Harare in a very overcrowded SPCA pick-up truck with pigs and turkeys as travelling companions and later there was a rapturous reunion with their overjoyed owners.

Ten days later the Kays finally managed to get permission and a police escort to go back onto their own farm. Kerry went up to the house while Iain and David were trying to recover some equipment, and she found the two remaining dogs, Jip and Bonzo. She even managed to get into their own home briefly, albeit escorted by an armed policeman. Kerry said she asked the policeman how they could do such terrible things and he answered: 'Things will change soon and by the way, Madam, I found pets' mince in your deepfreeze so I have been feeding the two dogs.' With that Kerry had burst into tears! The house had been looted and trashed and was a painful shadow of the beautiful new home they had built only two years previously. Iain was born on Chipesa Farm and had lived there all his life and now it had all been seized. The Kays' 44 goats had all been killed or hamstrung on the day of the initial eviction and their cattle had been stolen. Their nine horses were eventually rescued, but two had to be euthanased due to injuries.

Five years later Kerry wrote about the recovery of their pets and put into words the feelings that so many hundreds of other farmers had about Meryl and her dedicated team:

'Shumba died two years later but Bonzo, Jip and Sasha are part of the family again. Sasha was definitely a "Mummy's girl" and although still playful and loving, she has never really been quite the same since the trauma.

'One cannot describe the absolute desperation and devastation knowing that you have, by force, had to leave your pets unattended, essentially abandoned. The weeks leading up to the animals' being rescued were terribly emotional. Thank God for the courageous SPCA Meryl, Addmore and Misheck.'

Extracts from Meryl's Diary:

A conceited person is like the throat of a frog.
(Puffed up with his own importance.)
— Sindebele proverb

March 2002

Lion's Den:
Drove from farm to farm trying to find two puppies which had been seen on South African Television being carried away by war veterans who were looting a farmhouse.

After a few false starts and then the offer of a reward, the two puppies are tracked down and rescued – both appeared fine, just very thirsty. When the war vets saw we only wanted to help the animals they relaxed visibly and sent their children to herd all their animals to us. We then treated two young bulls for bleeding rashes and wounds; two sheep with foot rot and maggots; one goat with wounds on its feet; one black cow with screw worm in her ear; one brown cow and one young donkey. Left Malathion powder to be used on the rabbits.

Gweru:
Driving on my own from Harare to Gweru and there were several road blocks manned by police outside each town. They usually waved me through when they saw the SPCA logo on the truck but on this occasion two very aggressive army guys (armed) stopped me and wanted to search the back of the truck. As I started to get out an even more hostile police Inspector came over came over to the truck menacingly whacking his leather-bound cane onto his open hand. His face broke into a broad grin. The policeman rolled his r's when he spoke and he said: "Mrs Harrrison, I know you verrry, verrry well – I have seen you on TV!" Then, much to the annoyance of the army guys, he waved me through.

CHAPTER TWELVE

Major, the dog who drank and drank... and drank!

'A dog standing at his master's gate
Predicts the ruin of the state.'
— William Blake, 1757-1827

Twin Rivers Ranch, West Nicholson, April 2002
By the time Meryl and the SPCA prepared to make their first visit to Twin Rivers Ranch in West Nicholson, the situation was already extremely bad. Shannon Wheeler, his wife Rachel and their two children, Vilanda (16) and Eric (13) and their farm manager Sammy and his wife had been barricaded into their homes for 14 days by war veterans and settlers who were trying to take over the property. Meryl had been kept updated on events at Twin Rivers Ranch since the middle of April because there were seven adult Boerboel dogs and seven puppies at the Wheelers' house. Boerboel's are an indigenous South African breed, originally bred for guarding and protecting farms.

After being barricaded in for a fortnight, the Wheelers had begun running out of supplies and sent a desperate SOS to the SPCA for help. They had completely run out of food for their seven large dogs and all attempts to get more had failed. The war veterans had set up obstacles and barricades on all the farm roads and were turning back everyone who tried to get to the farm. No food supplies, either for people or animals, had got through for some days and it was obvious that the war veterans were absolutely determined to do whatever it took to put the Wheelers into a siege situation which would force them to leave their home.

The morning Shannon Wheeler spoke to Meryl he said that the security fence surrounding the farmhouse had been cut, his vehicle had been taken and the war veterans had switched off the water and electricity supplies to the house. As soon as Meryl heard how bad the situation had become, she offered to try and remove some of the dogs from the property, which would at least ease the crisis engulfing the family. Shannon Wheeler turned down Meryl's offer without hesitation. He said that the family had decided to sit it out together and that the dogs were part of the family. The Wheelers clearly needed help with food supplies for their animals and so Meryl immediately began to make preparations for the 600 kilometre journey from Harare to Beitbridge.

Meryl loaded the SPCA truck with all the donated supplies that had arrived from well-wishers: 60 kilograms of dog meal and cubes, eight litres of fresh milk and a bag of powdered milk. A cooler box full of pets' mince had been delivered to the SPCA by the Boerboel Club and hidden underneath all the animal meat were six packets of steak mince – all donated – which had been put in for the Wheelers. The steak mince had been labelled 'Puppy Mix' and would hopefully get past prying eyes and provide a few wholesome meals for the Wheeler family. Meryl was accompanied by her young colleague Addmore whose fearlessness would undoubtedly be a great asset on this mission and also by Tawanda. Tawanda was in his late thirties and had worked his way up the ladder in the SPCA hierarchy, starting as a kennel cleaner, then becoming a driver and finally an Inspector. Tawanda and Addmore had been on a number of rescues before; they knew the routines, problems and dangers and both did excellent work.

It was an exhausting seven-hour drive and because they didn't set out until after lunch due to the on-going pressure of work, they only arrived in Beitbridge well after dark. The road had been very busy because the following day was a public holiday and Meryl was utterly exhausted. Beitbridge was a place filled with bad and painful memories for Meryl and she was anxious and on edge.

'That road is hell in the dark, cattle and donkeys lying in the middle of the road, trucks parked on the verges with no lights, trucks coming towards you that won't dip their lights, scotch carts, etc. I was worried about the situation on the farm, and the fact that there was a Member in Charge who was new to me. My stress wasn't helped by the fact that I always hated visiting Beitbridge because my twin brother had, several years ago, been brutally beaten by Government agents there, and four days later died from his injuries.'

Thankfully accommodation for Meryl, Addmore and Tawanda had been sponsored at a local hotel and supper, a hot bath and an early night were much appreciated.

The following morning after an early breakfast Meryl headed straight to the police station to arrange for an escort onto Twin Rivers Ranch. This always took time but because the Officer In Charge was new to his post, it was more involved than usual. A meeting was called and it didn't take long for DISPOL (Officer in charge of District Police) to announce that they could not agree to Meryl being allowed to go Twin Rivers Ranch with food for the dogs.

'The situation at Twin Rivers is very tense,' the policeman said. 'The war veterans there are very aggressive and it would be much too dangerous for you to go there.'

600 kilometres, a seven-hour drive, 60 kg of dog meal and a cold box full of meat and all for nothing? No way! Meryl thought. To get turned away at this point was not an option and she was certainly not going to give up that easily.

'Look,' she said, 'I've driven all the way from Harare to ensure the well-being of the dogs on Twin Rivers. I am not interested in anything else at all. I just want to take food to the dogs.'

'But this is the problem,' DISPOL said, 'by going there with food for the dogs the war veterans will see that you are trying to help the Wheelers to be able to stay longer on the farm.'

'I am only going to protect the welfare of the animals,' Meryl replied. 'I have nothing whatsoever to do with the farm ownership. I am only concerned with issues relating to animal welfare.'

DISPOL digressed into a long explanation about the ownership of Twin Rivers Ranch and the government's intention with regards to land. He finished by saying, 'The Wheelers cannot stay there, Mrs Harrison. The government are definitely taking that farm and the house is going to be made into a school for the children of the war veterans and settlers.'

'Look,' said Meryl, anxious to get away from politics and back onto animal welfare, 'all I want is a police escort to go to Twin Rivers so that I can protect the welfare of the animals there. I give you my word that this will be a one-off visit with emergency food supplies for the dogs. If the dog food runs out again after this then I will not go back with more, you have my word.'

What Meryl didn't know was that the police had agreed to a mercy mission a few days earlier when well-wishers had begged to be allowed to take 'urgent' food supplies to the Wheelers. The police had agreed but when the war veterans had stopped and searched the vehicle they found whisky, beer and bananas amongst the groceries – hardly urgent, emergency food supplies, the policeman had said! Later Meryl found out that these supplies were looted and did not reach the Wheelers.

'Also,' the policeman said to Meryl, 'when we went to the farm just yesterday Mrs Wheeler was taking photographs of the police talking to the war veterans. This is not acceptable.'

It took over an hour of careful negotiations before the police finally agreed that Meryl could deliver dog food to Twin Rivers Ranch. They agreed to provide a police escort for the visit but made it clear that there wouldn't be another occasion; this would be a strictly one-off visit. The police also insisted that Meryl would have to meet with the Base Commander at the farm and eventually, after waiting another hour while the police found a vehicle, they finally set off.

For the first 60 kilometres of the journey Meryl saw little to feel positive about.

'On this main Beitbridge-Bulawayo road, for the first 25 kilometres the scenery is very depressing. The fences have long gone and everywhere there is red dust and just a few straggly bushes. All the river beds were dry and there were a lot of scotch carts belting down the road. Wherever possible we stopped the donkey owners and reminded them that the donkeys are not 4x4s and there is no need to continually whip them when they are going as fast as they can. There were also many carcasses of cows, donkeys and goats that have been hit by cars and it is only as you get nearer to West Nicholson that the countryside improves as you approach many of the large ranches.'

Twin Rivers Ranch had been bought by Rachel and Shannon Wheeler in 1986 and they had built it up into a very lucrative fruit and cattle farm. There were 15,000 citrus trees, 4,000 mango trees, 20 hectares of market gardening and 600 cattle on the Ranch. Under normal circumstances 50 permanent staff were employed on the farm and 150 men and women from the neighbouring Siyoka communal land were bought in for seasonal fruit picking.

Turning off the main road Meryl had been told to proceed for 23 kilometres along a dirt road that led to Twin Rivers Ranch. The nearest next door neighbour was 26 kilometres away. Meryl felt distinctly uncomfortable as she began to drive along the lonely gravel road. Everything about Beitbridge made her think about Colin, her twin brother who had died here 16 years before in 1986. It had been the Easter weekend and Colin had had a few drinks when the chance of a lift to Johannesburg came up.

Colin seized the opportunity to visit Meryl and her husband who were living in Johannesburg at the time and because it was already late in the day, an overnight stop in Beitbridge was arranged. Colin had a few more drinks as a passenger on the journey and was pretty drunk by the time they arrived at the Beitbridge Hotel where a party was underway. Colin joined in but his loud behaviour and merriment led some patrons to complain to the OIC (Officer in Charge) of Beitbridge police and the head of the CIO who happened to be off duty and drinking at the hotel bar. It wasn't long before Colin was being frog-marched by the two men to the police station which was just over the road from the hotel. Some hours later Colin, who suffered from a debilitating back condition, *ankylosing spondylitis*, was delivered by the police to the Beitbridge Hospital. He had been severely assaulted in police custody. Unconscious and in a bad way Colin was then inexplicably moved to an even smaller medical facility in Gwanda, 150 kilometres away. His condition deteriorated and then he was moved again, this time to Bulawayo.

By the time Meryl heard about the assault by police on her brother and got to Bulawayo, it was too late, Colin had passed away. The post mortem revealed that all of Colin's organs had been ruptured, his neck had been broken and he died from internal bleeding. A few weeks later the OIC of Beitbridge police and the head of the local CIO were arrested and charged with murder. Remanded in custody and before the trial even began, one of the two turned state's evidence and was released. On the day the trial of the second accused man was to begin, Meryl learnt that he too was free and clear, released under a Presidential Amnesty. Meryl had been devastated by the death of her brother. Being adopted and being twins, the bond between brother and sister had been very close. Knowing that Colin had been physically incapable of defending himself due to his back problem and that the two perpetrators had got away, literally, with murder, were facts that haunted Meryl. As she drove along the dusty roads now, 16 years later, Meryl hoped that one day Zimbabwe would have Truth and Reconciliation hearings similar to those held in South Africa, so that accountability could be demanded and then perhaps her brother could at last rest in peace.

There had been many tributes to Meryl's brother but the one she cherished most was that written by Colin's good friend, journalist Angus Shaw. Meryl remembered some of the words Shaw had written:

'*To countless Zimbabweans the name Colin Anderson is synonymous with fair play and a human integrity that is hard to find these days. Mr Anderson, a former social worker, had a fine intellect and a brand of wit. As a social worker, helping troubled youths of all races, Mr Anderson's even-handedness was legendary. He was no stranger to shebeens and the other haunts of his young probationers whom he stood alongside against the pressures of the time. He was an exceptional man.*'

Meryl sighed; the memories of 16 years ago were painful and oppressive. She shivered in the April heat and turned her thoughts back to the present. The dust rose up behind her truck as she headed towards Twin Rivers Ranch.

There were several illegal road blocks and booms across the gravel road and at the third one, both the SPCA and police vehicles were stopped by youths who disappeared into the bush to call a war veteran. While they waited a large crowd of settlers gathered to watch. Meryl noticed that most of them were women and youngsters. The youths were hostile and many wore dirty and torn Zanu PF T-shirts. The women seemed to just be curious and quite a few had babies on their backs and toddlers at their feet. When the war veteran arrived there was a lengthy discussion with the police and it was clear that he was not happy with the situation. It took some time but eventually the war veteran got into the police Land Rover and they set off to the farmhouse.

Shannon Wheeler came out of the house to meet them as soon as they arrived but Meryl immediately persuaded him against having any conversation with her at all. It had taken so much diplomacy to get this far, Meryl was determined that nothing should go wrong at this stage. If there was even the slightest suspicion that Meryl was friendly towards the Wheelers or if they thought she was giving or getting anything from them, then the entire mercy mission could be in jeopardy. It didn't matter what Meryl's own thoughts were, she had to be seen to be impartial and apolitical at all times. The war veteran who had travelled with the police came and watched as the dog food was unloaded from the SPCA truck and he said nothing when the cooler box filled with meat was taken to the house.

Meryl could hardly believe it was going so well but her thought obviously tempted fate. As so often happened, one moment everything would be fine, almost amicable, and the next it could turn chaotic or even violent, sometimes for no apparent reason at all. The equilibrium was clearly disturbed when a wheelbarrow was produced to carry the sixty kilograms of dog meal. Perhaps what had appeared as a small rescue mission to bring food for dogs suddenly looked like a bigger operation with the arrival of the wheelbarrow.

The war veteran suddenly went mad and started shouting furiously at everyone, ordering all the food loading to stop. His name was Matero, a stocky man, not well dressed and he'd clearly been drinking.

'It is too fast,' he fumed. 'You are going too fast and there is far too much food here. I won't allow all of this food to go in. I am in charge here, you know. I will tell you how much food you can give.'

Everyone stood aside while Matero ordered the farm manager Sammy to help him and they took away bag after bag of dog meal and cubes and dumped them back into the SPCA truck. Minutes later there was just one bag of food left in the driveway. Meryl watched in horror as the security of the dogs was taken away and so close to the end of what had been an exhausting journey. She could see a couple of the Boerboels in the garden and clutching at straws she pointed out the size of the dogs to the war veterans saying that the dogs would get through this food in no time at all. Boerboels are large dogs, similar in appearance to Mastiffs with a big head and docked tail and they need a lot of food – particularly when feeding puppies. Addmore joined in Meryl's effort and appealed that they at least be allowed to leave half the food they had bought. Then even the police intervened and at last they were given permission to leave all the food for the enormous dogs.

For the second time the food was loaded onto the wheelbarrow and while this was going on the Wheeler's 16-year-old daughter Vilanda came out to Meryl carrying a young Boerboel puppy with a swollen leg. Meryl saw immediately that Vilanda looked very distressed and close to tears and this siege was obviously having an enormous impact on her. Meryl did her best to treat the puppy and while she did she managed to whisper to Vilanda that the packets of meat in the cooler box marked 'Puppy Mix' were in fact steak mince for the family. What an appalling situation this was, Meryl thought. The stress and anguish was unbearable for the adults, the children and the animals and Meryl was filled with compassion as she watched Vilanda walk dejectedly back to the house, back to the siege, back to the nightmare that her life had become.

With all the food unloaded, Meryl had nothing more to do and so she and the police left Twin Rivers Ranch. It was hard to imagine how the situation on this farm would end. Both farm owners and war veterans were determined the property belonged to them and neither seemed prepared to back down. Meryl's thoughts were interrupted when suddenly the road ahead was blocked and they were confronted by the Base Commander and another man. These were obviously more senior war veterans and they were incensed that Meryl had been allowed to go the farmhouse.

'I was scared because the situation was noticeably getting out of hand. I was conscious that I was the only white person for miles and the youths had now also come back, attracted by all the shouting. For about 15 minutes the two men ranted and raved at both the police and at us. The youths shouted in Shona and waved clenched fists at us and all were outraged that we had gone to the farmhouse.'

When at last the shouting calmed down, Meryl explained exactly who she was and what the SPCA were empowered to do. At first the crowd was sceptical but Meryl handed out pamphlets in Shona which explained how to care for donkeys and gradually the tension eased. By the time Meryl was finally able to leave, she had given out medicine for foot rot, eye ointment, dog biscuits and dog meal. The war veterans were delighted with their acquisitions and they parted from the SPCA team as the best of friends.

In the following days the situation at Twin Rivers Ranch deteriorated dramatically. Shocking reports and heartbreaking accounts were exposed in local and international newspapers.

The Zimbabwean CFU (Commercial Farmers Union) reported that the pregnant wife of farm manager Sammy had been assaulted and abducted. The CFU reported that 700 tonnes of farm produce had been looted and 45 head of cattle stolen. It described how 75 war veterans and their followers, armed with traditional weapons, broke into the gate, went to the farm office and started removing the Wheelers' property. The UK *Sunday Times* reported how the Zimbabwean Minister of Home Affairs at the time had told war veterans and settlers just two weeks before that all the moveable assets on Twin Rivers Ranch belonged to them. Local, regional and international newspapers gave widespread coverage to the fact that the Minister of Home Affairs and his wife had taken over Twin Rivers Ranch. Of all the media reports, the hardest to read were the accounts written by the Wheeler children which were publicised by Jenni Williams, the CFU Public Relations official at the time.

16-year-old Vilanda Wheeler, a Form Four student at a Bulawayo senior school wrote:

'What started off as a peaceful holiday ended in a nightmare. Our water and power supplies have been cut off for the past 21 days. … I am dreading going back to school and leaving my home since this is the only home I have ever known and if I should leave I may never see it again. I don't want to leave my Mum and my Dad and my dogs… At night they [the war veterans and invaders] take turns in patrolling around our security fence, at times blowing whistles and beating drums… We will keep praying to God to give us strength in this time of trial.'

13-year-old Eric Wheeler, in Form One at a senior school in Bulawayo wrote:

'On the 20th there were at least 70 so-called war veterans and settlers, most of them under the age of 24 years, singing and beating drums and blowing a kudu horn. Thanks to our dogs they could not break into our yard…. We are all very grateful to our God for giving us the strength and courage and for keeping us safe. Thanks also for all the prayers and the very many phone calls we receive daily from people all over our beautiful country.'

Twenty three days later Meryl headed back to Twin Rivers Ranch but this time it was to rescue the Boerboels. The Wheelers had finally been forced out of their home and all the dogs had been left behind. Shannon Wheeler thought it would just be for a day or two but once they had him off the farm, neither the police nor the war veterans would allow the Wheelers to go back.

When the dogs had been left on Twin Rivers alone for a week, the need for their rescue was critical.

Meryl set out for Beitbridge immediately accompanied by Addmore and Tawanda. She had informed the police in advance and they were waiting for her when she arrived. On the dirt road leading to the farm, there was no doubt that the entire area was now controlled by the war veterans. The road was regularly piled with obstacles which served as road blocks – logs, planks and branches. Arriving at the farmhouse the property appeared completely deserted and the dogs raced around the garden barking frantically. In a run outside the security fence and farm gate was Major, a very large Boerboel. There was a broken sack of dog meal in the run which still had some food in it but his water dish was completely dry. Opening the gate to the run, Tawanda grabbed the dog's collar but there was no need to worry that the dog would run away. The huge Boerboel ran straight for Meryl's truck, dragging Tawanda behind him! Before anyone even had a chance to let the tail gate of the truck down, Major had scaled the back in one huge leap and sat waiting to be taken away!

With so many big dogs to carry and because Major didn't get on well with the other dogs, Meryl immediately drove the 23 kilometres back to the main road. The last thing she wanted was a dog fight in the back of the truck! The entire Wheeler family and some friends had gathered and were waiting anxiously on the main road. There was a tumultuous welcome for the huge dog. Tears and hugs mixed with patting, licking and wagging and then came the moment the dog had been so desperately waiting for – water! Everyone stood back and watched as Major drank and drank and then drank some more. Seven litres later Major looked up, drops hanging from his mouth. Seven litres to make up for a week of thirst. No one could know what sort of anguish the dog must have endured as his thirst grew from day to day over that long and frightening week. No one voiced the thought that undoubtedly filled everyone's minds – what kind of people were these war veterans that they could not even give a dog a drink of water.

Leaving Major reunited with his owners, Meryl headed straight back to the farm for the other six dogs still at the house. No food or water for a week, the six dogs could not be rescued soon enough. Arriving back at the house they were met by one of the war veterans who had been so obstreperous on Meryl's last visit. This time the man was relaxed and friendly. Wearing dark Rayban sunglasses he shook Meryl's hand warmly and did not offer any objection as she unlocked the gate. One by one they caught each Boerboel and lifted them into the back of the truck. It was no mean feat as the dogs were heavy and the truck was soon filled to overflowing. Moments before the dogs had just been big Boerboels, now they became individuals and much-loved pets as their names were ticked off: Mafinya, a male, and five bitches: Sofala, Sacha, Delta, Santie and Spookie. Spookie, the last bitch to be caught, lived up to her name as she was very nervous and difficult to catch. When Meryl finally got a rope lead over Spookie's head, the bitch flung herself crazily all over the place as if she was being murdered. At last though, with no room for niceties, Spookie was uncere-moniously dumped in the back of the truck where she landed upside down in a heap. The puppies had thankfully already been taken by the Wheelers when they left the farm and so last of all to be rescued was a beautiful dark ginger cat which meowed incessantly from the roof of the farmhouse making it quite obvious that it too wanted to be rescued! Meryl hadn't known about the cat but she couldn't miss it now thanks to its calls from above. How this pretty little cat had stayed so tame and loving in a house full of enormous dogs was a mystery but it was soon coaxed down and put into the front of the SPCA truck.

With dogs, a cat and people occupying every millimetre of space in the truck, Meryl was ready to leave Twin Rivers for the last time. She quickly walked across the garden and looked through the windows of what had been the Wheelers much-loved home. They were desperate to know if their posses-sions were still intact and Meryl dreaded having to tell them what she saw.

The house had obviously been looted and trashed some time in the last week. Every cupboard and drawer was open and what had not been stolen was thrown or smashed on the floor. The Wheeler's had left with just one suitcase of personal belongings and what Meryl saw was a shocking sight of mayhem and destruction. Meryl drove out of the farm and locked the gate behind her. She expected that there would be a confrontation and that the war veteran would demand the keys from her but he did not. Still wearing his dark sunglasses even though it was late in the afternoon, the war veteran smiled and wished Meryl a 'safe journey' and she knew that now the dogs were gone this man could cut the fence and get into the Wheelers home any time he liked.

With barely enough room to even operate the gears and pedals Meryl drove slowly back to the main road. It was a short journey, filled with colour – thanks to the cat!

'As we hadn't been told that there was a cat – we had taken our cat cage out to make more room for the dogs. So we had the ginger cat in the front of the truck with myself and the two policemen. There was no way we could put it in the back of the truck with all the dogs. He was struggling a lot and it wasn't long before their uniforms were covered in orange fluff and hair – they were not very impressed!'

Back at the main road the Wheeler family were anxiously waiting with a second truck to collect their Boerboels. With so many dogs it was a pretty chaotic reunion with hugs and tears mixed up with slobbery kisses and buckets of water being dished out everywhere for the desperately thirsty dogs. In the midst of all the stress and anxiety, and their fear for the rescue operation, the Wheelers had forgotten to tell Meryl about Sparkles, the beautiful ginger cat but now the cat was welcomed with great delight by the family. Then came the moment Meryl had been dreading when the Wheelers asked about their possessions. Meryl told Mrs Wheeler as gently as she could about what she had seen through the window of the house and both women cried and hugged on the side of the road. For now the most important thing for the Wheelers was that all the animals were safe and that they were all together again.

Meryl followed the Wheelers back to West Nicholson and watched the dogs all being settled in to makeshift runs for the night. Each dog was given an enormous dish of meat and maize porridge – a well-deserved meal after having had no food or water for a week. Major was presented with his food bowl and an enormous bone but was too excited to eat. The Boerboel seemed to be in love and was totally captivated with a young hand-reared giraffe that was gazing solemnly at him near his kennel! Love at the end of a very traumatic week for the dog.

Extracts from Meryl's Diary:

A bully is always a coward.
– Proverb

April 2002
Featherstone:
1 April. Farmer from Featherstone phones to inform me that his two children had been chased by an army truck down their farm road whilst they were carrying their pet cats. The cats ran away – children now on tranquillisers. Some time later we did rescue the pets after the family had left the farm.

Bromley:
Problems on a stud farm – takes many days to resolve.

4 April. Nick's birthday – managed to phone him before my day got too hectic. He's been in Melbourne for three years now and seems well settled. I know I probably got him in the middle of the night!

8 April. Phone call re: 49 pigs stolen by settlers from Gemini Farm.

CHAPTER THIRTEEN

Cuthbert, the tennis ball cat

'A leader of good judgment gives stability;
An exploiting leader leaves a trail of waste.'
– Eugene H Peterson

Waltondale Farm, Marondera, April 2002
Meryl's troubles started when she used the remote control to open the electric gate at Waltondale, the Cartwrights' Marondera farm. Meryl had arrived at the gate at a snail's pace, a great crowd of settlers and war veterans escorting her, walking in front of the SPCA vehicle. They were all armed with an assortment of weapons including sticks, stones and catapults

The war veteran in charge was a tall, slim man called Garesi. He was wearing a dark brown trilby hat with a wide brim and carried a large stick. He demanded to know where Meryl had got the remote control button for the gate and then wanted to know where the Cartwrights were. Meryl wasn't sure if Garesi accepted her answer that she didn't know where the farm owners were but as he said nothing more, she drove in and stopped the vehicle near the farmhouse. She had been asked to rescue six dogs and two cats from one house and two cats from a second house on Waltondale Farm.

Waltondale had been in the Cartwright family since 1934. It had not been designated by the government for redistribution but was obviously highly sought-after. The farm produced tobacco and maize and had 700 beef cattle. The Cartwrights had built a school on the farm and 400 children were enrolled in Waltondale Farm School.

At 5.30pm on 6 April 2002, Guy and Rosalind Cartwright concluded their day's work and set out to check everything was alright on the farm and to give their dogs some exercise. They went in the farm truck, dogs in the back, and stopped briefly at the tobacco barns. The first inkling of trouble came from the head barn worker who told Guy not to go onto the lands that evening – he'd heard they were about to be invaded by war veterans and settlers.

'Rubbish, we're going to be here forever!' Guy responded with conviction and they set out. Later Guy wrote about what was to be the last day of 68 years on Waltondale Farm:

'*It was nearly 6pm and we went to a particularly beautiful spot on the farm where we had been baling grass. From here we could see Wedza Mountain about 60km away – what a beautiful sight. After looking at the work done and a short inspection of the baler to see that it was in order for work on Sunday, we went across the dam wall and drove up the hill from the river and were heading for home. The car farm security radio came to life. It was our head of farm security telling us that we had been invaded. I said as calmly as possible that I would get to the farmhouse by the bottom gate but he said no, they are in your house.*
We had a dilemma. I mean what do you do when you have left your house open, the TV on and supper in the warming drawer? Straightaway Rosalind said, 'Poor Cuthbert and Macavity (our cats).'
I bravely said, 'Don't worry, I'll get them tomorrow.'
'I suppose they'll hide?'
'Of course they will,' I said calmly but I wasn't too sure as Cuthbert was 15 years old and was never blessed with a particularly good brain. Rosalind said he was slow because when he was younger he used to come on the tennis court and chase the balls. Once, unfortunately, he got hit by a ball on the side of the head, which seemed to shake him up! Definitely gave him a black eye.
The worry too was now: what about Douglas and Elke's dogs and cats? Their staff had fed them earlier that day, but what about tomorrow? Would anyone be allowed in to feed them?'

There was no tomorrow for the Cartwrights because they were not allowed back onto Waltondale Farm and it was Meryl who went to try and rescue Cuthbert, the tennis ball cat, his feline companion Macavity and the dogs and cats belonging to Douglas and Elke Cartwright, Guy and Rosalind's son and daughter-in-law.

The first dog Meryl saw was a Ridgeback who seemed delighted to see friendly faces and kind voices. This was Monty, a ten-year-old Ridgeback who came straight towards Meryl wagging his tail and was immediately picked up and put into a cage in the back of the SPCA vehicle. Meryl and SPCA Inspectors Addmore and Tawanda could see three Fox Terriers running around in the garden but they were nervous and would need coaxing, in order to be caught. There was a little child's chair outside the back door and Meryl squeezed herself into it and waited for the dogs to come to her.

She had a dish of food in her lap and kept throwing little bits to the dogs, tempting them, trying to reassure them and persuade them that their ordeal was almost over – or would be, if only they would let Meryl catch them and take them away. After a little while, as the trust became established, Addmore caught Lady, a 13-year-old black-and-white Fox Terrier with a fluffy coat. Shortly afterwards Meryl caught Twinkle, a ten-year-old Jack Russell bitch and then there were three dogs left to catch. These were two Fox Terriers called Heidi and Porkie, and Swartzie a black-and-white Jack Russell type, and they were all much more elusive. They were relatively new pets to the Cartwrights, having been given to the family by friends who had left the country just two months earlier, in February 2002.

When it was obvious that neither Heidi nor Swartzie were going to come close enough to be caught, Meryl and Tawanda put a trail of meat-balls on the ground. The food-line lead all the way into a laundry on the side of the house. Meryl filled a dish with pet food and put it at the back of the room and then, using the only thing that came to hand, she tied a green towelling dressing gown belt to the outside of the laundry door and waited.

After some time, hunger overcame Heidi's nerves and she followed the trail of meat, eating as she went. After two false attempts when she ran back out at the last minute, Heidi finally went right into the laundry and Meryl tugged the dressing gown cord and pulled the door shut. Then came the turn of Swartzie who appeared to have decided that as Meryl was the source of food she must be OK. Wagging his little tail frantically, Swartzie let Meryl pick him up and put him in the truck too.

With all the dogs that had been outside in the garden, now safely closed into cages in the SPCA truck, Meryl turned her attention to the house. There was still one dog missing and two cats, Sooty and Lucky, to find and catch. It had been four days since the Cartwrights had been forced out of their home – a long time for pets to have been left alone. Meryl had seen one cat through the window. The cat was in the kitchen, and judging by the description she'd been given, Meryl assumed this was Sooty. Meryl unlocked the kitchen door and handed the house keys to Addmore. She wanted to concentrate on only one thing and that was the cat. From the second she unlocked the door all Meryl's attention was focused on getting herself and the cage into the house without the cat running out. The more rescues Meryl conducted on invaded farms, the more aware she had become of the problems. Writing in her diary Meryl said:

'We had a definite routine for rescuing cats, knowing how nervous they can be with strangers. I had to make rules up at the start of the farm rescues and learnt the hard way all along.'

If the cat got a fright and ran, Meryl knew that she wouldn't get a second chance and the situation at Waltondale Farm was far from ideal. The farmyard was crowded with hostile war veterans and settlers and everything about the situation was extremely tense. Concentrating completely on the cat, Meryl heard some raised voices behind her but knew someone else would have to deal with it; she must stay focused if she was to succeed. The fracas, she later discovered, was with Garesi, the main war veteran. He had been following and watching, hovering like a vulture and when he saw the house keys being given to Addmore, he pounced. Garesi demanded that Addmore hand over the house keys, which he did. Luckily the woman police Constable, their official escort, saw what had happened and intervened immediately. She took the keys away from Garesi saying that he had no right to have them. Clearly getting the house keys was a major objective for Garesi and had been from the moment Meryl and her team had arrived.

While the keys were being passed backwards and forwards, Meryl had managed to catch the cat. Sooty, a beautiful black-and-white cat, showed no outward signs of distress; he sat in the passageway washing himself and Meryl easily lifted him into a cage where he would stay until he could be reunited with his owners. Boosted by the achievements so far, Meryl immediately started looking through the house for the other cat and last missing dog. Many of the windows around the house had been left open and so it was possible that the dog had got inside.

Everything in the house appeared to be in order – there was no obvious sign that anything had been taken or damaged. In many of the rooms there were several piles of dog faeces and puddles of urine, definite proof that the missing dog was somewhere in the house. Before long Meryl and Addmore found Porkie and he was clearly very distressed. He sat in the passage of what had been his home, head down and visibly trembling. The little Fox Terrier would not look at Meryl or Addmore and they had no way of knowing what may have happened to him to cause this behaviour but at least now he would be safe and the ordeal was over.

There was just one cat left to catch and Meryl and Addmore searched and called but there was no sign of Lucky. Just as Meryl was about to leave, one of the war veterans pointed to a cat sitting on the roof of the house. This must be Lucky! The cat was clearly frightened and it ran round and around before finally jumping down and back into the house through one of the open windows. Meryl and Addmore raced around, frantically pushing windows closed from the outside and then went back into the house where they found the cat in the main bedroom. Lucky growled and hissed and puffed her fur out but was eventually caught and closed safely into a cat cage and put into the truck. Meryl could hardly believe the success of her rescue. All the animals had been found and caught and, with any luck, collecting the last two cats at the second house on Waltondale Farm would be just as successful.

As they were about to get into the truck to leave for the second house, Meryl noticed that a large crowd of people had gathered and were coming up the driveway.

'What's happening?' she asked Garesi who was still following her as closely as a shadow. 'Who are all those people?'

'Oh,' Garesi answered casually, 'that is the MP for this area and with him is the Chairman of the Land Committee.'

Meryl watched in silence as the Member of Parliament, a retired army Brigadier, approached. He was followed closely by one uniformed police Constable, and a large crowd of war veterans and settlers. Meryl swallowed hard and mentally calmed herself; she knew she must show neither fear nor anger but it was obvious that this visit was not a chance arrival. Later Meryl wrote in her diary:

'I am positive that someone tipped off the Brigadier that we were at the house. It was a bizarre situation, as he had brought the police with him, but the police from Marondera Rural had been assigned to us for our protection!'

When the crowd came to a stop at the gate, Garesi asked Meryl to activate the remote control and open the gate. As Meryl activated the gate she heard Garesi say to one of the war veterans:

'Good, this will make our job much easier.'

Meryl knew things were rapidly deteriorating but there was nothing she could do about it. She introduced herself, Addmore and Tawanda to the MP and told him what she was doing at the farm. The Brigadier did not respond or extend a similar courtesy to Meryl. He was the former Ambassador to Yugoslavia and had won the Marondera West by-election in circumstances mired with numerous allegations of electoral irregularities. After his recent election victory the Brigadier was quoted in a South African newspaper defending the forcible occupation of land saying it was: 'a revolution given that those without land are prepared to fight for it' (*Mail and Guardian, South Africa*).

Meryl waited for the Brigadier to introduce himself or the people with him but he said nothing.

'Have you got all the animals then?' a woman in a large white hat demanded to know. She was short and fat and spoke good English but her manner was hostile. She didn't talk to Meryl but rather talked *at* her, hands on hips, the aggression palpable. She was, apparently, the Chairman of the Land Committee in the area, a powerful position to hold in these days. It was this woman who would decide not only who would be given land that was being seized from the commercial farmers, but exactly which piece of land a person could have. Obviously prime farms with beautiful homesteads and well-developed infrastructure were in huge demand – particularly by people of importance.

Meryl said that she had indeed finished getting the animals from this house on the farm but that there were still two cats to be caught at the second house on the farm. Both the Brigadier MP and the woman in the large hat wanted to know exactly where Meryl had got the keys for the houses from. When she replied that Mrs Cartwright had dropped them off at the SPCA, the Brigadier MP reacted with fury.

'They told me that the farm security had the keys,' he spluttered. 'Those farmers lied. Give me the keys now!' he ordered. Meryl was shaken at the reaction her words had caused but somehow managed to keep calm. Quietly and politely she refused to obey the Brigadier's order.

'I cannot give you the keys to someone else's home,' Meryl said. 'I am an Inspector appointed by the Government.'

'I don't care who you are!' the Brigadier spat at Meryl. 'I am a Member of Parliament and therefore I overrule you. Give me those keys now.'

Still Meryl refused saying that she had been entrusted with the keys on behalf of the SPCA and had no authority to let anyone have access to the houses on Waltondale Farm. Houses which were still furnished and filled with the owners' private belongings. The argument continued but the more Meryl remained steadfast, the angrier and louder the argument and demands became.

'Don't let them out,' one of the war veterans called out from the crowd. 'If she won't give us the keys, she will stay here, surrounded. We will not let her leave.'

Now the situation had reached breaking point and Meryl knew that she had pushed her luck, and perhaps her safety, right to the very edge.

'I will do what the police tell me, this is their decision now,' Meryl said, assuming that the police would do their job and protect the private property and belongings of the Cartwright family.

'You must give the keys to him!' the police Constable announced.

Meryl was shocked speechless. This was beyond belief. Seething with rage she had no choice but to do as the police Constable had instructed and she handed the keys over. Meryl was in SPCA uniform, in a marked SPCA vehicle and obviously on official business. It was the most sickening moment and Meryl felt terrible. What kind of madness was this? she wondered. How could this be allowed, sanctioned by the police – and under the name of land redistribution?

In silence Meryl drove to the second house on Waltondale farm to look for the last two cats. The sooner she could get this rescue finished and leave this place, the better, Meryl thought. If it weren't for the animals, she had no doubt she would have left a long time ago. Meryl's job was almost impossible now. The entire mob and the Brigadier MP had followed Meryl to the house.

'You will have to wait here,' Meryl announced to the mob, expecting them to ignore or laugh at her but amazingly they did as they were told. Most of the crowd stood around at Meryl's truck but two war veterans, who were both noticeably drunk, followed her to the house.

'I will find the kitty,' one of the drunks slurred repeatedly but his inebriated condition did not inspire confidence at all and so Meryl ignored him and opened the door to the house.

Meryl was looking for Cuthbert, a 15-year-old cat and Macavity, a 12-year-old Siamese. Cuthbert was apparently very fond of sunning himself on a deck and it was here that Meryl started her search. A big black three-legged cooking pot was standing over a fire that had been lit on the concrete floor of the verandah and several garden chairs had been placed around the fire. There were empty bottles of South African wine lying on the ground nearby; the contents must have been consumed by the war veterans. There was no sign of either of the cats and so Meryl and Tawanda searched the house, going from room to room, calling the cats and looking in every possible hiding place.

By now Meryl was being followed around by a large crowd and she knew the chances of finding either of the cats was miniscule. In the kitchen there were all the signs that the Cartwrights had left unexpectedly and in a hurry. There were two prepared dishes of cat food on the kitchen table which had both gone mouldy and it seemed more and more likely that the cats had run away. The terror of finding their loving and caring owners suddenly replaced by dozens of loud, drunken men would have been more than enough reason for the cats to run away.

When it was obvious that they were not going to find Cuthbert or Macavity, Meryl filled dishes with milk for the cats and then she prepared to leave. The main war veteran Garesi and his friends were sitting around the fire on the Cartwrights' garden furniture and the sight was one that was to become etched into Meryl's memory. As if it was not bad enough that these men had evicted the owners, seized the keys and entered a private home, it was truly shocking to see them now sitting around as if they owned the furniture too – clearly they did, as no one was even attempting to stop them.

Meryl was so angry that she hardly trusted herself to speak but when she got to her vehicle she turned to the Brigadier MP and asked him his name.

'You do not need to know that,' the Brigadier answered.

Meryl turned then to the woman in the white hat and asked her name. 'Meryl,' she said, 'I am not going to tell you.'

Finally Meryl looked at the policeman who had arrived with the MP and the woman and asked him his name, rank and police number. The policeman did not answer. Meryl asked a second time for his name and details but again the policeman just stared at her and did not respond.

'It is an offence for you not to provide that information,' Meryl said to the policeman but still he said nothing and so she walked across to the vehicle.

'Give me the keys to the house,' the woman in the white hat now demanded of Meryl.

'Why do you want them?' asked Meryl. 'It's quite clear that you have already been into the house and have already got your own keys. Why do you need these keys too?'

The crowd of war veterans and settlers had started gathering and the noise level increased. Meryl was beaten, she knew it. Later she wrote in her diary:

'Once again the crowd was growing hostile, in particular a tall war vet carrying a heavy stick who had earlier given instructions that the gate must be locked until I handed the key over or I was to be assaulted. I threw the key at the woman. I was crying out of anger and frustration, but kept thinking: at least we have a truck full of Cartwright pets!'

Meryl always worked hard at controlling and concealing both her temper and her emotions but this time it had all been too much. She finally drove out of the gates and left Waltondale Farm with her precious truckload of much loved pets. She had six dogs and two cats in cages in the back of her truck – she would have endured it all over again to save these animals; rescuing them made almost anything worth tolerating. Meryl headed for the Marondera police station to drop off the two police officers who had been escorting her. She might have been emotional, frustrated and upset, but she was determined to lodge a complaint with the Officer in Charge.

Very conscious of the precious and traumatised cargo she carried, Meryl parked in the shade and went into the offices. A tumultuous few minutes followed where one department blamed another, one individual accused another and telephone calls went backwards and forwards between the police and political and local government officials in the town. Meryl wanted to get to the bottom of the fact that a Member of Parliament had used the SPCA as a scapegoat to cover unlawful activities. She stressed that the ZNSPCA was a totally non-political organisation and should have been allowed to hand the keys of the house back to the rightful owners and not to a politician. One section of the police agreed that Meryl should not have been made to hand over the keys and said the matter would become a criminal issue. Another section of the police, in the same building, saw nothing wrong in Meryl being forced to hand the Cartwrights' house keys over to a mob headed by a politician. The District Administrator gave the classic reply notoriously used across the country and said, 'It is political.'

Meryl left the police station with the matter unresolved but knowing that she could do no more. After safely delivering all the dogs and cats to a nearby boarding kennel, Meryl delayed her return to Harare by taking Addmore and Tawanda to a local hotel for a pie and Coke. She was utterly exhausted and a mental wreck, her hands trembling and legs feeling as if they had turned to water now that it was over.

She did not know how she would find the courage to phone the Cartwrights and tell them that she had rescued their animals but had handed their house keys over to a Brigadier MP, a large woman in a white hat and a mob of war veterans. Oh God, Meryl thought, how can I do this? As she sat on the verandah of the Marondera Hotel and people walked and drove past going about their normal business, she felt like she had come from another planet. Everything seemed so normal, everyone behaved so naturally on this beautiful April afternoon. Was any of this hell real? Meryl wondered. Did anyone even care? she thought.

Meryl did find the courage to tell the Cartwrights about their house keys and they said they understood, said they knew that the war veterans would have broken in anyway and the keys were simply a courtesy for what was inevitable. After hearing what had happened, the Cartwrights instructed their lawyer and a warrant of arrest was issued for the Brigadier but nothing happened; the warrant was simply ignored. By the following morning all of the Cartwrights' personal belongings had been thrown out of the double-storey house and onto the lawn. Most of the furniture and breakable items had been thrown from second floor windows and smashed in the fall.

The Brigadier went to the other house and took possession of the fridges, furniture and stove and that was the finish of every last loving fibre of Waltondale farm. Guy and Rosalind Cartwright did get 'permission' to go back into their own home a few days later to look for their cats and both Macavity and Cuthbert were found and rescued. The Brigadier MP, despite having been quoted in the international press as saying that this revolution was to give landless people back their land, took over Waltondale Farm himself.

Extracts from Meryl's Diary:

He that would have eggs must endure the cackling of hens.
— Proverb

April 2002
Norton:
Investigated a case of two horses deliberately burnt by settlers.

Harare:
Office that Harare SPCA kindly offered me to operate from is painted — looks much better.

Chitungwiza:
Received a call re: a cow that is running amok in the densely-housed area of Chitungwiza — ends up in a residents' back garden — owner's terrified children are inside the house. Police refuse to destroy on the grounds that they have to find the owner of the cow first — that could take days — it was very stressed by the huge crowd — speak to DISPOL at Chitingwiza — cow shot by police marksman.'

Darwendale:
Addmore and I uplift 50 chickens from a farm and took them back to the Goromonzi office. For their own safekeeping we shut them in the kitchen for the night with food and water — couldn't leave them running around the garden. Quite a mess greeted us the next day — including eggs all over the place! Later we meet the owners at a garage in Norton and hand back their precious layers.

CHAPTER FOURTEEN

Alice

Fear can keep a man out of danger, but courage can support him in it.
— Proverb

Nyamsewe Farm, Guruve, April 2002
A dozen silky bantams, 10 laying hens, a black-and-ginger cat named '4 by 2' and a very nervous Siamese cat called 'Rix' were the animals that Meryl was asked to try and rescue from Nyamsewe Farm in Guruve at the end of April 2002. The farm owners, Peter and Vicky Bowen had been evicted a month before and all attempts to move back onto the property or even retrieve their animals or personal possessions had been stopped by the war veterans. Initially the Bowens' farm manager had been able to stay behind on the property and had been looking after the animals but when he was also thrown off by war veterans and settlers, Vicky contacted Meryl for help.

It was during that first phone call that Meryl was told about the bravery of Alice, the housemaid who worked for the family. Alice had been with the Bowen family for 15 years and had been beaten on several occasions by war veterans who seized Nyamsewe Farm. Vicky said that Alice suffered severe bruising, cuts and mental abuse during those assaults but she remained steadfast and loyal to her employers and dedicated to her work and responsibilities. On the last occasion Alice had been beaten by youths when she refused to hand over the keys to the Bowens' house.

It was a few days after Vicky's call before Meryl was able to go out to Nyamsewe Farm and it had been arranged that Alice would go with the rescue team. Alice had volunteered to accompany Meryl because she said the cats knew her and would recognise her voice and that the familiarity might make them less nervous and easier to find and catch. Vicky had given Meryl the keys to the farmhouse and with Inspectors Addmore and Tawanda in the back and Alice in the front, they set off to Nyamsewe Farm. Guruve, formerly called Sipolilo after a local Chief, is 150 kilometres north of Harare and famous for Tengenenge stone sculptures and large scale commercial tobacco production.

It wasn't tobacco or stone carvings that were on Meryl's mind as she drove. Instead, she thought about the astounding courage of the woman sitting next to her:

'Alice was incredibly brave to be going back to the very place where she had been beaten up a few days before – and all this for animals that didn't even belong to her – not many people would have done that.'

They stopped at the Guruve Police Station so that Meryl could get a police escort. The Acting OIC (Officer in Charge) confirmed that war veterans were in control of Nyamsewe Farm but said he didn't think Meryl would have any problems. Constable Norbert was assigned to accompany the SPCA team and he got in the front of the truck next to Anna and they set off for the farm.

Arriving at the farm road, Constable Norbert told Meryl to stop so that he could inform the Chairman of the Land Committee what the SPCA were doing on the farm. There were quite a number of huts near the road and while Norbert called for the Chairman, a crowd of people began gathering at the side of the road. After some time the police Constable, Land Committee Chairman and a few war veterans appeared. Without any hesitation or attempt to ask permission, they all climbed into the back of Meryl's truck. It was imperative that nothing was said or done that might upset the proceedings and so Meryl stayed quiet and drove on.

'The war vets had got into the car at the invitation of the Chairman – I was used to this sort of thing happening. Every rescue was different – you had to think on your feet – and if the rescues were to be successful you just had to go with the flow – do what it took to secure the release of the animals involved.'

Fully loaded, Meryl arrived at the Nyamsewe farm gate and was again instructed to stop. The Chairman of the Land Committee wanted to speak to the Base Commander and two other war veterans who were at the farm workshop. Alice took advantage of the absence of the war veterans to attract the attention of one of the Bowens' farm workers who was still on the property. She asked him if he could go to her house in the workers' village and fetch a jersey she had left behind when she and the Bowens had been evicted. Meryl, although exasperated by the incessant delays and huddled conversations, could do nothing but wait. The Base Commander indicated that he and the others wanted to speak to Meryl and so she parked the SPCA truck next to the workshop and got out. There were a number of youths standing around, some were tinkering with a tractor which belonged to the Bowens, and they all stared sullenly at Meryl as she approached. The Base Commander and another war veteran, both wearing green berets, told Meryl that she would have to wait while someone went to fetch a 'book' that they said she had to sign.

Addmore and Tawanda got out of the vehicle and chatted casually to some of the war veterans and Meryl leant against a tractor tyre and waited for what seemed like an eternity, wishing they would hurry up, wishing she could just get on with the rescue but staying still and silent, knowing that if she tried to hurry the process anything could go wrong. Her thoughts were also with Alice and she wondered if any of these youths had been involved in assaulting her:

'Alice did not get out of the car and just stared straight ahead although one or two of the settlers did go and greet her, clapping their hands in the traditional greeting.'

Meryl guessed that Alice was probably in her early 40s, a slim woman with a scarf covering her head. Alice wore a checked white, mauve and black skirt and a striped T-shirt. Meryl could clearly see the dark blotches on the woman's face, evidence of the recent abuse, the bruises from the earlier assault. Alice showed no sign of fear or aggression and displayed a stoic indifference to the youngsters who were milling around. While they all waited for the arrival of 'the book', Meryl asked Tawanda to start preparing the ground by informing the crowd that they shouldn't follow the SPCA to the house as this would frighten the cats and then they would have no chance of catching them.

After an hour 'the book' finally arrived but it wasn't shown or given to Meryl and police Constable Norbert told her that she could now drive up to the house. Meryl had no idea why she had been delayed for so long or what had really been going on all that time. She hadn't been able to see the Bowen's house from the workshop where she was parked and was just relieved that at last she could get on with finding and catching the animals. As Meryl started up the drive towards the house she saw that Tawanda, who was walking up behind the vehicle, was being followed by a great crowd of people. She called out to him saying that such a mob of people was exactly what they didn't want but Tawanda was obviously too frightened to try and stop them.

'Oh well! It seems they want to come with us,' he said, stating the obvious, much to Meryl's quiet annoyance.

Stopping the truck in the parking area near the house, Meryl told the crowd that only one person could accompany them, together with police Constable Norbert – if he wished. Meryl could hardly believe it when no one followed them at all, not even the police Constable, but a few minutes later one youth appeared and followed them around as they looked for the cats. Meryl didn't know much about the animals but had discovered that the cat called '4 by 2' had been named by Peter Bowen. He said the colour of the cat reminded him of the dirty colour of the four by two inch strip of cloth that emerged from the barrel after cleaning a rifle!

'The two Inspectors, Alice and myself walked around the entire outside of the house, calling the cats but there was no sight or sound. I then walked down to a cottage and checked all around that garden. Alice called me back to say that one of the cats was at an open window. It was '4 by 2,' the ginger/black cat. After some difficulty getting him through the burglar bars, Alice finally caught him. We continued to search for the other cat. A sprinkler was spraying water in the garden and I remember thinking: How pointless; the owners will never be coming back to enjoy or see their lovely garden again.'

After an exhaustive search Meryl asked Addmore to go and ask the war veterans for permission to go into the house. Even though Meryl had the house keys she knew that it was best to follow the protocol for the sake of the animals. The war veterans would only allow Alice to go into the house and she was inside for a long time, searching all the rooms and cupboards but eventually emerged saying that sadly Rix was nowhere to be found.

Meryl, Addmore and Tawanda walked across to the vegetable garden to try and catch the Silky bantams. They are strikingly attractive little birds with long, thin feathers which are curled and silky and give them a very distinctive, sophisticated appearance. As they approached the birds, just when capture appeared imminent, the Silkies suddenly ran and flapped out of reach and headed towards the stables. Once they were closed inside, the capture was a quick and relatively simple operation. The security guard had already told Meryl that there were no longer any laying hens to rescue as they had been stolen by the war veterans along with ten guinea fowl and a number of plain bantams. Over 40 birds were gone, presumed to have been eaten, and so with a dozen silky bantams and one cat, Meryl's work on Nyamsewe was done.

Before they left the farm the famous 'book' appeared and Meryl was told to sign it and state what she had taken and record all her personal details. Considering that she had been kept waiting for an hour while 'the book' was located earlier, Meryl assumed it would be filled with facts and figures, dates and details. She was wrong ! It was just a simple school exercise book which had nothing whatsoever written in it except the date. Meryl faithfully wrote her name and credentials, her ID number and description of the animals she had rescued. While she was writing she could hear some of the war veterans questioning Alice. They were trying to find out where she was living and where the Bowens were but Alice wasn't giving anything away and mumbled a vague address in Concession – a different town altogether and scores of miles away from where the Bowens were in fact staying. Meryl knew it was time to leave before the questions became more pressing and the demands more intimidating.

It was almost dark when Meryl and the team got back into Harare that evening and they went straight to the flat in the suburbs that was being rented by the Bowens. Meryl took photographs of what was a joyous reunion between the Bowens and their daughter and the much loved cat with the strange name of '4 by 2' – this was definitely a case of a cat changing a house into a home.

In the months ahead Meryl recommended that a Bravery Award be presented to Alice by the SPCA. At the time such an award was not in existence but during the land invasions and farm rescues Meryl had come across several instances where farm staff went beyond the call of duty to help the animals – often at considerable danger to themselves. Alice deserved to be recognised for her bravery – hers was the face that the world would never see and only Meryl and the Bowens knew what she had done. It was with great sadness that Meryl heard a few years later from Vicky Bowen that Alice never lived to receive her recognition. Vicky wrote:

'Alice very recently died at her home. She had failing health so we arranged for extensive tests that revealed it was AIDS. We accessed treatment with anti-retroviral drugs, antibiotics, vitamins and special supplements and at her insistence she returned home for a break. We feel due to the unaddressed stigma attached to AIDS she refused to take the drugs and got weaker and died as a result.'

Extracts from Meryl's Diary:

'He who wants to do good knocks at the gate;
he who loves finds the door open.'
– Rabindranath Tagore

April 2002
Bindura:
Cattle and horses need uplifting from Leopardsvlei farm as property taken over by Reward Marufu (President Mugabe's brother-in-law.) The owner had managed to walk his herd of cattle off, but left behind were a very large bull and a blind Jersey cow who would not have been able to walk the distance of some 15kms. We were

asked to collect the two animals in our horse box. Situation at the farm very tense, in spite of having a police escort. War vets and settlers prevented us from entering the yard where the livestock were being held. Whilst waiting for backup from Bindura Police Station, the crowd slaughtered the bull and many could be seen walking to and fro carrying lumps of fresh meat. Several hours later, after the intervention of a well-known war veteran by the name of Matangira, who had taken over the next door farm, we finally left with a very stressed Jersey cow.

Harare:
Received a parcel from Val Zangel today, have never met her but she has made the animals of Zimbabwe her cause. What a wonderful lady! She's single, a lawyer and lives in Johannesburg with her two dogs, Cavaliers called 'Lily' and 'Dash'. She was actually born in Zimbabwe, near Gwayi and her father was in the forestry field. In those days everyone used donkeys and that's where her passion for donkeys began.

When she heard about the SPCA's Zimbabwe Outreach programme, she asked me how she could help – what a fairy godmother! She has given countless items since then, from donkey harnesses to medicines, reflectors, foam rubber for padding the harnesses, gentian violet, vaseline, wound spray, de-wormers, bolt cutters, horse food – and all out of her own pocket too. Many thousands of animals in Zimbabwe owe their improved welfare and health to Val, she is a remarkable lady.

CHAPTER FIFTEEN

Marmalade

'Stolen bread tastes sweet
but soon your mouth
is full of gravel.'
– Eugene H Peterson

Danbury Park Farm, Mazowe, April 2002
Writing in *The Spectator* magazine, British editor Boris Johnson described how
he felt when he approached the gates to Danbury Park Farm in April 2002.

'Frankly, I am a bit nervous. Someone has said I'll get killed looking all white and
foolish out here in Mashonaland Central, and I am beginning to see why. We're only
a couple of hundred yards away from the thugs wielding pipes, swords and guns who
have been persecuting the local farmers. Three weeks ago they bludgeoned one of the
workers to death. Then they attacked Tommy Bayley, a farmer, and tried to throw
him on to a fire.'

Just two days after the visit of Boris Johnson, Meryl and two SPCA
Inspectors – Addmore and Tawanda – stood at the same gates. They had gone
first to the Marlborough Police station for a police escort because they were
going to need all the help they could get if they were to succeed in rescuing the
stranded pets.

Two families normally lived and worked on Danbury Park Farm in
Mazowe. Tom Bayley, aged 89, and his wife, Edith, aged 79, lived in one house.
They had come to Mazowe in 1936 and built the property up from virgin
bush. Tom, recovering from a hip operation, and Edith, suffering from Parkin-
son's disease, were not leaving Danbury Park Farm – this was where they were
growing old together. This had been their life's work and was now their retirement and pension. Their son Tommy, his wife, Trish, and their two-year-old
daughter lived nearby in a second house and together they worked the farm.
They employed 80 people who lived on the property with their families and in

normal times Danbury Park was a highly productive farm. The Bayleys were registered seed maize producers, planting 350 hectares of seed a year. They also grew soya beans and reared beef cattle, producing 90 tonnes of beef a year.

Both families were determined to make a stand and had refused to leave their homes. The war veterans, settlers and their supporters seemed equally determined not to go away and had set up camp in the Bayleys' garden, leaving the owners literally barricaded into their homes. It was a diabolical situation and had been going on for a month. By mid-April when Tommy and Trish Bayley were finally forced out of their home their hasty departure was witnessed by scores of war veterans, settlers and youths who had crowded into their garden. They had no choice but to leave their five cats shut in the house, not daring to risk trying to carry the animals through a mob of noisy and angry war veterans and settlers. There was no knowing how the mob might behave when they finally saw their prisoners of a month walking out.

There was a missing window pane in the dining room which at least meant that the cats could go in and out to hunt for rats, lizards and birds and Tommy and Trish left bowls of water and dry cat biscuits for the animals. It was the best they could do but the sooner the cats could be caught and removed from the house, the better it would be. The oldest cat, and the one Trish was most worried about because of her age, was a tortoiseshell called Mum. There were three ginger cats named Tigger, Apricot and Marmalade and a big blonde fluffy cat called Pinky. Trish thought that Pinky might have been kicked by the settlers at some time during the month-long siege because the cat had become very nervous lately and wouldn't be easy to rescue.

Tom and Edith had maintained their determination to stay in their house, even after Tommy and his family had been barricaded off the farm with only the pick-up truck they were in and the clothes on their backs. This had been their home for 70 years but it was hard to predict how much longer they would be able to hold out, or how much longer the war veterans and settlers would leave them alone. When Trish described the whole situation to Meryl, they agreed it would be wisest to try and rescue three of Tom and Edith's dogs from the barricaded house. They were Fox Terriers named Tiger, Dandy and Timmy and for almost the entire month of the barricading, the Bayleys had been forced to keep the dogs inside the house. It was a far from acceptable situation but the only safe option because whenever the dogs were seen outside, the war veterans and settlers bombarded them, throwing sticks and pelting the dogs with stones from catapults. The Bayleys knew that the extended confinement was not fair on the dogs and so when Meryl offered a rescue they sadly but gratefully accepted her help. The elderly couple decided to keep one little Fox Terrier bitch called Tiny with them for company.

Meryl arrived at Danbury Park Farm accompanied by Addmore, Tawanda and two policemen, a Sergeant in plain clothes and a Constable in uniform. The atmosphere was menacing from the start as Meryl described in her diary:

'On arrival at the farm we found a road block at the main entrance manned by six or seven war vets and settlers. There were two 44-gallon drums, several tree trunks and other paraphernalia across our path. The two police officers got out of my truck, explained our presence and after a few minutes the drums were rolled aside for us to proceed. I noticed the settlers had a large log fire burning at the road block and as we drove through, settlers and the police exchanged the traditional clenched fist salute of Zanu PF. Several of the individuals wore 3rd Chimurenga T-shirts and all carried a motley assortment of weapons ranging from iron bars to wooden poles and even catapults.'

Police impartiality was already in question but Meryl kept her face blank and her mouth closed. A youth wearing camouflage uniform guarded the next gate they came to. There was a chain across the road but the police Sergeant ordered it removed which the youth did – an angry, surly look on his face.

Meryl stopped in front of the double-storey house and took in the sight ahead of her. This was the house of Tommy and Trish Bayley and Meryl was glad they were not here to see it. There was a large fire burning on the lawn in the middle of the garden and several men – settlers and war veterans – were standing around it roasting maize cobs. This wasn't ordinary maize they were cooking, it was not grown for consumption but was seed. Seed maize which had been stolen from the fields and which was intended for planting across the country in just six months' time. These men were eating the seeds which would have ensured food security for the country for the following year. It was utterly absurd. Later Meryl wrote a few more details of what remained of the once beautiful farm garden:

'There were pots, pans, left over sadza [maize porridge] discarded on the ground, coats hanging up in the trees, all evidence that the "invaders" had well and truly moved in.'

Meryl wanted to start with the cats and she waited in the truck as her police escort spoke to the Base Commander and another man who stood nearby. The Base Commander, Jereven, was of medium height and sported a thin moustache. He was wearing a black beret and heavy overcoat. Makasa, the other war veteran who stood nearby and was second in charge, was heavily built with a plump, round face. Makasa was wearing a brown leather jacket and both he and Jereven spoke good English. Both war veterans were immediately dismissive of a rescue being needed and said there were no cats in the house but they agreed that Meryl and the SPCA Inspectors could go and have a look for themselves. Meryl didn't have keys to get into the house which, although making an animal rescue difficult, was a good thing. She would never have been able to stop all these people from storming the house if they had seen her going indoors. Meryl, Addmore and Tawanda walked all the way around the outside.

On the verandah there was a huge pile of wire snares that the Bayley's had been removing and collecting since the farm had first been invaded. The sight was chilling and the thought of all the animals that could have been poached was horrific. Through the windows it looked as if the contents of the house were intact. There were no obvious signs of looting such as Meryl had seen on other farms which had been hurriedly vacated. She did see a tin of peaches lying on the dining room floor which she thought was rather peculiar. Tommy later explained that whenever they left the house they put a tin on the inside of the door handle so they would be able to tell if the settlers had been trying the door handles – obviously this time they had!

Meryl soon found the missing window pane that Trish had told her about in the dining room. One after the other she called out the names of the cats. It was a strange roll-call, sounding more like a colour-coded breakfast itinerary but Meryl continued:

'Mum, Apricot, Tigger, Marmalade, Pinky!' she called again and again but not a single cat appeared. Meryl made meowing noises in a variety of ways but none worked. If the cats were there, they were not going to be persuaded out – at least not by those sort of noises! Bribery was definitely needed:

'We tried waving some smelly fish around through the narrow opening in the hope that they would smell it – but no response. Finally Addmore tried rattling the box of cat biscuits. It did the trick and 'Mum', the old tortoiseshell, came eagerly towards the window.'

Obviously the mere sound of the little cat snacks jiggling in the box was too tempting! Mum was clearly hungry and she devoured the biscuits that had been sprinkled through the window onto the floor. Mum looked longingly at the trail of biscuits which had been laid out onto the window sill. The cat was obviously suspicious and it took some time before her stomach got the better of her and she finally followed the trail of biscuits to the outside where she was caught and put into the cat cage.

There was no sign at all of the other cats and despite repeated calls, none appeared. Meryl left a pile of cat biscuits and several whole fish just inside the window and reluctantly left for the time being. She went and informed the Base Commander, Jereven, that she was going down to the house where Mr and Mrs Bayley Sr lived so that she could take away three of their dogs. For some reason Jereven got angry all of a sudden and lost his temper.

'You leave your truck where it is,' he said. 'I am in charge here. I am in control and no vehicles may go inside the security fence.'

Meryl took a breath and held her temper. She told Jereven that she understood that he was in charge but asked him to re-consider. She said it would be a long way to walk carrying the dogs and if they escaped she would have no hope of catching the Fox Terriers. Suddenly Makasa jumped up and joined in the abuse. His mouth full of stolen seed maize, Makasa blurted out angrily:

'That truck of yours does not move from here!'

Meryl looked to her police escort for support or intervention but both the Constable and the Sergeant had joined the war veterans and were also eating the seed maize. The police seemed completely uninterested in the argument that was raging and so Meryl, frustrated but persistent, turned again to Jereven and appealed once more. Finally the war veteran relented to a degree and said she could drive as far as a stone wall which surrounded Tom and Edith's garden but not into their gateway. Knowing that she would not be able to better this compromise, Meryl nodded her understanding and took a relieved and thankful breath. It was then she noticed that Jereven and some of the other war veterans were carrying what looked like toy AK rifles made of wood. Later she discovered the truth of these 'toys' and wrote in her diary:

'When I said to Tommy jokingly that the war vets looked so ridiculous with the wooden guns under their arms, he replied coldly: "There is a knife concealed inside every one." The hairs on the back of my neck stood up when he said that.'

Meryl and the two SPCA Inspectors drove down to the stone wall followed on foot by the two policemen and Jereven and Makasa. All of the curtains in the house were closed in order to stop the squatters and invaders from looking in the windows. Meryl knocked on the glass French door and as she did Jereven and Makasa hid behind a large palm tree in the garden. Edith opened the curtain and began unbolting the door. She looked strained and exhausted.

'Oh, you must be from the SPCA,' she said. 'Do you want to come in?'

'No, thank you,' Meryl answered hurriedly. 'We are being watched Mrs Bayley,' she explained, 'I think it will be safer if I don't come in.' Meryl knew the war veterans would be watching every move to make sure that nothing except dogs were passed out of the Bayley's house. Edith was extremely distressed and emotional as she handed her dogs one by one out to Meryl.

'We've been here for 32 days you know!' she said, her voice choked with tears.

'I know, my dear,' Meryl responded. 'We all send our love, everyone sends their love to you. The whole country is rooting for you.'

Meryl was sickened by her own words, they sounded so shallow and inadequate in such a dreadful situation but she didn't know what else to say. She took the dogs as gently as she could as they were handed out to her, knowing how heart-breaking this must have felt for the elderly lady.

'What about our tortoises?' Edith asked when all the dogs were safely in Meryl's care. 'Do you want to take our tortoises?'

Meryl hadn't been told about tortoises and thought that she would probably be pushing her luck to try. She knew from previous experience that she had to announce in advance to the Base Commander exactly which animals she had come for and then take only those animals. She told Edith the tortoises would be alright for the time being and with a heavy heart she said goodbye to the old lady. When she got back to the truck and had put the dogs safely away, Jereven and Makasa re-appeared and asked Meryl for her ID and cell phone numbers.

They said they would phone the SPCA if they saw the missing cats. Meryl gave them the details but didn't expect to hear from them. Driving out of Danbury Park Farm with her precious cargo of three dogs and a cat, Meryl passed a Zanu PF youth walking down the drive carrying an armful of stolen seed maize. The police Sergeant, asked for some and two cobs were handed over. Meryl made no comment about policemen witnessing and condoning theft or receiving stolen property. She also said nothing about the irony of strangers wandering around eating the Bayley's crop while the owners themselves were under siege in their own home and eating emergency food parcels provided by the International Red Cross. It all made so little sense and there was no understanding it.

Reunited with their cat Mum back at the SPCA kennels in Harare, Trish and Tommy Bayley were delighted that one of their pets had been found and desperate for whatever news Meryl could give them – about their parents, the other cats, their house. When Meryl began describing what she had seen in the garden – the fire on the lawn, coats hanging in trees and people lolling around eating seed maize, Tommy's eyes filled with tears and he turned away and looked out of the window. A little later when there was nothing more to be told, the Bayley's loaded up their parents' three dogs. Mum, the cat, sat regally in the front seat of the car. Tommy shook Addmore's hand particularly warmly, thanking him for his persistence and for climbing trees to look into upstairs windows for the other cats. When Tommy came to try and thank Meryl for everything she was doing, the emotion was too raw. Unable to speak Tommy just shook Meryl's hand before turning away. Meryl stared out of the window and watched them go. Their trauma and distress was palpable and Meryl recorded her own feelings in her diary:

'As they drove out of the gate of Harare SPCA, I felt outraged and incensed that these good folks' lives have been turned upside down and it appears there is nothing anyone can do to stop it.'

Nine days later Meryl returned to Danbury Park to try and finish the rescue that she had started. A lot of things had happened in those nine days as Meryl wrote in her diary:

'19 April 2002: I spoke to Trish and learnt that they had been back to the farm two days ago with the police and Land Committee – were subjected to major intimidation by the war vets but were able to recover another cat, "Pinky." She also told me that her father-in-law had fallen and broken his femur and had had to be moved out by ambulance. His wife had also left together with "Tiny", the Fox Terrier bitch – the latter had a wound on her back after being hit by a stone from a catapult.

23 April 2002: Tommy and Trish came in with a map of where to find the tortoises now that his parents had left the farm. They told us that the police had refused to provide an escort for the ambulance.'

The departure of Tom and Edith Bayley from Danbury Park brought an end to 70 years of farming and to a gruelling, barbaric five-week siege. The two families had endured so much but had maintained their dignity and been brave, principled and poised to the very end.

Meryl arrived at the gate to Danbury Park accompanied by two police officers and two SPCA Inspectors. The irony of having a police escort for tortoises when one had been denied for people and an ambulance, was striking. This was just one of the many contradictions that littered the land invasions. Meryl described another in her diary:

'On arrival at the farm gate the road block was still there, but more youths than war vets. At first one of the members told the police that they had instructions that no *"whites" were allowed through the road block. The police informed him that I was "different" and the drums and poles were then removed and we were allowed to proceed.'*

Meryl and her team were greeted warmly by the war veterans – as if they were old friends! It was an absurd but welcome reaction as Meryl was immediately given permission to go and look for the remaining cats and to collect the tortoises. Again they called out the cats' names and shook the biscuit box vigorously, but Tigger, Apricot and Marmalade did not appear. All the food Meryl had left on the last visit had gone and muddy paw prints were visible on the parquet floor but the cats were nowhere to be found. Meryl left food and water and went off to try and find the tortoises. Her police escorts were entrenched with the war veterans and were eating roasted seed maize but some youngsters who were hanging around went to help. Using the map they soon found nine of the twelve tortoises including one which was 75-years-old and had been in the Bayley family for over 50 years. The big old creature hissed and struggled all the way to the truck – resisting vacating Danbury Park Farm as vigorously as his owners had so recently done. With her job done, Meryl was about to leave when Jereven, the Base Commander appeared. He was wearing the now-familiar black beret and carrying the wooden gun and he treated Meryl like an old friend. She had obviously earned both the trust and respect of these rough men and Meryl felt slightly bemused by the attitude.

'I've still got your cell phone number,' Jereven said, 'I'll phone you if we see the other tortoises or the cats.'

Meryl nodded at the man, doubting she'd ever hear from him. She was ready to leave but he had more to say:

'You know there is no shelter for us here at the house,' Jereven announced.

Meryl said nothing. One of the others had already asked her when the Bayleys were coming to remove their belongings so that they could move into the house.

'It's very cold here at night, very cold,' Jereven reiterated. 'This is a human rights issue you know. We need blankets because it is very, very cold.'

Still Meryl said nothing, either about blankets or the issue of human rights. Knowing what had been done to the Bayleys made the irony of human rights complaints utterly ridiculous.

Not long after she had rescued the tortoises Meryl again wrote about Danbury Park farm in her diary on 1 May 2002:

'Tom Bayley senior died a week after leaving hospital where he had undergone a successful operation on his broken thighbone. The family issued this statement: "He was very tormented about the loss of his home. He had not been sleeping well as he had nightmares about his experiences while under siege."'

When Meryl heard from the Bayleys some time later, there were just two cats, Tigger and Marmalade, left to be rescued from the farm and she and two SPCA Inspectors, Addmore and Augustine, arranged one final visit. This was going to be last chance to find the two cats. The deadline for removing all equipment and property from the farm had arrived and the Bayleys would not be allowed back onto Danbury Park Farm after this day.

Arriving at 3pm Meryl found the farm to be a hive of activity. Neighbouring farmers and friends had come from all around to help the Bayleys get everything off the farm and there were people and trucks all over the place. While all the activity and assistance was fantastic for the Bayleys, Meryl knew that it would scare the cats and make her task even more difficult. It was so sad to see the dismantling of what had obviously once been such a busy and thriving farm and closing it down was an enormous operation.

On the lawn all the men and women who had worked on the farm, sat dejectedly waiting to receive their final pay packages. Like the Bayleys, these farm workers had also lost their jobs and homes now that Danbury Park farm had been taken over and they had nowhere else to go and no other way to earn a living – they too had to leave the farm today. Labour and Union representatives from GAPWUZ (General Agricultural and Plantation Workers Union of Zimbabwe) were monitoring and checking the last payments. Security guards were there too because of the large amount of money involved and police stood by watching it all. Jereven was there too, with his wooden gun, the one with the knife hidden inside, and he sat under a tree, watching and waiting, like a vulture preparing to move onto a carcass.

Meryl went into the house with SPCA Inspector Augustine. They checked every cupboard and room of the double-storey house, looking for and calling the cats all the time. In the bathroom on the first floor Meryl hesitated; she thought she had heard a faint meowing coming from under the bath. The bath was completely bricked in except for a small hole about a foot square, on the floor at one end.

'Tigger, Marmalade,' Meryl called into the hole but there was no response.

First Meryl and then Augustine lay down on the bathroom floor and put an arm into the hole under the bath but they felt nothing. If there was a cat under there it was obviously too frightened to move or make a sound. In desperation Meryl went downstairs and asked Tommy Bayley to come and try and call the cat. Perhaps the cat would recognise his voice and trust him enough to come out.

Back in the bathroom Tommy called the cats' names again and again but nothing happened. He lay on the floor and put his arm into the hole under the bath and called again. Suddenly he exclaimed in great excitement:

'It's licking my hand! There is a cat here and it's licking my fingers.'

Meryl described the effect of those few licks in her diary:

'As hard as Tommy tried, the cat would not move any closer to him. Tommy put his head on his arm and broke down. I think this was just the last straw, he knew that in about an hour he and Trish would be leaving the farm forever and now one of his beloved cats was destined to remain alone in the house, left to the mercy of the war vets. Tommy just could not take any more. I put my hand on his shoulder and gave it a squeeze – words at this moment seemed so inadequate.'

Meryl could see muddy paw prints around the toilet and on the window-sill. The cat had been surviving by drinking water from the toilet and saving the animal became paramount. Meryl and Augustine agreed that the only way to get to the cat was going to be to break down the wall surrounding the bath tub. Such drastic measures would need permission – absurdly not from the Bayleys who owned the house – but from the war veterans who were taking it over.

Jereven arrived in the bathroom, wooden gun in hand. He was with another man who Meryl hadn't seen on the farm before. For a moment Meryl couldn't help herself from staring at the newcomer as he had the most amazing hairstyle she had ever seen. The man's head was shaven bald but some clumps of hair had been left and they stood up in huge and strange tufts – almost like a Mohican! Meryl thought. When Meryl explained to them that there was a cat under the bath and that she wanted to break down the brickwork to rescue it, neither of the war veterans would give their permission for her to go ahead.

Meryl tried to get them to agree but they would not change their minds and she was getting desperate. It was beginning to get dark, the electricity had been cut off and time was running out. Meryl resorted to bartering. There was a good-looking Ridgeback cross that had been at the Bayleys' house since the beginning of the SPCA visits. It's name was 'Power' and it belonged to Jereven who said he'd bought it from a farmer who was leaving the country.

'Is Power vaccinated against rabies? It is a legal requirement, you know?' Meryl said.

When Jereven admitted that the dog wasn't inoculated Meryl thought this might be the inlet that she needed.

'I'll come back tomorrow and have him vaccinated for you if you'll let us destroy the side of the bath.

That wasn't enough and the war veterans weren't interested.

'It probably could do with de-worming as well,' Meryl said, but again there was no interest.

'What about blankets?' she asked, remembering how they had complained of cold last time she was here. 'If I bring you three blankets will you let me break down this wall and get the cat?' Meryl asked.

'Permission granted!' Jereven said immediately.

By then Meryl had also got increasingly anxious about Addmore who had disappeared. Later she found out where he had been:

'Unbeknown to me, whilst looking for the cats behind the sheds, Addmore had unexpectedly found tractors hidden in the bush, obviously stolen by the war vets. Later one of the farmers asked me if Addmore could write a statement for the police stating that he had seen the stolen tractors. I declined, reminding the farmer that our only role was to rescue animals.'

In the horror and trauma and high emotion of the farm invasions, few people really understood Meryl's absolute insistence that she would only assist the animals and not the farmers. But it was exactly this cast iron principle that enabled Meryl, Augustine and Addmore to begin destroying a bathroom to rescue one little cat. Armed with two large chunks of metal and with the bathroom door firmly closed, Meryl, Addmore and Augustine began to smash down the wall surrounding the bath tub. The noise in the small and crowded bathroom was tremendous, almost deafening. The combination of vibrations and noise must have been almost unbearable for the cat as it hid in the enclosed space under the bath.

Soon the room was full of choking dust and a mound of tiles, bricks and cement piled up on the floor. Meryl, Addmore and Augustine were covered in red dust from head to foot and not prepared when a cat suddenly shot out from under the bath. An orange blur of fluff streaked past them, raced around the room twice and then disappeared back under the bath. Success was now in sight and the work became suddenly easier! The next time the cat appeared, Addmore was ready. Wearing a pair of thick leather gloves, Addmore caught the cat expertly and immediately closed it into a waiting cage. Trish Bayley arrived, obviously alerted by the sudden silence coming from the bathroom and was overjoyed to see her cat. It was Marmalade and although thin and very traumatised, the cat set up an incessant meowing now that it was safely reunited with its owner. Seeing Marmalade reunited with the Bayleys made all the dust, noise and hard work worth it for Meryl. In typical Zimbabwean style there was no gushing emotion for Meryl as she left, but there was humour. It was humour that was undoubtedly tinged with respect, acknowledgement and appreciation. Meryl noted the brief exchange in her diary:

'As we reached the farm gate, several farmers were waiting there to make sure Tom and Trish got away safely. One of the farmers asked me how we had got on. I replied that the bathroom looked a bit of a mess – whereupon a tall bearded farmer said: "Is the SPCA not into interior decorating then?" to which I replied: "No, it's not what we do best!"'

Marmalade was sadly the last cat that was rescued from Danbury Park. Meryl returned with the blankets she had promised to Jereven. She remembered that she had three old blankets in her office that had recently been donated by a member of the public, and thought it was such a small price to pay for Marmalade's life. The vet from the Harare SPCA was with her and he vaccinated Power, the dog belonging to Jereven, while Meryl had one final look for Tigger, the last missing cat, but to no avail.

Barely three months after leaving Danbury Park farm, Meryl recorded the tragic news in her diary that the Bayley's had been involved in a car accident as they were driving to South Africa to have a much deserved break and Trish had passed away in the crash. The brave stance and exemplary courage shown by the two Bayley families is one that will stay in Zimbabweans' hearts forever, together with the story of how Marmalade was rescued from under the bath in exchange for three blankets.

Two years later, Meryl wrote about the Bayley family one last time:

'When I phoned Tommy to say goodbye he told me Marmalade was alive and well and living with him and his daughter in Harare. His daughter came on the phone and told me Marmalade was sitting next to her and was "fine".'

Extracts from Meryl's Diary:

'I'm a lean dog, a keen dog, a wild dog and lone,
I'm a rough dog, a tough dog, hunting on my own!
I'm a bad dog, a mad dog, teasing silly sheep;
I love to sit and bay the moon and keep fat souls from sleep.'
— Irene Mcleod

May 2002
Guruve:
Two farms needing assistance.

Johannesburg, South Africa:
Flew to Joburg to judge a dog show. Stayed with my ex-husband Dave Harrison and his wife. I had signed the contract to judge this particular show some 18 months before, not knowing at the time that I would be so heavily involved by then in farm rescues. The club involved, paid all my expenses, I was only away for the weekend — so it became a welcome break! Whilst there was interviewed by Patricia Glyn (SAfm Radio) who had been doing weekly interviews with me — broke down when I began to talk about the events at Danbury Park.

Harare:
Interviewing a prospective new vet nurse for Harare SPCA and took her on — she proved to be excellent. Spent the rest of the week with other Harare Inspectors checking on security dogs.

CHAPTER SIXTEEN

'Indulge me just once'

'Life is as dear to a mute creature as it is to man.
Just as one wants happiness and fears pain,
just as one wants to live and not die,
so do other creatures.'
– His Holiness the Dalai Lama

Umzururu Farm, Nyabira, June 2002

It was early winter when Meryl received a call for help from a vet concerning cattle on two farms in Nyabira that were in a very bad way. The vet said that the farms were teeming with war veterans and settlers and in the scramble for occupation of the property the cattle were being denied grazing, the bulls were fighting and wounded animals were going untreated.

The police station nearest to the farm was at Nyabira and Meryl started there. She was told that there were a large number of settlers on Umzururu Farm. Situated on the road to Chinhoyi and Kariba and less than 40 kilometres from Harare, Nyabira was a very desirable place to live. Close to the capital city and with a moderate climate, Nyabira was renowned for pedigree cattle breeding. While she waited for a police escort to accompany her to the troubled farms, she listened to the rumours that Umzururu Farm had in fact been delisted. In the first three years of the land seizures, scores of farms that had been listed for government acquisition were subsequently delisted as the owners successfully contested the seizures in court. The court rulings and delistings usually only offered a temporary reprieve however and the properties would be listed again and again. Some farms were listed and delisted as many as five times and each time both commercial farmers and settlers refused to move and the animals on these farms were stuck in the middle of the bureaucratic mayhem.

Arriving at the homestead for the first time Meryl was accompanied by SPCA Inspectors Addmore and Augustine and one police Constable. Umzururu Farm and the neighbouring Royden Farm were owned by Alastair and Fiona Smith but they had finally been evicted from the property some months before.

134

Alastair explained the last traumatic day in their home in December 2001 and how the police had refused to press charges against the perpetrators:

'In a culmination of events which lead to October 2001 a gang of 35-40 people lead by the Doornfontein group arrived late morning using Commuter buses [minibuses] and proceeded to break all the windows in our house. They then assaulted my secretary Margie thinking she was Fiona. In the meantime our domestic assistant, Emily, took Christie, our 18-year-old daughter, who was home studying for her A-level exams and locked her in a room upstairs. Emily had her arm broken by the invaders but she did not let on that Christie was in the house. The mob then proceeded to the workshop which they also trashed. Both Fiona and I were away in Harare for the day when I was informed via mobile phone of the events. I proceeded out to the farm to find the mayhem left behind but the intruders had vanished. The day that the house was trashed coincided with a Commonwealth delegation meeting at the Sheraton Hotel in Harare and I am sure that this whole event was a staged act. The police refused to open a docket on this incident and many others committed by this group, all in the name of land distribution.'

Meryl didn't know too many of these details when she went to the farm and perhaps it was just as well because the situation she found was very distressing. An old piece of earth-moving equipment had been dragged across the road to act as a barricade but Meryl negotiated a way around it and made her way to the cattle pens to meet the farm clerk John and cattle manager Marigo who were still looking after Alastair Smith's cattle on the farm. Both John and Marigo were second generation employees of the Smith family; they had been born on the farm, grown up there, been educated at the farm school and then worked their way up the ranks. Meryl did not need to be told the problem, she saw it immediately:

'The weaners were confined in a kraal with water but no grass. They were a mixture of Herefords and Red Angus. The hay looked old and the food in the troughs was a mixture of silage and chicken manure. One Red Angus was seen lying on its side; according to John it had been like that for two weeks – it was barely alive.'

Meryl took a photograph of the prostrate weaner and that action immediately attracted the attention of a man wearing a blue shirt who was standing nearby. He was the Base Commander and called himself 'Comrade Chungu'. Chungu was tall and dark-skinned. His eyes were bloodshot and his clothes tatty but he spoke good English. Chungu became hostile as soon as he saw Meryl's camera. She introduced herself and explained that the purpose of her visit was only to see to the welfare of the animals but Chungu wasn't interested.

'I am in control of this farm now,' Chungu said, 'and I want these cattle all removed.'

Meryl said that while she understood what Chungu wanted, those decisions were out of her control and in the meantime the animals must be allowed out to graze. At that point the police Constable who had escorted Meryl said that if the cattle were let out to graze it would cause a major problem for the police as there was a serious issue with stock theft in the area. The Constable said that the ex-farm workers were working with butchers in Harare to steal and slaughter the cattle. Realizing that she was making no headway Meryl told the Base Commander that she was going to remove the very sick Red Angus calf and one other calf, a Hereford that couldn't stand up but did seem able to eat.

As the two sick calves were being loaded for removal Meryl discussed arrangements for a return visit the following day. The farm clerk, John, asked Meryl to come with a vet, to bring rabies injections for the dogs and asked if they could go to neighbouring Royden farm and treat a number of cattle which were also in a very bad way. Apparently it had been over six months since the Government vet had last been in the area. The six month absence had come at the worst possible time; a period which included the rainy season when internal and external parasites built up to enormous levels and resulted in disease, suffering and death.

Government Animal Health Inspectors used to visit all the farms around the entire country once a month and had done so for over 40 years. They would check the general condition of livestock, inspect the animals for ticks and other parasites and check on the facilities and regularity of dipping. As the land invasions spread and the tensions rose, Government Animal Health Inspectors found themselves being targeted by war veterans and settlers. They became subject to verbal abuse, intimidation and even threats. They were called 'sell-outs' and warned to stay away from commercial farms. In many areas visits by Government Animal Health Inspectors had come to a complete standstill by the middle of 2002. With government vets chased away, private vets threatened or closed down due to lack of business, the burden of animal health on invaded farms fell more and more into the hands of the SPCA.

Unbeknown to Meryl, while she was making arrangements with John, Base Commander Chungu was issuing threats to the SPCA Inspectors:

'Don't come here if you don't know what is going on,' he had said. 'Otherwise when people come to look for you they will find you dead!'

The following day Meryl and Addmore did return to the farm and were surprised to see that the roadblock had gone, that the weaners had been let out to graze and that there was no sign of Chungu. Apparently, shortly after Meryl had left the previous day, a senior police Commissioner had arrived on the farm and told Chungu that he must not make any trouble and that the farm workers must not be prevented from doing their work. Unhindered by Chungu, the SPCA vet vaccinated six dogs for rabies and then they drove to neighbouring Royden Farm to see to the sick and wounded cattle there. What they saw on the drive left Meryl in no doubt that the troubles on Royden and Umzururu Farms were far from over.

'On the way there I could see a large bush fire raging through the paddocks. John explained that in the morning the farm labour had cut grass. This John had arranged would be baled the next day for the weaners that we had been so concerned about, but the settlers had set fire to all the hay. The farm labourers were too scared to put the fire out.'

The situation on Royden Farm for the remaining farm staff was ludicrous. War veterans had moved into the farmhouse and told the tobacco manager who lived there that they would all 'share the house'. The tobacco manager had no say in the matter: he had to either do as he was told or get out. The war veterans took over seven rooms and left the tobacco manager with just two rooms in his own house. For the animals on the farm the situation was even worse as Meryl recorded in her notes:

'The worst cattle were rounded up and put through the crush. Many of the cows – a mixture of Red Angus, Sussex, Senepols and Limousin had bad eye infections. One had an obvious respiratory problem. There was a cow with a huge wound on her udder. The worst was a Sussex cow, which according to John, the bulls had been fighting over. Her horn had been broken off, the hole was full of bloody tissue and maggots. All the flesh had been ripped off her tail too and she must have been in tremendous pain.'

After the cows had been treated Meryl promised to return with the vet the following week. When she did, Chungu was back but had changed dramatically. He was full of smiles and shook hands all round and Meryl wrote that 'Chungu had obviously had a crash course at charm school!' The reason soon became clear. Chungu said that he wanted Meryl and the vet to treat all the cattle as they were now *his*. Meryl was not going to be drawn into anything with Chungu and told him that they would only deal with emergencies. In the absence of the farmers, Meryl and her team always saw to all the animals when they visited and these two farms were no different. The SPCA vet treated all the livestock that were sick or injured and left extra medication with John to ensure continuity. John also had a humane killer and could destroy any animals that were too far gone for treatment. Fortunately this farm was not in a Red Zone area as Meryl recorded in her notes:

'In Southern Africa, when there is an outbreak of foot and mouth, the infected cattle are vaccinated and then kept contained in their existing area, known as Red Zones – unlike in the UK where all infected cattle and those in the surrounding area are culled. The plight of farmers whose properties are in Red Zone areas because of foot and mouth outbreaks is just heartbreaking because of these land invasions. Once the farmers are evicted it means that their entire herds have to go for direct slaughter, they aren't able to sell them at cattle sales. Many times we watched as entire herds, including pregnant cows, new born calves and pedigree stud bulls were loaded into trucks to be sent straight to abattoirs. At the height of the invasions the abattoirs were booked up months in advance causing another nightmare for beleaguered farmers who were being harassed on a daily basis to get their cattle off the farms but the abattoirs were taking no more bookings.'

Later, as they drove past Alastair's farmhouse on Umzururu, Meryl noticed the dramatic gap in the landscape – all the fir trees that lined the drive had gone – chopped down and sold. Years and years of growth, shade, habitat and wind-breaks gone for a few quick dollars.

This was Meryl's third visit to the pair of farms and the condition of the cattle had deteriorated in the ten days spanning her visits. The weaners had access to dry, dusty hay only, but no access to grazing. The dairy calves were looking very thin and in a poor state, hunched up and many with eye infections. They noticed a Hereford weaner who had pus pouring out of its ear and when Meryl saw the state of the sheep – her temper rose to boiling point.

'I noticed in one of the sheep pens that there was a ewe with a prolapsed anus. She could not put her left front foot on the ground. As there was no sign of the manager, John, we drove over to a neighbouring farm to look for him – settlers showed us where he was. Addmore found him making bricks – for himself.'

Without supervision or motivation or anything to look forward to, John had lost pride in his work. The settlers were out of control on the farm, the grazing was being burnt continually and John's perspective was clearly changing to one of self-survival.

Meryl, Addmore and the vet then followed John to Royden Farm to check on the sick and injured cattle they had treated the previous week. It was a relief to see that these animals were greatly improved but Meryl noticed immediately that follow-up treatment with a bright blue insect repellent, antiseptic spray had obviously not been made. Meryl was annoyed, particularly as she had left adequate supplies of the spray with John.

Before they left Royden and Umzururu Farms there was one last job to do. When they had been rounding up the cattle, Addmore had found a weaner lying in the field and he thought it would have to be destroyed. The weaner had come from a neighbouring farm and Meryl was incensed when she was told it had been attacked by a pack of dogs seven weeks before. She could not believe that John had not told her about the animal and what she saw was deeply shocking.

'We collected the weaner that had been attacked by dogs from the field. It was a heartbreaking sight. He had a large gaping hole in the nose, teeming with maggots and he was also very thin. We loaded him into the back of my truck and informed John that we would destroy him at the SPCA.'

On the drive back to Harare the calf seemed to improve quite a bit and was even eating hay hungrily. Meryl and the vet decided that they would try and save the calf. He was given a great cocktail of antibiotics and anti-inflammatory injections and then put in a paddock with a horse at the SPCA. In the paddock there was a little wooden shack and here Meryl left the calf quietly munching his hay, warm, safe and protected from the wind and weather. She began to have hope.

'13 June 2002. At 7am I rushed down to see how the calf was doing. To my horror I found him lying stretched out on the ground barely breathing and very cold. I immediately heaped piles of hay over him until the kennel-hands arrived and could help me lift him into the warmth of our ICU. I sat stroking his head, willing him to stay alive. He seemed to know I was there and every now and again, his beautiful brown eyes would blink. I prayed to God to indulge me just this once and allow this little chap to live and that I be allowed just one favour to compensate for all the horror that I had seen in recent months – but it was not to be. In spite of being cuddled up in blankets in ICU with a drip going, about an hour later his life slipped away. I was devastated.'

Even though Meryl had been too late to save this one calf, at least she had given it the last few hours of its life with warmth, food, medication and love – more than it could have got lying abandoned and suffering out there in the field on those warring farms.

Extracts from Meryl's Diary:

> *Sticks and stones may break my bones but words will never hurt me.*
> — Proverb

June 2002
Harare:
Received an award from the Board of Harare SPCA — a lovely surprise and much appreciated!

Truck and brand new horse box arrive from South Africa. A fantastic gift from the Zimbabwe Pet Rescue Project ladies.

Harare:
Returned to my office in The Harare SPCA late one evening straight from a farm rescue and the security guard handed me an envelope. He said that two men had come to the gates of the kennels and had said the guard must make sure that I received the envelope. A single piece of lined paper torn from a school exercise book was inside a brown envelope. The letter, spelling mistakes and all, read:

'Mrs Harrison,
Be warned that the days of cerving the interest of white at the expence of blacks are over. We know that you are 100% a rascist who does not deserve to leave in a liberated Zimbabwe. You are only interested in the plight of dogs and cats left by the white farmers. You love dogs and cats, at same time you heart blacks.
Your days in Zimbabwe are numbered. Take this seriously your given 24 hours to leave Harare where you are operating from.
Thank you for your racial attitude.
Vying for your head you are under spot-light.'

The letter was not signed.

CHAPTER SEVENTEEN

Ignorance is bliss

'All things bright and beautiful,
All creatures great and small
All things wise and wonderful,
The Lord God made them all.'
– Cecil Frances Alexander, 1848

Kalahari Farm, Mvurwi, July 2002

Meryl put everything on hold when she heard that dogs, cats, sheep and horses had been left on an invaded farm in Mvurwi. A neighbour had phoned to say that two dogs, four cats, three horses and 30 sheep were stranded. The neighbour wasn't sure of the numbers of animals so Meryl would need to check carefully when she was at the farm. The farmer, Stefan Le Roux, had left the farm, the country and the continent and the animals were the helpless and innocent victims.

Accompanied by Inspectors Addmore and Augustine, Meryl set out for Mvurwi – 100 kilometres north of Harare. Once known as Umvukwes and before that, Dawsons, the name Mvurwi was derived from the Shona word *'mvurivi'* meaning 'a heap of pieces', which referred to the great variety in the surrounding hilly countryside.

It was a very beautiful area and Meryl headed straight for the police station. She didn't know much about what went on at Kalahari Farm and at first the Officer in Charge was hostile when she explained why she wanted to go there and what she wanted to do. The OIC wanted to know who was going to be responsible for paying the farm workers since Le Roux had left and when Meryl said that was no concern of the SPCA's, the Inspector snapped back: 'Of course it is. You must know what is going on, on the ground.'

Meryl explained as patiently as she could that her information was from a neighbour of the absentee farmer and that the SPCA was completely non-political and that her only role was to collect the animals and take them to a place of safety. Meryl soon discovered that the Inspector knew a fair amount about the missing farmer already. He said that the farm workers wanted to hold on to Le Roux's possessions because they believed they were not going to get paid. The Inspector continued by saying that he believed Le Roux was still in the country as he had apparently said he was going to Harare to take his children to the airport. Whatever the truth was, Meryl was determined to go to Kalahari Farm and remove the helpless animals. When the Inspector said that Meryl and the SPCA team 'should be alright' to go to Kalahari Farm, Meryl was adamant that she wanted a police escort and had to insist until he at last agreed. Meryl smiled to herself as the OIC who had just said she 'should be alright' to go to the farm alone proceeded to provide three police officers and an army Sergeant armed with a FN rifle. As Meryl walked out of his door the OIC said, 'Good luck!' and then Meryl knew that things were probably far from being 'alright' at Kalahari Farm.

Arriving at the farm, they were greeted by a very forlorn sight:

'As soon as we arrived at the farm entrance, we saw a very dejected looking Jack Russell sitting in the middle of the drive. We guessed he must be one of the family dogs and had been on his own for several days. His name was "Orlow" and when I saw the little dog sitting in the middle of the long driveway – obviously waiting for his family to return, I was angry but also saddened that people could do this to a little dog who – through no fault of his own – had been abandoned by the people he loved.'

Orlow was immediately caught and put into a cage in the back of Meryl's truck. Arriving at the main house they found the gate closed and padlocked and Meryl hooted to try and rouse someone who could let them in. As they waited she could see the thirty sheep she had been told about. The flock were grazing around the tobacco barns and seemed unaffected by events taking place on the farm. The sheep had food and water and Meryl knew that she would be hard-pressed to find a legitimate reason to remove them from the property. At last a farm worker arrived and opened the gate. Meryl, Addmore and Augustine immediately began walking around and calling for the cats and another dog but their search was in vain, there was no sign of them at all. It seemed that Orlow was the only dog and the farm worker said it was possible that the cook, Dandaro, would know where the cats were as he fed them at night. One police Constable went with Meryl to the farm workers' village and they received a very hostile reception.

A crowd of about 20 farm workers swarmed around Meryl's truck and they had been drinking. They were noisy and menacing, particularly Dandaro who leaned in the truck window. He was wearing dark sunglasses, stank of alcohol and was obviously very drunk.

'Go back to Britain,' he slurred at Meryl, his breath stinking. 'Leave these animals alone on this farm and go back to Britain!'

Meryl knew there would be no reasoning with the drunken Dandaro and she left the police Constable to try and pacify him. She got the impression that a lot of his hostility and ranting was grand-standing for the crowd and she knew the wisest thing would be for her to keep her mouth shut and not get involved. After a little while the Constable had obviously had enough and he instructed Dandaro to get into Meryl's truck.

'Once back at the house, we asked Dandaro to help us find the cats. He told us that he fed them in the morning and now he did not know where they were but that they would be somewhere in the garden. Both the police and I were getting a little exasperated by Dandaro's evasiveness, not helped by his alcoholic state. Suddenly the army Sergeant, who had been very quiet up until then, just leaning against a mango tree in the garden and not taking part in things, exploded. He roared at Dandaro that he was wasting everybody's time and was just playing games.'

The army sergeant's outburst seemed to immediately sober Dandaro up and at that moment Addmore appeared from the side of the farm garden. Through a closed window he had seen two black cats sitting on the sink in the kitchen. Dandaro must have known all along that the cats were locked inside the house. Augustine and the drunken Dandaro went on foot back to the farm workers village to collect a key for the house from the maid.

In the meantime Addmore noticed that a catch on one of the windows was very loose and with police permission he climbed into the kitchen, followed by one of the Constables. The two black cats were apparently called 'Snoopy' and 'Foopy' and 'Addmore' caught them quite easily, passing them immediately through the window to Meryl who put them straight into the cage that she had ready and waiting.

The police Constable searched the house room by room and found the third cat, a tortoiseshell called 'Mischief' who had been shut into one of the children's bedrooms. Meryl thought the neighbour who had alerted her to the animals abandoned at Kalahari might have been mistaken about the numbers because there was no sign of a fourth cat anywhere in or near the farmhouse. Just as they finished putting the cats into the back of Meryl's truck, Dandaro appeared with the key for the front door – he was too late as the job had been done and the army Sergeant gave the drunk cook another tongue lashing before they left the farm.

On the way out of Kalahari Farm, Meryl stopped to look at the three horses she had been told about. They had access to food and water but did not look in good condition. One horse in particular was quite thin and its ribs were prominent. Meryl was worried and wanted the horses to be moved as quickly as possible. She knew from past experience that once the farmer vacated the property, the horses left behind were almost always ridden indiscriminately, sometimes even used for ploughing by the settlers.

Meryl left Kalahari Farm with her precious cargo of three rescued cats and the little Jack Russell dog and drove straight to Mvurwi Police Station to drop off the army Sergeant and three police Constables. She took a few minutes to go inside and thank the OIC for his assistance and co-operation and couldn't help but notice that he seemed surprised that they hadn't had any trouble with the farm workers. Meryl told the OIC that she could have done with the army Sergeant alongside the SPCA team at other farm rescues. How easily he would have dealt with some of the nastier encounters they had had on other farms – barricading and lock-ins, being surrounded and threatened by war veterans and harassed and intimidated by Youth Brigade members.

Once Foopy, Snoopy and Mischief were safely in the cattery at the SPCA and Orlow was in a kennel, Meryl went to her office where she was told of the frantic phone calls and messages that had accumulated for her. The neighbour who had asked Meryl to rescue the animals from Kalahari Farm had called repeatedly to say: 'Don't go to the farm, it's too dangerous!' Meryl smiled and shook her head: just as well she hadn't received that message, she thought – ignorance was bliss!

Several days later SPCA Inspectors Addmore and Augustine went back to Kalahari Farm with a representative from the Thoroughbred Trust to remove the three horses that had been left behind. Meryl had been called away to Bulawayo but later found out how the rescue had been concluded. Accompanied by a woman police Constable, the rescue team found everything to be quiet on Kalahari Farm but were dismayed to see that the horses had been ridden since the last visit. The horses were covered in sweat and salt which indicated that they had been ridden very hard and must have returned to the paddock sweating profusely.

One of the mares, a light bay, was suffering from azoturia, a condition of the hind legs caused by too much exercise undertaken too quickly. All three horses were covered in ticks and the rescue team were told that it was Dandaro and two other workers who had been riding the horses – apparently going backwards and forwards to the beerhall. Because all three horses could not be loaded into the one horse box, the police Constable gave instructions that the eldest of the three mares be walked by one of the workers to a neighbouring farm. Augustine wrote a note to the farmer explaining the circumstances and the remaining two mares were loaded into the horse box and taken back to the Thoroughbred Trust where the lame mare could be treated with anti-inflammatories. In the following weeks three cats: Foopy, Snoopy and Mischief and one little brown and white Jack Russell called Orlow were re-homed and at last their ordeal was over.

Extracts from Meryl's Diary:

'How can we be a whole human being
if the animals don't have rights?'
– Abraham Lincoln, 1864

July 2002
Harare:
I was in my office at Harare SPCA when a call was put through to me by the Manager. When I asked him who the caller was or what it was in connection with, the Manager didn't answer, just put the call through. A male voice said: 'We are coming to cut your throat because you are accusing the war veterans of cruelty to animals in the newspapers.' When I asked who was speaking, the caller rang off.

This threat frightened me much more than the written one had. Immediately phoned and reported the call to Braeside Police Station. CID (Criminal Investigation Department) came and took a statement from me but I never heard anything more. For a while I stopped working late at the kennel in the evenings, but with time I forgot the whole incident.

8 July. Invited to give a talk on the farm rescues at the Rotary Club of Harare West and was presented with an award. [Meryl was given a Service Award which read: 'For devoted and selfless service to the recovery and care of livestock and domestic animals from commercial farms, in the face of considerable personal danger.']

Bulawayo:
Drove to Bulawayo as Roly not at all well, his doctor wanted to see us both. While I was holding Roly's arm and slowly walking into the doctor's surgery my cell phone rang – it was a man from Harare and he was quite put out that I couldn't deal with his problem then and there. Even at a time like this I am not spared the intrusions. The Doctor said that Roly must have his leg amputated otherwise he would die. At first Roly absolutely refused but after further discussion he finally agreed. Went to see the specialist who would be operating and by 2pm Roly had been admitted to the Mater Dei Hospital. Two days later Roly's right leg was amputated above the knee. As I sat

by him in the Recovery Room after the operation, I remembered the letter that I had written to The Bulawayo Chronicle just the year before:

'The man that I love and share a home with urgently needs a complicated by-pass operation in South Africa as it cannot be carried out here in Zimbabwe. As there is no forex [foreign currency] in this country (I wonder why?) he sits and waits. If he should die in the meantime, I will hold Robert Mugabe responsible.'

The letter was published but the lifeline of forex never came and now his circulatory system was breaking down. In his usual stoic way he tried to play the whole thing down and didn't want any fuss made.

Remained in Bulawayo for another week – doing my best to work from home but was receiving many calls, especially from the Mvurwi area.

Had to eventually leave. Went to Masvingo where we had a court case involving a professional hunter who had been using donkeys for live bait in order to attract lions for his overseas clients to shoot. He was found guilty.

CHAPTER EIGHTEEN

Upside down chickens

'Animals are such agreeable friends –
they ask no questions, they pass no criticism.'
– George Elliott

Benwell Farm, Bindura, August 2002

Roger Birdwood made contact with the SPCA in August 2002 some weeks
after he had been forced off Benwell Farm in Bindura. Roger, distraught at
being evicted from his farm and home and with no idea of what he was going
to do or where he was going to live, had reluctantly left his two little Pekinese
bitches, Lucy and Emily, on the farm while he tried to get some stability into
the chaos that had become his life. The dogs were being looked after and fed
by staff who were still on the farm and who the dogs knew. Roger's wife had
recently passed away and nothing was safe or familiar any more; survival came
by taking just one day at a time.

Everything changed when Roger got a phone call from a neighbouring
farmer to say that a man kept coming and parking outside the gates to Benwell
Farm. The man would sit staring at the house for long periods of time, sometimes
talking on his cell phone, but mostly just looking at the farmhouse. This had
gone on for some time but then came the news that the war veteran had given
up looking from a distance and had now actually moved into Roger's house.
Most of Roger's furniture was still in the house but this had not deterred the
man who had decided he was the new owner, not only of Benwell Farm, but
also of Roger Birdwood's house and possessions.

The two little Pekinese bitches, Lucy and Emily, lived in a courtyard
off the main house and if a stranger had indeed moved into the house, Roger
knew it would be a huge problem. Knowing his dogs and how they behaved,
Roger knew that Lucy and Emily would not take kindly to seeing and hearing
strangers in the house, one wall away from them. Roger was sure that his dogs
would bark incessantly and that the noise would soon anger and annoy the
strangers. Roger was desperate to rescue his dogs. He couldn't bear to think of

them getting hurt but he knew that he couldn't do it himself; he couldn't go back onto Benwell Farm. Aside from the fact that it would be almost unbearably painful to see what had happened to his farm and to see strangers in his own home, Roger had been warned by his neighbours that it was not safe for him to return to Benwell Farm.

Accompanied by SPCA Inspector Augustine, Meryl set out for Bindura Police Station where she collected a young police Constable. He was to be her escort and they headed for Benwell Farm immediately without any of the standard arguments or problems. The Constable was shy, quiet and obviously very inexperienced, having only been out of Depot training for six months. This made Meryl a little nervous but rather than delay the rescue and leave two little dogs at risk of being hurt, she carried on. It was not the best of days to conduct an animal rescue and Meryl felt distinctly ill at ease. Later she wrote:

'I was most definitely nervous going to Benwell. Normally, whenever possible, I tried not to do farm rescues at the weekends because of the increased consumption of alcohol by the settlers. At weekends there was also a decreased chance of support from the police if we got into any real trouble. On this occasion, it was a Saturday and also a public holiday.'

Just before the turn off to Benwell Farm, Meryl saw a truck parked half way across the road and a man stood in the middle, flagging them down. At first Meryl thought he might have been the farm foreman but she soon changed her mind. The man was aggressive and arrogant, his questions hostile. Later Meryl discovered that he was one of the settlers who had taken over Benwell Farm.

'Who are you?' the man asked abruptly. 'What do you want here?'

Meryl explained that she was from the SPCA and had come to collect Mr Birdwood's dogs from the house but her explanation annoyed the man.

'Why hasn't he come himself?' the settler demanded. 'Why has the farmer sent the SPCA and the police when he should just come here himself?'

Meryl had hoped for support from her young police escort, but soon realised she was on her own. The young Constable was clearly nervous and didn't say a word. Meryl, familiar with such situations, said: 'Mr Birdwood is an elderly man you know. Maybe he wasn't feeling well and not up to coming all the way out here by himself.'

The settler didn't answer. He got back in his car and drove away and Meryl breathed a sigh of relief at another hurdle crossed and drove on towards the farm. A little further down the road there was a man carrying six live chickens upside down. The birds had their feet tied to a stick and were flapping pathetically as they hung over the man's shoulder. Everything was put on hold

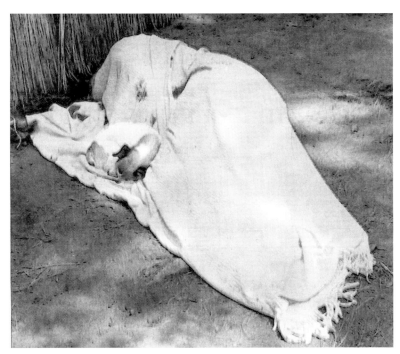

Terry Ford, a farmer living 40 kilometres west of Harare, was dragged from his vehicle, brutally assaulted and shot in the head. This was the sight that awaited those first on the scene: Squeak, his Jack Russell, curled up beside the lifeless body of his dead master. It was an image, distributed by Reuters throughout the world, that summed up the true horror of the land invasions in Zimbabwe. *(Linette Frewin)*

The manager's house, Charleswood Estate. The house was burnt by settlers, the family escaped but the cat was burnt to death. *(Roy Bennett)*

The vehicle in which Meryl and her team travelled thousands of miles throughout Zimbabwe on their missions to rescue animals. *(Nick Dean)*

Vet Rob Gordon reunited with his beloved dachshund, Bob, who was rescued from Nyapi Farm, Chinhoyi, along with eight other pets. *(Belinda Bowie)*

Becky Parsons and her favourite horse 'Chianti' in happier times. In 2003 Spring Farm in Karoi was invaded and the Cochrane family brutally assaulted. After a 4-hour stand off Meryl and her team were able to get the horses off the farm. *(Jenny Parsons)*

Marmalade, the ginger cat from Danbury Park Farm. He was rescued by Meryl and Addmore after many days of hiding behind a bath when invaders took over the farmhouse. His owners had been violently evicted and were unable to return to rescue their beloved cats. *(Tommy Bayley)*

The elderly owners of these tortoises had been barricaded in their house by war vets for 35 days. The family asked Meryl to rescue their nine pet tortoises. *(Lisa Hywood)*

This chimpanzee, known as Buffy, had been confined to a miserable life of solitary confinement in a wildlife park outside Harare. Meryl managed to get the chimp transferred to the world-renowned Chimfunshi Wildlife Orphanage in Zambia. (Sue Roberts)

A leopard killed by a poacher's snare at Masapas Ranch. *(Deirdre Reichard)*

Chalkie with Ben and Storm as they settle in at the new farm: a happy outcome after very protracted negotiations. *(Sandie van Schalkwyk)*

The brutal effect of a snare on a hand-reared giraffe at Wasara Ranch. *(Gary Warth)*

We rescued 57 sable antelopes from the quarantine bomas at Beatrice that had been confined for 3 years while legal battles over ownership went on. *(Chris Milligan)*

A farm worker helps Meryl examine a calf that settlers had stolen – they had tied its legs together with barbed wire until they were ready to slaughter it. *(Brent Stirton/Getty)*

Attacks on livestock were common and were carried out to intimidate farmers off their farms. This cow on the Wasara Ranch had been slashed with a panga. *(Theresa Warth)*

This fine Limousin bull at Charleswood Farm was chased by thugs into the river where it was repeatedly beaten. Efforts were made to save it but there was no option but to put him down. *(Roy Bennett)*

Emaciated cows at Collingwood Farm, Concession, one of the top dairy farms in the country. The farmer was forced at gun-point to leave his herd of 436 animals. These photos taken some months later show how the herd was now suffering from neglect. The cow on the right had a prolapsed udder infected with mastitis. *(F.J. Gaisford)*

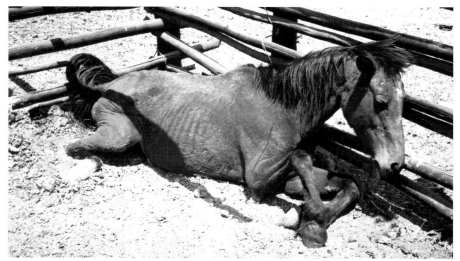

ABOVE: Data Farm, Bromley: after a year of running wild and hungry, picking up barbed wire and even a fencing post, we were called in to round up 14 horses. All were in very poor condition. The farmer had been forced off his land leaving the horses behind. *(Mark Evans)*

We managed to squeeze all the Kay family's pet pigs into the back of this truck on their way to a new home! *(Kerry Kay)*

An axe head lies embedded in the back of a cow in the Lowveld. The axe was extracted and the animal recovered. *(Gary Warth)*

Happier times: 'Cannon' with Russell, the nephew of Ian and Jo Cochrane. When war vets invaded their farm in Karoi two of the horses were set on fire. Cannon later had to be destroyed. *(Jo Cochrane)*

Swartzie, rescued from Walton dale Farm. In spite of a very hostile reception from war vets on the farm, Meryl and Addmore managed to rescue all the dogs. *(Ros Cartright)*

Denver, the little chestnut pony who gave the team such a hard time as they tried to catch him and seven other horses at Mapora Farm, Odzi. Later he led them all calmly onto the truck. *(Claire Evans)*

Cuthbert, one of the cats rescued from Waltondale Farm. *(Ros Cartright)*

ABOVE: Shumba the Staffie rescued from Chipesa Farm in the Marondera area. *(Kerry Kay)*

LEFT: In between farm rescues the team travelled to rural areas to treat donkeys and give advice to owners. Here in Zvimba, Mugabe's home area. *(Joy Stevens)*

Nandi, fully recovered from her ordeal at Two Tree Hill Farm, and enjoying her twilight years in her new home in South Africa. *(Lenie de Jager)*

Meryl at the BBC Animal Awards ceremony in 2002 with Fiona Bruce (left) and Gaby Roslyn (right). This was a joint award for both Meryl and Addmore for their work rescuing stranded animals on Zimbabwe's abandoned farms.

as Meryl stopped the car. She could not abide any sort of cruelty to animals, even if the animals were soon to be slaughtered for food. A few minutes later the man and his chickens were in the back of the SPCA truck and had to find space alongside the cages, buckets and veterinary supplies that went on every rescue. The chickens' legs were untied but the birds had obviously been incapacitated for some time as they were weak and flailed around, unable to stand up. Meryl left them loose in the back of truck so that they could move around and start to get their circulation going again.

Arriving at last at the gate to Benwell Farm, a security guard strode across to the vehicle with a shotgun slung over his shoulder. Meryl explained who she was and the reason for her visit and the guard opened the gate. He pointed out where Roger Birdwood's house was and warned Meryl that war veterans had moved into the homestead.

Feeling a little apprehensive at what she would find and not encouraged by having such a young and inexperienced Constable as her police escort, Meryl drove up to the farmhouse. Built on a hill to get the most of the breeze and the best of the views, the house was over 80 years old. Every single brick and piece of timber used in the construction had been painstakingly brought up from South Africa in 1920. It was no wonder that Roger could not bear to come back to the farm now. In her diary Meryl wrote of the magnificence of the house:

'The house was so beautiful, white, with large Dutch Gables at either end, wooden window frames and a pretty courtyard. Apparently it had been designed by Sir Herbert Baker, a well known architect of the day. The view was so typically Zimbabwean: panoramic scenes of Msasas, kopjes and a dam in the distance. The garden was obviously once much loved and cared for, but was now beginning to show signs of neglect.'

Meryl hooted at the gate which was locked and after a while a sour and sullen-looking settler sauntered across. He was middle-aged, thin and scruffily dressed. The man had blood-shot eyes and was dour and hostile.

'I am Chief Inspector Harrison of the ZNSPCA, appointed by the Zimbabwean government,' Meryl announced, using her full and official title. Her words were met with indifference and silence. 'This is my ID,' she said holding out the tin disc for inspection but the man seemed totally uninterested. 'I've come to get the dogs,' Meryl said.

Thankfully any further monologue was unnecessary because at that moment Roger's trusted and long-standing cook, Philip, arrived at the gate. Philip had the key for the small gate of the security fence surrounding the house and garden. Philip unlocked the gate for Meryl and while she drove in and parked, he went to the house to get the dogs. This sequence of events was not new to Meryl as she later recorded:

'I found that the war veterans and settlers very often, at the beginning of an occupation, would let the domestic workers keep the keys. This was to show that they had not stolen anything but of course they could always break in whenever they wanted to.'

Meryl could not see any of the war veterans although she suspected they were probably watching her from inside the house. Philip carried Emily out in his arms whilst Lucy came running across the lawn straight towards Meryl. The two little Pekinese dogs were both very good looking – not surprising as Meryl later learnt that they were imported, pedigreed and registered. Emily was a rich, deep tan colour and slightly smaller than Lucy who was a pretty golden colour. With their tails characteristically curled up on their backs the two Pekes were obviously delighted to see Meryl. Lucy especially was beside herself with excitement; she went bananas!

The little dog skipped delightedly around, wagging and wiggling and barking, overjoyed at all the sudden friendly attention. Emily, the other little Peke, was not anywhere near as trusting or forthcoming and was much more cautious about accepting yet more strangers. Emily had a frightened look in her eyes and was trembling a little but when Meryl bent down and picked her up, she began to relax. Meryl stroked the little dog, talked to her softly and called her by name and Emily must have realised that her ordeal was coming to an end. It must have been a terrifying few weeks for the two little dogs. They had been surrounded by strangers, their owner had gone and they had been closed into the courtyard all the time, virtual prisoners in the place they had always known as home.

Philip had done a fantastic job of looking after the two dogs. Their long, fine haired coats were clean and brushed and both dogs looked well-fed and healthy. Philip came out to the SPCA truck with the dogs' baskets, blankets, brushes and leads and his emotion at having to say goodbye to the dogs was almost too painful to watch. Every day Philip had fed and groomed the little dogs, calming them, caring for them and cleaning them and now suddenly the little dogs were going.

Philip and the few other farm staff still there stood around watching as Meryl prepared to leave. The pain and sorrow was palpable. The staff knew that the departure of the dogs meant the end of Benwell Farm for sure. Now everything really had come to an end, Philip's job, his home and his future. Nothing would ever be the same again for Philip or any of the people who

150

had worked on Benwell Farm; life was suddenly filled with uncertainty and insecurity.

The atmosphere was filled with anguish and emotion and Meryl turned away. Lucy was going to have to go in the back of the truck and by the look on her face, wasn't too happy at being closed in with chickens. Lucy, true to the breed description, clearly lost her sense of humour and went into 'dignified' mode as she was lifted into the vehicle! In the back of the truck, sitting patiently awaiting his fate, was the man Meryl had apprehended earlier, the man with the six upside-down chickens! Meryl warned him about cruelty to animals and then dropped him off at his destination before setting out for Harare.

An hour later she was in the suburbs of the capital city and headed straight for the new home of Roger Birdwood knowing that an emotional welcome was waiting for the two dogs. It was a joyous reunion on all sides and Meryl wrote about it in the closing sentences of her diaries on Benwell Farm:

'When we got to Roger's place, he came out to the truck with a big grin on his face, which soon turned to tears of relief when he realised that his beloved dogs were at last safe and sound. They gave him a few quick licks, tails wagging and then they were off round the flat and garden, checking out their new home. They busily pottered around the garden flat as if they had always lived there!'

A few days later a donation for the SPCA and a card arrived for Meryl. 'Thanks Meryl for bringing my two little girls back. What a fantastic service. I was scared stiff. Thanks again, Roger.'

Extracts from Meryl's Diary:

He conquers who endures.
– Proverb

August 2002
9 August. The date the government had set by which all farmers had to be off their farms. We drew up contingency plans for the animals.

Bulawayo:
Drove to Bulawayo over the weekend to see Roly.

Save/Runde River, Mahenya:
Went to Mahenya, the confluence of the Save and Runde Rivers in the lowveld for the start of the Blue Cross Challenge. The Blue Cross began as an argument in a pub

when Colin Anderson and his mates disagreed about the lowest point in Zimbabwe. Colin searched maps and identified the two extremes of altitude in the country: the Save-Runde confluence at Mahenya which is just 150 meters above sea level and Mount Inyangani which is the highest: 2.593 meters above sea level. The distance between the two points is 500 kilometres and in 1996 The Blue Cross Endurance Challenge began.

Colin combined his love of the bush and outdoors with his passion for animal welfare and challenged walkers and cyclists to cover the 500km distance, going from lowest to highest altitudes and raise money for the SPCA in the process. Eight walkers and 16 cyclists took part in 1996 and from then on the gruelling challenge passing through wild, remote and beautiful parts of Zim grew in popularity and became a most prestigious event – even attracting competitors from outside Zimbabwe. All the money raised goes to the various individual SPCA centres – the event has raised millions of dollars over the years & has enabled many of the centres round the country to keep going (especially the smaller places).

For several years I've been coming down to the lowveld for the start of the Blue Cross – usually arrive in time for the departure of the walkers which is always a few days before the cyclists set off. It gives us a good opportunity to treat donkeys along the way and also to go to the more remote growth points that we would never normally get to, in order to give them help with their animals such as dogs, rabbits, goats, poultry, the occasional cat, and of course their donkeys, without which they would not be able to plough, cart firewood, take maize to the grinding mill and sick relatives to the nearest clinic which could be many miles away.

It's at these little centres that the exhausted Blue Cross walkers collapse for the night – joined by me and Addmore! Sometimes we all slept on the floor in school classrooms or I sleep in the back of the truck whilst Addmore sleeps in the front.

This is a special year because Patricia Glyn (Presenter of 'Patricia's People' on SAfm Radio) is coming up from South Africa for the Challenge. She's been interviewing me for weeks already about the farm rescues and even though we've never met I feel like I already know her – a lovely, warm and professional lady – passionate about animals and Zim.

[Patricia Glyn, writing later from South Africa, described her involvement with Meryl and her reasons for getting involved in the Blue Cross Challenge in 2002:

'The listener response to our interviews was the most overwhelming that I've had in 13 years of broadcasting. Meryl always manages to convey the essence of the human and animal tragedy in a balanced and professional manner.

'Meryl's compassion and bravery inspired me. Together with 13 of my listeners we embarked on the Blue Cross Challenge to raise funds for her projects. Whilst on that long and gruelling road, we had a chance to see Meryl and Addmore at work – treating donkeys that had become victims of neglect or cruelty. It was here that I learned to admire this woman – her patience with people who I would have smacked for what they did to their animals – her intuition, her tact and her gritty determination to help against all odds. Meryl was a reluctant heroine, someone who had been thrown into the limelight and wasn't completely comfortable with it. She constantly stressed the help she got from her friend and colleague Addmore, along with many other brave people who risked life and limb to rescue the voiceless from Zimbabwe's farms.

'Through donations from SAfm listeners I managed to raise about R300,000 and got a medal for the most money raised that year (and I suspect ever – not hard as I had access to radio!)']

Harare:
Meeting at the racecourse with representatives from SPANA (Society for Protection of Animals Abroad) who are based in the UK, together with vets and other concerned members of the equine world. We were increasingly worried about the number of horses being left behind on farms.

Bromley:
More trouble on a stud farm. Spend many days negotiating with war vets and settlers for the release of over 60 confined horses.

CHAPTER NINETEEN

Pumba, Mufasa and Zazu: dogs under house arrest!

'Nowadays we don't think much of a man's love for an animal; we
laugh at people who are attached to cats. But if we stop loving animals,
aren't we bound to stop loving humans too?'
– Alexander Solzhenitsyn

Kinghamdale Farm, Mutepatepa, August 2002
Meryl arranged to meet Peeps Reid at the Bindura Police Station on 23 August 2002 so that she could get exact directions to Kinghamdale Farm in Mutepatepa. Meryl had been asked for help in rescuing two big brown Boerboel dogs named Pumba and Mufasa and a little brown and white Jack Russell bitch, Zazu. The dogs had been named by the Reid children after characters in *The Lion King* and when Meryl got the call for help from Peeps, she agreed to help immediately. The Reids had left Kinghamdale farm early on a Saturday morning thinking they would be gone for just a night or two. Peeps was totally unprepared for anything longer and said:

'We barely took anything. I really thought it would be just for the weekend and by Monday we would be back, but our children never went home again.'

The Reids' youngest son, Kingsley, was eight and for him the trauma of being away from home was compounded by a desperate longing for his pets – the dogs and cats and his two brown house snakes. The Reid's maid, Beauty, was still on the farm and able to get into the house to feed the animals but for a little boy that wasn't enough: he needed to be able to see, touch and cuddle his animals. Meryl must have heard the desperation in Peeps' voice because she made arrangements for a rescue as soon as she could.

Meryl had had dealings with the Officer in Charge of police in

Bindura in the past and, as she had found before, the OIC was helpful and very co-operative and provided Meryl with three police officers in a Land Rover Defender. In the vast majority of farm rescues, Meryl didn't see the farm owners on their properties because they had either been forcibly evicted or had been warned and threatened not to return to their farms. With Kinghamdale, however, the situation was different. In fact everything about this incident was unusual, or perhaps absurd would be a better description. Stuart Reid was one of the farmers who had been arrested for farming in the chaos that dominated agriculture in August 2002.

In May 2002 the government had amended the Land Acquisition Act and stipulated that 2,900 farmers had 45 days to stop production and another 45 days to leave their properties. The combined 90 days was a grossly insufficient time to stop producing almost all crops – even short-term horticultural projects. It seemed that no recognition was paid at all to the long-term planning, advance purchasing of inputs and land preparation that went into farming. Having 90 days to stop livestock farming was even more absurd and clearly did not take into consideration calving and lambing seasons, gestation periods or weaning and fattening times.

For Zimbabwe this mass eviction of farmers could not have come at a worse time. The UN World Food Programme estimated that 6 million people (half of the total population of Zimbabwe) were going to need food aid over the next year. The Commercial Farmers Union warned that if the evictions proceeded, 1.2 million farm workers would be forced out of their homes and jobs; 65,000 hectares of cropping land would be involved, including large hectarages used for wheat, maize and tobacco. The evictions were also going to affect 800,000 cattle and uncountable numbers of sheep, pigs and chickens.

Those 90 days expired in the first week of August 2002 and Meryl was hoping for the best but expecting the worst when it came to the animals on those 2,900 farms. With two years' experience of animal rescues Meryl knew that the days before and after a commemorative public holiday were always the worst. Anniversaries like Independence and Heroes Day were invariably mired with political rhetoric and with 2,900 farmers set to be evicted this Heroes Day it seemed the pattern was continuing. Heroes Day, in 2001, would forever be remembered for the great swathe of farm lootings in the Chinhoyi district and now Heroes Day in 2002 promised a mass of arrests.

Meryl tried to prepare for what might happen to the animals if the arrests and evictions took place. A notice appeared in the press six weeks ahead of the deadline and the farming unions also sent out the request on their bulk mailing lists.

'URGENT APPEAL:
Being cognizant of the approaching deadline by which time owners of farms who
have been served with Section 8 Notices are required to cease farming operations, we
are appealing to all parties concerned to do nothing to compromise the welfare of any
animals, particularly livestock, remaining on these farms after 25 June 2002.
We appeal to all those concerned to ensure the provision of adequate food, grazing and
water for livestock animals at all times.'

The country held its breath as the deadline for the mass evictions came
and then went.

On the whole people seemed to think that such massive evictions would
not happen and it was estimated that only 300 of the nearly 3,000 affected
farmers actually did leave their farms in anticipation of the deadline. The
trouble began just a week later. The first news items were that six farmers had
been arrested, taken to a police station and been given warned and cautioned
statements. By the following day the number jumped to 49 farmers arrested and
in the following days the numbers rose to 147. By 22nd August, 217 farmers
had been arrested. Some of the farmers were held in police custody, others were
released on bail and in some areas the arrests were forcible and farmers were
denied access to food, life-preserving medication and access to lawyers.

Stuart Reid was one of the farmers arrested and although he had been
granted bail, one of the conditions was that he was not allowed to go anywhere
near Kinghamdale Farm. Apparently at first the gates to the farmhouse garden
had been locked and the farm workers were not allowing anyone in. The maid
Beauty had initially been able to come and go and to feed the animals but soon
even this arrangement came under threat.

Meryl's rescue couldn't have come at a better time and she was expecting
to only meet Peeps Reid at the police station and was surprised to see Stuart
there too. He had been given permission by the police to go and collect personal
items from his home but had to be off the farm by 4pm. They were delayed
for a while as the police Inspector showed Stuart a list of other farmers in the
area who were supposed to have handed themselves in to face being charged
with 'farming illegally'. Meryl kept quiet but thought this the most bizarre
encounter. The police wanted Stuart's help to arrest his farming friends while
he himself had been arrested by these same police! It made no sense at all.

Normally Meryl only rescued animals when the owners were unable to
do so themselves but on this occasion, in view of both space and time restric-
tions and knowing that dogs, cats and snakes were involved, Meryl decided
to continue with the rescue. Accompanied by a three-man police escort, the
ZNSPCA team and the Reids arrived at Kinghamdale Farm and at first the

place appeared deserted. After a little while Moses the rose manager appeared. He had been coming onto the farm at night and watering the roses under cover of darkness – doing whatever he could to try and save the plants and what was left of the business and his job. The two Boerboels, Mufasa and Pumba, and Zazu the little Jack Russell, were clearly delighted to see their owners and they rushed around excitedly, barking and panting, tails wagging and tongues hanging out. Two cats also strolled out across the garden to wind themselves around the legs of their owners and a bleak and deserted scene was immediately transformed into one with life and love and noise.

Because Meryl was only able be involved with animals she could not help the Reids and so she just stood out of the way, watching and waiting until it was time to load the three dogs. They had decided the cats would not be taken this time after all because Beauty was confident she could take care of them and there was plenty of food still in the house. Until the Reids were settled in their new home, it would be better for the cats to stay in the familiar environment of the farm. The ginger cat was called 'Kluesner' and had been named after the red-headed South African cricketer. Kluesner was apparently a very cheeky cat but on this occasion he just curled up in the sun and went to sleep – oblivious of the problems of his owners! Meryl watched the dogs, the cats and the Reids and thought how tragic this all was. She could not imagine how it must feel to be arrested for farming or how you would choose what to take and what to leave behind if you were given just a few hours to get out of your own home.

'Stuart and Peeps immediately started piling up the two trucks with personal posses-sions. I noticed Stuart's first priority was his golf clubs! Peeps was more concerned with retrieving the children's school trunks and uniforms as the schools were going back the following week. It was so sad watching them trying to pack a lifetime into two trucks in the space of two hours. Other farmers' wives told me how difficult it was to decide what to take – especially when you are under pressure – sometimes the war vets came into their bedrooms and threatened them as they were trying frantically to pack. Another wife told me how she struggled out to their car with her sewing machine – not knowing what the future held for them, she thought she could always turn her hand to sewing clothes to earn a living for the family. Nearly all wives were unanimous in telling me that photographs were always one of the most precious possessions to take – even if they could take nothing else.'

At one point in the afternoon, and for no apparent reason, one of the farm workers locked the gates, closing everyone in. When Stuart asked him why he had done that, the worker replied, 'I don't know!' It made no sense but was so typical of farm invasions where rules were being made up all the time and no one ever really seemed to know who was in charge or what to do. Meryl thought about how Peeps had described the farm and could not imagine how painful this eviction must be. Surrounded by hills, Kinghamdale was 2,500 hectares and the Reids grew tobacco in summer and wheat in winter. Stuart also reared cattle for beef and Peeps had two hectares of roses which she grew for export. There were wild animals in abundance on Kinghamdale too: kudu, sable, zebra, waterbuck, duiker and impala. The animals were not fenced in but they mostly stayed on Kinghamdale and even leopards were not uncommon.

It was well after the 4pm deadline when the Reids had finished loading every square inch of their two trucks and had crammed in as much as they could – including finding a safe and secluded space for Kingsley's two brown house snakes. Meryl was about to start loading the dogs when her cell phone rang. It was her partner, Roly, calling from a hospital in Bulawayo – hundreds of kilometres away on the other side of the country.

Roly was still in hospital after having had his leg amputated. Meryl had stayed with Roly for the first few days after the operation but had to leave as the situation on the farms got worse and more and more animals needed rescuing. Amazed that Roly had been able to get through to her at all, Meryl heard just one brief sentence before the phone cut off: 'I am freezing my arse off out here!' Meryl immediately phoned a man in the same ward as Roly and discovered that nurses had wheeled Roly out into the garden and then forgotten him out there! Unable to attract the attention of a nurse to help him, in desperation Roly phoned Meryl. A nurse was summoned, the rescue effected and Meryl smiled sadly. Zimbabwean nursing at its best, she thought, as she turned her attention back to the animal rescue.

Meryl, Addmore and Augustine loaded Pumba, Mufasa and Zazu and, with the police in the lead, the vehicles left Kinghamdale Farm in convoy. They didn't get very far:

'Half way down the drive the police Land Rover Defender packed up. Stuart offered to tow them as far as the tarred road with a chain, but reminded them that it would be illegal for him to tow them on a main road using a chain. I don't think they were too happy about that!'

It was dark by the time Meryl and the Reids arrived in Harare and they headed for a house in Mount Pleasant which they were using as a base. Meryl did not stay for long but she felt so moved when she saw the reception given to the dogs by the Reid children. She closed her records on Kinghamdale farm with a rare but most welcome happy ending:

'Pumba and Zazu leapt out of the back of our truck but Mufasa had to be gently lifted out as Stuart informed us that she had a plastic hip. There was a joyous reunion between the three dogs and the Reid children.'

That was a day that Peeps Reid would never forget because even though they had lost their home, business and farm, the family were together, reunited with the pets who meant so much. No one knew the effect these traumatic times were having on the children of the farmers involved but Meryl was convinced that being able to have their pets would help them to adjust and cope and begin to feel safe again. Peeps described the feelings of that memorable evening:

'It was a fantastic reunion, we were a family once again, all together! Kingsley had already planned where the big dogs were to sleep and set about putting their baskets in place and of course they all fought over who was having Zazu in their bed that night! We later inherited a very large brown house snake from friends when they left Zimbabwe and his name was Julius Squeezer! This gave Kingsley plenty to do in finding lizards and grasshoppers in the garden.'

In the weeks ahead Peeps was able to go back to Kinghamdale a few more times to tend to her roses. She always took the dogs with her for security and they clearly loved being back, racing through the grass and treading old familiar tracks. On one occasion Peeps caught the cats and took them back to Harare and was glad she did this in time as her visits soon came to a shocking end. Checking the greenhouses with a rose consultant one day, news came that the war veterans were locking them in.

The rose consultant managed to get out of the only farm gate without incident but Peeps was too late. She loaded the dogs into her truck and followed Moses, the dedicated rose manager on his motorbike, driving blindly through the bush. It was a journey Peeps will never forget:

'He escorted me on a track that went to our neighbour's farm. There was no road, I was literally driving through tall grass! I made it and he waved me goodbye and went back to work whereupon he was beaten up and took an axe to the head from the war veterans for getting me off the farm. We managed to get him into Bindura to a private hospital where he stayed for a week. The wound was about 10cm long at the top of his head. He was so lucky to survive and I will always be indebted to him for that.'

Tragically there was not a happy ending for Beauty, the Reids' maid who had been so dedicated and loyal and had faithfully fed and cared for the dogs and cats in those last weeks after everyone else had gone. Beauty died of cerebral malaria a few months after the Reids had been evicted – there had been no telephone, no ambulance and no one to turn to for help.

Extracts from Meryl's Diary:

'If I be the first of us to die,
Let grief not blacken your sky,
Be bold yet modest in your grieving
There is a change but not a leaving.

Close your eyes
Breathe,
Listen for my footfall in your heart
I am not gone but merely walk
Within you.'
– Source Unknown

August 2002

25th August. Roly phoned on his cell phone several times from the hospital during the day, the last time at about 8pm when he told me that he was feeling 'yuck'. When I asked him why, he said he didn't know and that he felt nauseous. I told him that I would phone him first thing in the morning.

26 August. Mater Dei Hospital in Bulawayo phoned at 5am to say that Roly had passed away.

His death came as an enormous shock to me. I know an amputation is a major operation, but the whole point of it was so that Roly would no longer have all the circulation problems and that the op would improve the quality of his life so that he could move on. Death was never an option.

I was so unprepared for it. When I put the phone down I did not know what to do, who to phone first – at 5am most folk would still be asleep and I didn't want to disturb anyone. I called Nick in Australia, his phone was on voicemail – then Tim in Bulawayo – he was fast asleep.

I just couldn't take it all in.

Then the Mater Dei hospital phoned back to know when was I collecting the body that morning because they could not keep it – there is no mortuary there. Phoned a few close friends, one who came round to make me some sandwiches for the journey to Byo.

About two hours after I had received the news from the hospital that Roly had died and I had made all the necessary phone calls, I got in the truck and left my cottage to drive to Bulawayo. As I drove through Ruwa Petrol station to get onto the Mutare road, my thoughts very much pre-occupied, I saw a scruffy-looking vendor, trying to sell some guinea fowl to people who were queuing for petrol. Nobody seemed very interested – some told him in no uncertain terms to push off. As he was holding the poor, bedraggled birds upside down, I felt I just could not drive past. I called him over to my truck, wound the window down to speak to him about the birds and within seconds he had put them on the front seat for me to look at; I think he thought his luck was in and that he had made a sale at last! I then showed him my Inspector's badge, informed him that I was confiscating them and drove off – not the way I usually do things, but my mind was very much elsewhere. At the same time, I was saying sorry to Roly that once again work had somehow intervened – but I could just hear him saying 'My darling, I wouldn't have wanted you to do anything less.'

My next thought was – what the hell was I going to do with five guinea fowl? They sat on my front seat looking very sorry for themselves and I remembered that my very good friend Linda Ainsworth worked in Ruwa and I thought I could deposit them with her. As soon as Linda saw my truck, she ran out to give me a huge hug (I had phoned her a little earlier with the news about Roly). I then let her know the reason for my visit. Linda being Linda just smiled and said, 'Right let's get them into my office.'

Unable to delay my journey any longer and knowing that I had to face the terrible reality ahead, I set out. As I drove I played tapes that both Roly and I enjoyed – tears streaming down my face. Other cars on the road hardly made any impression on me. I passed through Chegutu, Kadoma, Kwekwe, Gweru – barely noticing the towns. I didn't know what I was going to do without him, he was my rock, always there in the background, always so supportive. On the other hand I knew how much he dreaded the future with only one leg. He would have found it very difficult being disabled and two days before he died, the specialist had hinted that in all probability, the other leg would have had to be amputated. I knew that it was very selfish of me to want him to go through any more pain, stress and trauma. I don't know that he would have been able to cope.

CHAPTER TWENTY

'The pigs were not co-operating'

'We shall have to repent in this generation,
not so much for the evil deeds of the wicked people,
but for the appalling silence of the good people.'
– Dr Martin Luther King

Nyamanda Farm, Karoi, September 2002
Meryl and Addmore cut the padlock on the gate into the pig-sty area at Nyamanda
Farm in Karoi and were greeted with a sight of utter horror. There were pigs
wandering around everywhere and many were blistered with sunburn. Farm
owners Chris and Eleanor Shepard had been evicted from the property by war
veterans two days previously. The farm workers, frightened, intimidated and
then encouraged by the war veterans, had gone on strike for massive retrench-
ment packages and no one had tended to the pigs for two days.

There was no sign of any water and so Meryl opened a tap and just let
it run. Within seconds dozens of pigs came running from all directions. They
pushed and jostled and squealed as they desperately sucked up the water as it
ran out onto the bare ground. As Meryl and Addmore moved around they saw
that quite a number of the pigs had been let out and this was a relief as at least
they had been able to forage for roots and leaves and what was left of the grass.
Others were far less fortunate and there were many young weaners that had
not been released from their sties for nearly three days and had not had any

food or water. This was a very long time for animals used to being fed twice a day and particularly as they were unable to get out and forage for themselves. Meryl and Addmore immediately released all the pigs. Lying in the passage of one set of sties they found a third boar. He had obviously also been involved in the fight and was badly injured. The boar had large and gaping wounds which were crawling with maggots and the animal made no attempt to move as Meryl stepped over him. In her diary Meryl later wrote how death would come as a merciful release for another pig she came across:

> 'In another sty, I found a dying sow who was very thin and too weak to move. It wrenched at my heart to see her lying there — uncomprehending as to what had happened, waiting for death to come.'

While Meryl and Addmore had been walking around the pig sties a large crowd of farm workers and war veterans had gathered at the farm gates and were making their presence known. The sound of drumming and singing could be heard. The drumming was a bad sign; it indicated that people were getting worked up into an excitable state and anything could happen. Meryl was enormously relieved to receive a call on her mobile phone to say that the arrival of the first truck coming to remove the pigs was imminent.

She and Addmore opened the doors of the store room where the pig feed was kept. They let as many of the starving pigs as possible feed from the pig meal which they threw from the bins onto the floor. There were 500 pigs on the farm and Meryl knew it was going to be an enormous operation removing them all. The truck seemed to be an awfully long time in arriving and the reason soon became clear. Another call came on the mobile phone, this time to say that the large crowd of war veterans and workers who had gathered at the farm gate were refusing to allow the truck to enter. The driver had been threatened and told that no trucks would be allowed onto the farm and if any came they would be set on fire.

The young police Constable who had been assigned to escort the SPCA team went to the farm gate to try and resolve the problem but returned half an hour later having made no progress at all. The war veterans were adamant that no trucks were going to be allowed in. Exasperated, hot and frustrated Meryl phoned the most senior police official in Karoi who seemed surprised that the rescue of the pigs had still not been effected. Another policeman was dispatched and in the hour that it took the police Sergeant to arrive, the drumming and noise from the crowd at the gate was incessant. By now there were two trucks sitting at the gate and lengthy negotiations between police, war veterans and farm workers continued. While they waited, Meryl and Addmore checked all the pig sties and looked for sick and injured animals. Meryl found a tiny piglet dragging its hind legs and thought it must have been stood on or crushed in the chaos. Without asking anyone's permission, she scooped up the piglet and popped it in the front of her truck with some food and water and closed the door.

Finally at 2.30 in the afternoon, four and a half hours after they had arrived, Meryl was relieved to see the first truck being allowed into the gate. Conditions had been negotiated: only sick and injured pigs could be taken, and although some of the farm workers had agreed to help catch and load the pigs, they would only do so if they were paid. It was extremely hot and Meryl and Addmore were both exhausted and parched by the time the loading began – they'd had nothing to eat or drink since they'd arrived at Nyamanda Farm. Meryl and Addmore pointed out the sick and injured pigs which they wanted loaded first. The handling was rough and the pigs screamed and grunted and were very vocal – obviously enormously stressed.

Loading continued all afternoon, one truck was filled and another arrived. The second truck bought blessed relief for Meryl and Addmore when a farmer, not allowed onto the property himself, had put a flask of iced water on board and the drink was heavenly, like pure nectar!

The afternoon developed into a nightmare as the pigs became more and more stressed from the constant chasing. The screaming from the pigs never stopped and the more the animals ran, the rougher the handling became. Meryl watched helplessly as eight pigs were hit full in the face with pieces of PVC piping or lengths of wood.

'The pigs were not co-operating!' a worker announced in response to Meryl's shout to stop.

There was nothing Meryl could do or say. It was such a dreadful situation already and getting the pigs loaded and off the farm was the utmost priority. Piglets became separated from their mothers and several of the very large sows collapsed from sheer exhaustion, their sides heaving as they tried to get their breath back. Meryl knew that if she complained the workers would immediately stop and so she said nothing. She poured water over the exhausted sows and wept for what was happening to them.

At one point in the afternoon some workers came over to Meryl and asked if they could have the meat of the sow that had died in the morning. Swallowing hard, Meryl said, 'I suppose Mr Shepard has no need for the animal now.'

She watched as the workers immediately stacked hay around the carcass and set fire to it – apparently to burn the hair off. In a very short time the sow had been chopped up and carted away. In her diary Meryl wrote:

'I find it hard to describe this. The pig died because of their actions and now they were benefiting from that unnecessary death – it just all seemed so wrong. I guess it seemed an insult to treat her like that, but she was after all dead so nothing more could hurt her.'

Later Meryl learnt that in fact the farm workers didn't get any of the meat. The war veterans on the farm, the ones drumming and stirring up sentiments at the gate, took all the meat for themselves. The war veterans apparently told the workers they could have no meat in punishment for not attending an all night pungwe [political re-education meeting].

As it began to get dark the trucks, thankfully, continued to drive in and out. Everyone was utterly exhausted but at least the pigs were being moved off the farm slowly but surely. A phone call came from the farm owner Chris Shepard asking that as much pig food as possible be loaded in one of the trucks as the farmer who was receiving the pigs did not have anywhere near enough feed. Meryl and Addmore began filling sacks with pig food themselves as the farm workers were pre-occupied and continued to argue amongst themselves over who was going to get the meat from the dead sow. Time was against them and the sun had sunk below the horizon already. Finally, just before 7pm, the last truck was loaded. Meryl made a list of all the workers who had been loading pigs so that they could be paid and she prepared to leave. As she drove through the farm gates, war veterans stopped the SPCA truck. The Base Commander leant in the window.

'SPCA – finish your duty in the morning and come and take all the animals,' he said and then stepped away.

Once off the farm and on the road, exhaustion began to take over. Meryl dropped off the policemen and headed back to the home of Kelvin Weare. Throughout the rescue at Nyamanda Farm, Kelvin had been a tower of strength in the background for Meryl. He wasn't a farmer himself but a leading figure in the community who somehow managed to keep tempers cool and unite the farmers in the neighbourhood.

Kelvin had phoned Meryl repeatedly throughout the day, checking if she was alright, letting her know she was not alone, passing on messages about trucks and drivers and giving Meryl continual moral support. The little piglet with damaged hind legs that Meryl had rescued earlier was now wide awake. Once they arrived at Kelvin's house, his wife swept the little pink animal into her arms and immediately put a bottle of milk into its mouth. Meryl and Addmore sank into chairs in the kitchen and had a most welcome cup of tea, something they'd been desperately longing for since 10 o'clock that morning.

As Meryl drank her tea and watched the little piglet sucking on the baby bottle, memories of another pig from happier times came flooding back. Babe had unquestionably been a pig with attitude! She had been just a few days old when Meryl found her, a little one-eyed scrap lying in thick mud, freezing cold and barely alive. Meryl gently lifted the tiny piglet out of the filth, wrapped her in a blanket and drove back to the kennels with the little bundle nestled in her lap. Lying on a heating pad, surrounded by warm bottles and wrapped in towels, the piglet's temperature began to rise.

When she was warm enough to be cleaned up, they started on her face. The caked mud was gently washed off and there was her missing eye – it had been completely sealed up with mud! That night, clean and warm, the piglet went home with Meryl – snuggled up in towels in a cat basket! Every couple of hours Meryl bottle fed the piglet and gradually Babe began to take an interest in life. With each passing day she grew stronger and more adventurous and soon became everyone's favourite animal at the SPCA kennels in Bulawayo.

During the day Babe spent her time in a cage in Meryl's office and what a life she had! Lying on a blanket with a heating pad underneath her, bottled milk provided at regular intervals and it wasn't long before everywhere that Meryl went the little piglet was sure to follow! Doing her rounds of the kennels to checks on dogs and cats, birds and livestock, the little pink piglet trotted happily along behind Meryl, oblivious to surprised stares, raised hackles or barking dogs. Two or three of the kennel dogs which had always spent their days curled up asleep in Meryl's office were soon ousted as the piglet took over completely. When Babe arrived in the office, the dogs would leave rapidly – head butted out of the door – piglet power ruled!

At night Babe went home with Meryl, sleeping in a cage next to the bed. Once she had learnt to drink from a dish on her own, Babe would trot off during the night to help herself. Often Meryl would wake up in the night to hear little stiletto-like piglet hooves clicking across the parquet floors – Babe was heading off for her midnight snack! A soft sigh, loud schlurping and then a contented quiet would descend over the house again.

Babe seemed to like the weekends best of all. She would spend hours playing with Meryl's dogs – Staffies – and they would all tear round and round the garden. Babe decimated flower beds, pruned pot plants and trotted paths all over the lawn. One night on her way home from work, Meryl stopped at a cross-road next to a tired-looking businessman in a Mercedes. Babe was asleep in the passenger seat next to Meryl.

Waiting for the traffic lights to change the piglet suddenly woke and sat up, staring out the window at the Mercedes – just her little head visible. The driver looked, looked again and then burst out laughing: the lights changed and the brief encounter was over – but undoubtedly not forgotten!

When Babe became too big to sleep in Meryl's office, she was relocated to the livestock enclosure at the kennels. She soon made it quite clear that she didn't want to be there and constantly dug her way out and headed straight to Meryl's office. By then an enormous sow, Babe would stand in the doorway staring straight at Meryl, an enquiring look on her face. At home Babe would squash herself into the dogs' basket at night. If there was already a Staffie in the basket Babe just lay down on top of them – heaved a huge sigh and went off to sleep – leaving an indignant, squashed dog struggling to get out. Those happy memories of normal times gave a moment of sanity to Meryl and she wondered if anything would ever be right again in Zimbabwe.

The next morning by 8am Meryl and Addmore were back at the gates to Nyamanda Farm. This time they went without a police escort and the war veterans unlocked the gates and let them in without any problems. The next stage of the rescue was for cattle, sheep and horses and Meryl began by paying the workers who had helped load the pigs the day before.

Ready to begin loading cattle, Meryl waited for the truck that had been arranged to arrive but the problems of the previous day had resurfaced. A large crowd of war veterans, settlers and farm workers had gathered on the road and weren't allowing any trucks onto the farm. Meryl fumed. One day the war veterans were telling her to hurry up and get all the animals off the farm, and the next they were turning back cattle trucks. With no police on hand, Meryl and Addmore left to go to a neighbouring farm where a horse had been deliberately set on fire, to move the remaining horses to safety. It was some hours before they got back to Nymanada and by then the war veterans had made another decision. Now, they said, the cattle could only be taken off the farm on foot. This was a far from ideal situation as there was a major highway to cross to the neighbouring property which had offered refuge to the animals but there was no choice.

The cattle had been without water for two days and were very vocal as they were finally walked off Nyamanda Farm. As had been the case with the pigs, the farm workers who knew every animal on the farm and had earned their living tending the animals, now only agreed to assist in herding the cattle if they were paid in cash. They knew these were not only the dying hours of the farm but most likely also their last chance to earn a few more dollars.

An hour later 250 head of cattle and calves were gone and Nyamanda Farm was becoming eerily quiet. Then 70 sheep were walked off the farm to another neighbour and the SPCA team drove behind with all the newborn lambs. Slowly the lifeblood was ebbing away from this 2,000 acre farm which had employed 250 people, grown 220 acres of maize, 200 acres of tobacco and reared pigs, cattle and sheep.

When all the pigs, cattle and sheep had gone, Meryl's job was almost done and she turned her attention to the dogs and cats. They were caught and loaded into the SPCA truck, their names becoming the last roll call from the farm garden. The dogs: Shadow, Jody, Spud, Shandy and Fudge; the cats: Thumper, Casper and Bluebell. As soon as the pets were loaded Meryl and Addmore drove to Karoi to reunite dogs and cats with Chris and Eleanor Shepard who waited in a car park, their lives in shattered fragments. The reunion was fairly chaotic as Meryl later recalled:

'It was all a bit hurried because I was worried if they jumped out of the car on their own we would never see them again – being farm dogs. So it was all a bit of a mad scramble with Chris, Addmore and I trying to grab legs and collars etc. I am sure there were lots of joyful greetings from the dogs once they were safely in the Shepards' car.'

On the very last trip to Nyamanda Farm, Meryl rescued the bantams which crowed and flapped in the back of the truck. By then the seven horses had been walked to a neighbouring farm and now it was almost over. Meryl and Addmore took one last drive around the barns and farmyard to make sure that no animals had been missed. Beside the barns they found a cow that had just given birth to a calf but there was no way the mother and baby could be moved and so Meryl had to leave them. As they went down the drive for the last time they saw a large crowd of women wearing Zanu PF clothes – shirts, scarves and dresses – going through the security fence and towards the farmhouse. Within minutes they were peering through the windows of Chris and Eleanor Shepards home.

Meryl's last diary entry about Nyamanda Farm was a bleak and sad testament:

'Only a week before, this had been a thriving and productive farm and now it stood empty and silent, not an animal in sight except for the mother and calf – the latter's fate unknown. The pig sties, stables and sheep pens stood empty – children's toys scattered on the lawn. In the distance a barn door blew open and shut – would this farm ever be the same again? I doubted it and it was with a very heavy heart that Addmore and I drove away from Nyamanda Farm in Karoi for the last time.'

Extracts from Meryl's Diary:

'Work is love made visible.'
– Kahil Gibran, 1923

September 2002
Goromonzi:
Move ZNSPCA offices from Harare SPCA to Goromonzi where a local farmer has offered a house on his property at a nominal rent. It has accommodation upstairs for the Inspectors and an office on the ground floor.

Manage to get the entire place fenced for free thanks to a generous donation and it will be ideal for keeping our equipment and give room to keep any livestock that we may need to look after.

Harare:
One evening on the way home I decided to collect some dry grass that the Municipality had cut near the Sheraton Hotel. Since we always have livestock with us on a temporary basis and because we can't afford to buy it, I'm always stuffing my truck full of hay whenever I see it lying in a public place. It was almost dark and I was very preoccupied with gathering up the dry grass and pushing it into the back of the truck. I thought I had the place to myself when suddenly I heard a voice with a deep Welsh accent asking, "Do you come here often?" It was the husband of one of the ladies at work; he'd seen the SPCA truck parked on the open land and wondered what the hell I was doing!

Bromley, Horseshoe Block, Darwendale, Norton, Karoi:
Addmore and I travel all over as the farm rescues continue unabated. Fortunately it leaves little time to think about my personal life.

CHAPTER TWENTY-ONE

Cannon

Cruelty is the first attribute of the devil.
— Proverb

Renroc Farm, Karoi, September 2002

Meryl and Addmore arrived at Renroc Farm in Karoi on a hot and dry day in mid-September 2002. They had been in the middle of rescuing animals from Nyamanda Farm but when the situation there became too tense to operate in and while they waited for police reinforcements, they visited the Cochranes' farm in the same neighbourhood. Renroc had been a highly productive farm growing 70 hectares of tobacco, 50 hectares of maize and 20 hectares of coffee. There had also been a 400-strong herd of beef cattle on the farm. When Meryl was asked to help, it was in connection with the horses on Renroc Farm. Reports were that one horse had been burnt to death by the farm invaders and there were fears that other animals could be in danger as the situation worsened on the farm.

Things had been building up for five days previously with frequent visits from war veterans, men in an army vehicle and large groups of people, at times up to 200, trying to intimidate Ian and Jo Cochrane and their family into leaving their home. A number of the war veterans were seen by the farmer to be armed and in the three days prior to Meryl's visit, there had been numerous serious incidents involving shooting, arson and looting. It was only later that Meryl would get to read the reports written by Ian Cochrane and even the briefest of extracts were chilling:

'I saw one man, armed with a shotgun, walk up to my house.'
'My mother was held at gunpoint, they took her pistol and radio.'
'One man opened fire on me.'
'One man had a loud hailer ... "Pamberi ne Zanu", "Pasi ne Cockren", "Today we are going to kill you Cockren."'

'The vehicles were full of people and weapons. ...10 weapons ... at least 100 people.'

'Joanne tried to undo the poles of each loosebox to free the horses.'

'The mob started climbing over the fence and were coming towards me.'

'They started firing shots, first into the air and then towards us.'

'They started lighting the hay bales and paddocks around the houses as well as surrounding both houses in large numbers.'

'Shots continued to be fired for a considerable time.'

'My sister's house had been looted.'

'The farm trailer was destroyed.'

Meryl and Addmore found a bleak scene when they got to Renroc. Thin blue smoke still hung in the air, the smell was acrid and the atmosphere extremely tense. Ian Cochrane was preparing to speak to his 40 farm workers who were sitting on the ground near his tobacco barns. Describing how serious the situation had become, Ian said:

'Members of the CIO were visible in the crowd. The Support Unit had been sent to calm the situation on the insistence of the British Embassy after Jo contacted them and asked for assistance as she is a British National.'

As Meryl waited to talk to Ian she looked at the scene where such mayhem had unfolded. It was hard to imagine what the view may have been just a few days before. Perhaps it had been one of animals grazing, tails flicking at the incessant summer flies, piles of hay, brimming water troughs. Now the sight was of desolation. Several of the paddocks surrounding the homestead had been burnt very recently by the war veterans and the sight was of blackness: scorched shrubs, burnt grass and everywhere just ash and dust.

What had once been a large stack of rolled hay bales had also been incinerated by the land invaders and only the smouldering remains were left. Meryl could see that there was nothing at all left for cattle or horses to eat in these paddocks – both natural grazing and supplementary hay were gone. For the animals this was a desperate situation and had come at the worst possible time of year. With the rainy season a good month away, it would be many weeks before there was any natural grazing for the animals. Meryl already knew that the only option was going to be to remove the animals from Renroc Farm altogether and as soon as possible.

Ian took Meryl to the stables to show her what had happened to his horses and in particular to Bella and Cannon. To Meryl 'Bella' and 'Cannon' were just names but to the Cochranes they were friends, animals who were part of everyday life and with whom many happy memories had been made. Bella was Jo's horse, her first horse, and an integral part of her life on Renroc Farm as she described:

'Her full name was Serilla Bella. She was the first horse we had on the farm and she came with a companion – another unwanted horse of the race track. Bella was 11 years old when I got her and had been playing polocrosse, but she was an excellent show jumper also and was well schooled. Not being a terribly competent adult rider, I wanted a horse that I could trust and she turned out to be just that. She was also a chestnut, like Cannon, and was very sweet to me during the 10 years that I had her. I used to take her on long outrides on the farm with the children on their ponies and sometimes we would help to round up the cattle and bring them in for dipping. We would sometimes take the horses and ponies swimming in one of the farm dams and go for moonlit rides at full moon. I built a jumping arena on the farm and used to jump her a bit and even entered her into a three-phase event on neighbour's farm where we competed; we didn't do very well but we had a lot of fun. I had built paddocks very close to and surrounding my house so that wherever I looked I could see the horses on the farm. The horses and the cattle became my whole life.'

Cannon, a big 16-hand chestnut was also an ex-racehorse. When he first came to Renroc farm he had been thin and run down but soon responded to the carefree days on the farm, the wide open spaces and plenty of food. A special bond soon developed between Jo's 10-year-old nephew, Russell, and the huge horse. Russell taught Cannon to jump and to do gymkhana and sometimes they would go out and round up the cattle in the late afternoons. When Cannon got horse sickness one year Russell spent all his time in the stables, tending to the animal's every need and the two became very special friends – a big retired racehorse and a little boy, both living a carefree life on a farm.

Ian and Jo Cochrane were both at home on the farm on that terrible day when the war veterans and land invaders started burning and shooting; luckily their children were not there. Ian told Meryl what happened when he and Jo had gone to the stables late in the afternoon to feed the horses.

'The horses were each in their own individual looseboxes eating when two vehicles drove up to us. The vehicles were full of people and weapons (approx. 10 weapons). More people ran up to us. There were at least 100. Joanne tried to undo the poles of each loosebox to free the horses while I monitored the situation. The mob started climbing over the fence and were coming towards me, shouting and behaving in a very threatening manner. Jo abandoned her attempts to free the horses and moved back towards me.'

Shots began to be fired, first into the air and then at the Cochranes and the couple had no option but to run for their lives, hoping their animals would be ignored by the crowd. The couple locked themselves into their house but Jo feared the worst. She could hear but not see or intervene to help the horses:

'For a couple of hours we knew that one of the horses had been hurt because as we raced away from the stables after trying to feed them we could hear the horse's screams as we scrambled through our gate and locked ourselves in our yard. We couldn't see what was going on though as they had set fire to the huge hay stack in the paddock between our house and the stables and the fire and smoke obliterated our view of what was going on.'

Some time later one of the grooms radioed the house to say that Bella and Cannon had been burnt in a fire. By then it was dark and Ian and a friend who had come to help, crept out into the night, hoping that the war veterans had gone and that they were not going to be shot at. They went down to a paddock where they found Cannon in a paddock with the other horses, dazed, shocked and in a dreadful state. Ian and his friend led Cannon away from the other animals and shot him immediately.

The memory of that horrific day was still vivid in Ian's mind as he walked alongside Meryl who wrote in her diaries what was left to see two days after the event:

'They believe two of the horses had hay put around and on top of them and were then set on fire. Jo later told me she heard a scream from the direction of the stables, from Cannon – a beautiful chestnut thoroughbred with a white blaze. Bella sustained minor burns but managed to break out. Cannon was very badly burnt and when the siege was over he was found still alive but in a very poor state. He was blind and had fluid coming from his nose and mouth indicating that his lungs had been damaged.'

Meryl took photographs of Cannon's body and the evidence of the barbarity was still there for her to see.

'The burnt grass and straw could still clearly be seen on his back where his attackers had piled it. A shocking unnecessary death of an innocent animal caught up in this political mayhem.'

Meryl urged Ian to lay charges against the perpetrators under the Prevention of Cruelty to Animals Act and then they discussed the fate of the remaining horses. There was no option and it was soon agreed that all the horses should be moved off Renroc farm and taken to a neighbouring property. Meryl and Addmore went into action immediately.

'To get the five horses up to the house, where the horsebox was, we had to walk the horses past the stables where the incident had taken place. Without exception, they all became very jittery and we had a job to hang on to their bridles. Once past the stables, they settled down again.'

As Meryl and Addmore loaded the horses, other people arrived to help and even after such horror Meryl felt encouraged by the spirit of unity and togetherness.

'Ian's mother came out with a lovely framed photo of Cannon and her grandson in happier times. She said that he had the most wonderful temperament and the whole family was devastated at what had happened to him. Chris Shepard had come over to help with Ian's horses and three trips later all horses were safely on a neighbouring farm. At the same time another friend of Ian's was helping to get his tobacco off the farm – once again I was impressed by how the farming folk continue to rally round and help a neighbour in times of trouble.'

Meryl closed her records on Renroc hoping that one day in the future there may be a Cannon Memorial Race at Borrowdale Park. She wrote:

'I believe this was one of the cruellest acts perpetrated by the government-sponsored land invaders – and we must never forget.'

Extracts from Meryl's Diary:

'When it hurts to look back and you're scared to look ahead,
you can look beside you and your best friend will be there.'
– Anon

September 2002
Goromonzi:
Now that I am on my own it makes sense to find a place of my own in the Harare area. This is where I need to be almost all the time as the majority of the farm invasions are in the Mashonaland area. I have been staying with various friends all these months – Pat Webb, Stella Killick, Mike and Angela Neighbour, Nigel Wilson – I will always appreciate it, they've been nothing but kindness to me.

I have rented a cottage in Milne Park in Ruwa. Coincidentally it was my father who had been the driving force behind getting these cottages established for retired folk many years before. Little did we know that one day I would benefit from his earlier vision. The cottage that I am in has a plaque on the wall that reads: "The Leslie Anderson Block" — my father!

Centenary:
Out to a farm with a vet to destroy a 15-year-old thoroughbred stallion. Owners evicted and not allowed to return. Farm apparently been taken over by a woman, a political 'bigwig'. Arrived to find signboard being repainted with name of woman who has taken over. Women in farmer's garage making peanut butter. Find the horse in shocking conditions. A single shot brings a quick and merciful release.

CHAPTER TWENTY-TWO

In Memory of Stompie and five hundred others

Four-Feet:
I have done what most men do,
And pushed it out of my mind;
But I can't forget if I wanted to,
Four-Feet trotting behind.

Day after day, the whole day through –
Wherever my road inclined –
Four-Feet said, 'I am coming with you!'
And trotted along behind.

Now I must go by some other round –
Which I shall never find –
Somewhere that does not carry the sound
Of Four-Feet trotting behind.
– Rudyard Kipling, 1932

Tredar, Mashonland West, September 2002
When Meryl was called in to help hundreds of dogs at Tredar, she walked into a nightmare. It was to go on for nearly three weeks and involve many people, all of whom would be deeply, permanently scarred by the events that were to follow. This is not a story of bravery and heroism and fluffy cuddly pets. It is a story of horror but also of mercy. It is a true record of what happened and is written in memory of all the dogs.

Tredar was a security association providing guards and dogs to farms in Mashonaland West. It was not a farm nor had it been seized by the government. It was not closing down or going into liquidation but at the beginning of

September 2002 the security guards suddenly began making the same demands as farm workers on seized land. The guards said they wanted to be paid what had become known as 'packages'. These payments, stipulated by a newly introduced Statutory Instrument (S16 of 2002), required farmers whose property was being seized by the government to pay large amounts of compensation to their farm workers who were also being evicted from the land.

Despite the fact that farmers were being evicted without receiving any compensation for their homes, buildings, infrastructure or businesses, farm workers were in a similarly desperate situation. In many cases the farm workers had been born and spent all their lives on a particular commercial farm. They were men and women with their families and even extended families, who had no other homes to go to, no other way of earning a living and no qualification aside from farm work.

The farm workers, suddenly redundant and abandoned by government were left with only one direction to turn to for money – their employers – the very farmers who were being evicted. As 'packages' were calculated, assets sold to raise capital and meetings held with Ministry and Union officials, workers often became suspicious and anxious at the delays. They resorted to angry demonstrations, barricaded farmers into homes and offices, and kept up a continuous barrage of shouting, whistling, drumming and banging, accompanied by threats, taunts, insults and other crude tactics designed to intimidate and harass. These frightening encounters were known as 'jambanja' and just hearing the word was enough to cause the hairs on the back of your neck to stand up.

Paul Hopcroft was the CEO of Tredar and had been involved in the company since the very beginning as he explained:

'In 1987 the farmers in the Trelawney/Darwendale (hence the name Tredar) farming areas decided to form a Security Association to combat the ever-increasing crime in the areas. I was contracted as a Security Consultant to start the Association off. It belonged to all the farmers from the beginning until the end. I started with four dogs, two men and a second-hand Land Rover in March 1987.'

By September 2002, just before the trouble erupted, Paul was changing his personal circumstances and going to live in Ruwa, a small country area north east of Harare. Paul was to remain the CEO of Tredar and commute to Banket regularly and an assistant had been engaged to deal with the day-to-day running of the company. Tredar had grown into an enormous undertaking by then, employing 1,000 security guards and with 650 trained dogs, 18 pick-up trucks and two cars.

Despite the fact that Tredar was not being acquired by government or closing down and after weeks of meetings, the Workers' Committee representing the security guards would not be moved and continued to demand packages. Paul explained that if Tredar was forced to pay these packages then the Association would become insolvent and all moveable assets would have to be sold to meet just a part of their demands. The guards obviously did not believe Paul and responded by saying the Association was rich because it had lots of vehicles and if Tredar could not pay, then the farmers were rich and so they must pay.

Desperate and often heated negotiations, meetings and representations were made and for the next 11 days every attempt was made to save the company, the employees and the dogs from a shocking end. It was not to be. The security guards were demanding more money than the company could pay. Requests for arbitration from the Ministry of Labour were met with delays and then more delays until finally the guards took matters into their own hands.

Over the weekend of 21 and 22 September 2002, a total of 602 Tredar security guards left their posts, abandoned their dogs unattended on farms and returned to the Tredar bases. That weekend Paul and his wife were held under house arrest by a mob of striking guards. On Monday 23 the Ministry of Labour made a ruling, ordering all Tredar guards to resume work immediately. The guards refused. Paul and the Tredar Transport Manager were held hostage again for two hours until the police effected their release.

The following day Paul, his wife and two senior executives were subjected to 15 hours of continual verbal abuse, shouting, whistling and banging on tins and drums by over 100 guards who had surrounded the company house. The following morning Paul walked out of the house and saw that the striking guards had dug three shallow graves in the garden and placed crosses and flowers at each one. The graves were for Paul and Di Hopcroft and the Tredar transport manager. It was a crude and frightening intimidatory tactic frequently used by war veterans during the land invasions to try and scare farmers into abandoning their homes. These symbolic graves provided further evidence of the outside influences involved in the Tredar situation.

Paul knew the writing was on the wall. He contacted Meryl because by then hundreds of dogs had been left abandoned on farms for two days. It was hard to believe that security guards who worked day in and day out with dogs would desert their animals – their partners and protectors – but they had. Almost from this point onwards, Meryl would be on her own when it came to the Tredar dogs as Paul later explained:

'In effect I was under house arrest from 21 September to 10 October and Di got out on 28 September. House arrest meaning we were guarded in our house at night and if

I had to go anywhere I had to have an "escort" in case I ran away!'

After Paul's phone call, Meryl went out to the Nyabira Base to see for herself what the situation was. It was 24 September, the problems had been going on for three weeks and she expected trouble. Meryl had Addmore with her and a police Constable as an official escort. On arrival at the Nyabira Base they came to a boom across the driveway and attached to it was a battered piece of cardboard with a crudely written message: 'Closed for packages'. Those three words told a tale that was being repeated on hundreds of farms across the country.

Despite the sign, Meryl drove in. The only person at the Tredar Base in Nyabira was a Tredar security guard, Sergeant Jimmy Zuze. Jimmy had not joined his striking colleagues and had been undertaking an enormous task on his own which Meryl described:

'Jimmy had been trying to feed and water all the dogs at the base by himself – he had even borrowed a bicycle to get to dogs that were deployed on farms in the area. Sgt Zuze said that the rioting guards had destroyed all the company records, including the deployment book and so it was very difficult to know which farms had Tredar dogs on them. When the guards had gone on strike, they had abandoned all their dogs, leaving them chained to trees, gates, etc; they had also destroyed the radios, telephones and commandeered all the vehicles.'

As Meryl stood talking to Jimmy she began to realise the enormity of the task ahead. Over six hundred dogs were deployed on 480 farms – but which farms? Meryl knew that some farms had more than one guard and that other farms had guards without dogs – but she did not know which was which. It was hard to know where to start but Meryl began by thanking Jimmy for everything he had managed to achieve single-handedly. She promised him a vehicle and an SPCA Inspector to help by the following morning – at least then they could get out to the farms where they thought the dogs were.

As they stood talking, a Tredar vehicle raced into the yard. It was one of the vehicles that had been commandeered by the striking guards and was crammed with the angry workers, many of whom appeared to be drunk. Meryl took a breath and mentally braced herself for a confrontation.

She knew that earlier the Tredar Dog Master, accompanied by a police escort, had tried to get onto the base to attend to the dogs but things had got out of hand very quickly. The angry, striking security guards had grabbed the policemen's hats and kicked them around like footballs and then chased them away. The Dog Master and police had run for their lives, jumping onto the truck and racing away moments ahead of the mob.

Meryl was determined to stand her ground and asserted her authority immediately, putting some sanity into a situation which could only be described as anarchy. Meryl warned the striking guards about taking care of their dogs, saying the SPCA would charge them with cruelty if the animals suffered during the wage negotiations. There was silence as Meryl spoke and then, when asked, she leant on the bonnet of her truck and put her words in writing for the men to take away to tell the other guards. It was a short confrontation, some of the guards were openly hostile, but the meeting passed without incident. Meryl could only hope that her warning may help the stranded and distressed dogs who had been left shackled and without food and water on remote and unoccupied farms. Later she learnt that the message contained in her scribbled note had spread like wildfire and all she could do was pray for mercy and compassion for so many innocent victims.

For the next two days the SPCA team visited dozens of farms giving food and water to stranded dogs. On some farms, realising that the Tredar security dogs had been abandoned, the farmers fed and watered the dogs themselves, but there were many cases where the dogs had been left totally alone. In these cases the dogs were taken back to their respective bases. Soon there was no option but to chain some of the dogs to trees in the bases as kennel space ran out and after just two days the enormity of the task at hand was almost overwhelming.

Tredar had a main base, known as Group Headquarters, which was in Banket town and six sub-bases located in a vast farming area stretching from Darwendale, just west of Harare all the way to Doma, north east of Karoi. The sub-bases were at Trelawney, Nyabira, Raffingora (Ayrshire Club), Banket (Weltevrede Farm), Umboe (Fupi Farm) and Doma (Doma Club). At each base there were offices, communication systems, guard accommodation and kennels for the dogs. Each base operated independently, deploying dogs and guards into the surrounding farming areas. Meryl called for the help of her friend and colleague Chinhoyi SPCA Inspector Belinda Bowie and more staff came out from Harare too. Between them they could at least spread out and cover more ground.

Meryl and Belinda went to the Umboe Base and began to get an idea of what to expect:

'There were still one or two loyal guards who were feeding and watering the dogs, but no cleaning of the kennels was being carried out. They did their best to try and remember where various dogs had been deployed and we started compiling a list of dogs to be uplifted. Whilst we were doing this several of the striking guards came into the office. One of them, very drunk, asked me what we were doing there. "Doing *your job!" I replied. He didn't seem to like that remark very much and unleashed a stream of obscenities at me. With that his more sober companions dragged him out of the office.'*

Meryl, Belinda and Addmore visited as many farms as quickly as they could. There were lists and lists of them – farm names and dog's names and it was a mammoth task exacerbated by no records, radios or vehicles and the fact that there were nowhere near enough people to help. At one of the first farms they visited they found the dogs chained up in different rooms of a derelict building – without food or water and lying in their own urine and faeces.

The dogs were overjoyed to have the company, attention, a friendly word and a pat; they desperately gulped mouthfuls of food and water. Working from the memories of the few guards who had not gone on strike, priority lists were compiled: dogs that were alone, shackled, confined and in need of urgent uplifting. That night sleep was slow in coming for Meryl.

'I lay in bed that night at the motel in Chinhoyi and thought of all those dogs out there that must be wondering where their handler was. They would be hungry, thirsty and in many cases had no shelter from the sun beating down on them during the day – I wept for them.'

Meryl and her team spent the whole of the second day driving over an enormous area, looking for dogs abandoned by their handlers. On one farm they found Alice, a Black Labrador, who had been chained to a tree for two days.

On another property they found Mukiwa, a Boxer bitch, fed and watered but without exercise for some days. At other farms the dogs had been taken by the striking guards but no one knew where they had gone. One dog stood out on that day:

'We went to another farm that we had rescued dogs from during the trashing and looting of last August. There we found Stompie, a very aggressive Boerboel cross – his handler had been gone for several days. Addmore was usually brilliant at handling and calming down the most aggressive of dogs, but there was just no way that Stompie was going to let Addmore get into his kennel. All his hackles were up, he was growling and snarling at him. Whilst I was wondering how on earth we were going to get Stompie into my truck, Addmore had a very bright idea. He went and found the missing guard's Tredar overalls and once he had them on, Stompie greeted him like a long lost friend and Addmore was easily able to remove him from his run and put him in my truck.'

Soon all the kennels at all the Tredar Bases were full and the point came where no more dogs could be taken in. Under normal circumstances the dogs were continuously deployed out on the farms, only coming back to their respective bases every 6 weeks to rest and recuperate. As dogs came in, others that had been resting at the base kennels would go out on deployment. It was never intended or even required that all the dogs from one particular base would have to be housed all at the same time. Each base had kennels for just half their complement of dogs. The system of rotating and resting the dogs also applied to staff and at any time one quarter of the guards would either be on leave or in training. Meryl and the SPCA team and Belinda and her husband put everything else in the background and travelled to as many farms as they could, feeding and watering the dogs on site as there was literally nowhere to move the animals to. By then Paul had met with the Minister of Home Affairs and appealed for intervention. The attempt was fruitless as Paul explained:

'We had more guards (610) on the ground than ever before and this was explained to the Minister on 26 September 2002. He explained to me that irrespective of the numbers, there would only be 12 white commercial farmers on the land so I had "better close down".'

After the meeting with the Minister, Paul knew that the end had come and there would be no salvation for Tredar, the guards or the dogs. Meryl and Paul then made the joint decision that the majority of the dogs would have to be euthanased. There was no one to feed, water, exercise and look after hundreds of dogs. Most were frightened and traumatised by their abandonment and even though what had been done to them by the guards was heartlessly cruel, they were now in situation that could not be allowed to continue. It was literally impossible to get to all the dogs every day with food and water. The Tredar bases were full to overflowing already and the SPCA did not have kennel space for so many dogs either. Clutching at straws, Meryl explored every possibility but none was feasible:

'The sudden re-homing of over 500 dogs was just not possible logistically – who would house and feed them in the meantime? Re-homing is regarded seriously by the SPCA which takes time to check out respective new owners and their properties. All the dogs would have had to be sterilised before re-homing. And then there was the fact that the dogs had been trained to be aggressive – they could not have been re-homed with children. All the dogs would have had to be assessed for their temperament – the logistics of all that were just not feasible. I had always had the greatest of respect for the veterinary profession in Zimbabwe, and the fact that local vets were offering *their services without charge, to help with the euthanasia, confirmed to me that they realised no other decision could be made and that trying to save all those dogs was just not an option.'*

Once the shocking decision had been made, Paul and Meryl both tried to focus on what had to be done. For Meryl the logistics of the job ahead were vast. All the dogs would have to be relocated from the farms to the Tredar bases. Large quantities of Euthapent (the drug used for euthanasing animals) were going to be needed and it took some frantic phone calls and desperate pleas to arrange this.

'Laying our hands on enough Euthapent or Euthatol was a huge problem; there just wasn't enough to destroy that vast number of dogs in the whole of Zimbabwe. Initially, I begged and borrowed from other SPCAs and private vets until the consignment from South Africa arrived, courtesy of the Zimbabwe Pet Rescue Project – what a star Anne Kempen and Estelle Walters were in sourcing the drug so quickly for us. Several vets also donated some bottles. We made do using needles and syringes several times over, until new supplies arrived. This was obviously not something that happens in the normal veterinary world, but there was nothing normal about the situation we were dealing with.'

Paul had to try and sell all the company assets in just a few days to raise some of the capital being demanded by the guards. There were not enough assets and the negotiations were volatile with Paul regularly being verbally abused, held hostage in his home or office and threatened with death by the guards. Paul was never allowed to drive anywhere without an escort from the Workers Committee and he was unable to help Meryl at all. Paul described the scene when he arrived to make a partial cash payment at the Tredar headquarters in Banket:

'On arrival at the HQ the number of guards, most of them drunk, amounted to some 800 and caused havoc on our arrival at 6pm. The police had to fire two teargas grenades and 2FN rounds in order to quieten them down.'

On Friday 4 October 2002 as Paul dealt with angry guards, Meryl, Addmore and vet Ant Donohoe had a police escort of two Support Unit members and it was a day none of them would ever be able to forget. There were none of the normal or familiar trappings of a veterinary surgery here – no clinical surgery, smell of antiseptic or discreet voices of white coated assistants. With a table carried out from the security base office and placed under a tree, they got on with the grim task.

'We worked as a team, each one with their own role. Addmore firmly but gently held each dog. I stroked and talked to each one. Ant expertly administered the lethal injection into a vein in the dog's right foreleg which took the drug straight to the heart and other vital organs. He always checked with a stethoscope that there was no longer a heart beat and it was all over in a matter of seconds. Later with the help of a local farmer who loaned his JCB, a large mass grave was dug. My truck was continuously loaded with the limp bodies and I drove to the site to off-load them.'

54 dogs were euthanased and buried at the Umboe Base on Friday 5 October 2002.

That night as Meryl walked into the foyer of the motel in Chinhoyi the bar was packed with good-looking, well-dressed people laughing and joking as they sipped from frosted glasses. Seeing them bought Meryl close to tears. These people and their lives were so far away from the reality of what was happening in Zimbabwe – of the brutal events that were taking place just a few miles away. Meryl could not bear to be near them. Her head swirled with anger and despair and she felt totally alone and utterly out of place. For a moment she wondered how these people had spent their day, and if they knew or cared how she had spent hers. Meryl asked that a meal be sent to her room but when it came she barely touched it. Alone with her thoughts, the horror of what she had had to do was vivid. In silence Meryl drank a Scotch and soda and sat numbly in a chair – she could not get the events of the day out of her head.

There was no rest from the horror even on Sunday as there were far more dogs than kennels at the Nyabira base and the situation had reached crisis proportions. Dogs were tied to trees and doubled up in kennels. There were then 111 dogs at a base which had only 50 kennels. Fights were breaking out all the time and none of the dogs were getting any exercise at all. Addmore and Jimmy had managed to feed and water all the dogs but there had been no time to clean the kennels so the dirt and flies were building up to serious levels – made worse by the searing October heat. Meryl had enlisted the help of Rose Nurse, the Chairman of Harare SPCA, Dr Richard Reynolds, a vet from Marondera who volunteered to help, and Addmore.

The four of them worked as a team. Rose, a level-headed ex-nurse, prepared and laid out the syringes. Addmore held the dogs, Meryl stroked, talked to and calmed the animals and Richard slipped the needle into the veins. The work was heartbreaking for everyone present on that sweltering October day. Meryl tried to talk to each dog by name; if she did not know the name, she made one up – it was the only comfort she could offer in those last moments of life. Almost all the dogs were calm, trusting and accepting, wagging their tails to the last. A couple had to be muzzled, Rottweilers and Ridgebacks, as they were a bit aggressive – perfectly understandable after what they had been through. As before a local farmer supplied a JCB and a mass grave was excavated. Again Meryl was there to the last and she watched, shocked and numb as the dogs were tipped into the giant hole. No one spoke but the emotions were palpable, raw, tortured. So many dogs with names and personalities – all had served so loyally and now it ended like this.

76 dogs were euthanased and buried at the Nyabira base on Sunday 6 October 2002.

At 8.30 the next morning Meryl and Addmore travelled out to farms in the area collecting more dogs who had been abandoned by their handlers when the strike had begun sixteen days before. A little after midday Meryl, Addmore and Dr Ant Donohoe started on their desperate task again. Everyone was quiet; numb with shock and trauma but there was no time for emotion and the work continued.

26 dogs were euthanased and buried at the Nyabira base on Monday 7 October 2002.

In the meantime the situation at Tredar headquarters remained very volatile. The local Bank Manager informed Paul and the Worker's Committee that the ten cheque books ordered (to pay 1,000 workers) were not available on the promised date due to a problem at the printers. The Worker's Committee were enraged, saying this was a 'secret' between Tredar and the bank. It was tragic and absurd beyond words that while this went on, healthy, loyal dogs were being put to sleep in their scores.

The next morning Meryl and Addmore moved on to the Ayrshire base in Raffingora where Dr Richard Reynolds took over from his colleague. They worked swiftly and as soon as they could they moved on to the Trelawney base. The situation there was utterly desperate. The dogs had not had food or water for two days and were all extremely stressed and were barking anxiously. The notes that Meryl recorded in her diary described a picture of such cruelty that it was hard to believe any man could do this to a dog, let alone a dog who had been a faithful partner.

'Where the kennel doors were broken, dogs had been chained inside the kennel, some so tightly that they could not even sit down, never mind lie down. Another 16 dogs had been chained to trees. Some, in their effort to escape, had gnawed through the branches. Near the kennel block we found a Rottweiler that had been chained to the pipe of a reservoir. At some stage he had fallen in and was standing up to his neck in cold water. One of the striking dog handlers stood idly watching the dog's frantic efforts to escape – but the surrounding wall was too high and he kept falling back into the water. The whole scene was a nightmare.'

Release for these dogs could not come soon enough and so the small team set to work. Making sure that no dog was euthanased in front of another dog and that all the bodies were carried out of sight of the kennels, they put the dogs to sleep as humanely and respectfully as they could – each given a stroke, a pat and one last sound of its name being spoken. Some of the dogs were so stressed and overwrought that they had to be muzzled. One large black-and-white dog was so aggressive that they injected the Euthapent drug into a lump of meat and waited for it to take effect and calm the dog to the point where it could be handled. The task was enormous, the daylight faded but the team worked on.

'We then turned our attention to all the dogs chained to the trees. It was now dark but there was no way we could leave until all the dogs had been seen to. I drove my truck close to where Richard was working and put my headlights on. We moved from tree to tree, each dog receiving the same gentle handling. Somehow it just seemed all the more poignant, putting dogs to sleep in the dim light.'

When everything was done they turned back to the big black-and-white dog who had been unapproachable before. He had eaten the drugged meat and was slightly subdued but was still not letting anyone near him or into the kennel. The dog was lying next to the wire and so Richard injected the drug into a muscle of his leg. Because the drug had not gone into a vein it took a little longer to reach his heart but eventually it did. The dog lay down, at peace at last, and drifted away. The Trelawney base was eerily silent, the work was done.

'At least 40 dogs were euthanased at the Trelawney base – maybe more, by the time we finished so late that night, I just couldn't go round counting them – many lying out there in the dark. Some of the dogs that had been left by the dog handlers chained to trees, we left – their now still bodies at the foot of each tree – their suffering was over at last.'

At the end of that horrific day and in the dark as she drove out, Meryl had one last encounter with the striking guards:

'As we drove out of the base a group of very inebriated dog handlers were weaving their way up the drive, all laden with shopping and boxes of shoes and new bicycles – purchases from their "packages". In a week's time they would have nothing left of their retirement payments. The OC of the base came to the window of my truck. I wound down the window and asked him why he had not seen to the dogs at his base before he went to Chinhoyi to go shopping and drinking. He just laughed.'

Later that evening, alone in a motel room in Chinhoyi, Meryl got a call from Robert Hardman, a well-known journalist with the UK *Daily Mail*. Meryl was exhausted, in shock and emotionally broken but this story, she knew, had to be told. The Tredar dogs were the innocent victims of a country gone mad and so she told the journalist everything. A few days later the *Daily Mail* told the story in a double page spread: 'Tragic Dogs of War – they are the forgotten victim's of Mugabe's war against white farmers – dogs condemned to death by his henchmen.' As the world read of the horrors, Meryl carried on with the job that no animal welfare worker anywhere, at any time, should have had to undertake.

20 dogs at the Ayrshire base and more than 40 at the Trelawney base were euthanased and buried on Tuesday 8 October 2002.

There was just one Tredar Base left to attend to but before they went to Banket, Meryl and Addmore spent a day travelling to remote farms, making sure no dogs had been missed and that none were still tied to trees or shackled in the baking heat without food or water. They rescued five dogs that day – taking them to the Tredar base in Banket.

Amidst the enormity of the tragedy of events unfolding at Tredar bases, there were smaller and more personal agonies also at play. Barricaded into their home and not allowed to leave, Paul and Di Hopcroft were held hostage by the striking security guards. The guards refused to let the Hopcrofts look after their own dogs or even take them into the house with them. For two days the dogs had no food or water and were sporadically stoned and beaten. Di watched helplessly as her dogs hid underneath the cars until at last she was able to get hold of Belinda Bowie. Belinda arrived with a police escort and rescued the dogs, taking them at first into kennels and then, when the dogs were at risk again, Belinda took them to her own home in Chinhoyi.

There were hundreds of guards and dog handlers milling around at the Banket headquarters. They were waiting for their final payments and the mood was tense and ugly. Tredar was now completely crippled. Money had been borrowed and a potential buyer had been found for the fleet of Tredar vehicles – together this would be enough to pay the guards. When the potential buyer arrived with police and drivers to take the vehicles away, the guards smashed his windscreen and both tail lights.

Nearly four hours later, persuaded not to cancel the deal, the buyer returned with police Support Unit officers. They found that all the vehicles' tyres had been let down and it took another two hours before that was resolved and the vehicles were moved. While all that was going on and hardly out of sight, Meryl, Addmore and Dr Ant Donohoe once again got on with their task. As they worked, guards walked passed on a number of occasions – whistling, calling out and shouting in derision.

115 dogs were euthanased and buried at the Banket base on Thursday 10 October 2002.

On the last day of this most horrific affair Meryl again worked at Banket, this time with another vet, Dr Astrid Heulin, who had offered to help. In her diary Meryl recorded the final details:

'I could see this affected Astrid deeply and most of the time her eyes were full of tears as she carried out this unhappy task. By lunchtime we had finished and we headed back to Harare. Mt first port of call was the boarding kennels where I went to collect my own dogs that I had had to leave there for over a week. That night they got extra hugs and treats. To see their sheer joy at being home again took some of the pain away.'

39 dogs were euthanased and buried at the Banket base on Friday 11th October 2002.

In the following days and weeks Meryl received anonymous hate mail and in the government-controlled *Herald* newspaper she was referred to as 'that murderess from the SPCA'. In that same week, however, vet Ant Donohoe was quoted in the press as saying that his practice was putting down an average of 60 pets a week as people left the country. Even though she knew that there had not been any other option for the Tredar dogs and that the most compassionate thing had been done for the animals, the memories and accusations hurt Meryl beyond words.

Three months later, in January 2003, Meryl was in Chinhoyi and went to check on the welfare of some of the few remaining Tredar dogs that had not been euthanased. Mostly these involved cases where farmers were still on their farms and had begged Tredar that they be allowed to keep the dogs. There was no way of knowing or checking on the fate of many other Tredar dogs who had been stolen by the ex-security guards before Meryl and her team had got to the farms in October. These dogs were never to be seen again.

If Meryl had doubted the decision to euthanase the majority of the Tredar dogs in October, what she saw three months later convinced her the right thing had been done.

'When I returned to Chinhoyi at a later date to check on dogs that had remained on farms it was to find that in some cases the ex-Tredar dogs, were now living in appalling conditions. This had come about because they now didn't really belong to anyone – not to Tredar and not to the commercial farmer. Whilst guards from other security companies were now guarding those farms, the companies involved took over the

dogs, but because they were based many miles away in Harare, there was now no Dog Master going round the farms on a regular basis to check on their welfare. In some cases warnings were issued and in one case a farmer was charged with cruelty.'

Over 500 dogs were euthanased in those first 10 days of October 2002. Meryl had only recorded three hundred and seventy. It had become just too painful to keep reducing lives to numbers but to each and every dog Meryl gave a last moment of human affection and a merciful and dignified death. For the dogs it was over but for Meryl, the SPCA team and the vets, the horror would remain as a tormenting memory for the rest of their lives. Writing about it four years later Meryl said:

'Even today I have nightmares about the euthanasing of all those hundreds of healthy dogs, but the alternative, I later discovered was worse. In Zimbabwe, with such chaos on the farms and so many people leaving the country, there was just no alternative. Perhaps the real tragedy was that ironically, many of those Tredar dogs were family pets of farmers who, on leaving the country, had donated their pets to Tredar rather than face having to have them put down.'

Finding peace after Tredar was not easy for Meryl or any of the people who had been involved in the events of October 2002. There were few positives but one came in the form of Jimmy Zuze, the Tredar guard who had refused to join his striking colleagues and had single-handedly fed and watered scores of dogs. Jimmy was offered a job by Meryl at the ZNSPCA. Jimmy accepted, was trained and went on to become an excellent Inspector for three years.

Sadly he passed away from AIDS in 2006 but his last years had been spent giving comfort and relief to many animals and showing other people to do the same.

The foreign press called them the 'Dogs of War', but to Meryl the Tredar dogs were the innocent victims. They were friends, companions and loyal protectors who worked on farms during the worst of times in Zimbabwe's land invasions. Closing her records Meryl wrote:

'The tragedy of Tredar was one of the worst spin-offs from the farm invasions, but I know we did the right thing. It was a harrowing decision to make — but with the passage of time, I still believe it was the right one. We could not promise the dogs a good life but we could promise them a good death.'

Extracts from Meryl's Diary:

*'If there are no dogs in heaven,
then when I die I want to go where they went.'*
– Anon

October 2002
Harare:
After Tredar I knew more than ever how we couldn't have done this work without the tremendous support of South Africans, the NSPCA and in particular the Zimbabwe Pet Rescue Project in Cape Town. Ann Kempen, Estelle Walters and her group of friends have done so much. Ann first contacted me in 2001 and she wrote later and explained how it got going:

'Estelle had read about the plight of the animals and so she raised some money among family and friends and sent a donation. We then realised the extent of the danger facing the animals as well as the difficulties facing the ZNSPCA and from that we saw this was an ongoing and horrific crisis and that we could not stop at one donation.

We then decided to spread the word as far and wide as possible by asking friends and family to send emails and the photographs that we had to everyone they knew. Gradually it was picked up by people on the internet and they started publishing our letters on their websites. We then wrote to local magazines and newspapers in an effort to gain more awareness. The bulk of the publicity came from email press releases to newspapers and radio stations and we also held events. We even had a horse-riding event along the main road from Fish Hoek to Cape Town; this attracted a lot of interest.'

Between them they did so much to raise money and awareness for the plight of the animals left behind on the farms. The farm rescues would never have been such a huge success without their fantastic support. They gave so much including a Nissan pick-up truck; a double horse box; essential equipment including sterilisers, operating equipment, syringes, needles, sutures, rubber gloves, de-wormer and dip and the essential drugs that we were so desperate for including: Bomathal/Thiopental, Ketamine and Acepromazin injectable, Parvo vaccine, ACP tablets, antibiotics, Cortico, Prednisalone, Atropine, Tominol and Ivomec. They even sent a consignment of animal food when we were desperate.

Of course for the work at Tredar it was Ann and her friends that donated the many, many bottles of Euthapent and Euthatol that we needed.

Johannesburg, South Africa:
The BBC fly me to Joburg for the day to interview me for their 'Country File' programme on TV. This day trip necessary because the Zim government will not allow the BBC into the country.

Bulawayo:
A friend in Bulawayo pays my electricity bill – had completely forgotten about my own domestic issues!

Johannesburg, South Africa:
Addmore and I drive to South Africa with 'Nandi' who is to be handed over to her new owners. Work with the BBC production team who had to fly into South Africa to film the footage they wanted on Addmore and myself in preparation for the fact that we had been nominated for the BBC Animal Awards. The filming took two days and when it was all over I had to say goodbye to my beloved Nandi.

28th October. Tim's birthday. I phoned him before I went off for the day and had sent a parcel a couple of days before. Headed off to Darwendale with a vet to destroy some horses that had been left behind by a farmer. Later collect the two horses belonging to an Air Vice Marshall that we have confiscated.

November 2002
Norton:
Abandoned horses need assistance.

Bromley:
More problems at the stud farm. Settlers have ploughed up most of their grazing.

Rusape:
Uplifted four stranded dogs. Had a vet destroy 13 of the abandoned horses – a heartbreaking day.

Glendale:
Collect cats from a farm.

Tengwe:
Go with Inspectors Augustine and Addmore to Tengwe to rescue seven dogs, two cats, one rabbit and seven tortoises – owners have been evicted and realise they aren't going to be allowed to go back... Saw a large crowd of workers at the barns but drove past without looking at them... On the back verandah we found the six tortoises and a rabbit in an aviary and the seven dogs: 'Jessie' – Doberman; 'Ginger' – Daxie; 'Brutus' – Miniature Pinscher; 'Patch' – Fox Terrier; 'Chloe' – Labrador bitch; 'Shannon' – male Lab; and 'Hooch' – a Boerboel. All very excited to see us, lots of

tail wagging and jumping up. Soon had them all in the back of the truck, tortoises and rabbits into cages and found the cats sunning themselves on the wall... Very large crowd of workers gathers... Addmore manages to establish that they were very angry because they had not been paid their packages and were not going to let us take the animals... One of the female domestic workers whispers to me that Caleb the Cook is not to be trusted...

Crowd outside the gate swelling and shouting growing louder... Augustine leaves through a small pedestrian gate out of sight of the mob to get help, Addmore and I let dogs out of the car, put rabbits and tortoises in the shade and prepare for a long wait...The cook informs the crowd that I am not from the SPCA but a friend of the farmer – tells them he saw me here having coffee on the verandah with the owners! All this incenses the crowd... Brutus, the Min Pin very worried by all the noise and sat on my lap shivering and shaking – other dogs did not seem unduly worried and lay down on the floor next to me – only too pleased to have some company.

Augustine returns with two workers who had spoken to police... now a very large crowd at gate who will not listen and who barricade us in. They drag an enormous piece of farm machinery and chain it to the gate and then pack large branches on top... Augustine gets away and goes for help again...

Two hours later police arrive with Support Unit and dogs. A Sergeant stands on the back of the police vehicle and tells the crowd in no uncertain terms that they are being very stupid and that animals don't have votes. He asks them what they will achieve if we leave the animals behind and they die because there is no food for them... He tells them to dismantle the barricade and let the SPCA go... Quickly re-load all the animals and get going. Out of sight of police we come across another barricade of tree trunks, lumps of metal and bits of farm implements. We dismantle it quickly and are finally on our way...

Dropped off our precious cargo of animals In Harare... dropped Augustine and Addmore in Goromonzi and it was after 9pm that I reached my cottage in Ruwa. I was utterly exhausted. 'Supper' was a packet of crisps and a scotch and soda – I woke up after midnight having fallen asleep in the chair.

December 2002
UK:
The BBC fly me to the UK for the Special Award for Outstanding Work in Animal Welfare that Addmore and I have been jointly nominated for. The BBC had suggested that just one of us come over and attend the event on behalf of both of us. ZNSPCA Chairman suggested that I attend and Addmore remain to continue with the rescues.

It was a fantastic, memorable evening, one of the main reasons being that I met just about everyone in animal welfare that I have admired and held in high esteem for many years, from David Shepherd to Saba Douglas-Hamilton, Jenny Seagrove, Daphne Sheldrick to David Grant the well-known vet in the BBC's Animal Hospital, Rolf Harris and Celia Hammond who runs her own Animal Trust Sanctuary in Sussex.

Had to be at the BBC London Studios by 6pm for a Champagne Reception, having been picked up by taxi, then on to a train, then another taxi to take us to our hotel – everything organised fantastically by the BBC and sponsored by More Th>n Insurance and there were many of us from all over the world. We then went through to the studio where we were seated at circular tables – sitting at my table were Saba Douglas-Hamilton, Celia Hammond, Jenny Seagrove, a vet and a lady from WSPA. Short films on each nominee were shown – all very touching and it just brought home the fact that there are so many fantastic people in the world who give their all for animals.

The BBC rep that I had been dealing with ever since I first heard that Addmore and I had been nominated – came to me and suggested that I prepare an acceptance speech in case we won. But as she had told me that there were three other people in the category, I thought, We don't stand a chance! I felt it was such a privilege just to be here and to lap up the fantastic atmosphere. Little did I know that all along they knew that Addmore and I were in a category of our own – The Special Award (Individual or Organisation), so when my name was announced by newsreader Fiona Bruce – I was absolutely stunned and speechless.

As Meryl walked to the podium to receive the awards for herself and Addmore, she was given a standing ovation by an audience of her peers – great, famous and highly-respected people in the world of animal welfare and conservation. Many had tears in their eyes but also enormous respect for this woman and her young colleague. There had been film footage of Meryl and Addmore at work and the young SPCA Inspector's words summed it up so well.

Addmore had said: 'Sometimes I do feel frightened to go onto the farms but we can't turn back, we have to help those animals.' Meryl gave a short speech in thanks and acceptance of the joint award that had been given to her and Addmore:

'I'm very touched and very humbled and very honoured to receive this Award. I'd also like to accept it on behalf of Addmore. It is great having him as a colleague; he never gives up if there are animals to be rescued and his courage is matched by genuine concern for the animals left behind on the farms.
I'd like to dedicate this to the memory of all the animals in Zimbabwe who've died,

who've been starved, bludgeoned, burnt and axed. You name it they've had it in this utter chaos that's been going on in the name of land reform in Zimbabwe.'

After the presentation we returned upstairs for the 'Award Winners and Finalists Celebration Party' and what a celebration it was: superb hot and cold snacks and a seemingly endless supply of wine. I wandered around with my friend Joan Gadd who I had been staying with in the West Midlands, speaking to all sorts of wonderful people in animal welfare, had my photo taken with Rolf Harris for OK magazine – David Shepherd wrote in my programme: 'Full of admiration – we must NEVER give up!' Eventually the coach driver came and reminded us for the fourth time that the coach was waiting and we reluctantly took our leave. A fantastic experience that I will never forget and one that I felt very privileged to have been able to attend.

14th December. Two days before I leave UK I receive an Award: 'In recognition of her work rescuing animals in distress' from The Staffordshire Bull Terrier Club. It is a beautiful crystal rose bowl which was presented to me by their President Mrs Barbara Beaufoy. It came as a wonderful, unexpected surprise.

Harare:
More problems with my heart. They are getting to know me at the Trauma Centre now!

Chivhu:
Checking on horses left behind at sale pens.

Masvingo:
Spend most of the month with Addmore and Inspector Happson from Masvingo SPCA, continuing our outreach programme with donkey owners in the area. Treated many donkeys. Mended harnesses and many education pamphlets in the vernacular given out.

Harare:
25th December. My first Christmas without Roly. Friends in Harare very supportive.

Ruwa:
26th December. Boxing Day – spent eight hours in a fuel queue at Ruwa – eventually left empty-handed. I am sure this is due to all the cars that were pushed into the front of the queue (while the security guards looked the other way!).

January 2003
Mvurwi:
New Years Day! Drove to Mvurwi with Jimmy after receiving reports of over 300 cattle that had been rounded up and fenced into a small area – most of them had

apparently already died. Went to Mvurwi Police Station — found two Constables on duty both drunk — in uniform too. One Constable sitting on the counter eating a mango... Both very hostile... The police Community Relations Officer sitting in a side office reading a Bible — he gave us directions to the farm and said he didn't think we would need an escort... Arrived at the farm but shunted around from one section to another... everyone very reluctant to talk to us...

Finally spoke to an assistant who told us that two weeks earlier, a war vet called Padzi had instructed the farm workers to go on strike 'for packages' ... workers confined 1,000 head of cattle to a small area on the edge of a soya field to pressurise owners to pay... we found a thickly-wooded area totally devoid of grass... workers had surrounded area with barbed wire and confined cattle — mostly weaners... there were several deep gullies full of rain water- ... sides were steep and slippery with mud... over 300 had died here — starvation, drowning, stuck in the mud, exhaustion... Tracks could still be seen where tractors had gone in to drag out the carcasses — they had apparently been burnt — piles of bones could still be seen, many of them appeared to be of very young cattle... It was the most depressing sight and I felt utterly sick to my stomach... There is apparently a government-to-government bilateral agreement with this farm... If there is a change of government the people involved in what went on here must be prosecuted — all those responsible. This must rank as one of the most heinous, deliberate crimes against a number of innocent animals that has ever been recorded. ... one of the worst things I have ever dealt with...

Harare:
Visit to Blair research laboratories to check on the living conditions of mice, guinea pigs, etc.

Goromonzi:
After a particularly harrowing week friends invited me to a braai (barbeque) and people were talking about bridge, book clubs, what they'd just bought at a craft fair, their husbands fishing trips to Mocambique, etc. I wanted to shout: 'Do you have any idea what's going on out there? What the farming community is facing? What the animals are going through?'

I needed to talk about what I had experienced but no one was interested. I feel as if I have nothing in common with so many people any more and feel very isolated.

CHAPTER TWENTY-THREE

'Dial 999 for Emergency!'

The iguana is not shut in.
(You cannot put fear into the heart of a courageous person.)
— Sindebele Proverb

Spring Farm, Karoi, January 2003

'Sport and Politics don't mix?

'Today, Alan Parson's wife Jenny went out to the farm [Spring] with son Andrew Parsons and friend Tim Withers (both 17), and daughter Rebecca (11). They were confronted by Mliswa, who has claimed the farm as his own, even though it has only received a Section 5 order. He demanded to know what they were doing there since it was no longer her farm and he was allowed by the police and DA to be there. Jen informed him that his occupation of her house and farming of her land was wrong. He exploded at that point, calling her "fucking white bitch" etc. He told her to read today's newspaper to find out what was really going on and how things had changed on the ground. She waited until he was finished, and told him that he was illegally on the property.

'Mliswa exploded again, told her that she was to get into her car, and that they were going to the police station. As she was approaching the car, he came up behind her and slapped the back of her head, snapped her necklace, and pulled her earrings off. The Parsons got into the car and started driving out of the security fence, they were suddenly surrounded by about 30 youths. Men were jumping on the bonnet, trying to grab the keys out of the ignition. They punched Andrew though the window, and Mliswa dragged Jenny out of the car by the neck and tried to steal her cell phone, but she managed to hide it under her shirt. He slapped and punched Jen a lot.

'Andrew asked them to leave his mother alone and they started hitting him whereupon a couple of others set upon Jen (about five of them), Mliswa called out to them saying, 'No marks – no marks!' – A youth came to beat up the son, who had now been

196

beaten to the ground and was begging them to stop hitting him and his mother. Four of them laid into him, punching and kicking. Tim was slammed into the canopy face first, and has suffered severe bruising, numbness and a very painful ear. They separated the three whilst kicking and punching them preventing them from helping each other or Rebecca in the back of the truck.'

– Canada Free Press

On 11 January 2003, Meryl got a call from Jenny Parsons desperate for help to rescue four horses from Spring Farm in Karoi. Jenny did not have to tell Meryl why she could not remove the horses herself, Meryl had seen the press reports and was shocked to have read the horrific details and to know that a woman, a young girl and two teenage boys had been set upon by a mob at Spring Farm. Jenny told Meryl that her daughter Rebecca was very traumatised after what had happened and was desperate to see her horses safely removed from the farm.

Meryl knew that this would most likely be a difficult and dangerous rescue mission and so she arranged for as much support as she could get. Meryl phoned Belinda Bowie, her friend and colleague at the Chinhoyi SPCA for help with the logistics and assistance with the loading and removal of the four horses. Meryl would bring one horse box from Harare and asked Belinda to arrange for a second. Belinda was also asked to contact DISPOL (Officer In Charge of District Police) in advance so that the SPCA team would be ensured of having an armed escort onto Spring Farm.

There was also the usual crisis situation with finding enough fuel for the return journey as the country was again crippled with petrol and diesel shortages. With this requirement Jenny Parsons could help and she arranged for Meryl to collect a donation from the ZTA (Zimbabwe Tobacco Association). When all the arrangements were made, Meryl left Harare towing a horse box and was accompanied by SPCA Inspector Jimmy Zuze. Their next stop was to be Chinhoyi where they would meet Belinda and on the drive Meryl thought about what she knew of the man who had taken over Spring Farm.

Temba Mliswa was a man in his early thirties and well-known in the sporting world, particularly in rugby circles. He had coached rugby in England during the 1991 World Cup and later coached in America but many published sources had little good to say about him. Writing in the *America Rugby Times* magazine, Foster Niumata said that one fellow rugby coach called Mliswa 'a smash and grab artist' and another referred to him as a 'snake-oil salesman'. In 2001 Mliswa set up a Recruitment Agency in the UK where he was charging Zimbabweans who were trying to get into the UK a thousand British pounds in exchange for immigration clearance.

In 2002 Mliswa's Recruitment Agency was closed down by the British government and Mliswa was deported back to Zimbabwe. Back in Zimbabwe, Mliswa continued to make news as a controversial figure. Sometimes called a 'personal fitness trainer', even the State-controlled press described him as: 'a controversial Zanu PF member who has been implicated in a number of underhand business dealings in recent years.' In early 2003 Mliswa nominated himself as the manager of the Zimbabwe Football Association and for a time seemed to be a law unto himself.

Meryl and Jimmy arrived in Chinhoyi and met up with Belinda and all the arrangements were well in hand. Belinda had two local SPCA kennel hands with her and two of her own grooms to help with the loading. The grooms were given ZNSPCA uniforms to wear to give them some protection and there was some comfort in the team of seven people who were about to travel to Spring Farm.

Belinda had already spoken to DISPOL who said that when they were ready they should see the OIC (Officer in Charge) of Karoi Police Station and he would provide whatever escort the SPCA team needed. As prepared as they could be, Meryl and Belinda in two vehicles, each towing a horse box and with their team of five helpers, set out for the Karoi Police Station. They got off to a slow start:

'On arrival at the station, it was to be told that the OIC had "gone to town for some shopping" and we were told to wait as he wouldn't be long. Whilst we were waiting outside the police station, Support Unit arrived with several police dogs in the back of the enclosed truck and promptly parked the vehicle in the boiling sun. I pointed out that with a little thought the driver could move the Land Rover Defender forward a few feet and park in the shade of the trees. This was done and the previously heavily panting dogs soon settled down. Also at the police station was a harassed-looking white farmer and his wife who apparently had just bought a quantity of maize quite legitimately from the GMB (Grain Marketing Board) to feed their workers on the farm, but were being told by the police to return it to the GMB. Just then a Sergeant from Support Unit came out of the station. He immediately recognised me – he had been very helpful in getting us released when we had been barricaded in at Zimyewe Estate in Tengwe. When he heard why we were waiting he immediately offered to escort us onto Spring Farm!'

A few minutes later they were on their way! In the lead was Sergeant Ngwenya driving a Land Rover Defender. His vehicle was packed with members of Support Unit and they were wearing helmets and protective visors and carrying baton sticks and Sergeant Ngwenya was armed with a pistol. The two ZNSPCA vehicles followed towing the horse boxes and Meryl was relieved and encouraged; this was more than she had hoped for and it had happened so quickly too – perhaps this was going to be easier than she had previously feared.

When they arrived at Spring Farm the gates were locked and being guarded by two surly youths. Sergeant Ngwenya ordered the youngsters to open the gates and the three vehicles drove in. Meryl couldn't help but smile to herself when another man appeared carrying a panga in his hand.

> 'The Sergeant mocked him and said: "What do you want that for? Put it away!" Sgt Ngwenya then explained that we had come to collect the horses and that there was to be no trouble. He pointed out one youth to me that he said was "a Border Gezi youth and in charge of security". He then informed the youth that he "would roll (he didn't say how!) if Mrs Harrison was stopped from removing the horses". With that Sgt Ngwenya wished me a cheery goodbye and said he was "off to the farm next door where there was trouble". I thought this had all been too good to be true!'

Meryl asked Sergeant Ngwenya to leave one police officer behind which he did and he said that if she had trouble he should get the Constable to call him on the radio. The Constable looked as apprehensive as Meryl felt and so she didn't delay another minute and drove straight down towards the barns where they could see the four horses grazing. Halters, food, experienced grooms and a quiet approach and in no time at all four horses were caught. Loading them was a different matter altogether!

Chianti was first. Twice they got him up the ramp but at the last minute he reared up and rushed out backwards. Chianti was a very good looking part-thoroughbred horse and he and 12-year-old Becky Parsons apparently made a fantastic pair, barrel racing in the Karoi district. Becky was the youngest member of the team and it was hard to believe that this same horse, so obedient and obliging with a young teenage girl, just wasn't going to be loaded by Meryl and her team!

They turned their attention to Tickey. She was an old bay mare and Meryl thought she looked the quietest and most sensible of the horses – and she was! With one old horse loaded so easily they turned their attention to the other old lady, Misty, who was over 30 years old. Age, it seemed meant nothing when it came to getting into a horse box:

> 'Misty's age and wisdom did not go together! About a dozen times we got her up the ramp but only by us methodically lifting each foot one at a time and pulling on a rope around her ample backside. But at the last minute she would come hurtling out, sending us all scattering. In her day Misty had apparently excelled in Pony Club events

even going to South Africa and wiping out the opposition. And to think that she was behaving as if she had never been in a horse box before!'

With just one of the four horses loaded and temperatures beginning to rise, Meryl noticed that the crowd of war veterans and youths at the gate was getting considerably larger and noisier. The one-and-only Support Unit Constable was being given a hard time; Meryl could hear the youths taunting him and demanding his particulars. Meryl told Belinda and the team of helpers that they needed to do whatever they could to speed things up. She could already see that they were going to have a problem when it came time to leave with the horses. Standing next to the horse boxes was a hostile-looking youth who was wearing a "3rd Chimurenga" T-shirt and he had a note book in his hand.

'Just relax!' Meryl said to him calmly, 'I'll give you my ID card and any other details about me that you want when we've finished.'

The youth didn't say anything but Meryl thought he looked a bit easier and perhaps this would buy her a little extra time.

Turning her attention back to the attempts to load the horses, now it was the turn of Jack. He was a good-looking part-Arab chestnut and he wasn't too difficult at all. By then some old 44-gallon drums had been found and had been put alongside the ramps to make it look less flimsy and intimidating for the horses. Jack resisted the ramp for a minute or two but a groom walking ahead with a bucket of food did the trick. The rest of the team kept a tight pull on the rope behind the horses' hindquarters and Jack was soon loaded. With two down and two to go, they turned back to Chianti who had calmed down by then. He resisted to the very end!

'We had several more abortive attempts, one of which resulted in him rearing up and taking some skin off his head but finally Chianti was in and we turned our attention to dear old Misty who was grazing unconcernedly nearby.'

With success and departure so close at hand, the youths got increasingly aggressive and began demanding that Meryl hand over 'documents' to explain why and where she was taking the horses. Meryl explained that she didn't have to give them any documents at all as she was acting under the Prevention of Cruelty to Animals Act and had permission for the entire exercise from the police in Karoi. As she talked to the youths Meryl could hear the three horses getting more and more restless in the horse boxes. It was a very hot and humid day and she felt the sooner they could get away the better. Turning away from the youths and trying to ignore their pressing demands, Meryl and the team tried again with Misty. As they had before, they moved her feet forward one at a time with their hands and finally she was in. They quickly managed to hook the chain up behind her tail so that she couldn't reverse out again and then Misty too was safely loaded. At that moment the Chairman of the ZNSPCA rang on Meryl's cell phone which was fortuitous as Meryl said she thought they were going to have problems leaving with the horses and at least now someone knew. The Chairman said she'd call again in 10 minutes.

The two vehicles, each towing their precious cargo in horse boxes, drove towards the main gate out of Spring Farm. The crowd of war veterans, Border Gezi youth and government supporters, was now very large. The mob closed and locked the gate and ordered Meryl to stop several metres before the gate.

Meryl did as she was instructed and was exasperated to be told that she was not going to be allowed to take the horses off the farm after all. The solitary Support Unit Constable repeatedly called on his radio, desperately trying to raise Sergeant Ngwenya and get some back-up but his increasingly frantic calls went unanswered. Inspector Jimmy got out of the vehicle and went to talk to the youths in an attempt to try and calm them down and Meryl and Belinda began raising the alarm. A call went to Kelvin Weare who had been Meryl's knight in shining armour during other Karoi farm rescues. When the ZNSPCA Chairman called again, Meryl asked that she contact the police. The situation was deteriorating rapidly and the tension was palpable:

'Several of the youths surrounded the two vehicles and were swishing the ground with sticks and kicking the ground close to the vehicles – all intimidatory tactics. The Border Gezi youth who had been threatened by the Support Unit Sergeant Ngwenya, had now changed out of his green uniform and was mingling with the crowd – possibly in the hope that we wouldn't recognise him and hold him responsible for the barricading. Our Constable was now standing on top of a trailer, trying to get a better radio signal and at one stage he asked me to dial "999 for emergency" on my cell phone! Belinda was now sitting in the front of my truck with me – we sat chatting, trying to look as unconcerned as possible.'

It was sweltering sitting in the car surrounded by dozens of angry, loud and aggressive youths but Meryl did everything she could to keep her self-control. From the very beginning of the farm rescues Meryl had learnt that it was imperative that she appeared to be in control at all times and did not take orders from the war veterans and farm invaders. She needed to continually re-assert her authority and that of the SPCA and even when she was personally frightened, Meryl worked very hard at maintaining the outward impression of calm and control. She noticed that many of the youths were holding two-way communication radios and appeared to be taking instructions from someone and Meryl was sure she knew who it was, even though he wasn't showing his face. Meryl knew he was responsible for this blockade. Even with the car windows wound right down, Meryl and Belinda felt as if they were melting in the sun. The horses were getting increasingly restless in the trailers, they could feel them moving around and hear them stamping their feet in discomfort.

Meryl was getting more and more desperate to bring relief to the horses, youths were leaning in the windows of the car, watching their every move, listening to the conversation and seemed to be totally unconcerned about the obvious agitation of the animals. Meryl, as an aside to Belinda, said, 'Who the hell are these people to tell us what to do?' Her words caused an instant storm:

'An older man in a khaki shirt and trousers who I later found out was Felix, Temba Mliswa's manager, who had been standing near my truck, had heard me. He exploded – demanded an apology from me, shouting that I had insulted the people, that I must get out of the truck and go and apologise – said that I had sworn at them, etc. I apologised as I didn't want to make an already explosive situation any worse.'

As the time dragged past and extended into hours, midday came and went and still there was no sign of relief or rescue. News of the barricading was spreading and Meryl received more calls – from John Worsley Worswick of JAG (Justice for Agriculture) who offered moral support and encouragement and from journalists who wanted information and details of what was happening. This was the second time in a week that Meryl and the SPCA team had been threatened and subjected to abuse while on farm rescues and now her concern escalated at the obvious distress of the horses.

'The two grooms were having a very hard time trying to pacify the horses who were now very restless. It must have been like a sauna in the horse boxes but we dared not let the ramps down to give them more air as it would have made them very vulnerable to attack and injury from the crowd.'

Felix came to the window of the car several times and each time he screamed at Meryl and Belinda, demanding that they let the horses out, saying that if they did then they would be free to go. Meryl was having none of it and she refused each time.

There was no way she was leaving without the four horses and she told Felix that she would wait for the police to come. They did, however, seem to be taking an awfully long time to arrive, Meryl thought, wishing they would hurry up!

'Twice a grey twin cab pulled up outside the gate – the driver we were told was Mliswa's business partner, but he made no attempt to come in. I noticed that the hostile youth with the note book rushed outside to the gate to show him my ID and Inspector's Certificate. A short while later a tractor and trailer drew up outside the gate and Felix came and told Belinda that she must move her truck and horse box out of the way.

'This was impossible as she had the day before lost reverse and fifth gear. This seemed to really annoy him and sent him off on another tirade against us. I told him that as Inspectors we are appointed by the Government. Felix said he also worked for the Government. I said, "Doing what?" This was met with silence and a glare. I asked the youths who continued to surround the truck what they wanted the horses for. One replied, "To look at every day". I explained that they cost a great deal of money to look after correctly; another youth then said that when Mrs Parsons left she had put them in charge of "everything including the horses".

It was a futile conversation and Meryl wondered how much longer it would be before the youths' impatience erupted into violence. The stand-off at the gate had been going on for almost three hours when at last help arrived:

'Inspector Khupeta and his men came in several police trucks and he immediately ordered the youths to unlock the gates and release us. He asked me to point out the chief troublemakers and said that they would be arrested.'

Suddenly, as quickly as it had started, it was over. Belinda got back into her truck and the two vehicles pulling their trailers drove out of the gates and away from Spring Farm. Meryl's hands gripped the steering wheel as she drove and a wave of emotions engulfed her. She was elated that they had saved the horses, something which had been far from certain as they had been sitting surrounded by a hostile mob.

'Once off the farm we stopped at the main road to check on the horses. They were pouring with sweat, so much so that the floors of both horse boxes were very wet. I thanked all of the SPCA team for their exemplary conduct. I was so very proud of each and every one of them. No one had lost their cool or panicked during the nearly three hours that we had been locked in and the grooms had an especially hard time under very trying conditions. We stopped near a farm store where there were quite a few trees, affording plenty of shade for the horse trailers. We let down the ramps at the back and opened the side door of each trailer allowing the breeze to blow through.'

Belinda had bought great piles of sandwiches and cold drinks for everyone and they ate quickly, no one wanting to be anywhere even remotely near Spring Farm! Before long the two trucks and trailers were on the road again, heading for a farm in Banket where the horses were to be dropped off. Meryl called Jenny Parsons on her cell phone and told her the good news and that they were on the way. Jenny was thrilled and told Meryl that both she and Alan would drive out from Harare so that they could be there to meet the team when they arrived in Banket.

With the end of the rescue now in sight Meryl suddenly felt herself swamped with exhaustion. Delayed shock began to set in and her hands started to shake on the steering wheel. A tearful and joyous reunion between owners and horses was just around the corner – that made it all worthwhile for Meryl but this was a rescue she was exceedingly glad was over!

Three months after rescuing the horses from Spring Farm, Meryl was shocked to learn of renewed violence at the farm. The press reports were chilling and Meryl knew just how lucky she and the SPCA team had been to get on and off Spring Farm without being hurt. Even the government-backed *Herald* newspaper carried the report on 10 April 2003:

'Sports personality Temba Mliswa was arrested on Tuesday for allegedly assaulting three police officers, a messenger of court and two commercial farmers. Police said Mliswa (31) and 10 workers at the farm became violent when police officers and a messenger of Court, Mr Brighton Chimba, tried to effect a High Court order.'

Meryl closed her notes on Spring Farm with a postscript – written in capital letters – as if to remind herself of just how bad things were for the Parsons family and could have been for her and her farm rescue team:

'THREE MONTHS LATER ALAN PARSONS, JOHNNY COAST, ZRP INSP KHUMALO AND THE MESSENGER OF THE COURT WERE SEVERELY BEATEN BY TEMBA MLISWA AND HIS GANG – ALL WERE HOSPITALISED.'

Extracts from Meryl's Diary:

The man who has confidence in himself gains the confidence of others.
– Hindu saying

January 2003
Harare:

As a result of the barricading at Spring Farm, I have now developed a close working relationship with John Worsley Worswick – CEO of JAG (Justice for Agriculture). Someone must have told him that we were in trouble there at Spring Farm and whilst I was sitting in the front of my truck with Belinda, he phoned. It was so reassuring to hear what was soon to become his familiar, deep voice, talking me through the whole thing. He reassured me that I could handle the situation and gave me such moral support – just as Kelvin Weare had done some months ago at Nyamanda and other farms in the Karoi area.

By now John was nearly always the first person that farmers got in touch with and he would immediately let me know if there was a hostile situation where the owners were being prevented from removing their animals. Our meetings were haphazard – depending on what was going on at the farms. He has an open plan office with a large, deep settee (that I always have great difficulty in getting out of!). It is always manic in his office with farmers coming in and out, swapping experiences of their latest jambanjas. John is always on the phone and always has a cigarette in his hand!

It was vital for the safety of the ZNSPCA team that John was able to give us a sitrep on what the situation was on a farm that we were planning to visit. John usually knows pretty well what sort of reaction we could expect from the police in a particular area – and of course the attitude of the local war vets and base commanders. John could also warn me of a possible deterioration of security in a particular farming area so that we could begin to make plans to evacuate animals. It was rare that I was able to get his undivided attention straight away – and even when we did start chatting there were always constant interruptions!

Concession:

Request to rescue seven dairy calves and five beef calves from a farm. Owners unable to return, stepson has been badly beaten up by war vets and settlers on the property. At the police station a Sergeant with an extremely bad squint finally appears and says he will accompany us – 'after his tea'! He disappears with a loaf of bread and reappears 25 minutes later and finally we get going... The familiar Zim flag has been planted and is fluttering on the end of a very long gum pole. Several posters with the President's face have been tied prominently to the farm gate... Angry workers, hostile war veterans, much shouting and arguing... finally get three small calves into the back of my truck and the mothers into the cattle truck... As we finished loading the mob *appeared round the corner. Troublemaker is a pink-shirted youth smoking a cigarette made from newspaper... Dropped our precious cargo at a farm in Bromley... Directed to a paddock of thick, lush green grass... Adults quickly unloaded and calves carried from the back of my truck to a joyous reunion with their mothers. Farm owner Sally very kindly gave Jimmy and me a box of grapes each and the owner of the cattle gave a very generous donation for the ZNSPCA.*

CHAPTER TWENTY-FOUR

Bart

'No society can survive, no civilization can survive,
with 12-year-olds having babies,
with 15-year-olds killing each other,
with 17-year-olds dying of AIDS,
with 18-year-olds getting diplomas they can't read.'
– Newton Gingrich, 1994

Duiker Farm, Beatrice, January 2003

'No secrets!' the youngster who called himself 'Taliban' shouted at the girl, 'No secrets with the white!'

'Taliban' was one of the more aggressive Border Gezi youths in charge of guarding Duiker Farm in Beatrice. His accusation and reprimand was directed at one of his fellow youth brigade members, a teenage girl, who he had seen talking to Meryl. Perhaps it was the girl's apparently friendly conversation that Taliban objected to or perhaps he'd been instructed to allow no contact between the youths and white people. Whatever the reason, Meryl thought Taliban's comment and reprimand was childish and she told him so, saying they were talking about the girl's late father who Meryl knew as he had once worked for the SPCA.

Meryl had seen nine of the Border Gezi youths when she arrived on the farm – five males and four females. They were so young that really they could have been described as boys and girls: most looked to be barely 16-years-old. They were all dressed in the menacingly familiar olive green uniforms which were obviously brand new, the shirts and trousers still distinctly creased on the folds, new from the factory. They all wore green floppy hats pulled down over their eyes and carried sticks – presumably to make them look threatening, mature and experienced but their age, behaviour and mannerisms (particularly that of the girls) gave them away. Even the police Constable accompanying Meryl commented on their age.

207

'Ah – these children are too young for this job!' he had said, his voice laden with scorn, almost contempt.

Meryl wisely said nothing in response. At that point there was little to choose between the young Green Bombers, as the Gezi Youth were popularly known, and the police Constable when it came to outward appearances. When Meryl arrived at Marirangwe to collect the police Constable assigned to be her escort, he was nowhere to be found. Eventually a villager located the Constable who was in the beer hall. Emerging in torn shorts, flip flops and with his shirt hanging out, the Constable had not bothered to change his clothes and didn't apologise for his attire or appearance. Dressed like this the Constable accompanied Meryl as her official 'police escort' and this in itself spoke volumes for the state of law enforcement in the country.

Meryl knew that this particular group of Green Bombers were newly arrived at Duiker Farm. She had been told whilst at the police station, and probably inadvertently, that the previous contingent of Gezi Youth brigade had been warned and then 'removed' from the property. Apparently the youngsters had been joy riding on purloined tractors up and down farm roads in the area from dawn to dusk. One of the youths had recently had an accident, careering into an oncoming truck and was then charged with 'driving without due care and attention'.

The situation at Duiker Farm in Beatrice was as complicated and tense as it could be and exacerbated by a squabble over occupation between war veterans and politicians with the youth militia being used by both sides. Beatrice, 54 kilometres south-west of Harare, had originally been named after a gold mine which was worked for 50 years until 1945 when ore reserves were depleted. The area went on to become a lucrative cattle-producing district with lush dairy farms and rich green paddocks visible from the main road.

En route to the farm for the first time, the view had changed considerably thanks to the farm invasions and Meryl tried to get her head around the facts that she knew. The farm owners had already left the property after being evicted by war veterans. They had sold all the cattle, including a working bull, to Obbi, a prominent figure in the country and a well-known supporter of the government and the land redistribution exercise. The deal had been concluded, the cattle had been moved off the farm but the Border Gezi youths refused to let the bull be moved with the others.

They said that because the bull was not listed on 'the invoice' they would not allow the animal to be moved. The 'invoice' was a detailed list of which animals were to be transported and the omission of the bull was simply a clerical error. The owners of the farm had been given 'permission' by the man who was taking over the farm to remove their furniture and personal possessions. This man, Russian, was a member of the CIO (Central Intelligence Organisation) and also a war veteran with a fearsome reputation. Russian had not given permission for the bull to be removed and so the animal remained stranded on the farm. The bull was obviously a desirable prize to whoever finally claimed Duiker Farm and all attempts to remove the animal were being firmly resisted.

Things became complicated when government Land Committee officials arrived on the property and said the farm was too big to have been given to one man and it should be subdivided. The confusion and animosity deepened when, according to the police Constable accompanying Meryl, 'some "Chef" in the CIO has taken over the farm', a fact that clearly did not go down well.

A cottage near the main farmhouse was being leased by an elderly man, Mr Van Heerden. Evicted from his cottage by Gezi Youths without notice or warning, Mr Van Heerden had left his pets behind, sure the situation would calm down and that he would be able to collect them the next day. When he tried to return Mr Van Heerden was turned back by Gezi Youths and in desperation, after four days, he asked Meryl to help rescue his two dogs and a cat.

Meryl, now in the middle of it all, was as informed as she could be of the disputes and complications. She knew that Duiker was a very dangerous place to be and that the situation was filled with tension and hostility. In her diary in her usual frank and casual manner, she wrote:

'Fortunately the police at Beatrice took my request for an escort seriously, the Inspector going twice to Duiker with a whole truckload of Support Unit to calm things down. The fact that he gave me two members of Support Unit and a police Constable – both armed with AKs – shows that he definitely knew we would be faced with aggression and hostility and I do believe he did his best to help.'

'Impartial' was Meryl's middle name and neutrality was her only safe route and so she turned her thoughts to Jock, a very old Staffordshire dog; Bart, a young Boerboel cross Ridgeback dog; and Smokey, a black-and-white cat. These were the pets which belonged to Mr Van Heerden and their rescue took priority. Meryl negotiated her way through Border Gezi youths and Land Committee officials and finally approached the farmhouse.

Before there was any chance of the cat getting scared and running away, Meryl called in the help of Mary, a house worker who knew the cat. Smokey was quietly caught, put in a cage and moved to the safety of the SPCA truck. Then it was the turn of the dogs and Meryl had to smile at the behaviour of Bart. The young Boerboel, who Meryl described as a very handsome chap, was hurling himself repeatedly at the gate and looking very aggressive, obviously taking his role of protecting the property with great seriousness! In the background, Jock, the old Staffie was barking himself hoarse at all the commotion and Meryl decided he should be first. Bart had whipped himself up into such a frenzy of noisy rage that he could well have attacked if anyone came too near. Eventually, deciding that she could get past Bart without being bitten, Meryl negotiated her way through the gate, past Bart and straight to Jock. The little Staffie was scooped up immediately and carried to the back of the truck.

Bart, the big, noisy and fierce beast that he was, took one look at his little mate sitting in the back of the SPCA truck and seemed to suddenly realise that he was on his own in this business. Bart shut up very rapidly, went to the truck and jumped into the back alongside Jock! There he sat panting loudly, tongue hanging out – the show was over and he had more than done his bit in defending the property!

Meryl had done what she came for but when she tried to take a few bantams that were running around the garden an uproar broke out. None of the onlookers were happy and said the birds were to be part of a 'poultry project'. Meryl knew that was extremely unlikely and her authority won the day.

'I did rescue the bantams – there was no way I was going to leave them behind. I took them out to our office at Goromonzi where they just about took over the house and the garden and thrived.'

On the way back to Harare Meryl phoned Mr Van Heerden with the good news that she had two dogs and a cat on board and he was thrilled. Again and again he thanked Meryl and she could hear the tears of relief and gratitude in his voice.

Just two weeks later the situation on Duiker Farm changed again and Mr Van Heerden was able to return to the farm. Violent altercations and threats had ceased and so Mr Van Heerden went back to the farm and took the dogs with him. The calm did not last long; just a fortnight in fact. War veterans and youth brigade members soon decided that sharing the farm and working together were not what they wanted and they barricaded farm workers into their homes and would not let them go to work. Other youths left the gate to a second homestead on the farm open and Jock, the old Staffie went exploring. Tragically he fell into the swimming pool and drowned.

As the bad feelings grew, Bart came under the spotlight for negative attention. Whenever he barked and tried to protect his property and territory, the youths pelted Bart on the head with hard, unripe avocados. It was clearly an untenable situation and so Meryl, accompanied by Inspector Jimmy, returned to Duiker farm for a second time. She was shocked to see how much weight Bart had lost since she had last seen him just a month before. Bart barked a little when Meryl arrived but he must have remembered how this operation worked and this time did not need any tempting or persuading to get into the truck.

Many of the youths had gathered around to watch and Meryl was struck by how young they were. The girls were smiling and giggling and had their arms round each other – just the way young teenage girls do when they are with their best friends or out on school adventures. How tragic that these girls were witnessing and assisting in the seizure of another person's property and then guarding it to prevent him from getting it back. This wasn't just farms and land that were involved here. It was personal belongings: clothes, furniture and private property.

As Meryl left with Bart in the back of her truck, she was filled with sadness at the thought of the youths and what would become of them and of the people whose lives they were destroying. Today's youths were tomorrow's leaders and to Meryl the future of Zimbabwe looked very bleak.

A few weeks later Meryl learnt with great sadness that Mr Van Heerden had passed away. The emotional strain of the last few months and events on Duiker Farm had all been just too much and had taken their toll on the elderly man.

Meryl's work on Duiker Farm was not over however because as the ownership and occupation wrangles deepened, there were still animals to be moved from the property. Some were luckier than others. When Meryl was called in again it was in connection with the Simmentaler bull, still stranded on the farm and still being used as the pawn in the ownership wrangle. Confined to a small paddock, sick, weak and helpless, the bull's only hope lay with the SPCA rescue team.

The first time she tried to rescue the bull Meryl was assured by the police that there'd be no problem at the farm. A cattle truck had been arranged and was waiting at Duiker to transport the animal, Meryl had police permission and a police escort, but the Border Gezi youths were having none of it. As soon as Meryl said she'd come for the bull, the youths went into a total frenzy. They shouted and ranted, waving their fists angrily and saying that the bull was staying exactly where it was and would not be leaving the farm. Meryl described the hostile atmosphere later in her records:

'Many of the Green Bombers were holding rubber sjamboks (whips) – including Daniel and Taliban – and I honestly believed they would have used them if I'd insisted on taking the bull.'

211

Trying to keep her calm Meryl talked to the youngster who seemed to be in charge of the gang of Gezi youths and whose name she discovered was Daniel.

'Daniel,' she said, 'I have just come from Beatrice Police Station. The police have given their full agreement that this bull be moved from here.'

Her words resulted in a torrent of angry bellowing:

'I don't care who gave you permission. I don't listen to police and I don't care who gave you authority but I am in charge here and I don't allow this bull to be moved.'

'Are you above the law, Daniel?' Meryl asked

'Yes!' he shouted back triumphantly. 'Not even the police can tell us what to do here on the farms. I am in charge here, I told you.'

'OK, OK, just calm down, Daniel. Can't you stop all this shouting and screaming? I'm not shouting at you, am I?'

Amazingly the rebuke calmed the youngster down immediately. Perhaps embarrassed or even ashamed at having been told off by this white woman, old enough to be his grandmother, Daniel stammered an explanation: 'I, I can't help it. My voice is always loud like this. It is not my fault, I just have a loud voice. It is loud even when it is idling!'

Meryl could not help smiling at Daniel's choice of words, barbaric as the situation was, Daniel was just a boy underneath it all, a boy with a sense of humour!

The arguing, pleading and negotiation continued for some time but Meryl was getting nowhere fast. The Border Gezi youths were not going to let her remove the bull and the best she could get was permission for the police Constable to go to the paddock and look at the bull. The youths wouldn't allow Meryl herself to even see the animal. When he returned, the Constable told Meryl the bull was in poor shape, it was lying down and looked very tired and weak. An hour after she had arrived Meryl left without the bull – with victory cheers, whistling and shouts of derision from the Border Gezi youths as she drove away empty-handed.

The following day Meryl set out yet again to Duiker Farm, absolutely determined one way or the other to bring the matter of the sick and stranded bull to an end. She had phoned Obbi's manager and discussed the problem with him, telling him the bull was sick, lame and deteriorating by the day. Obbi's manager gave Meryl permission to have the bull destroyed if it was suffering and said that it was going to be slaughtered anyway as soon as it was removed from the farm. With grim determination Meryl collected two armed members of the Support Unit from the police station a little after 2pm. One of the two, a Sergeant, sat in the front of the truck with Meryl and he appeared to be either high or drunk – a situation which didn't inspire confidence for the business that lay ahead, not to mention personal safety and security.

They stopped at Marirangwe Police Post to collect a Constable, and the Sergeant jumped out of the vehicle. There was meat and fish cooking on a fire in a thatched kitchen next to a beer hall and the Sergeant hurriedly helped himself to everything that was left. Eventually he climbed back into the front of the truck still chewing and sucking on greasy bones.

Meryl drove on in silence. When they arrived at the farm Meryl was surprised to find the gate open and not being manned by the usual contingent of Green Bombers. It was pouring with rain and the Border Gezi girls were in the implement shed, huddled around a smoky fire roasting and eating mealies. Again the Support Unit Sergeant climbed out and went to help himself to more food. The Green Bomber boys had gone to a nearby farm store and the more senior boys were apparently with the war veterans. Meryl was relieved that she wouldn't have Daniel shouting at her and Taliban harassing her and announced that she had come to check on the bull. None of the girls seemed to know what to do and so they agreed Meryl could proceed to the paddock.

Meryl and the police officers walked in the pouring rain across the paddock to where the bull was lying in the field. He was a magnificent Simmentaler bull but clearly in considerable distress and he struggled to get up as they approached. The bull was sandy coloured, thick set and with a typical enormous Simmentaler head. Without a doubt he had been a superb animal before this horrific situation had evolved. His right hind leg was hugely swollen and he was not putting any weight on it. There was no water in the paddock and no sign that any of the various occupiers or youths had been bringing water to the bull. Obviously unable to walk far, the bull must have been very dehydrated and he stood with his head hanging down, obviously sick, weak and utterly miserable.

Meryl's heart went out to the bull, an innocent and uncomprehending victim of this man-made situation. Meryl watched as he made a very half-hearted attempt at grazing but she knew already that there was really only one thing she could do, the kindest release for the bull. She knew that the dispute over occupation of the farm would continue as neither war veterans nor CIO were showing any sign of backing down. Obbi had already stated that if the bull was made to leave the farm it would be sent for slaughter and so, stay or go, there was no hope for the poor creature.

Meryl made the decision she always hated and reluctantly decided the bull should be destroyed then and there – rather than being subjected to the stress of being loaded and transported for a journey that would only end in slaughter. With the decision made Meryl wanted to get it done as quickly as possible – before the Green Bomber boys or war veterans returned – she knew that they'd cause trouble and prolong the suffering of the bull even more. Meryl knew that if Russian were to suddenly arrive, there would very likely be an explosion of anger and a strong likelihood of violence. Meryl showed the youths and Support Unit members the legislation which empowered her to have the animal destroyed [The Prevention of Cruelty to Animals Act Ch 19:09 Section 11(1)] and she asked the Support Unit Sergeant to shoot the bull for her. On so many of the farm rescues, the situation on the ground was hostile and it was too dangerous for Meryl to carry a humane killer in the vehicle. If it had been found it could easily have been mistaken for a gun, giving the impression that the SPCA team were armed or, even worse, it could have been seized and used against them.

Meryl always tried to establish if the farm staff were still on the property and if the livestock manager had a weapon with which to destroy animals when necessary. On Duiker Farm this was not possible and so Meryl asked the Sergeant to carry out the task. He agreed immediately and Meryl turned her back. After all her years in the SPCA and having seen the most unimaginable suffering, this final act was still one that Meryl was unable to watch. In her diary she wrote:

> 'Two shots rang out in rapid succession and he later said that he had "put it on automatic to make sure he killed the bull". I turned round and saw to my horror that the bull was still standing, blood pouring from its nose. The bull then slowly turned round whilst this apology for a marksman emptied three more bullets into it. This time thankfully the bull went down with an enormous thud and was dead. The Sergeant then leapt on it and began cutting its throat with his bayonet. This was so blunt that it would have had a job going through melted butter. As he was sawing away he informed me that: "This was meant for fighting, not cutting animals' throats".'

Meryl's hands were shaking with rage, with sadness and with utter despair. She took photographs and walked out of the paddock towards her truck. Her tears ran with the rain down her face. It was such a sad end for such a magnificent animal and Meryl wondered how much more of this she could take. She wept for all the animals of Zimbabwe who had lost their lives because of the madness of land reform. On that sodden January day Meryl felt as if her heart was breaking.

A short while later Meryl received a letter from a relation of the owners of Duiker Farm. The words lifted Meryl a little:

'Thank you so much for your help with trying to get our bull off Duiker Farm. It is refreshing to find people like you in this country, still with determination and the ability to go on under extremely difficult circumstances. You are an example to everyone who still wants to make a life in this country.'

Extracts from Meryl's Diary:

'They (Holsteins) also have a compulsion to lick and
mouth things and to manipulate objects with their mouths.
Their behaviour is so extreme that if a tractor gets left in their field
they'll lick the paint off and chew up all the hydraulic hoses –
they'll destroy it, whereas beef cattle will just sniff it!'
– Temple Grandin, 2005

February 2003
Harare:
Repeated visits to National Parks trying to obtain paperwork and a permit to remove the remaining chimpanzee in Zimbabwe ('Billie') to the Chimfunshi Sanctuary in Zambia.

Concession:
Get to know the inside of the Concession Police Station very well as I begin a series of very long and fruitless meetings trying to get permission and an escort for a huge dairy farm in the area which has been taken over by a doctor of alternative medicine who says he is going to grow herbs to cure diseases such as HIV/AIDS... Fred and Denise Gaisford, as owners of the farm, were forcibly evicted in December... 400 head of Pedigree American Holstein dairy cows (180 being milked) and 50 calves... Two dogs stranded – a German Shepherd male and Fox terrier bitch... two cats also stranded... cattle desperately need vaccinating for Lumpy Skin disease and Rift Valley Fever... bull calves should be being sent to Mount Hampden... no dipping is being done...

First visit to farm, the Doctor comes to the gate, greets Jimmy and the police Constable. Then stepped closer to me, until his face is a few inches from me and says: 'GO AWAY' in very menacing tones... he starts shouting at Jimmy that he shouldn't have bought 'the white'... the Doctor grabs a stick from one of his workers and advances towards me and says : 'I will show you how rough I can be'... PC nonchalantly sits on the ground chewing a piece of grass and ignores threat... He won't let me take the dogs or go and inspect the cattle...

Another visit with two ZNSPCA Inspectors, a government vet and Animal Health Inspector... Arriving at the gate the Doctor says, "Gentlemen, drive up to the house, but the white stays behind.' He then starts shouting at me that I was an MDC spy, that I was spying for the farm owners, that the whites were responsible for sanctions (don't know what that had to do with things!)... In order to make progress I go back and wait at the police station. The two ZNSPCA Inspectors return alone to the farm to try and just get the dogs and cats... a long wait of over two hours before I saw my truck approaching the police station – there were no animals in the back.

CHAPTER TWENTY-FIVE

Kitty Kitty

'The smallest feline is a masterpiece.'
– Leonardo da Vinci, 1452-1519

Concession, March 2003

Meryl's eyes widened as she saw the response to the old man's voice. He had very few, if any, teeth left in his mouth and stood outside the tobacco barns summoning his charges.

'Kitty, Kitty!' he called out.

'Kitty, Kitty!'

Almost immediately cats came streaming out of the bush and from the surrounding sheds and they ran towards the old man. Within minutes there were at least 30 cats milling around and they followed the old man into the barns. Plastic milk bottles had been cut in half to serve as food containers for the cats and lay all over the floor. A big black pot of food for the cats stood on offer on the barn floor; it was full of yellow, crusty, dried out sadza (maize porridge). There was also an old fridge which had some milk and three packets of pets mince in it – not much to feed so many cats.

Meryl had come in response to a call from a farmer's wife who said they had been thrown off the farm two months ago and she wanted the cats to be caught and removed. The woman said the cats were her husbands' hobby and were 'tame' but Meryl was sceptical, it was a phrase she'd heard many times before but one that was seldom true of cats living in barns and outbuildings on farms. There was hardly a farm in the country which didn't have some cats, wild or half-wild living in the barns, sheds, store-rooms and dairies. The difference here was that there were so many cats and that they had grown dependant on food provided by the farmer – who was no longer there.

According to the farmer's wife, the property had been taken over by two people: an army major who was 'quite co-operative' and also an accountant from Borrowdale [an up-market suburb in Harare] who was apparently 'very unpleasant'. When it was clear that the farmer wasn't going to be able to go and sort out the cats herself, Meryl took over. Initially the farmer's wife asked Meryl to destroy the cats but said she might want to keep a couple of them but two days later changed her mind and told Meryl to have all the cats put to sleep.

The farm was in Concession, 55 kilometres north of Harare in the heart of the Mazowe valley and it was a much sought-after area. Concession, like so many other centres in Zimbabwe, had opened up in 1914 with mining being the main attraction – gold and chromite mostly. In later years it was found to be a prime agricultural area and ideally suited for crops such as maize, cotton, soyabeans, tobacco and winter wheat. Meryl had already made some decisions and was mentally and logistically prepared for what she had to do when she went out to the tobacco farm in Concession in March 2003.

'I had decided not to put the cats through the stress and trauma of putting them all in cages for the long, hot drive back to Harare SPCA, where they probably would not be euthanased until the following day. Instead I had brought our Vet Assistant with me to euthanase the cats on-site.'

Meryl and the Vet Assistant followed the old man and all the cats into the barns. They were instantly hit by the pungent, heady smell of cat faeces which lay in piles everywhere on the floor of the barns. Meryl knew almost immediately that this was a mission of mercy and undoubtedly the right thing to do. She saw that most of the cats were in a poor condition and infested with fleas. Most were very thin and several had respiratory infections and symptoms of cat flu which would undoubtedly spread to the others. Because the cats were feral, none of the females had been sterilised and would continue having litter after litter of kittens – more hungry mouths, more fights between the toms and more injuries all round. It was clearly an untenable situation. Meryl poured cat biscuits into the feed containers and the cats immediately began eating hungrily. In her diary she described the task ahead:

'The Vet Asst prepared several syringes of Euthapent, and then the difficult part began. These cats were not tame at all and whilst we could catch them fairly easily whilst they huddled round their dish full of biscuits – once we caught them the biting, scratching, hissing, spitting and yowling began. I went and fetched a very thick pair of gloves from the truck, but none of us came off unscathed. We wrapped each cat up in a towel so as to have more control over it, but sadly, there was no gentle, dignified way in which to handle them. We began by spraying a small amount of the drug into their mouths; whilst they hated the taste of it, it did help to calm them down before finally finding the vein to put them to sleep. It still took two of us to hold each cat down – albeit as gently as we could. I felt very distressed at having to end their lives in this way – but given the situation there was no alternative.'

With so many cats, Meryl knew there were most likely going to be kittens too and she asked the old man if he had seen any litters hidden in the bush. The farmer's wife had already told Meryl that she had instructed the old man to 'blalah' (kill) any kittens that he found but even so his descriptive answer as to how he killed the kittens was truly shocking. It horrified Meryl and is not one that can be reproduced here.

By 4.30 that afternoon 20 cats had been euthanased and the light in the barns was fading and so the work stopped for the day. Meryl wrote in her diary:

'I felt so sad looking at the row of little bodies lined up on the floor, but knew that we had removed them from a pretty miserable existence.'

A few days later Meryl, SPCA Inspector Jimmy and the Vet Assistant returned to the farm to finish what they had started. Some of the cats were hanging around the barns and again the old man called out as he done before:

'Kitty, Kitty!' he shouted and soon they counted 15 cats waiting for food. Even though the cats began to eat the biscuits Meryl had bought, they were much more nervous than they had been the last time. The Vet Assistant began drawing up syringes of Euthapent and laid them out on a little wooden table. Three hours later they had euthanased 13 cats and more had hidden in the enormous flue pipes that had been piled up on the floor of the barns. It took another hour to find, catch and euthanase the last two cats. One ginger cat had scrambled up into the rafters of the roof and was 20 feet up. The Vet Assistant stood on Jimmy's shoulders, lunged and caught the cat and then they all fell to the ground – luckily landing on a big pile of empty sacks.

The last cat was a large, dark tortoiseshell that Meryl had seen earlier in the morning and he took some finding.

'We began by dismantling the huge pile of flue pipes and throwing them in another corner of the barn. The noise was deafening and the air was thick with dust. After about ten minutes he shot out, obviously absolutely terrified and we were able to catch him. As with so many of the others, we first sprayed Euthapent into his mouth and let him calm down before administering the fatal dose.'

By 4 in the afternoon, 18 cats had been put to sleep and their bodies lay in a corner of the barn covered in plastic sheeting. The silence was eerie. As they were packing up the truck Meryl saw a grey cat some distance from the barns in the long grass.

'It was tempting to head back to Harare as we'd had nothing to eat or drink all day but I felt we could not leave this one by itself. We set the cat trap in the long grass with half a packet of pet mince and waited – and waited.'

For a moment Meryl thought there might be a problem when they heard a truck approaching. The old man, who was hankering to go off home as it was late, said, "ma war vets are coming!" In fact it was just settlers from another property taking a short cut and Meryl knew the warning was just an attempt to get her to hurry up and go home.

Meryl wandered around the deserted barns and implement sheds and was struck by the sights, the desolation and the neglect.

'Only a few months ago this had been a busy, productive tobacco farm bringing in much-needed forex [foreign currency] for Zimbabwe. Now the many tractors and trailers stood with flat tyres, long grass growing around their wheels. Barn doors blew open and shut in the wind – it was all so sad and unnecessary.'

When the last grey cat had been caught in the cat trap, it too was gently held, calmed, euthanased and laid with the other cats – waiting to be buried. Before they left Meryl wanted to confirm how the litters of kittens were destroyed and so she asked the old man again. He called another worker who gave Meryl a graphic description and a mock demonstration. What Meryl saw and heard from the two workers convinced her she had done the right thing in euthanasing all the cats on the farm. Coming to terms with it all was not so easy.

'By the time we left the farm the sun had gone down, it was getting cold – but my heart was even colder – I felt so traumatised by the day's events. When I finally got home my own two dogs, 'Genie', a Japanese Shiba Inu, and 'Jethro', a French bulldog, got extra special hugs and treats – but sleep evaded me most of the night.'

Meryl and her team gave a dignified death and merciful release to 39 cats in March 2003. Once again, Meryl had not been able to promise the cats a good life, but she could provide them with a good death – it was all she could do.

Extracts from Meryl's Diary:

A man fights jumping.
(One has to be wise in dealing with an adversary)
— Sindebele proverb

March 2003

Concession:
Hear from the dairy farm owners that they have finally managed (after lawyers' letters) to get onto their property and remove most of their furniture and rescue their two dogs and one cat – the Siamese could not be found... The farm owners desperate about the dairy herd.

For the next 18 months I would be involved in this saga but without success. Despite endless meetings, negotiations, confrontations, lawyers, government ministers, land committees and permanent secretaries, the Doctor was all-powerful.

Bulawayo:
Had to return to Bulawayo to deal with many issues and able to work from my office at home. Before he became so ill, Roly had turned one of our spare rooms into an office complete with desk, phone, files, typewriter, etc – this was so typical of him.

Bulawayo:
Had lunch with Chairman of SPCA Bulawayo and handed over drugs and medical equipment that had been donated by Zimbabwe Pet Rescue Project ladies in SA and by Vicky in USA.

Harare:
Had a meeting with the Minister of Environment and Tourism concerning sable and other issues. Tea in beautiful bone china cups!

Ruwa:
Ran a week-long training course for Inspectors at Ruwa Country Club. Chairman Rose Nurse gave us very good hire rates and the meals were excellent. Participants did well and later, after sitting their exams, we welcomed 3 new Inspectors onto our team.

Ruwa:
Spent the last Sunday of the month sitting in yet another petrol queue – this time for eight hours.

CHAPTER TWENTY-SIX

Shumba

'The darkest day is the turning point.'
− Shona Proverb

Mabvuku, Harare, March 2003

Things were always worse at weekends and most people dreaded the time from midday on Friday to the start of business on Monday morning. It was during these two and a half days that political violence and farm invasions always reached critical heights. Farmers and members of the opposition knew that if there was trouble or you were arrested anytime after lunch on Friday, you were on your own. Lawyers, magistrates and judges were often not available, police superiors were not in their offices, bail hearings were not held and the chances of a reprieve or rescue from trouble were very slim. Meryl hated having to respond to calls for help on weekends − not because she had anything of a personal life left after having been in the forefront for so long, but because she knew getting help, back-up and support was so difficult.

> *'On Saturday 23 March 2003 I received a phone call from a concerned member of the public who had been visiting injured members of the MDC at the Avenues Clinic. They had been assaulted during the night by members of the Zimbabwean army who had stormed into the high-density suburb of Mabvuku. The caller informed me that one of the injured mentioned that a neighbour's dog had also been badly beaten. I later found out that the injured informant had herself experienced horrific brutality at the hands of the soldiers − she had been raped and suffered many other injuries.'*

Meryl's SPCA rescue team were all off for the weekend, having a well-earned break and so Meryl phoned ZNSPCA Inspector Jimmy who lived nearest to her in Goromonzi in the hope that he would be able to accompany her. Meryl was sure that she was the last person Jimmy wanted to hear from on a Saturday but half an hour later they were on their way to Mabvuku. Meryl had already phoned the Mabvuku Police Station to check on the situation there and been told that it was 'all quiet'. She was shocked at what she saw as they drove into the suburb.

'Although it had been like a war zone the night before now it was quite eerie, there was just no one around. We saw much evidence of rocks and bricks strewn all over the road, but very few residents could be seen – the atmosphere felt very tense.'

This mayhem on the streets was the final result of a two day national strike that had been called by the opposition. Petrol prices had increased by 91%, telephone charges by 100% and inflation was officially quoted at 208%. The opposition were determined to air their grievances and show their discontent and it seemed the safest and most effective way of doing so was to call for people to stay at home. Over 80% of shops, businesses and factories had been closed for the two days and the government were furious, threatening to seek out and find the organisers of the strike and punish them for what they said was 'economic sabotage'. When Meryl and Jimmy went into Mabvuku that Saturday morning, they witnessed the results of an angry government.

It did not take long to find the right address and Arthur Gwatidzo met Meryl at the solid metal gate to his home and let them in. A pretty little tan-coloured Collie-type dog followed Arthur and although she seemed pleased to see the visitors, the little dog visibly flinched when Meryl bent down to pat her. Arthur told Meryl and Jimmy what had happened the night before.

Arthur and his wife were ardent supporters of the opposition MDC and Mrs Gwatidzo was the Chairperson of the Mabvuku branch of the party. At about 2.30am they had been woken by a great deal of shouting and noise and were horrified to see soldiers jumping over the wall and into their property. Arthur had a six-foot wall but this was no obstacle to the determined invaders. A large army truck had parked parallel with the wall and the soldiers just climbed over it and jumped down to the ground.

Arthur came out of the house to protect his property and face the trespassers and as he did one of the soldiers bent down, picked up a bowl of uneaten dog food and threw it into Arthur's face. Disorientated and struggling to see, Arthur bent down to wash his face at a nearby tap and the soldiers laid into him beating and kicking him all over his body. The little Collie, appropriately called 'Shumba' [lion], immediately tried to protect her master and chase away the attackers. Shumba barked furiously and darted in and out amongst the soldiers but she was hugely outnumbered and her behaviour infuriated them. Eight soldiers, all in uniform, attacked man and dog, beating them with rubber whips and kicking them with their booted feet. Arthur couldn't protect himself or his dog and then the soldiers went inside the house where Mrs Gwatidzo became their next victim. She was subjected to a prolonged beating and her arm was broken in the process. When the soldiers finally left, the traumatised residents of Mabvuku began emerging. The Gwatidzos were not the only victims. Many others had also been beaten and brutalised. Neighbours, friends and relations joined together and helped to get everyone who had been injured to hospitals and clinics.

Meryl and Jimmy loaded Shumba gently into the SPCA truck and told Arthur that they would take the little dog to the vet to be thoroughly checked over. Arthur was grateful and immensely relieved at the assistance being offered and could not have hoped for more attentive carers for his brave little dog. Shumba was just seven months old and still a puppy. Meryl and Jimmy went straight to the Kamfinsa Veterinary Hospital where they were always welcomed very warmly by vet Ant Donohoe and Shumba was seen to immediately.

This particular veterinary surgery had become a familiar and most welcome place of safety and sanity for Meryl. Often the animals were terrified, traumatised, bleeding, beaten or with broken limbs. Ant and his colleagues worked with great care and compassion, knowing only a fraction of what the animals had been through as innocent victims caught up in political violence and land invasions.

Meryl had lost count of how many animals she had bought to Ant for help during the farm rescues, everything from kittens to horses and there must have been hundreds of them. Ant never once sent a bill for the work he and his staff carried out – he told Meryl it was his contribution to animal welfare in Zimbabwe and Meryl knew that his magnificent gesture had saved the ZNSPCA countless thousands of dollars. The vet on duty X-rayed Shumba and treated her for shock and decided to keep her in for observation for a couple of days. Shumba winced wherever she was touched on her body but it was thought, and hoped, that her thick, fluffy coat had protected her to some extent.

A few days later Meryl took Shumba home and there was a delightful reunion with her owner who was also recovering from his wounds. Arthur was thrilled to have Shumba home again and overjoyed when he saw the wonderful assistance that Meryl had bought. People regularly made donations to the SPCA for pet owners who were in need and Meryl gave Arthur a kennel for Shumba, together with blankets, a collar and lead and enough dog food for several weeks.

Arthur's property had no garden and there was not much space for Shumba to run around in and nowhere for her to shelter which was why Meryl offered such welcome assistance. She also hoped that the gift of a collar and lead may encourage the family to take the dog for walks and she promised to return in about a month's time to collect Shumba and take her for vaccinating, de-worming and spaying. Meryl could see that Shumba could do with the extra help and care and was more than happy to help.

> *'Five weeks later I collected Shumba and she was delighted to see us. I delivered her to the vet for spaying. Returning at the end of the day to collect her, Ant came through to tell me that during what is a very routine operation, little Shumba had stopped breathing. Fortunately, after working frantically on her for several minutes, he got her breathing again but was sure it was the result of the severe beating that had damaged her lungs. You would never have thought so as she dashed off to the ZNSPCA truck that she immediately recognised!'*

Meryl felt a special bond with Shumba so in the following months, when she was in the area, she often called in to see the family. Arthur and his wife had both made a good recovery and Meryl always had a box of treats for Shumba – the very brave little dog who at just seven months old risked her life to protect her owners.

Extracts from Meryl's Diary:

> *'If I had a donkey that wouldn't go,*
> *Would I beat him? Oh no, no.*
> *I'd put him in the barn and give him some corn.*
> *The best little donkey that ever was born.'*
> *– Nursery rhyme*

April 2003

Nick's birthday. He arrived from Australia for a quick visit and we went straight from the airport to the house in Harare that Roy Bennett was renting so that I could collect a drum of diesel that Roy had very kindly donated to ZNSPCA. Nick enjoyed meeting Roy as even in Australia there had been quite a bit of coverage on his courage and his fight for Charleswood.

The next day Nick and Tim and I drove up to Hwange for a couple of nights. It was so great for the three of us to be together again, though they got extremely fed up with me continually stopping on the way there and back to treat donkeys, mend harnesses, etc!

When Nick got back to Australia he wrote such a moving piece which a couple of newspapers published. The last paragraph I am sure said it all for so many Zimbabweans – farmers and others:

Innocent Victims

On my final morning in Zimbabwe I ran along a dirt road through my grandparents' former farm. Mist was rising from the vlei, there were fresh jackal tracks in the dust and the doves were calling. Those who have spent any time in the African highveld will appreciate the perfection of such early autumn mornings. As the sun rose through the msasa trees I reflected on Karen Blixen's lines on the opening page of Out of Africa, 'I had a farm in Africa.. in the highlands you woke up in the morning and thought: here I am, where I ought to be.' In Zimbabwe one may have had a farm, but one no longer belongs. More significantly for the country's future economic prospects, after the experiences of the past three years, a large number of people, black and white, are unsure whether they now even want to belong.

Harare:
Begin investigations into organised dog fighting in Harare. These fights are for money – huge amounts change hands in the form of betting on the outcome. We had known for some time that it had been going on but had no proof.

CHAPTER TWENTY-SEVEN

Puss–Cat

'I love little Pussy,
Her coat is so warm,
And if I don't hurt her
She'll do me no harm.
So I'll not pull her tail,
Nor drive her away,
But Pussy and I
Very gently will play.'
– Nursery Rhyme

Hidden Valley Farm, Mazowe, April 2003
Meryl didn't know much about the cat at Hidden Valley Farm except that it was an old mink-coloured female that had arrived on the farm as a stray and had decided to stay. Hidden Valley was owned by Paul and Jenny Hill and was a rose farm, growing flowers in greenhouses for export. Paul and Jenny were evicted from the farm by war veterans in September 2002 but Paul had desperately tried to keep the business going as it was his only source of income.

There was much political posturing at this time about existing commercial farmers and new farmers working the farms together, sharing the land and 'co-existing'. In almost all cases this was wishful thinking. Mostly it seemed to be just diplomatic talk proffered by the President and his senior Ministers to appease the critics as little, if anything, was done to facilitate any co-existence. The Hills moved off Hidden Valley when the situation became untenable but Paul tried to continue farming from a distance – commuting backwards and forwards.

For a while this worked but in April 2003 even that collapsed. Paul was held hostage by the war veterans occupying Hidden Valley Farm and was then ordered off altogether. The war veterans warned Paul never to come back. When Jenny asked Meryl for help it was for a mission of mercy. Jenny said that the family didn't know where they were going to live or how they were going to make a living and had therefore reluctantly decided that the cat should be put to sleep. Jenny told Meryl that the cat didn't have a name, not that they knew of anyway.

Meryl went to Hidden Valley Farm in Mazowe with an SPCA Veterinary Assistant. It was a short and scenic journey, just 38 kilometres north of Harare. Originally famed as the site of ancient gold mines and smelting works and where fragments of old Delft pottery had been found, nowadays the name Mazowe was synonymous with fruit juice. Famous for its citrus estates and particularly for oranges, this was a prime agricultural area with maize, cotton and tobacco being produced in summer and irrigated wheat in winter.

Arriving at the farm they met the Hill's gardener, Jason, at the greenhouses. Jason got into Meryl's truck and talked incessantly all the way to the house. He wasn't at all happy with the way things were turning out for him and the other farm workers who had all lost their jobs when the Hills had been evicted by the war veterans. He said the war veterans had told all the farm workers that they had to work for them from 1 May but that the workers had all refused.

Jason told Meryl that the war veterans were only prepared to pay a minimal salary which would not even be enough to buy one bucket of maize (approximately 12kg). With an adult eating a minimum of 15kg of maize meal a month, this proposition from the war veterans would not even keep the farm worker himself in basic food, let alone his wife and children and not to mention clothes, school fees, medicines and any of the other things needed for a basic existence. Meryl let the man talk, she said nothing – there was nothing really that she could say. This was a situation being repeated all over the country and Jason just needed someone to tell.

Arriving at the farmhouse Meryl recorded what she saw:

'The place looked sadly deserted with the remains of looted goods lying all over the lawn. The war veterans had stolen all the electrical goods and also clothes. The war vets vehicle – a white truck – was piled high with stolen timber but apparently would not start and was now abandoned on the front lawn, a tattered tow rope still attached to the bumper.'

It didn't take Meryl long to find the cat which the Hills has asked her to euthanase. Jason had taken to calling the stray Puss-Cat and she was a beautiful, long-haired Siamese. Puss-Cat was lying on the patio in the sun. Jason told Meryl that Puss-Cat hadn't had any food for a week and Meryl immediately rectified that situation.

'Puss-Cat seemed very pleased to see us. We could see that she was beginning to show her age and when I picked her up she felt very thin. As always we had some cat biscuits with us and I felt that Puss-Cat had every right to have a full stomach again before she was euthanased – she finished up every last bit of it before being put in the SPCA cat cage.'

With the cat safely loaded Meryl and the Vet Assistant drove back to the greenhouses, again accompanied by Jason. The gardener continued to complain about the occupation of the farm by the war veterans. Jason called the war veterans 'ma-rubbish' and said they had no idea how to grow roses and had only utilised a very small section of the farm to plant a few mealies but the rest of the place was derelict. Again Meryl just listened and nodded and she thought about all the thousands of farm workers in the same situation as Jason – homeless, unemployed and completely at the mercy of the war veterans and farm invaders.

Meryl said goodbye to Jason, leaving him at the greenhouses on the Farm. It was a hot day and didn't take long for Meryl to decide that she was not going to subject Puss-Cat to a moment's more distress than necessary. It was unlikely that the cat would be able to be put to sleep until the next morning which meant a night in a cage at the SPCA – a strange place, new smells, frightening noises and an already crowded cat house.

'I believed that Puss-Cat deserved better than that. When we reached the Eskbank fruit and vegetable kiosk I pulled off the main road and parked in the shade of some giant gum trees. I took Puss-Cat out of the cage and sat on the front seat with her in my arms, stroking her and telling her what a beautiful, very special cat she was. The Vet Asst slipped the needle into the vein in her leg, her head sank slowly on to my arm as her loud purring gradually stopped.'

Meryl wrapped Puss-Cat in a blanket and later buried her at the ZNSPCA complex in Goromonzi. Puss-Cat may have become another statistic in the long, long list of animal victims in the land reform programme but to Meryl, she was the sweet and gentle cat who was loving, trusting and purred to her very last breath.

Extracts from Meryl's Diary:

> *'It is the friends you can call up at 4am that matter.'*
> *— Marlene Dietrich*

May 2003
Harare:
Finally moved baboons from their spartan living conditions in cages at the University of Zimbabwe, where they had been living all their lives (only coming out of their cages for tests to be performed on them) to the Lion and Cheetah Park. They had never seen trees and grass before – it was so good to see them out in the sunshine – the result of many, many meetings.

20 May:
Had a very bad night with my heart and for once stayed in bed the next day. As always my neighbours are concerned and supportive. Jimmy and Mignon Dodds live right next door to me and help me in so many ways. Jimmy has come to my rescue so many times when the car battery has been flat; helped me with a cobra in the bathroom and once with a particularly large and hairy spider that was lurking in the corner of the lounge! So comforting to have friends like them.

Harare:
Collected much-needed desks and a filing cabinet for our office in Goromonzi – these had been donated by Gerry Jackson, a friend for many years, who was having to leave the country after the government closed down her station, Capital Radio.

CHAPTER TWENTY-EIGHT

Sassy and Charlie

'Memories are hunting horns
Whose sound dies on the wind.'
– Guillaume Apollinaire, 1912

Wychwood Farm, Mvurwi, May 2003

Ed and Pat Cumming had just 24 hours to pack up their entire house and farm and get off the property that had been home for 14 years. Two hand-reared duiker and 26 geese were in their garden. The house was still fully equipped with furniture and personal belongings and the farm outbuildings held all the equipment that went with running a fully functional tobacco farm. To get everything packed and removed in 24 hours would be almost impossible and friends and neighbours from all around had come to help.

The crisis at Wychwood Farm in Mvurwi came to a head on 29 May 2003. War veterans and settlers who had invaded the property came to the homestead and demanded that they be given the title deeds to the property. When Ed Cumming refused their absurd demand, the invaders gave the couple just 24 hours to get off the farm. To a non-farmer or non-Zimbabwean, such a situation would be utterly ludicrous and laughable and you would just call the police to get the people making the demands arrested. On the ground in Zimbabwe, however, it simply did not work like that!

Since February 2000 there had been no law and order when it came to farm ownership and occupancy. As absurd as it may seem, the lives and jobs of hundreds of thousands of farmers and their employees were literally dependant on the temperament and whim of mobs of men who arrived at the gate saying they were war veterans and were taking over the property.

The not-so-funny phrase that some farmers used to describe this horror was to say that some arbitrary bloke on a bicycle had pitched up and announced he was taking over. Other farmers said, "A bloke on a bicycle – hey, you were lucky, I lost my farm to a chap pushing a wheelbarrow!" For the farmers and farm workers, when this happened, there were not many options. Some farmers tried police, others tried lawyers and courts and others tried politicians and government ministers but it was all to no avail. Sometimes a farmer would be able to negotiate for a few more days or weeks but invariably the day came when the bloke on the bicycle had the final word.

A friend and neighbour of the Cummings contacted Meryl for help with catching and finding homes for the duiker and geese. Already appeals had been made to three other animal sanctuaries but no one seemed able to help; one promised to phone back – but never did. Meryl agreed to help immediately, her only problem was finding enough diesel for the SPCA vehicle.

Yet again she turned to businessman Richard Maasdorp who did not let her down. His company's regular donations of fuel had become a vital lifeline for Meryl who knew that many farm rescues would have been impossible without his help and generosity. That evening Meryl rang Pat Cumming to get directions to Wychwood Farm. The situation had not eased at all and it seemed a reprieve was not going to happen.

'Pat sounded very stressed and tense. She said the war vets had been waiting at the main gate all day for them to get out.'

First thing next morning Meryl made her final preparations for the 100-kilometre trip to Mvurwi. This wasn't going to be an easy rescue at all as it didn't involve obedient dogs or cats but noisy, aggressive geese, skittish and nervous guinea fowl and two hand-reared but very timid wild animals. Because there were so many geese and two duiker to transport, Meryl arranged for two vehicles to make the journey. She and SPCA Vet Assistant Elias would go ahead in one vehicle thanks to the diesel that had been donated and SPCA Inspectors Sternford and Jimmy would follow later once they found petrol for the second truck.

On the way through Harare Meryl stopped at the veterinary surgery of Dr Ant Donohoe and collected three syringes of tranquillisers that Elias would need for the duiker. Meryl and Elias did not talk much on the journey. They passed a few scotch carts laden with fire wood and stopped every time to check on the condition of the animals pulling the loads and to give out education pamphlets in Shona advising the owners how to care for their donkeys. Meryl was passionate about this cause and was never too busy to do it.

'I always worked on the theory that I may never have the opportunity of seeing that donkey again, and it could have a very bad wound from the usual homemade harnesses or be very ill, and it would be left untreated with possible dire consequences.

The Inspectors travelling with me were not very happy about my continual stopping – with the exception of Addmore, who usually spotted the scotch carts long before I did!'

With the message of animal welfare passed on, the journey continued and the urgency of the visit to Wychwood became apparent as soon as they arrived:

'On arrival at the farm it was to find a bunch of very hostile-looking war veterans and settlers waiting outside the locked gates. Once inside the security fence, we parked our truck on the lawn and saw the now-familiar sight of a removals pantechnicon close to the house. Beds were being dismantled, packing cases lay everywhere and several neighbours and friends were directing operations. By the barns and implement sheds there were more scenes of great activity as neighbouring farmers had brought their trucks and workers to help move all the farm implements and equipment.'

Although there was movement and noise and activity all around, the atmosphere was filled with emotion and despair. The Cummings' home and business lay out on the lawn, waiting to be wrapped in grey packing blankets and brown paper and pushed into a truck. A life, home and business were being forcibly closed down by a handful of aggressive and hostile men and there was nothing anyone could do to stop it.

Pat Cumming led Meryl and Elias through the chaos and dust of the half-packed house. The walls were suddenly bare as pictures came down, the windows exposed as curtains were unhooked. Home suddenly had an echo.

There, outside in the front garden amongst the shrubs, were the two little duiker. Pat called them Sassy and Charlie. Standing just knee high, the little grey/brown animals were both adult females and each weighed only about 20kg. Charlie had been with the Cummings for almost ten years, rescued as an orphaned lamb on a friend's farm during the devastating drought of 1992/93.

Game Scouts on the farm had heard a noise in the grass and found the duiker lamb, emaciated, dehydrated and near death. The lamb's mother had been killed in a snare and so the baby duiker was taken in by the farmer. With nothing else on hand the baby was fed on baby formula milk powder but it soon began to scour badly.

The situation was not good by the time Pat was approached to try and save the lamb. Pat had hand-reared orphaned baby impala before and hoped that this was a similar enough species and that her knowledge and experience may help save the duiker.

Those first few days were ones that she would never forget:

'Fortunately we had Bill Howells with us. He was a game ranger in Hwange and is a wild life expert. Charlie needed 24 nursing shifts to pull her through and she survived! Bill and I took shifts through the nights. She was a right "charlie", hence the name!'

Charlie grew stronger and thrived in the Cummings' garden. For a while she was joined by other animals orphaned in the drought who had been taken in and given sanctuary. At times there was quite a menagerie in Pat's garden and a clear browse line stood out on her garden shrubs. There was a steenbuck rescued from Mutorashanga, an oribi from Barwick and a duiker from Kariba. Five years later, in 1997, another duiker came to Wychwood, and Pat remembered this arrival with great affection:

'Sassy came from Msasa Farm down the road. She had followed the sheep and lambs into their pens, and with all the human pressure in the area we decided her safest haven was with Charlie. Sassy was already weaned so was much easier to rear. She was named Sassy – she really was a little sassy, full of beans and fun!'

Sassy and Charlie thrived in the Cummings' garden. Roses were their favourite food and so Pat planted more roses – for the food the leaves provided and not the flowers in a vase! They loved bananas too and maize and, when they were really being spoiled, home-made rusks!

Having to part with Sassy and Charlie was almost unbearable for Pat Cumming but there was no choice. The two duiker would never have survived in the wild, they were too tame. They knew only the Cummings' garden, and their dogs who they curled up and slept with at night.

Meryl did not know any of the background to Sassy and Charlie on the day she went to Mvurwi to rescue them. She knew only that they had been hand-reared but were very shy. Meryl and Elias got to work immediately.

'We had had no experience in tranquillising wild animals – this was always left to the Veterinarians, but few, understandably, would come out to farms where there was a hostile situation. They would obviously have to charge for their services, so we just had to get on with it and time was not on our side. We would not have been able to dart the duiker, that is a job for the professionals and requires a licence, which is why we had to get up close to them so as to be able to administer the injection. Catching them was as difficult as I had imagined it might be. We enlisted the help of several workers but an hour later the pair had still eluded us. We then used a long piece of chicken

mesh to corner Charlie, the larger duiker. She was then unceremoniously rugby tackled to the ground and Elias administered the tranquil is er. In order to give the drug a chance to become effective, we left both duiker alone for a little while. To our surprise the drug had absolutely no effect and an hour and a half later she was still tearing around the garden.' [Later, speaking to Viv Wilson from Chipangali – a world expert on duiker – he told me that duiker are always tricky and need as much tranquilliser as an adult eland that weighs approximately 450 kg!]

Time was moving on and no progress was being made at all and so a phone call was made to the Government Wildlife Vet in Harare. The vet on duty told them to use ACP (*Acetyl Promazine*), a general tranquillising drug that the SPCA team always had with them in tablet and injectable form. ACP would normally be used to calm a frightened animal that needed to be loaded into a vehicle or to quieten a terrified or aggressive animal that had experienced a very stressful situation such as being hit by a car or stuck in a drain. Hopefully the ACP would be effective on the duiker.

Armed with another loaded syringe Charlie was caught for the second time but the stress on both animals and people was mounting. It took a protracted chase before the duiker could be caught and in the process she ran into a fence, cutting her face and biting her tongue. With the drug administered to one of the duikers and nothing to do but wait, Meryl sat with Pat on the verandah. All signs of a once calm and beautiful home and garden were gone. The lawn had been churned up by the removal trucks and farm workers casually helped themselves to oranges and bananas from Pat's garden as they walked through. The whole system was disintegrating.

Relatives and neighbours had provided lunch for everyone and people ate on the move or sat for a few minutes on the remaining chairs that had not yet been packed. There was so much to do still and time was fast running out. Ed Cumming arrived to eat when most had finished. He had been having protracted arguments with war veterans who were insisting that the Modros (portable drying rooms for tobacco) had to be left behind for them. Ed was having none of it. At that time the law still stated that farmers could take moveable assets and Ed had no intention of giving his equipment away.

After lunch and reinforced by the arrival of Jimmy and Sternford, the SPCA team got back to work. The first duiker that had been injected, Charlie, still showed no sign of quietening down and when Meryl approached her she stood quite meekly until the last minute and then darted away.

The team turned their attention to Sassy who was also chased, tackled to the ground and the drug then injected into her fat little rump. She too was then released to give the tranquilliser time to work. After frantic phone calls the night before, a home had been found for Sassy and Charlie outside Harare and now just the capture and journey remained as obstacles. While they waited again for the pair of duiker to get sleepy Meryl and the team turned their attention to the birds. A neighbour had offered to take the guinea fowl and so it was just the geese to deal with.

The geese, every farmer's perfect watchdog, were wandering around the barn area constantly getting in the way of trucks and activity and were screeching loudly at the intrusion into their territory and trying to chase off the trespassers. The SPCA team herded all the geese out of the barns and into the garden and then steadily caught and loaded them into one of the SPCA vehicles. The process was accompanied by much hissing and lunging and mock charges from the males – and probably quite a few nips to the backs of knees and calves too! With 26 geese on board, Jimmy and Sternford left for Harare where the birds were going to a new home in the suburbs.

By then it was almost 5pm and Meryl knew that their time had almost run out. The two duiker still showed no signs of sleepiness at all.

'I decided we would just have to catch them again and put them in sacks for the journey back to Harare. With the help of the farm workers both duiker were cornered, caught and not very easily put into large sacks. I had threaded a bandage through the neck of each sack so that we were able to leave their heads sticking out and then we tied the bandage as securely as we could. They were then carried to my truck and you would never know they had been tranquillised at all as they both struggled a great deal.'

Meryl had only known the Cummings for a few hours and yet she felt overwhelming sympathy for the couple. She and Pat embraced like old friends and Pat was very tearful to see her beloved duiker going but knew this was for the best. Meryl had no doubt that if Sassy and Charlie had been left behind they would have been slaughtered and eaten by the next morning.

As Meryl drove out of Wychwood Farm she couldn't help but see the war veterans. They stood at the gate, sour and sullen-looking and Meryl, always impartial, controlled and dignified, was filled with anger.

'They were still outside like vultures waiting for the pickings of a kill. I mouthed, "You bastards!" at them, something I have never done before but it had just been one displaced farmer too many.'

Driving down the road Meryl was at the end of a long procession of tractors towing all sorts of farm implements and several low, flat bed trailers which were carrying the Modros that Ed had been determined he would not leave.

Sassy and Charlie struggled quite a bit at the beginning of the journey and Meryl could hear them flopping around in the sacks but she did not stop and soon they settled down. They arrived at the plot where the duiker were to be rehomed at 7pm. It was already dark and there was a distinct wintery chill in the air. The pair of duiker were gently lifted out of the truck and at last, the drugs had taken effect. Both Sassy and Charlie were now much quieter thanks to the ACP. Meryl phoned the next morning and was delighted to hear that both the duiker were walking around, eating grain and wild fruit and exploring their new paddock.

Four years later the memories of that day at Wychwood Farm were still clear in Meryl's mind. For Pat Cumming the journey of healing was still going on as she wrote from her new home in Botswana:

'The sounds of axes on live mombies [cattle] *and the bleating and breathing sounds of my hand-reared orphaned duikers, Sassy and Charlie, when Meryl and her wonderful team were trying to dart them are sounds I'll live with for ever. The numerous tablets that my friends had me swallow dimmed my emotions – but could not block out those sounds.'*

The pain of it all was deep and vivid but Pat was also left with good memories of her beloved duikers Sassy and Charlie and said: 'I always felt so privileged to be able to rear them successfully and have them in our lives.'

Extracts from Meryl's Diary:

*'One reason a dog is such a comfort when you're downcast
is that he doesn't ask to know why.'*
– Anon

June 2003
Interviewed by Peter Godwin – he's been commissioned to write an article on my work with the farm rescues for the Readers' Digest *(UK). Then onto another interview with John Reed of the* Financial Times *(SA).*

Ruwa:
Put my dogs in boarding kennels and headed to Mutare for a meeting with the stakeholders in the timber industry and the baboon poisoning. Stayed overnight with

Alan and Fiona Boyd. (Fiona is the Vice Chair of Mutare SPCA.) Later had a bad time with my heart and Fiona had to cart me off to the Trauma Centre in Mutare. She insisted I stay on the next day and not drive back to Harare – felt too washed out to argue with her!

Miss my own dogs so much when I am away. I love walking them – no matter how early I have to leave, I always walk them round the large garden area of Milne Park in Ruwa. Often end up getting my dressing gown and slippers soaked with dew but the dogs just love it – they have the whole complex to themselves at that time!

CHAPTER TWENTY-NINE

Pamberi! A1 versus A2

The black ant may swallow a giraffe.
(Many little things can overcome a big thing.)
— Sindebele proverb

Bains Hope Farm, Goromonzi, June 2003

Meryl was on home ground when she saw a cattle truck loaded with very thin cows and calves in Goromonzi in June 2003. She had two SPCA Inspectors with her and they could all see that the animals were in very bad condition. Meryl stopped the truck and asked to see the Animal Movement Permit (a legal requirement when moving livestock). The driver didn't have a permit and grew hostile as Meryl questioned him. When he said he was moving the cattle from Bains Hope Farm to a plot in Ruwa, Meryl was instantly taken back in time.

Meryl had come to Zimbabwe (then Rhodesia) with her twin brother Colin and adoptive parents, Pam and Leslie Anderson, when she was just eight years old in 1948. Adopted at birth in England, Meryl and Colin received their primary education at a boarding school in East Sussex. Although Colin never talked about it, Meryl had very bad memories of those early days, she hated the school and remembered the staff as being very abusive.

It was an unhappy time that would not last. Two years later her parents left England, travelling by sea to South Africa and then by train to Rhodesia and lived for the next nine years in Highlands in Salisbury. Meryl and Colin were put into boarding school for the remainder of their junior education and their parents visited many schools in South Africa to find what they considered the best senior education for the twins – also boarding. They settled on St Anne's Diocesan College for Meryl and Hilton College for Colin, both in Hilton Road in Natal.

In 1959 Meryl's father bought a virgin farm in Goromonzi. He built a house, tobacco barns and various outbuildings and took on a full-time farm manager. The Andersons named the farm 'Ndirande' after a mountain in Malawi that they had been able to see from their home when they had lived in Blantyre in the 1920s. Meryl and Colin came home to Ndirande for the school holidays and they were the happiest of times. Meryl's parents had a very full and active social life together, and often the two teenagers would go off on their own, horse riding and visiting friends, either on neighbouring farms or at the Ruwa or Goromonzi Clubs – the hub of all social and community life. Meryl had two very clear memories of her teenage years in Goromonzi, one was of dancing and parties and the other of young love! Square dancing was all the craze in the late 1950s and every weekend someone in the area would host a dance – a wonderful social life was virtually guaranteed. For the Andersons, keeping up appearances and being in with the right social scene was very important and Meryl was presented as a debutante to the then-Governor of Southern Rhodesia, Sir Peveril William-Powlett.

She was also sent to a finishing school in the UK where she met and became engaged to the Master of the Southdown Hunt. He was quite a bit older than Meryl and the Andersons seemed quite impressed with the match but it didn't last and the engagement was broken off when Meryl returned to Rhodesia. In later years, Meryl wrote that the end of the relationship with the Sussex farmer was probably just as well and said:

'His love of hunting would have very soon come between us, as I became less naïve and began to realise that all animals are sentient beings.'

In the meantime, Colin was also sent to the UK, to the Royal Agriculture College in Cirencester. The Andersons' attempt to turn Colin into a farmer were not to be. He was far more interested in the social life and parties. He had some pretty wild friends including Julian Cayo-Evans who, at the time, apart from his studies at Cirencester, was also involved with the Free Wales Army. Years later, Meryl received a letter from Julian who wrote: 'Panda and I were such good friends and we had a lot of fun at Cirencester. We used to go off to London in an old Austin 7 that he had got hold of. I hold such happy memories of him, for me the world was a better place knowing him.'

At times Colin's 'fun' at Cirencester got out of hand and he was finally asked to leave after he and a friend 'borrowed' a tractor and fully loaded muck-spreader from the institution and proceeded to drive through the picturesque town of Cirencester – spattering cow dung on the pretty shop fronts and in their wake! The twins seemed destined for Rhodesia and had their joint 21st birthday party at the Ruwa Club in February 1960 and Meryl would never forget that night – or the next morning!

'It was a huge bash, complete with the BSAP band! [British South Africa Police] Presents included an MG sports car for Colin and a more sedate brand new Anglia for me. The following morning the phone lines were all red hot as our traumatised parents swapped notes on what time and in what state their offspring got home!'

Bains Hope Farm held fond memories for Meryl as not only was it on the boundary of Ndirande farm but Meryl was madly in love with the young man who was working there as a Farm Assistant to the owners, Jack and Molly Hughes. Every day an employee from Ndirande would walk to Bains Hope to get milk from the dairy. Walking through the bush was the quickest way to get to Bains Hope and became the perfect way for Meryl and her young man to exchange passionate love notes! Once twin brother Colin discovered that it wasn't only milk being carried from one farm to the next, he began intercepting the 'postman' and seizing the love letters and would then tease and taunt Meryl for the rest of the day! In the end Meryl would ride almost all the way to Bains Hope herself to collect and deliver the love letters and she knew every inch of the farm. Her young love went on to become a leader in agriculture in Zimbabwe, holding high office in the CFU when the land invasions began.

Bains Hope had been in the Hughes family for three generations and over more than 60 years they had built the business up to one of the finest dairy farms in the country. William Hughes' grandfather bought the farm in 1932 when there was just a shack on the property. When William's father, Jack Hughes, started farming on Bains Hope he had only one animal – a cat called 'Livestock'! The dream however was for a dairy farm and it began when 22 Jersey cows were bought in Natal, South Africa and railed to Rhodesia, all being milked twice a day on the train journey! William took over the running of the farm when his parents retired and the business thrived. In 1999 he wrote:

'We have slowly, over the years, built up what my grandfather started, and my parents nurtured. Bains Hope is very much a family farm, and we hope it will continue to be so with our children in the years ahead.'

This was not to be because in 2003 the Hughes family were evicted from Bains Hope in the land seizures and not long afterwards Meryl came back into the picture of the farm so familiar to her from her childhood.

At first when they seized Bains Hope, the Zimbabwe government divided the farm up into small plots and allocated these to what they called A1 settlers – peasants practising subsistence agriculture. Later, for some unknown reason, the once prime dairy farm was re-allocated to commercial farming (which was what it was in the first place!) and given to what was called an

A2 farmer. The A1 settlers who had been allocated and started developing their small plots refused to move and they clashed almost immediately with Mr Bayisa, the A2 farmer who had been allocated the farm. Both sides claimed ownership of Bains Hope Farm.

Mr Bayisa was a dairy farmer with 15 years experience and already had a smallholding but he had been given an 'offer letter' from the Zimbabwe government and began to move his cattle onto Bains Hope Farm in April 2003. Offer Letters were about as official as it came and were literally letters which named an acquired farm and the prospective new farmer the government of Zimbabwe was offering it to. Offer Letters were of course much sought-after and many forgeries emerged which resulted in a deepening of the chaos on the ground.

On Bains Hope the A1 settlers who had planted little squares of maize and beans and vegetables on their plots could not protect their crops from the dairy cows but were not prepared to move. Mr Bayisa, with his Offer Letter from the government and 260 Holstein dairy cows said he was not moving either as the property had been allocated to him.

It was a shambles that had become the norm on hundreds of commercial farms around the country. Clashes and chaos were inevitable and for two months the fight for occupation of Bains Hope continued. The A1 settlers repeatedly confined Mr Bayisa's dairy cows to small paddocks and refused to allow the animals to graze on the farm. Mr Bayisa brought his cattle workers to live on the property but that made no difference to the situation – the workers were intimidated, threatened with violence and stopped from doing their work at every turn by the A1 settlers. In total, 260 Holstein cows were stuck in the middle of a bitter dispute and were losing weight and condition dramatically.

As the stalemate continued and there was no solution in sight, Mr Bayisa had no choice but to save his cows. By June the grass was dry and brown, it was winter and the dairy cows that were strong enough were walked off Bains Hope and back to Mr Bayisa's smallholding, eight kilometres away in Ruwa. The cows not physically capable of the walk were moved by truck and it was during the second trip that Meryl became involved in the affair. Meryl followed the truck to Mr Bayisa's 12-hectare plot in Ruwa and she found a dire situation there too:

'The remainder of the herd were confined in a very small area and being fed on cauliflower and broccoli. Mrs Bayisa explained that her husband's truck was going into Harare twice a day to pick up vegetables that were too old to be sold in shops. Two of the dairy cows had already collapsed and had been "down" for several days. I suggested that they be destroyed as in our experience once a cow has gone down it *is almost impossible to get it up again. The weight of its body puts enormous pressure on the various organs and it soon develops pressure sores.'*

Despite the long-standing personal association Meryl and her family had with Bains Hope Farm and regardless of the issue of the seizure of the property by the government, Meryl offered to help. She could see the dire state of the dairy cows and knew that urgent action was needed. Meryl managed to see past the history and friendship, past the rights and wrongs of land seizures and past the legalities of title deeds and ownership – she saw only the needs of the animals.

Meryl went to the Goromonzi Police Station with SPCA Inspectors Addmore and Misheck and she spoke to the Officer In Charge. The police Inspector listened to what Meryl had to say and agreed that the A1 settlers must move off Bains Hope Farm. He said that these settlers had in fact been allocated plots on another farm in Enterprise and should not stay in Goromonzi. Meryl soon discovered that this same police Inspector was regularly seen drinking beer with the settlers at the weekends. Impartiality was clearly in question and there seemed little, if any, chance that the policeman was going to instruct the A1 settlers to leave Bains Hope Farm. Meryl tried another angle and went to see the DA (District Administrator) hoping that the political hierarchy may be able to assist in providing a solution that would save all those cows which were getting thinner and weaker by the day.

'The DA, Mr Madombo, was very polite and concerned and I had high hopes that he would use his authority to sort the matter out, but as it turned out there was no way that the settlers or war vets, especially the one known as Bishi, were going to listen to him, and in the end he seemed powerless.'

Meryl had two police officers and two SPCA Inspectors with her when she went to Bains Hope on 23 June 2003. There was no sign of any of the A1 settlers near the homestead but some of the Hughes' farm workers were still living at the farm village – they had not been allocated plots on the farm but had nowhere else to go and so they had become little more than squatters in what had been their own homes. All Meryl's hopes for an easy or amicable end to the stalemate between A1 and A2 settlers were dashed almost immediately.

'As we drove back down the drive, a very hostile-looking youth accompanied by two other men, came storming towards the truck demanding to know what we were doing there. He had a red scarf tied around his head and a '3rd Chimurenga' T-shirt on that was long overdue for a wash.'

Having explained why they were there, Meryl was told to wait and the youth disappeared towards the A1 settlers' complex on the other side of the Goromonzi road. When the youth reappeared he told Meryl to leave her truck where it was and follow him, which she did, making sure that both SPCA Inspectors and police were following too.

'We wended our way down a dusty path until we came to a large settlement of huts and a tuck shop. This doubled as a beer hall, evidenced by the fact that all three war veterans we were introduced to were very drunk. They offered me a chair to sit on but I declined – preferring to speak to them at their level. The two police officers and I tried to explain the reason for our visit: i.e. that the DA said that they had to move but we were mostly drowned out by the political lecture that we were subjected to by all three war vets. The most vociferous was from the man who called himself Bishi – their leader and notorious in the area for his hold over the locals. The gist of all their aggression was that there was no way the government or anyone was going to move them off the farm. Our police escort (both of whom were in uniform) disappeared into the beer hall for a drink of Chibuku [beer], re-appearing a few minutes later wiping the white residue from around their mouths.'

There was no question at all now about the ability of the police to be impartial and the situation for Meryl, whether she acknowledged it or not, was extremely dangerous. A white woman, out of sight of the main road, in a beer hall in a settlers village, surrounded by angry and drunk war veterans and with her police escort drinking beer whilst on duty and in uniform – it all made for an explosive situation. Meryl did not have a radio in her vehicle and although she had her cell phone with her, there was no signal and so things could not have been much more dangerous at that point.

'I realised that we were making absolutely no progress plus I was tired of the smell of alcohol being breathed at me as the war vets stood inches away, "in my face", screaming at me. We departed back to the police station and then on to the DA's office where I had another meeting with Mr Madombo. He reiterated that the settlers must go and that he would arrange for the police to meet ourselves and Mr and Mrs Bayisa at Bains Hope the following day.'

The A1 settlers had obviously understood that something serious was happening because when Meryl and three SPCA Inspectors arrived at Bains Hope the next morning the driveway had been blocked off with boulders. With some difficulty they managed to roll the boulders off the road and Mr and Mrs Bayisa arrived shortly afterwards. Mrs Bayisa told Meryl that two more dairy cows had died and it came as such sad news because the cows had already suffered so much. There was still no sign of the police and so they all stood around waiting but were soon spotted.

'After about 15 minutes three very hostile-looking youths arrived, including our friend with the dirty 3rd Chimurenga T-shirt, and a tirade of abuse was directed at me – including informing me that I was "an animal and a dog". Elias, our youngest and most hot-headed Assistant Vet, was seething and looked as if he was about to take a swing at the youth but he was restrained by Addmore and Sternford who told him not to react.'

There was still no sign of the police and at the first opportunity Meryl left and went back to the Goromonzi Police Station where she requested the Officer In Charge to accompany her back to the farm. She knew she was pushing her luck and was completely bowled over when the Inspector agreed and bought a member of PISI (Police Internal Security and Intelligence) along too. The police were in the vehicle with Mr and Mrs Bayisa and Meryl in the SPCA truck with her team of three. The two vehicles stopped at the farm entrance on the main Goromonzi road where a path led off to the settlers' compound. Within minutes a large crowd had arrived, many were women and youths. A confrontation seemed inevitable.

'Once again the 3rd Chimurenga T-shirt was there – axe in hand – marching up and down, singing Chimurenga songs and doing a very good job of getting the crowd psyched up. One of the women was behaving as if she was possessed – flinging herself around and shouting. The situation was very tense. At this moment a Chibuku lorry arrived and delivered a large quantity of "scuds" [brown, barrel shaped, plastic beer containers] which were soon opened by the crowd and the contents downed.'

It was only 10 in the morning and Meryl had the distinct feeling that they were in for trouble – despite the presence of the high–ranking police official. She was right!

'We sat down on some rocks and waited for Inspector Marangarire to address the crowd which was now very hostile – the frenzy-makers having done a good job. However, before Marangarire was given a chance to speak, a youth in a blue dustcoat – with "Duly's" [a well-known vehicle sales and maintenance company] written on the back – also with axe in hand, shouted "Pamberi ne Zanu PF". [Long live Zanu PF] Everyone responded except SPCA Inspector Augustine and myself.

'This incensed the axe-wielding youth who screamed at Augustine to leave immedi-ately. Augustine stood his ground and said why should he – he is a member of Zanu

PF anyway. The youth, once again with clenched fist in the air, repeated the slogan: "Pamberi Zanu PF" – the crowd responded, including Augustine, but I did not. The Duly's youth then turned his attention to me and with the handle of his axe prodding at my face, screamed at me to shout the party slogan. (Of course not a word of protest from the most senior policeman in the area.) I decided that this was not the right time to refuse on principle, so I shouted the party slogan. "Duly" was still not happy and screamed that my clenched fist had not been raised high enough – my second effort seemed to satisfy him.'

Once the obligatory slogans had been shouted and clenched fists raised to the satisfaction of the youths, police Inspector Marangirire addressed the A1 settlers. He tried to explain that the Agriculture Minister wanted Mr and Mrs Bayisa to run Bains Hopes as a dairy farm and the settlers to go to another farm in Enterprise. The policeman's words were continuously drowned out by shouts and taunts from the crowd who were getting angrier by the minute. After a few minutes Inspector Marangarire realised he was getting nowhere and gave up. Meryl again became the focus of attention:

'Once again the youth with the axe came at me, the handle centimetres from my face, yelling that if I ever came to the farm again people would hear on News Hour [ZBC TV main evening news bulletin] what happened to me.'

With the crowd of angry A1 settlers shouting and screaming that they should leave immediately, the police Inspector, Meryl and the SPCA Inspectors and Mr and Mrs Bayisa walked as slowly as they dared back to the vehicles. Several of the youths pushed Mr Bayisa around as he passed; he was not a young man and not in good health but thankfully he did not react and this prevented an open outbreak of violence.

Later Meryl went back to the DA but he said there was nothing more he could do and she was filled with despair for the fate of the cattle – it seemed no one else cared that the animals were malnourished and starving and growing weaker with every day.

In the following weeks Meryl regularly visited Mr Bayisa's plot in Ruwa to check on the condition of the dairy cattle. At the start of July, in the middle of Zimbabwe's winter, she found a very depressing sight. The dairy cows had lost a great deal of weight, two more had collapsed and Meryl gave instructions that they must be destroyed. The cows that were stronger were grazing on a nearby piece of land that Mr Bayisa had managed to rent; the cows too weak to walk to that land were munching dejectedly on old broccoli and cauliflower. Meryl was frustrated and in despair as to how to help the dairy cows and she phoned

Mrs Bayisa and warned her that the situation had deteriorated to critical levels and that the couple should do whatever they could to improve the conditions for the cows before it was too late. On her next visit to the plot Meryl found that another dairy manager had been employed and he was bringing in a better quality of supplementary feed but she knew this was only a temporary measure. If Mr Bayisa could not find a long term solution to sustain the big dairy herd, de-stocking would have to be undertaken.

A few days later Meryl decided to visit the war veteran Bishi at Bains Hope Farm to see if there was any hope that the A1 settlers would move. Bishi was not at the farm and so Meryl asked Addmore to call some of the settlers from the compound, including the woman who had appeared 'possessed' on their last visit. It didn't take long for an angry tirade to be launched at Meryl.

'As soon as they saw the ZNSPCA truck they started shouting that we were in the pay of Bayisa, that there was corruption in the allocation of land (they were right there!), that they had been told to see the Governor in Marondera but that they had refused to do so. They said they wanted President Mugabe to come and see them, that the Government could bring guns and dogs but they would NEVER leave Bains Hope. I noticed since our last visit that all the good grazing had been burnt – there seemed little hope that the dairy cows would ever get back to the farm.'

For the next few weeks Meryl could do nothing for the animals on Bains Hope or any other farm as her heart condition resulted in an emergency operation in South Africa but the plight of the dairy cows remained on her mind and in her diary.

In the first week of September 2003, over three months after first getting involved with the starving dairy cows and Bains Hope Farm, Meryl phoned the Governor of Marondera in absolute desperation. She had known him for many years and impressed on him the suffering that the cows were going through because no one in authority seemed prepared to take a stand against the A1 settlers. Meryl told the Governor that she may have to consider prosecution under the Prevention of Cruelty to Animals Act. When the Governor told Meryl that he was aware of the situation and the urgency, Meryl felt a glimmer of hope. As asked, she then submitted a written report detailing the suffering of the dairy herd and then could do no more and so again she waited.

'Ten days later as we passed the farm entrance on our way to Harare, we saw a large crowd which included Bayisa, members of the Land Committee, police and several recognisable war veterans and settlers from the Goromonzi area – maybe something had happened at long last – maybe the Governor had succeeded.'

A few days later Meryl received the good news. The A1 settlers had finally been moved off and Mr Bayisa's dairy cows had been walked back on to Bains Hope Farm. Meryl was told that war veteran Bishi had been outraged and had rounded up some of the A1 settlers to go and slash and axe the cattle but the police returned with reinforcements from Support Unit and the mob were sent packing. Meryl had good reason to be proud of the closing entry in her diary about the condition of the dairy cows on Bains Hope farm:

'It is so good to see the dairy cows back in the paddocks, and fences being mended. Over the following months we continued to monitor the welfare of the herd. The Bayisa's had now taken on an excellent dairy manager who had previously worked for a commercial farmer who had been evicted from his farm. It was so good to see these previously emaciated cows now looking fat and sleek with full udders. If we had not stopped the Bayisa's truck all those months ago, we may never have been given the opportunity to save most of the herd.'

Extracts from Meryl's Diary:

A courageous man eats his own strength.
(One who has worked reaps the reward of his toil.)
— Sindebele proverb

July 2003
Odzi:
Problems on farms in the Odzi area so drove through with Addmore — he stayed at the Mutare SPCA and I went to the Boyd's again.

Bromley:
Saturday morning and thought I'd treat myself to a cooked breakfast for a change and then get on with mountain of paperwork. Phone interrupted plans and it was an urgent request for help with over 1,000 ostriches on a property approx. 15 kilometres away from me. War vets and settlers and in particular a man called Bear who works for the Harare Municipality have barricaded farmer into his house and no one allowed to feed or water the ostriches. Phoned Addmore to accompany me — he was asleep and thought he was going to stay that way most of the day!

Me, Addmore and two police Constables finally arrived at the farm at 9am… a large crowd of settlers surrounding the house, all singing Chimurenga songs and dancing — they had been there all night and had no intention of releasing the farmer who was inside the house. In nearby paddocks we could see hundreds of ostriches pacing up and down the fences — obviously looking for their food which was long overdue… Bear emerged from the crowd wearing a huge brown overcoat and reminded me that he knew me from when we had worked together with the Municipality on Dog Control By-laws. When I asked him if the ostriches were being fed? – he made the fatuous remark 'I won't comment on that'... Tried talking to Bear but he became increasingly hostile... Police wouldn't go with me to talk to the workers so Addmore and I walked down the winding path on our own. Workers confirmed that they were being stopped from going to work...

Bear appeared looking intimidating and I informed him that we now had confirmation that the ostriches had not been fed since the previous morning. Told of the possible severe consequences for him and the settlers if the ostriches were not given food and water. Bear agreed that two workers could attend to the ostriches – it would probably take them all day but it was better than nothing. ... Much jeering and cheering from the rent-a-crowd as we drove past them down the drive and out of the farm gate.

They thought they had won but I was satisfied that at least we had achieved our objective. Dropped police off at their post, Addmore at Goromonzi and went home. Later heard that the beleaguered farmer phoned his mother-in-law to tell her that he had watched our confrontation with Bear through his bedroom window and wanted to thank us for our intervention. It was of course beyond our powers to have gone to his assistance and he understood that. Breakfast turned into brunch and then I knew the paperwork would have to be tackled.

Ruwa:
11th July. Another bad time with my heart. Rose Nurse phoned an ambulance and then came with me as they rushed me to the Avenues [Hospital]. They had no spare beds in the Cardiac Care Unit, so once my heart had been stabilised I was taken to the hospital at Dandaro at about 1am. I was absolutely freezing – I still had my uniform on and no jersey. The staff were very kind, made me a cup of tea and bought me a hot water bottle. Won't forget seeing Rose standing in the Resuscitation Room – a concerned look on her face as she stood with my boots that I always wore for work hanging around her neck where she had knotted the laces!

Was allowed home the next day, Saturday, but at 6am on Sunday morning had another attack and once again found myself being rushed to the Avenues by ambulance. The pain was the worst I had ever known it. I was given morphine but it didn't ease the pain – later they gave me more but it just made me sick. I don't remember what happened after this, they told me I had another attack. The next day Linda and I flew to Johannesburg.

CHAPTER THIRTY

Heart beat

'I no doubt deserved my enemies,
but don't believe I deserved my friends.'
— Walt Whitman 1819-1892

July 2003

By the second week of July 2003 Meryl's body finally forced her to stop. More and more often she was being rushed to trauma centres and hospitals with friends or by ambulance. Meryl knew what was wrong with her. She had a heart condition called Paroxysmal Atrial Tachycardia which was the development of a short circuit which made her heart's rhythm change – in Meryl's case it made her heart beat much too fast. During an attack, Meryl's heart would race from the average 50-100 beats a minute to anything between 140-240 times a minute! The attacks could last for just a few seconds to several hours. In Meryl's case the attacks lasted several hours. Her breathing became difficult and she felt as if her chest would explode with the pain. Meryl had started having these attacks in 1995 and had medication which helped to some extent. She had also identified some of the things that could trigger an attack – food, drink (especially coffee), stress and exercise.

There was certainly nothing at all about her job of rescuing animals from invaded farms that could be said to be helping her heart condition – there was little doubt that this way of life was making things far worse for Meryl. Just flicking through her diaries, it was easy to see why! In the last three and a half years Meryl had been onto hundreds of invaded farms. She had driven thousands of kilometres, criss-crossing the country repeatedly; she was constantly in places and situations of danger, dealing with threatening and aggressive people and she had rescued an uncountable number of creatures from birds and reptiles to fish and mammals – tame and wild. At last her body had had enough!

Meryl's doctor told her things couldn't go on like this and advised her that she needed an operation to regulate her heart condition but when she learnt that this could not be done in Zimbabwe, Meryl presumed she was sunk. After years of working for the love of animals with a welfare organisation, Meryl had only ever received a minimal salary. All the savings she had accumulated had been completely exhausted with the huge medical bills incurred the previous year with several operations that Roly had needed. Meryl wrote:

> 'I did not even have the money to pay for Roly's funeral. It was only months later when I went to the undertakers in Bulawayo to tell them that I would try and pay them off in instalments, that they informed me that the bill had been paid by an anonymous well-wisher.'

It would be months before Meryl finally found out who the well-wisher was, and there were no words, then or now, that adequately expressed her deep gratitude.

Without savings or foreign currency, a trip to South Africa, fees for a specialist, a heart operation and a stay in a South African hospital were all totally out of the question. What Meryl didn't know, however, was just exactly how desperately people in Zimbabwe, and neighbouring South Africa, wanted to help her. For three and a half years Meryl had been our hero, the brave woman on the front line, facing the dangers and fears and doing what we could not do. We had heard her voice so often on Short Wave Radio Africa at night. Started by Gerry Jackson and staffed solely by Zimbabweans in exile, this was the radio station which broadcast from the UK after its original brainchild, Capital Radio, had been shut down in Harare by the government.

Sitting by candlelight during the nightly electricity cuts, battery powered radios brought Zimbabweans the stories of what Meryl was doing. Meryl had become our eyes on farms and in districts that had become 'no-go' areas. Often listeners would be reduced to tears as they heard Meryl tell of what she had seen: cattle that had been burnt, pigs starving to death, dogs terrified, beaten, abducted, abandoned. Zimbabweans had seen Meryl's name in the local papers too as she spoke out whenever she could about the desperate plight of the animals caught in the land seizures.

Sometimes we even saw Meryl drive past, headed to or from remote areas – in a dusty pick-up truck, cages crammed in the back, people squashed in the front – but we hadn't known how to thank her or acknowledge what she was doing.

When Meryl's heart finally forced her to stop, here at last was a way for people to thank her. An email appeal was sent out by the National Chairman of the ZNSPCA on 23 June 2003 and within a couple of days it was flooding computer screens and it seemed everyone knew that Meryl was in trouble.

'Sadly but not surprisingly, the strain of the last three years have taken their toll on our valiant Meryl, who continues bravely to head the rescues in Zimbabwe under increasingly difficult conditions. Our "60-something" Chief Inspector has suffered from a heart condition since she was a young woman but has always kept her condition, and the pain and discomfort she experiences, hidden from most. She has on several occasions been rushed to hospital to stabilise her heart rate but the incidents have become increasingly frequent and it is now essential that she undergoes the necessary "keyhole" surgery (electrical ablation) to prevent a potentially fatal attack.

In recognition of the invaluable role that Meryl has played in rescuing and safeguarding literally hundreds of thousands of animals, we would like to do all that we can to help our brave champion. We realise how generous and supportive everyone has been with contributions towards the valiant work of the rescue team but are confident that you will help if you can or pass this on to anyone in a position to assist that Meryl will be able to continue with her outstanding animal welfare work in the future.'

Everyone wanted to help and from around the country calls and pledges began to pour in. Aside from Meryl's work with the SPCA, her long-standing association with the Kennel Club and judging dogs raised even more awareness and soon dog lovers and owners in Zimbabwe, South Africa, the UK and Australia were stepping forward to help.

International awareness escalated thanks to the article of journalist, Fred Bridgland in the *Sunday Independent*, a South African newspaper. 'Ailing animal activist braves Mugabe's war vets,' was the headline of Bridgland's 29 June article and it told of Meryl's most recent harrowing encounter on Bains Hope farm. It made for compelling reading and towards the end of the article Bridgland mentioned Meryl's need for a heart operation and quoted the high praise proffered by her boss, the Chairman of the ZNSPCA:

'The keyhole operation she needs is unavailable in Zimbabwe and the ZNSPCA is trying to raise funds for her to be operated on at a private clinic in Johannesburg. "I just cannot tell you where we would be without this remarkable lady," said the ZNSPCA chairperson. "Without her, animal welfare would be set back for good in Zimbabwe. Her life has been at risk more times than she's told you about. But the number of times she has been rushed to the hospital to stabilise her heart rate have become increasingly frequent."'

The day after Bridgland's article appeared in the South African press, Meryl got a call on her mobile phone. It was John Robbie, a very well-known current affairs talk show host from Radio 702 in South Africa. John Robbie had read the newspaper article and wanted to talk to her on his radio programme about the situation regarding animals on seized farms in Zimbabwe. Robbie said that he had not thought about fund raising for Meryl but his listeners took the decision into their own hands! Meryl was staggered at what happened next:

> 'John Robbie came on the phone and wanted to interview me. He chatted to me about my work and then mentioned the op – he said something like: "Well, maybe we could help." Before the interview was over, some man rang in from Krugersdorp to say that he pledged R500! As I was driving to Goromonzi about half an hour later John phoned on my cell phone again to give me the news that the entire amount had been raised... I pulled over and stopped the truck at the side of the Goromonzi road and just burst into tears – I was just so overwhelmed.'

John Robbie was equally surprised:

> *'We were staggered at the response of our listeners. Within half an hour listeners had pledged aeroplane flights, ambulance trips, hospital time and money – from business people donating R10,000 to the ordinary listener giving R5 – and we had covered the cost of Meryl's operation. It was overwhelming.'*

At the same time as radio airwaves were being flooded with offers in Johannesburg, Juanita Crawford, also in South Africa, dedicated the annual publication, 'Stafford World', to Meryl and wrote an editorial whose title spoke for so many: 'Meryl, we salute you,' she said. Without a doubt this testimony to Meryl engendered even more support and although Crawford did not specifically ask for donations, she said that the SPCA had put out an appeal for help. People who knew Meryl, and undoubtedly many who did not, could not help but be inspired and motivated by Crawford's words:

> *'Meryl's work has taken her beyond anything you or I could possibly imagine. She continues to go beyond the call of duty on a daily basis, tirelessly bringing relief to abandoned, tortured, mutilated and deprived animals. Her determination and courage not to let such vast numbers of animals suffer needlessly, has personally cost her dearly, not only financially, but physically as well... Today Meryl stands the SPCA team in good stead, despite the most awful of circumstances, as a pillar of strength and a tower of fortitude. Her willpower is immeasurable and her courage immense.'*

A tidal wave of support, empathy and concern had begun and the momentum kept building. Cherry Grobler, editor and owner of South African magazine *All About Dogs* interviewed and wrote about Meryl's work, and

253

her need for financial assistance with her medical condition. Cherry's articles spanned two months and in the July 2003 edition, in one sentence she revealed the secret ingredient that so few people had been able to understand – the very reason that Meryl and her small team of SPCA Inspectors had been able to achieve so much.

'The ZNSPCA is adamant it will continue to work for and on behalf of the animals of Zimbabwe, whatever political party their owners belong to. As one of the senior war vets, a Base Commander said to me recently: "Mrs Harrison – at present we are at war but one day, you and I will eat cake together in Harare."'

A month later Cherry Grobler ran another full page on Meryl Harrison in the magazine *All About Dogs*.

'In in a bordered box came the summary of the gifts given to the woman everyone admired so much:
Meryl Harrison's operation sponsors included the following:
BA/Comair provided two return tickets to get Meryl to South Africa.
Milpark Hospital provided hospital services free of charge.
Cardiologists Dr Graham Cassell and Dr Prof Obel provided their services free of charge.
Medtronics donated Meryl's R25,000 pacemaker.
Avis Rent-a-Car provided a vehicle and driver for the duration of Meryl's stay and some money for herself.
Hotel bills were paid for by Talk Radio 702 from donations received.'

Meanwhile, back at home, the emails kept flying! The ZNSPCA appeal had gone far and wide very quickly. It had originally been estimated that between 60-70,000 Rand would be needed. Far more had in fact been raised, both at home and away, and then, as it turned out, almost everything that was physically possible had also been donated in kind!

Meryl knew nothing of the details of the fund-raising and finances, or of the excess realised: everything was left in the hands of the Zimbabwean and South African SPCA's. By now Meryl was spending more time than she could spare at the Trauma Centre and doctors frantically tried to get her off her medication and stable enough to travel and be assessed.

When Linda Townsend phoned Meryl to see how she was, she heard, for the first time in their long-standing friendship, a Meryl she didn't know.

'Meryl said she was going to have to go to Jo'burg for a heart procedure and she told me she was very apprehensive. Meryl always came across as independent, resourceful and absolutely able to cope with whatever arose. I'd never heard apprehension from her before. I put the phone down, spoke to Brian and ten minutes later phoned Meryl back and asked her if she would like me to go with her! Meryl immediately said yes!'

Two days before she flew to South Africa, Meryl found a note on her desk. It was short and to the point but meant a great deal:

'Have a nice trip to South Africa. I wish you a successful operation.
From Addmore and family.'

Meryl and Linda left for Johannesburg, South Africa, flying on donated tickets, on 14 July 2003. They had been told that an ambulance had been arranged and would be waiting at the airport to take Meryl directly to Milpark Hospital – it wasn't! Linda began to get worried when they had been waiting for nearly two hours and still there was no sign of an ambulance or anyone else to take charge. Because the heart specialists needed to be able to assess Meryl's exact condition fully, she had not had any medication at all and was beginning to feel distinctly unwell. Linda didn't panic – she isn't that kind of person – but she did admit to feeling very anxious by now! She found a wheelchair and manoeuvred between her sick friend, their combined luggage and telephones – no mean feat in a crowded airport in a strange country with a seriously sick friend at her side! At last Linda tracked down Marcelle, the head of the South African NSPCA, who came to their rescue.

For the next two days Linda camped out at the Milpark hospital while Meryl was monitored and the preparations for the procedure were made. On the third day everything was ready and Linda got to the hospital early in the morning and walked alongside the stretcher which carried Meryl to the theatre. It would be seven hours before Linda would be allowed to see her friend again. Later Meryl explained the procedure that had taken place during the operation:

'Once I went into theatre I had an angiogram, then an electrical ablation – that is when the surgeon inserted a catheter into the chamber of the heart to deliver pulses of energy that destroy the area that is short-circuiting in the heart muscle. They ended up by destroying all the electrical pathways between the atria and ventricle and then I had to wait quite a long time whilst they sent for a pacemaker. I remember lying on a stretcher type bed in a passageway for what seemed like ages. It was freezing cold

– every now and again, Graham Cassell would come and have a chat to see how I was doing.'

Eight days later, after eight years of discomfort and pain, Meryl was discharged from Milpark Hospital in Johannesburg. Saying 'thank you,' to doctors, specialists, nurses and the hundreds of people who had donated in cash and kind, felt so inadequate and insufficient to Meryl; it seemed like such an understatement. What Meryl did not understand was that for every day that she had put her life on the line to rescue a cat or a dog, a pig, cow, sheep or horse on an invaded farm or a violent township, thousands of people had felt so inadequate when all they could do was say 'thank you'. What goes around had come around!

For the next week Linda and Meryl stayed in Johannesburg, taken backwards and forwards to the hospital and wherever they needed to go in a donated, chauffeur-driven, Avis car. The next week was not easy:

'Although I was discharged, I had to return to the hospital every day for physiotherapy. After the op I developed incredible back pain, could only sleep sitting up in a chair in the hotel room. Graham and Prof Obel didn't know what was causing it, so thought some physiotherapy might help. I really felt lousy that whole week at the hotel. Linda was a fantastic friend during that time. The only time we went out, apart from our trips to the hospital, was on the last day.'

Linda knew when Meryl was back to normal when her friend started talking about the excellent second-hand shops in the suburbs of Johannesburg. Meryl loved going to these sort of shops and to jumble sales and had always furnished her homes with items picked up in this way. She'd always felt quite at home with second-hand things and had a knack of making them look as if they'd always belonged. Linda didn't think Meryl was up to that kind of shopping just yet – not after a heart operation, so using the money that had been so kindly donated by Avis they went on a small excursion close to the hotel:

'I persuaded Meryl that we should go on a little shopping trip. Meryl was always so frugal with her purchases and I had to really urge her to spoil herself and buy some toiletries and make-up and smellies!'

On 26 July, ten days after they had flown out of Zimbabwe, Linda and Meryl went home. Linda had phoned ahead and asked her husband Brian to cook a chicken and meet them at Harare airport. It was just as well that she did because as much of an international heroine as Meryl was, no one else was there to meet them. Meryl was home, no fuss, no fanfare, just another day.

Brian met the two women at the airport and they drove straight out to Meryl's cottage in Ruwa. Neighbours had brought bread and milk for her and the chicken went into the fridge. Linda, thoughtful to the last, checked on linen, made sure Meryl was OK and then they left to pick up lives that had been set down just ten days before. Life in Zimbabwe, regardless of who you were, had become like this, very matter–of–fact!

Six days later, on 1 August Meryl sat in her SPCA truck as a passenger. Inspector Sternford was driving and they headed for Maplanka Farm in Mtorashanga to rescue three dogs abandoned after the property had been taken over by the army. In her diary Meryl wrote: *'I did not feel 100%!'*

Three months later, Meryl drove to Bulawayo to have her pacemaker checked. The pain and attacks in her heart had stopped but the stress and worry were back with a vengeance and she was again working full-time on farm rescues. Every month Meryl had a shortfall on her medical aid and every month she struggled to find the money to pay for the stabilizing medication she had to continue to take. Inflation was already at 430% and by Christmas would be 600%.

Extracts from Meryl's Diary:

> *'Most people walk in and out of your life, but only friends leave footprints in your heart.'*
> *– Anon*

August 2003
1st August: Back in the truck, still had a dressing over the wound and not allowed to drive. Went to a Maplanka Farm in Mutorashanga as a passenger and rescued three dogs. Farm had been taken over by army.

Marondera:
Tom and Sheila Holden badly beaten up and robbed at their rented farm. Both are in hospital in Marondera and are in a bad way. Their daughter called us in because in the ensuing mayhem one of their Scotties had run away and could not be found. Got to the farm and found that one Scottie, 'Lizzie' had been found, but the other, 'Timolena', had been beaten by one of the thugs and had a nasty wound on her back – although still very nervous she was so good as we treated her.

Mutare:
Invited for the weekend by the Vice Chair of Mutare SPCA to give a short course on

Policy and Procedure to their Committee – accompanied by Addmore.

26 August: A year since Roly died. When friends ask me how I am – I always reply 'fine' – but inside I am not, I miss him and his quiet support so very much.

September 2003

Norton:
Trouble at the Lion and Cheetah Park – manager phoned to say they might need help.

Three local war vets had accused the manager of disturbing an old burial ground and of breaking some pots on the graves – this inside the boundaries of the Lion and Cheetah Park. Of course he had done nothing of the sort, it was just an excuse to invade the park.

Goromonzi:
Had Roly's beloved Staffie, 'Rosie' put to sleep. I had given her to Roly when she was just a tiny puppy. He began showing her and was hugely proud when she went on to win Best In Show in Mutare. She was never the same once Roly died and her health just deteriorated – our vet suspected a tumour on the brain. I was with her as she gently went to join Roly.

South Africa:
Drove to Johannesburg on the 19th as this was always the best way of bringing back the many donations of dog food, etc that had been collected for us by the NSPCA in South Africa.

Flew down to Cape Town to receive a joint award from the International Fund For Animal Welfare (IFAW) and the South African Animal Talk magazine. The award was called the Animal Rehabilitation Superhero! There were several other recipients. The occasion was held at a Breakfast in a local restaurant in Cape Town, a very pleasant occasion and the awards were different – very ethnic – a wooden fish on a wooden base with an engraved plaque.

Attended the All Africa Humane Education Summit organised by a wonderful lady, Louise van der Merwe. She had invited people from all over Africa to attend and it must have taken a tremendous amount of organizing. It was a great success. Five days later drove back to Zimbabwe with the truck packed to the roof with donations.

Collected my dogs from the kennels and once again they went quite mad with delight when they saw me!

CHAPTER THIRTY-ONE

Poisonous fish

'Oh what a tangled web we weave,
When first we practice to deceive.'
– Sir Walter Scott, 1771-1832

August Hill Farm, Goromonozi, August 2003
Abby and Humphrey were the much-loved Abyssinian cats of Dr Sandy Murray
and his wife, Ann, but in the noise, frantic activity and confusion of a 24-hour
farm eviction, the cats disappeared. Dr Murray was a well-known radiologist
and in his 70s but neither of these things spared him from the land invasions.
Meryl had been told that the Murrays' August Hill farm in Goromonzi had
been taken over by a man called Munjanja, a retired member of the CIO
(Central Intelligence Organisation) who had businesses in the nearby town of
Marondera.

August Hill Farm had been purchased by the Murrays in 1968 and
in a local history book on the area, the Murrays told the story of their home:

'Work on our house as it is now was started in 1974 with much of the building
material being produced locally. The front door was from the Old Meikles [Hotel]
"Corner Bar". All of the roofing material, ex Meikles Hotel, originally came from
Washington, USA in 1927. Three teak doors came from the old Prince's Theatre
and another from a demolished post office. Our staircase of Burma teak came from the
Midlands Hotel in Gweru.'

The house and its components on August Hill Farm were not the only
things steeped in history. Sandy Murray believed that people had lived there
for many hundreds if not thousands of years. He said the faintest pigmented
lines could still be seen on rock faces in the two caves on the farm – perhaps
the drawings of passing San hunters and gatherers. In recent times a builder,
Thomas Nyakudya, had worked on many of the farm projects with the Murrays
and he told them that his family and his great-great-great grandfather had once

lived in this valley. Thomas told the Murrays that his forefathers had been chased away after the first Chimurenga and that he hoped that one day his family might be able to come back to the area. The take-over of August Hill Farm this August 2003 had nothing to do with any of Thomas's relations.

Meryl had been told that the eviction of the Murrays from August Hill Farm had been accompanied by violence and a driver had apparently been severely beaten. Even though this was home turf as it was near where Meryl lived and where the ZNSPCA offices were, she proceeded with caution.

'I was a bit worried for the team as we all lived in the area, but we had always received good co-operation and help from the locals in the past and Munjanja was not from the area himself.'

Meryl and Addmore loaded the truck with two cat cages and a large packet of cat biscuits and arrived at August Hill Farm to find the main entrance and then the second gate barricaded with large poles. Between the two of them Meryl and Addmore managed to drag the poles off the road and drive to the security fence that surrounded the house. The gate was chained and padlocked and being guarded by a surly-looking man holding a gun. He was tall and thin and had blood-shot eyes and had obviously been tasked by Munjanja to guard the farm. Meryl explained to him who she and Addmore were and the reason for their visit. She handed over their ID cards for inspection and pointed out the cages and cat food in the back of the truck. Eventually the armed man grudgingly let Meryl drive in. They immediately saw that Munjanja had left his own dog at the house and the guard told them that the dog chased the two cats whenever they appeared. This was going to make Meryl's job much more difficult.

Still carrying his gun, the guard led Meryl and Addmore into the Murrays house and upstairs to the main bedroom. Leading off from the master suite was a verandah which overlooked a magnificent garden. Even though Ann and Sandy Murray had been chased off August Hill, their employees continued to look after the garden as best they could and it was still in immaculate condition, giving a strangely surreal impression of normalcy.

Meryl knew this wouldn't last long as daytime temperatures were warming up and soon the garden would need water – the one thing the employees could not provide. The electricity had been turned off which meant that water was not being pumped from the borehole and Meryl had come with plastic containers of waters for the animals. The armed guard told Meryl that one of the cats was frequently seen here, sleeping out in the warmth and fresh air, undisturbed and safe. Meryl looked around at her surroundings and the fragments that were left of a life.

'The house was magnificent with a beautiful garden, the rooms now empty of furniture, pictures and personal effects. The electricity had been cut off, the invaders had plundered all the bee hives and the fish ponds were starting to dry up.'

The goldfish in the ponds were huge and Meryl was worried that the settlers might attempt to kill and eat the fish – after all they had shown no respect for the bees and their hives – so she told the guard that the fish were poisonous and that it would be very dangerous to eat them! Meryl's intention was to keep the fish alive until she had time to catch and move them. Goodness knows what her son Nick, with a BSC in Ichthyology and an MSC in Aquaculture would have made of his mother's mumbo-jumbo about goldfish! Amazingly, however, Meryl's words were believed because from then on each successive guard at August Hill Farm solemnly told Meryl each time she visited that these fish were very dangerous to eat!

Meryl and Addmore set the cat trap in the main bedroom with a large dish of cat biscuits and informed the guard that they would come back the following day. As they were leaving Meryl noticed that Munjanja's dog had neither food nor water. They found a sticky plastic container that had obviously been used by the invaders to dispense honey and cut it in half, filling one half with water and the other with food.

The following day Meryl and Addmore returned to August Hill Farm to see if the cats had been caught. Already the tragically familiar signs of the looting of the land were visible.

'As we drove up the long drive we could hear the loud buzzing of timber saws and found an enormous lorry from Marondera loading poles and logs. The "new owner" Munjanja was there directing operations. All the beautiful pine trees surrounding the house were being felled. A tractor with a huge chain attached was dragging the cut trees across the drive, flattening shrubs, plants and smaller trees in its wake. One tree had fallen across the security fence, smashing it and making it very difficult to open the gate.'

Munjanja approached Meryl. She got the impression that he was a 'smooth operator', wearing casual shirt and trousers and driving a fairly smart truck.

'I'm the new owner of this farm,' he announced. 'I will be moving in soon you know.'

Meryl nodded and even though she found it nauseating it was also necessary and so asked for Munjanja's permission to go into the house. Meryl's only priority was to achieve the objective of rescuing Abby and Humphrey – the much-loved cats. Munjanja gave his permission and instructed his gun-toting guard to go with them. The cats had not been caught in the cages but Meryl could see that one had been clever and managed to eat all the food without springing the trap. The food dish was re-filled, the trap checked and another packet of pet food left for Munjanja's dog. Preparing to leave, Meryl saw Dr Murray's young gardener having a whispered conversation with Addmore. As they drove out she asked Addmore what had been going on. Apparently the gardener had hidden what he called 'important papers' that he thought Dr Murray might need and had asked that Meryl and Addmore meet him on a nearby road. Arriving at the designated road Meryl parked under some gum trees and it wasn't long before the youngster appeared out of the thick bush carrying a large box. Then followed a most peculiar encounter which Meryl would never forget.

> 'The gardener looked quickly up and down the road to make sure no one had seen him before putting the box in the back of our truck. He then asked Addmore to assist him with the remainder of the boxes. They appeared to contain mostly old X-rays and medical reports – but it was thoughtful of him to think that Dr Murray might need them. Finally he handed me something wrapped in newspapers – it was a human skull! He whispered to me that if Munjanja, (being CIO) found this, then the Doctor would "be in big trouble."
>
> The skull was obviously an old relic from Dr Murray's medical days, but I could just see the headlines of the government press: "White farmer found with human skull"! The state sponsored press would have a field day.'

Meryl and Addmore were on their way to Harare and would have to go through at least two road blocks so quickly agreed it wouldn't be wise to be travel around with a human skull in the car. Meryl headed back to her Goromonzi office so that she could leave the skull somewhere safe until she could get it back into its rightful 'medical' hands!

> 'On the way I wondered whose skull I had on my lap and if they had been male or female, young or old. The ZNSPCA had rescued a wide variety of animals over the last few years – but this was bizarre! I was quite sure that whoever's skull this was, they wouldn't have wanted to stay at August Hill any longer. Once it had been a happy family home – no longer so now.'

A couple of hours later Meryl collected the skull again and delivered it to a close friend of Dr Murray's who knew all about it and confirmed that it was from the Doctor's medical days. It was a relief to Meryl to have the incident behind her as she was only too well aware of how the situation could so easily have been misinterpreted. If the wrong people had found the skull at a time when the mood in the country was so volatile, there could have been dangerous consequences for the Doctor – not to mention for Meryl and Addmore. The quick thinking of a young gardener had prevented a nasty incident but even so Meryl was glad to have got rid of the passenger in her lap!

When Meryl and Addmore next visited August Hill Farm, the guard at the gate had gone and they were approached by a relation of Munjanja's who informed them they could no longer drive up to the house but had to walk instead. If this would ensure they could keep looking for the cats, Meryl was happy to go along with the new instructions. For the following two weeks they visited the farm every day with food and water. Sometimes they changed the position of the cat trap and other times they switched to a different brand of cat biscuits to try and tempt Abbey and Humphrey to the cage.

As the days passed Meryl and Addmore also kept checking on the condition of the gold fish. A beautiful man-made stream ran through the garden, around shrubs and across once lush lawns. There were little waterfalls and pools in the stream and there had obviously once been a pump which kept the water moving. If Meryl closed her eyes she could almost hear the cool and calming sound of water trickling and bubbling across the garden. Without electricity the stream had fallen still and silent and in the warm August sun evaporation had begun to take its toll. The water level in the pools was dropping and in one pond there was hardly enough water for the fish to swim in. Meryl and Addmore caught the legendary 'poisonous fish' and took them back to the ZNSPCA plot in Goromonzi where an old enamel bath became their new home. It was a far cry from their once cool and beautiful stream on August Hill but at least it was life.

Three weeks after first visiting August Hill farm, success was at last achieved. The Abyssinian cat Abbey was caught in the trap and delivered to a neighbouring farmer who already had the Murray's bantams. Two months later news came that Sandy and Ann Murray had won their court case and that Munjanja was to be evicted. Meryl hoped that the return of the Murrays to the house may mean that Humphrey, the missing cat, would return home but sadly this was not to be. Ann and Sandy Murray did return to their beautiful home but it was short-lived and not long after they were again violently evicted. Humphrey was never found.

Extracts from Meryl's Diary:

'He that has no children knows not what love is.'
— Proverb

October 2003
Mombasa, Kenya:
Masvingo SPCA Inspector, Happson and I went to Kenya where we had been invited to attend a workshop organised by WSPA (World Society for the Protection of Animals) – all expenses paid by WSPA. It was the African Member Society Development Workshop and was held at an hotel in Mombasa and attended by animal welfare folk from all over Africa. I had been asked to give a presentation – of course on the farm rescues. Happson and I went back a long time. He was one of the first Inspectors I had trained back in 1995 and he is very good on law and knows the Prevention of Cruelty to Animals Act better than most.

We always got on very well together. Happson is slim in build and always impeccably dressed. I remember once we were treating donkeys together at Ngundu Halt. It was an incredibly hot day. I was covered in dust and gentian violet and my shirt stuck to me with perspiration. Happson still looked immaculate with his jacket and tie on! He is married with children and has a great sense of humour. We were in Kenya for a week and it was the best animal welfare workshop I had ever attended and Happson and I left feeling we had learnt so much.

28 October. Tim's birthday – phoned him before I left for work – he sounded very happy – his boss and the girls at work always spoilt him on his birthday.

Another very busy day for me – started off with a meeting with the Magistrate at Goromonzi, then to Stockit Farm in Mazowe to check on starving cows on the invaded farm. On the way back call in at Danbury Park to check on the zebra there.

November 2003
Harare:
Tipped off about a possible dog fight in Harare Central. Managed to get several police officers from Harare Central armed with tear gas to accompany us but when we arrived there was no sign of the participants, though plenty of evidence of previous dog fights.

Marondera:
Addmore and I go to a farm accompanied by a vet to destroy four wild stallions that are causing havoc on a stud farm. We never knew who owned the stray stallions – they had apparently been roaming round the area for literally months.

Norton:
More trouble at the Lion and Cheetah Park – manager and his family violently evicted. Went out there to give an injection to a baby jackal and to uplift a baby monkey that the manager's wife was hand rearing.

December 2003
Goromonzi:
Christmas card from Addmore on my desk:
'To Mrs Harrison and Tim. Merry Christmas and a happy New Year! It was very nice to work with you. You have taken me to hotels which I will ever step my foot. (Think he means that without me taking him to hotels when we are away on rescues, he would never have set foot in them!) Looking forward to have nice co-operation from you. I will never find another boss like you. I don't want to lose you. From Addmore and family.'

Christmas Day:
Spent a very happy Christmas day with friends. All of us on our own due to death or divorce. I paid for Tim to come up from Bulawayo on the Blue Arrow coach – was lovely to have a couple of days with him again. He had bought one of his watercolour paintings with him to show me – he'd done it for one of his clients in Bulawayo. It was a bunch of Cosmos flowers and was really brilliant. Tim always much in demand when he comes – several of my friends had waited for him to come up from Byo so that they could get their hair cut by him! He also does all the cooking during his visits to me and he makes an excellent spaghetti bolognese, also several chicken dishes including Coronation Chicken – his speciality. Today we were being spoilt though and only had to take a pudding!

January 2004
Ruwa:
1st January 2004. New Year's Day! A chance to catch up on some of the ever-waiting paperwork and later out for lunch with friends.

Harare:
Spend the first week of the month in investigations of a pet shop where conditions are bad – even worse at the owners home where many of the animals and birds were kept. Called in the City Health Dept. and needed assistance from the police because of the owner's aggressive attitude. A docket to be opened and he is to be charged with Cruelty and Obstruction.

Harare:
Routine inspection of police horses at Morris Depot. Gave the 2 i/c of Equitation several boxes of suturing material as theirs was very out of date.

Nyazura:
Went to a farm in the Nyazura area – family had already been evicted, but rescued their poultry.

February 2004
Goromonzi:
Went with Vet Ant Donohoe to a farm to euthanase two lovely Bull Mastiff X Boerboel dogs – 'Oscar' and ' Chloe'. Their owners were in the process of being evicted and didn't even know where they were going themselves, never mind the dogs. It was a heartbreaking scene, I sat on the verandah with my arms round the teenage daughter who was sobbing, whilst Ant gently slipped the needle into the first dog's vein – the burly farmer knelt beside his beloved dog and sobbed.

Chimanimani:
Repeated trips to Charleswood Estate to help with Roy and Heather Bennett's cattle.

Harare:
Trouble at Mbizi Lodge on the outskirts of Harare – owner's violently evicted – we uplifted parrot, cat and tortoise.

Harare:
Backwards and forwards to the doctors for blood tests – am on Warfarin but for some reason the blood test results were all over the place and they kept changing the dosage to stabilise it.

Mount Hampden:
27 February. My birthday: spent all day with Game Management Services and Johnny Rodrigues in the Mount Hampden area capturing impala and zebra for relocation to a safer area away from the main Kariba road – now that the fencing has all been stolen. I was very impressed with the helicopter flying skills of Mike Le Grange of Game Management Services as he darted low between the many trees, driving the impala and zebra towards the boma

29 February. Fly to the UK – ticket sponsored by British Airways. Have been invited to give a presentation during Crufts week at The International Forum. Thought I would give a power point presentation (something I've never done before), Jan Whyte who edits the Air Zim Inflight magazine offered to prepare the whole presentation for me and did an excellent job.

March 2004
UK:
During Crufts week, I was interviewed by the Chief Reporter of Dogs World and also did a radio interview with John Peel (respected and much-loved BBC presenter who died a few weeks later). Delivered my presentation at The International Forum on ZNSPCA and the current situation in Zimbabwe to quite a large audience.

9 March. Travelled to the RSPCA Headquarters in Horsham, Sussex, to be presented with the RSPCA Overseas Gallantry Award by Jackie Ballard – the Director General of the RSPCA. Whilst there – I asked the head of the Overseas division if we could have a donation to enable us to purchase protective wear ie: gumboots, hats, winter jackets, etc. they readily agreed.

CHAPTER THIRTY-TWO

In her shoes

'Comment is free but facts are sacred.'
– C. P. Scott, 1846-1932

March 2004

At a viewing point on the Zambezi Escarpment there is a plaque commemorating Rupert Fothergill and Operation Noah which was the largest animal rescue operation ever undertaken anywhere in the world. Lake Kariba lies below and the Matusadona mountains and National Park shimmer through the heat haze on the distant horizon. Some of the five thousand animals rescued from drowning by Fothergill and his team of game rangers as Lake Kariba filled and flooded the valley are listed on the plaque.

Antbear 48	*Buffalo 78*
Duiker 527	*Waterbuck 120*
Scaly Ant Eater 6	*Hyaena 3*
Rhinoceros 44	*Hare 43*
Grysbok 345	*Warthog 585*
Bushpig 44	*Jackal 2*
Wild Cat 5	*Porcupine 47*
Genet 21	*Bushbaby 1*
Baboon 268	*Bushbuck 320*
Elephant 23	*Klipspringer 28*
Kudu 300	*Civet 5*
Monkey 172	*Sable 105*
Squirrel 6	*Night Ape 10*
Badger 12	*Mongoose 14*
Dassie 21	

Operation Noah started in December 1958 as the flood waters of the Zambezi River began to rise. Rupert Fothergill, four game rangers and 20 assistants had been tasked by the Department of National Parks to: 'take such measures as they thought necessary to save animals which were endangered by the rising water'. Five years later Operation Noah came to an end on 30 June 1963 when the water stopped rising and Lake Kariba settled into her new bed.

The similarities between the achievements of Rupert Fothergill in the late 1950s and Meryl Harrison some fifty years later, are numerous. Both worked tirelessly, day after day, year after year, to save the animals of Zimbabwe. Fothergill faced fangs and teeth, stings, horns and kicks while Meryl's adversaries took on a human and political face and carried weapons. Both had very few resources, sacrificed their personal lives completely and tackled a mammoth undertaking with determination, courage and grit.

By all accounts Rupert Fothergill was a shy and humble man and the classic one-line entry in his diary, as related by author Keith Meadows, said it all:

'Sunday 8.3.59: Frank gored by buffalo.'

A similarly matter-of-fact entry in Meryl's diary, such as that in July 2000, contained a few more words but was laden with possibilities of danger which did not deter but rather motivated Meryl to action:

'July 2000. Addmore and I travel to Concession and rescue four border collies, one old cat and three owls. The farmer had been physically beaten by war veterans and the son was not allowed back to the farm to feed the dogs.'

By March 2004 Meryl had been going onto invaded farms and rescuing stranded animals for four years. She and her small team of SPCA Inspectors had come up against men and youths armed with guns, knives, whips and pangas. They had dismantled road barricades, dragged branches and stones off blocked roads and Meryl had driven hundreds of thousands of kilometres to virtually every part of Zimbabwe, no matter how remote.

Meryl had stood up to men who were drunk, drugged, hostile, threatening and aggressive. She had used every tactic she could think of, from asking and insisting to talking and negotiating – and sometimes, if it meant saving an animal, she even offered rewards: a few dollars, a pack of cigarettes or one occasion she even bargained with blankets to save a cat!

She had spent what amounted to hundreds of hours in police stations – in meetings, waiting for meetings, waiting for police escorts and being endlessly passed from one person to another. Meryl met and approached politicians, Members of Parliament, cabinet ministers and top government officials.

She spoke to reporters and journalists representing newspapers, magazines, television and radio stations from around the world, always emphasising that the work of the SPCA was totally non-political and they were only there for the animals. She didn't have a fancy office, private assistant or even the luxury of a computer or email. She earned a very small salary, most months dipping ever-deeper into her rapidly dwindling personal savings to get through to the end of the month, to buy food and the most basic essentials.

Meryl's personal and family life had become almost non-existent after four years of farm rescues and yet still she carried on. It was impossible for most people to understand why she did it and in some cases ignorance as to her motivation led to jealousy and then attack. In this regard also, the similarities between Meryl Harrison and Rupert Fothergill were apparent; he too was accused by the spectators and armchair critics of looking for glory and fame. Author Keith Meadows could have been describing Meryl when he wrote:

'There are people who say that any one of the men in the rescue teams could have led the operation. That may be the case. But the fact is that it was Rupert Fothergill who was there, from beginning to end.'

Half a century later, the same truth applied and the fact is that it was Meryl Harrison who led the rescue of hundreds of thousands of animals from Zimbabwe's invaded farms.

'Fearless, courageous, single-minded, determined. A heroine to all the animals in Zimbabwe.'

These were the words used by a colleague to describe Meryl. This woman knew, perhaps better than many others, what Meryl saw and did when she went out to invaded farms to rescue the animals that had been left behind.

While Meryl was in England in March 2004 where she was receiving the RSPCA Overseas Gallantry Award, her colleague, Inspector Nadia Marabini took over for a fortnight. She described a gruelling and traumatic 14 days in an occupation that is not for the faint-hearted at the best of times but that had been made almost unbearable during the times of farm invasions:

'I received a call about a herd of cattle starving to death on a farm. I proceeded to that farm with two Inspectors. I was met by the horrific sight of dead and half dead cattle, 50-60 of them, maybe more. What to do? Prevent suffering... captive bolt pistol to the head of those lying in their death pits and a sharp knife to slit their throats. Their

eyes looking at you, the smell of blood caught on the wind, ending up in the nostrils
of the next to die. How many did we kill that day?

'Such decisions.

'Another call: Horses in the ground behind Pomona Quarry. Ex-farm horses, one
of them lying half dead but still alive. Again the decisions: call a vet – euthanase
– decisions. What shall we do with the bodies?'

'We heard of another "situation" on a farm. On that day I was faced with the
possibility that I may have to go where there were a group of war vets. I had never
been in such a situation and I was scared. I had to keep reminding myself of Meryl's
advice: "Don't make eye contact", "Tell them you are mandated by Government
– you're just here for the animals", "Don't be intimidated".'

Nadia also saw what was going on behind the scenes and her words
hinted at a deep anguish, of a life that Meryl never spoke of and an image that
she never displayed:

'I don't know how she has continued... her shoulders must be broader than even I
knew. She didn't care what people thought abut her, she had only one mission. So
many malcontents thought that she loved the glory and the fame and that that was her
real motive. Those small, weak-minded cowards who would never have done what she
did – their guilt now sits miserably on their shoulders.

'One day when the people of Zimbabwe gain some courage and strength, those innocents
who lost their lives should be remembered in a special day to honour both them and
Meryl Harrison. No one has done more for animal welfare, animal awareness and
animal rescues than Meryl.'

Nadia understood Meryl's passion for animals and their well-being. She
knew the realities of the work and the hard decisions that constantly had to be
made. Sometimes Meryl's colleagues out of town were called on to provide a
bed for a night or two and would then witness at first-hand the perils Meryl
faced and the lengths she went to. Joy Stevens, herself training to become an
SPCA Inspector said that Meryl seemed to have eyes everywhere and nothing
escaped her notice:

'Meryl noticed farm animals in distress even when driving and would, on her own,
release them from tangled fencing wire. Even if she was on her way to sort some other

problem, she'd never drive by and think to sort it later!

'*She was amazing with the farm rescues! How she didn't lose her life is a miracle! Once when she was staying with us in early 2002 she had to go into a hostile rural area in Chegutu to rescue a farmer's cows who'd strayed onto a farm that had been taken over, and had had their mouths wired up. It was getting dark and late and I was extremely concerned as I hadn't heard from Meryl. I'd learnt that it may be because she had been side-tracked in assisting another animal, but as time dragged on, I really did worry. What relief when she finally arrived late; she'd had no signal to call me and had had a really rough time.*'

Later safe and sound and with a much-needed and most welcome Scotch in her hand Meryl told Joy what had happened:

'*Cattle belonging to a local commercial farmer had strayed onto an invaded farm (because the fences had been cut) and we received a report that the settlers had tied up the mouths of several cows with barbed wire because they had eaten some of 'their' maize. Once on the invaded farm the police and one of Joy's kennel hands went to look for the cattle. The police told me they were going to be walking through the bush, so I should wait for them by the settlers' recently-constructed village.*

'*Darkness fell and still I waited. I felt pretty nervous, so put the interior light on in the truck and tried to concentrate on reading the paper. The settlers didn't take much notice of me and I watched as they lit their fires and began preparing their evening meal. Finally, just as I was beginning to think that I should possibly try to find my own way back to Chegutu, I heard voices. They were back, but had not found the injured cattle. Later, fortunately, it turned out to have been a false report.*'

Perhaps one of the most amazing things about the farm rescues, and certainly one that was cause for considerable admiration, was Meryl's ability to be impartial and to communicate with all sides. She witnessed extreme cruelty and barbaric events and yet she kept calm and steadily set about leading her team of Inspectors to do the best for as many animals as possible. No one really understood how she managed to talk to men who were often armed, almost always hostile, aggressive and threatening. Men who were very often drugged or drunk and who always outnumbered her and the SPCA Inspectors by dozens.

What was it that Meryl had, did or said that resulted in rescued animals? She achieved results where farmers, lawyers and union officials had failed and no one really knew why this was the case. Meryl said it was because she was completely apolitical and her most commonly used phrase was: 'I'm only here for the animals.' There must have been more to it though, some facet of her personality, a trait from within. Meryl was the kind of person who always had an abiding need to help and to put something back into life. The fact that she was adopted played a big part in what made Meryl tick and what motivated her. She said she always felt unworthy, vulnerable and emotionally needy and thought these feelings were a result of being adopted. Meryl had been in touch with other people who were adopted and found that a sense of rejection was a common feeling.

Perhaps in Meryl's case the fact that she and her brother had been sent to boarding school from an early age had added to her insecurity. Undoubtedly the death of her twin brother also contributed to her feeling of vulnerability and need to help others. Meryl hated injustice of any kind, to people or animals, and always found herself identifying with people less fortunate than others. She had been a Samaritan in both the UK and Rhodesia and later became a founder member of the Randburg Crisis Centre in South Africa.

Undoubtedly the skills of listening, diplomacy and negotiation that she learned then were put to their best advantage in the farm rescues. Kelvin Weare who was in the background of many of Meryl's rescues in the Karoi area and gave moral and practical support whenever he could, said that it was her passion that led to success:

'The community of Karoi will forever be indebted to Meryl. Without fanfare or reward, she did so much, risking her own well being, for the rescue of countless farm animals in the district. Meryl's passion and conviction in the job she had to do was unflinching. She showed compassion and understanding with those who were sickened by the abuse and disregard for the welfare of the animals on the farms and found the controlled diplomacy and rationale to deal with those who orchestrated this mass cruelty.'

Linda Ainsworth, a long-time friend, had an insight into what drove Meryl:

'Undoubtedly Meryl's strength was her greatest asset in Zimbabwe's farm rescues. When an animal's life or safety were at risk, Meryl would never back down or give up. She knew that she was only human and could save some, not all; that sometimes to eliminate suffering, you unfortunately have to bring that life to an end in order to do what is right for the animal. Too many so-called animal lovers were harshly critical of Meryl's actions. Stunned and appalled by the decisions and choices she made. They openly and publicly condemned her, verbally attacked her, insulted and denounced her.

273

'At times when the security situation was really tense, she would appear to compromise to diffuse the hostility – if only to ensure the safety of her team and herself, so that they had a chance to try another approach. This was often what made the difference to the eventual outcome – the adversary would think he had won, meanwhile Meryl was already planning an alternative way to get the animals to safety. Diplomacy was vital, no matter how gut wrenching it was. To others caught up in the fracas – the farm and animal owners – it must have been unpalatable, but Meryl always remained neutral.'

Linda was one of just a few who saw at first hand the effects on Meryl of the brutality and barbarity that she saw on the farms, of the aggression and hostility that she faced every day and of the euthanasing she had to call for and witness again and again and often in vast quantities.

'Meryl wore an "armour" that was crucial to her survival and it was a heavy and costly garment to wear. When the wall of defence came down, Meryl was often alone. She returned from farm rescues late at night, and no one from the Society checked to see if she was safely home. There was no proper security offered to her, no two-way radio system, no-one keeping track of her movements. Imagine arriving home late at night, still recovering from your ordeal on a farm and having to face an empty house with no one to talk to. Who could she talk to that would understand? How could anyone really understand unless they had "lived it"?

'The aloneness could be more frightening than facing armed and aggressive men. More painful than any physical blow. More brutal than any insult suffered. Alone she faced her own set of demons including constant mental reruns of the horrors she had encountered and trying to comprehend such cruelty and abuse of innocent animals. Then there were the faces of the victims she hadn't been able to save. She didn't need all the photographs to remind her – they were ingrained into her memory.

'The harsh reality of what Meryl personally survived produced a demon all of its own. Often she said that when driving home from an "incident" when the adrenalin had calmed down and reality kicked in, her legs would begin to shake or she would break down and have to pull over until she calmed herself.'

Meryl herself said that she rarely, if ever, let the SPCA Inspectors see how stressed she was. On the occasions when she did break down, Meryl always maintained her self-control until after Addmore and the others had been dropped off and she was on her own. She said she felt she had to be strong for everyone in the team. When they were going on rescues that Meryl knew could be particularly dangerous, she would always offer the Inspectors an out, saying they weren't obliged to accompany her because these were dangers far beyond the call of average duty. Never once did any of the SPCA Inspectors choose not to go with her.

Someone else who understood the grim realities of the farm rescues and what Meryl was witnessing and having to cope with every day was Claire Evans. She and her husband Mark had started up a rescue unit for horses in 2002 when farming friends had been evicted and the couple took in their 10 horses. Claire and Meryl often worked together to rescue horses that had been abandoned on invaded farms and they made a good team. It wasn't just war veterans and settlers who caused the occasional scare either, as Claire remembered:

'I knew Meryl had a pace-maker and one day we were out in her truck and driving along a badly corrugated road when Meryl put her hand to her chest. She said the trouble with her pace-maker is that it is programmed to speed up when she runs but it can't tell the difference between that and a bumpy road! I had an anxious drive, waiting to grab the steering wheel should the need arise!'

As Claire and Mark took in more horses, the need continued to grow and then their own farm was taken over. They leased another farm but that too was seized. Eventually a property with 15 acres of land, stables and two houses was found. It was small but would have to do.

'Meryl and her team helped us and we walked most of the horses to the new property and thanks to Meryl and the ZNSPCA horse box we were able to move the weaker animals. It very soon became clear that horse rescue was a full-time job, we were funding the whole unit ourselves... food bills, wages. I got together a booklet of pictures and stories and sent them to all the major animal charities who deal with horses. There was little or no response. Because Meryl could do no more, Mark and I arranged a meeting with the Chairman of the ZNSPCA. She arrived, marvelled at the work we had done, and I showed her horses we had got back into work, which I allowed her to take photos of. Then she told us we could become our own branch of the SPCA but that they would not help fund our running expenses. Horses are not cheap to keep and we put down far more than we rescued, but here was the death knell for all of them. At that time I had 32 horses in my care, huge lists of other horses needing help. We could do no more.'

In the short time that Claire and Meryl's paths had crossed in their common attempt to save the animals that had been left behind, Claire soon found all the pitfalls Meryl had been battling for years. Claire encountered the bureaucracy and lack of funding at grass roots level; funding that was critical to keep the animals fed and alive. While talk was cheap and praise was nice, neither paid the bills or enabled Claire to keep doing the work.

After four years of farm rescues the support given by Meryl's friends undoubtedly kept her going. In some cases it was emotional support in the form of a shoulder to lean on, a sympathetic ear or a glass of wine with a friend. In other cases it was the practical day-to-day things that Meryl needed help with. Pippa Cory used to cook and freeze meals for Meryl so that when she got in late at night from a rescue all she had to do was heat the meals up. Pippa dealt with paper work and accounts, she helped with packing and moving and she worked ceaselessly in the background to help with the nitty-gritty's of fuel and money that often literally kept Meryl going from one week to the next:

> 'When Roly was alive and working it didn't matter too much but when he died Meryl was virtually a pauper. Several people gave me money for her and one family who was leaving the country tithed 10% of all the money they got from selling things they got off the farm and their furniture.'

In 2004, the Bulawayo SPCA which was Meryl's home ground, presented her with an in-house award. Coming from her colleagues, this recognition meant a great deal. Meryl was the first to admit that she was impatient; a perfectionist who didn't suffer fools gladly and she knew she can't have been easy to work with. The citation on the in-house award read: 'Certificate of Acknowledgement – For Unwavering Dedication to the Welfare of Animals in Zimbabwe.' Many of the staff had signed and written comments on the Award and they were words that Meryl treasured particularly because they came from people at the coal face. The vet, Dr Anele Dube wrote: 'Your tenacity in the pursuit of animal welfare is unsurpassable'; Inspector George Masuku wrote: 'To a respected colleague of long standing. Your many years of work are an example for others to follow'.

Meryl herself held the real answer as to what it was that kept her going back onto those farms. She had often been asked what it took to be an animal rescuer but there weren't any simple answers. There were no specific job qualifications or college degree requirements but there was a deep passion. Meryl said it was a passion that became the heartbeat of her life and her identity.

In Zimbabwe in 2004 that were not many, if any, who could walk in her shoes and when she came back into the country after her trip overseas Meryl found that she would have to go on alone without Addmore. There were other issues too which were recorded in her personal dairies and they made for the most distressing reading.

Extracts from Meryl's Diary:

Truth and oil are ever above.
(Truth will always rise above any attempts to conceal it.)
– Proverb

April 2004
Harare:
Arrived back to find that Addmore had been arrested by the police for the theft of a large quantity of items from the ZNSPCA complex. This was not the first time he had been in trouble with the law and it was with great sadness that I had to dismiss him. He'd had so many warnings and it would not have been fair to the other staff to keep him on just because he was so good at his job. His work with animals was outstanding. He risked his life on several occasions when carrying out farm rescues and with him at my side I knew we would succeed, however tough things got. We went through a lot together and there was no one else I would rather have had 'watching my back.' I am so sad about this ending and it's been such a difficult decision to make but there really is no other choice.

Harare:
1 April. April Fool's Day! In court all day regarding a cruelty case.

4 April. Nick's birthday.

Harare:
Photographer arrived from the USA to take pictures of me working in the field – these are to go with the Peter Godwin/Readers Digest article.

7 April. In court again for another cruelty case.

Goromonzi:
A man brought several of his donkeys to our office at Goromonzi for treatment – it is really great when something like that happens.

Harare:
More court cases and more blood tests – hate needles, so wish things could be stabilised!

Chimanimani:
Sternford and I go to Charleswood again – injured cattle and stranded dog. Rose Nurse phoned me the night before – she does this without fail every single time I am due to go onto Charleswood – knows how nervous I am about this particular farm. Both she and my very close friend Esme Smithwhite always phone just to say good

luck and that they're thinking about me.

Raffingora:
To a farm to rescue three Ridgebacks left behind on a farm – removed two, the older dog had died the night before.

Harare:
24th April. Attended Colin Anderson's funeral in Highlands. A wonderful man who did so much to support SPCA's in Zimbabwe through the Blue Cross Ultra Marathon which has raised thousands and thousands of dollars over the years for all those that cannot speak for themselves. I always had a soft spot for him, because he had had the same name as my twin brother who was also Colin Anderson! Whilst everyone quietly filed into the Highlands church for Colin's funeral, I sat in my truck in the car park and reflected on all the good that Colin's fund-raising had done for animals in Zimbabwe and the SPCA in particular. So many people pay lip service only to how passionate they are about animals – but after wringing their hands about how they abhor cruelty to God's creatures they do no more about it. Colin was different – his love for all creatures great and small has left a legacy in Zimbabwe. The church was packed, with many athletes attending with the much coveted Blue Cross medals hanging round their necks.

May 2004
Harare:
To ZDI [Zimbabwe Defence Industries] to collect a letter giving me permission to go on to Charleswood to check the condition of the weaners.

Mutare:
Sternford and I leave Ruwa at 5am for a court case in Mutare against a butcher we had charged with cruelty for the way in which he transported some calves and goats. He is found guilty and fined. Dropped off drugs and supplies for Mutare SPCA and then on to Chimanimani to Charleswood. Treat calf with arrow wound – arrow had been made from an iron fencing standard. Also inspected 191 weaners – condition very poor. Left wound spray, etc. for treatment of cattle.

Masvingo:
On the way back from Chimanimani went via Masvingo SPCA and dropped drugs etc off for them and then back to Harare. Collected my dogs the next day from the Boarding kennels. Found that Annie Wilkinson had done her usual when I got home. She and Freddie are always there if I need them. Freddie helps me when my truck won't start and both he and Ken Scott take it in turns to walk out to the gate to unlock it for me when I get back late at night – so that I don't have to get out and do it myself as this could have been unsafe in these days. Annie has such an excellent sense of humour and she quite often puts little soaps in the bathroom for me if I've

been away for a few days or leaves a little vase of flowers for me (probably picked from my own garden!).

Odzi:
Put my dogs back into kennels. Drive to Odzi – Police said it was 'too dangerous' to go a particular farm where the owner had been shot two days before, so we were unable to rescue the three dogs and three cats stranded there. As a temporary measure, we met the farmer's maid, Mandy, at the police station and gave her some dog and cat food. Then drove her through Kondozi to get as close as we could to the farm. After some distance she told us it was not safe to go any closer and we watched with concern as Mandy disappeared down the road carrying the bags of food on her head. We later heard she got back to the animals safely – another very brave lady!

Bulawayo:
Drive to Bulawayo for an appointment with the Cardiologist – another blood test.

June 2004
Beitbridge:
Drive to Beitbridge – treated donkeys all the way down, arrived at the B&B as it was getting dark.

8 June. Hold Donkey Clinic at Mikado Police station – many villagers attended with their donkeys and scotch-carts.

9 June. Deliver to Bulawayo, Gweru, Kwekwe, Kadoma and Chegutu SPCAs – five litres of Dip and 200 de-worming tablets each.

17 June. Precious diesel is pouring out of my truck – head straight to a friend's garage – nothing too serious, soon repaired and I am back on the road.

Johannesburg, South Africa:
Drove to Jo'burg – stayed with my ex-husband, Dave, and his wife overnight.

Durban:.
Flew to Durban – ticket paid for by my old school – St Anne's Diocesan College at Hilton Road in Natal. They had invited me to attend their old girls reunion day and to present me with the St Anne Award: 'for dedicated service above and beyond the call of duty'. After attending a chapel service I was asked to give a speech to all the girls in the school on the work of the ZNSPCA and the problems we were facing on the farms. When I had finished, several girls (who were from Zimbabwe) came up to tell me that in fact I, unbeknown to me, had rescued their pets or their father's cattle.

Johannesburg:
Before I left to return I packed the truck with stacks of items donated by that wonderful South African lady – Valerie Zangel (who I still haven't met!). Val had had all the items delivered to Dave's house. There was medicines, baby formula, syringes, de-worming tablets, disposable gloves, cotton wool, bandages, assorted horse tack, dip, savlon, etc. Also met a representative of the South African NSPCA at the airport when I arrived and he handed over some cat traps that they had donated. My truck was pretty full and I only got through the border at 7pm. Headed back to Harare the next day, I dropped off some of the donated items at the various SPCA's on the way.

Harare:
Get a phone call from a lady who asked me to call in at her travel agents office as there was a something waiting for me – called in to find she had left a carton of wine for me – with a card attached saying 'This is a small Thank You for all the incredible work you do for Animals – Kind Regards.' – Things like this go a long way in helping me to keep going!

Tengwe:
Sternford and I spent some time in the Tengwe area trying to rescue a herd of sable belonging to a commercial farmer. After weeks of trying, we had to concede defeat.

Beatrice, Norton, Banket, Concession:
Many visits to farms rescuing or attempting to rescue herds of cattle, domestic pets and wildlife.

Harare:
Another blood test!

Harare:
Meeting with Minister John Nkomo to voice my concern over the condition of the dairy herd at Collingwood Farm.

July 2004
Chimanimani:
Sternford and I to Charleswood to monitor the loading of Roy Bennett's cattle by ARDA. After a long drive back which included deviating off to Chipinge to collect an abandoned security dog, I was home by 8pm, having collected my dogs.

Karoi:
News from farmer in Tengwe to say 'it was all systems go' for the relocating of his sable. After meetings on the logistics we go Karoi to discuss matter with Karoi police (very hostile reception).

Harare:
Phoned Minister John Nkomo to tell him I wanted the photos back that I had left with him concerning the dairy herd at Collingwood. He told me that they were with the Permanent Secretary.

Harare:
Meeting with Parks about the van Schalkwyks' lions.

Tengwe:
To Tengwe Estate with vehicles, etc. to uplift sable. War vet Changiva, other resident war vets and settlers all very hostile. Police arrived – Game Management team and farmers' representative. War vets and workers had said they would kill the farmer if he went to the farm. Sternford and are I left with the rabble while all officials go off to Urungwe District Council. War vets eventually calmed down – probably from boredom! By 5pm when there was no sign of the relocation team, we headed back to Karoi.

Harare:
Another meeting with Parks about lions.

Harare:
Invited by 'Golfing and Giving' to their annual presentation of donations to local Harare charities. Wonderful team of ladies, who raise money through their golf matches throughout the year. They had contacted me a few weeks earlier to enquire what sort of items we would like them to purchase with the money allocated. I suggested protective winter clothing, now that it's midwinter and our Inspectors in the field are desperately in need of warm items of uniform. That evening I was given much-needed gum boots, winter jackets and jerseys, enough for all of us – what stars these ladies are!

Harare:
South African 702 Radio phoned for John Robbie to interview me again – wanted to do an update on how we were getting on with the farm rescues and to enquire whether my pace maker was still OK.

Chimanimani:
Sternford and I to Charleswood again to monitor Roy Bennett's cattle. Just before the turnoff to Odzi, we noticed a donkey lying at the side of the road. We realised it had been hit by a car and its back was broken but it was still alive. Whilst Sternford drove to the police station to get someone to come and shoot it, I gave the donkey some water to drink and provided some shade for it – it had obviously been lying there for some time.

Harare:
31 July. Excellent lunch party held for very dear friends who had been kicked off their farm in Bromley. It was Pip's 80th birthday and many ex-farming folk attended.

August 2004
Harare:
1 August. Diane from Coast Radio station in South Africa does a phone interview on the farm rescues.

3 August. Called to a meeting by the ZNSPCA at the new office. Only four members of the Executive in attendance. Meeting had been called to haul me over the coals. Chairman told me that I had bought the name of ZNSPCA into disrepute because I had complained in public about so much money being spent on the proposed new headquarters.

One board member shouted at me: 'We told you to say that the house was donated!' They hadn't and anyway I wouldn't have lied for them.

The ZNSPCA Board purchased a house to be used as an Admin/Education centre. It is in a very upmarket area of Harare, cost a great deal of money. They later approached the State Lotteries and got a donation of 37 million for a gate and front wall. Later I was accused of having complained to officials about the donation – I had done nothing of the sort.

Being at the coal face as I am and in a 3rd World country that is economically in a state of melt-down with white and black families leaving every day, I was totally against the purchase of the house. I felt what was urgently needed was mobile clinics, vaccines, drugs, dip, fuel for the vehicles, etc – ie funds that would directly improve the welfare of Zimbabwe's animals. The house would have been a great idea 10 years ago or 10 years hence, but I felt this was not the right time for the organisation to indulge in purchasing new headquarters. Months later, a member of the Board, still trying to convince me – said, 'But don't you see, we are buying this for YOU?'

A member of the public on hearing that the board had been looking for a place to have as a headquarters, approached me and offered us the bottom half of her house rent-free. The Chairman said that we didn't want to share and another board member said that it was the wrong side of town – Milton Park, an older but very nice residential area.

Mapora Farm, Odzi:
4 August. Went to Odzi with Mark and Claire Evans and some of their grooms from the Horse Care Unit to start catching horses that had been left behind. Found seven

horses – two of them ponies, one of which was dragging a wooden fencing pole behind it with a great deal of barbed wire wrapped round its legs. She was very nervous and frightened, but with incredible patience and using the Monty Roberts' method of approaching a nervous horse, Mark managed to get right up close to the pony, remove the wire and pole and treat a nasty wound on the leg. Then the idea was to drive them all into an old dip tank area that we had cleared. Each time we got them moving roughly in the right direction, a small chestnut pony with a long mane and tail would lift his head up and go thundering off in the opposite direction, followed by all the other horses. Mark and Claire later named him "Denver". They had started naming all the rescued horses whose names we didn't know – after towns in the USA.

It was very, very hot and Claire and I went back to clearing the dip tank area, which was very overgrown, leaving Mark and the grooms to try all over again. After what seemed like hours, Claire and I saw a small procession in the distance – headed by little Denver being walked in a head-collar by one of the grooms. Also several beautiful Palaminos, these had been owned by Landros who was now in jail. He accidentally shot and killed a war vet when he was struggling to protect himself as he was being beaten. The war veterans then beat him up very badly, resulting in both his hands being broken.

He was subsequently arrested and put inside. Through his parents Landros got a message to me to say that I had his permission to destroy his horses – they were now all thundering from one farm to the next and it was only a matter of time before they were injured or killed... Mark once again showed endless patience in getting the horses through the now-derelict spray race, up the ramp and into the truck.

We then took them to a farm on the outskirts of Mutare to rest and recover for a few days, Mark leaving one of his grooms at the farm to look after the horses and to assess which should be destroyed – two or three of the Palaminos were very wild and the chances are that given the present circumstances, it would have been a mistake to try and re-home them. We finally got back to Ruwa well after 10pm.

Ruwa:
9 August. Heroes' Day – public holiday. Had a bad turn with my heart, so spent the day in bed. Received a call from the owner of a thoroughbred stud farm in Bromley re: youths/settlers arriving 'to plough' their horse's paddocks up. Also, another phone call this time from Karoi to say that their workers had gone on strike and were refusing to feed their 25 horses.

Ruwa:
10 August. Public holiday – Invited out to lunch but declined as I was still feeling very shaky.

Harare:
11 August. Went to my doctor – she said that my blood pressure was high. Meetings with Director of ARDA to complain about the way they were looking after Roy Bennett's cattle, and then later a meeting with the Permanent Secretary in the Ministry of Lands.

Harare:
13 August. Meeting with Permanent Secretary in Ministry of Environment and Tourism on various wildlife matters.

Montclare, Nyanga:
14 August. Memorial service for Colin Anderson. I couldn't go but later saw extracts from the obituary:

'The people involved in Blue Cross were introduced to the magical terrain through the eyes of a man who really loved it and to a country he served with passion.

It was Dad's dearest wish to see the Blue Cross grow from strength to strength, not only in its main purpose to raise funds for animals in need but also in fostering camaraderie amongst the participants and organisers, regardless of race, colour or creed.'

Bromley:
16 August: To a farm in Bromley where three cats had been left behind following violent eviction of owners the previous night. They had run away amidst all the noise, so we left cat traps at the house. These of course have to be checked every day – tragically two of them were caught a few nights later, but a settler took them from the traps and threw them in the well before we got there in the morning. We asked police to arrest the settler and he was charged with cruelty.

Odzi:
Went with Mark Evans back to Mutare where we decided to destroy five of the Odzi horses, they were just so stressed at being confined. With so many people leaving the country and very few safe farms to move the horses to, we knew it was the best decision. There was no one I trusted more than Mark to do this job. As they were so wild, we had to get them into the crush to do it, but I was able to keep the other horses out of sight of the one being shot. We returned to Harare feeling very heavy-hearted, but with Denver and one of the Palaminos in the back of the horse box – where once we got to the Horse Care Unit, their stables had been prepared for them and their food waiting – it must have been many months since they had been spoilt like that!

Harare:
18 August. To Parks to collect permit for the lions – at last!

Chegutu:
To Chegutu to collect horses from a farm where owners had been evicted. Take horses to Mark and Claire Evans Rescue Unit – they are always so well-organised. It doesn't seem to matter how late I get to their place at night after having towed the horse box for miles, they are always ready. The stables have always been prepared with deep straw on the ground, a hay net and bucket of water waiting. Claire personally oversees the feeding of each and every horse according to their individual needs. She prepares meals of horse food, bran and chopped carrots for the horses. As we start off-loading horses their cook appears through the darkness down by the stables with a beautifully cooked meal for me to take home – organised by Claire before we'd set off in the morning.

21 August. Moved the lions.

Harare:
22 August. Meeting to wind up the affairs of The Terrier Club of Zimbabwe. I had started it in 1989 and remained the Chairperson for the next eight years. It became one of the most successful specialist dog clubs together with The Terrier Rescue Scheme which I also started in 1988. With so many people leaving the country, membership dropped drastically and there was no alternative but to put the Club in mothballs until better days. Pleased to know that my friend Michelle Fuller will take over Terrier Rescue, and continue to run it. I know that I couldn't have left the scheme in better hands.

Harare:
Fuel is getting increasingly difficult to obtain – help came in the form of two drums of diesel donated by Roy Bennett. Made me think of Roly who used to move heaven and earth to source fuel for my truck and purchased several large plastic containers so that I would always have reserve fuel. He'd also purchased a strong torch for me to use on those late returns – just like him – always so thoughtful.

Mutare:
Meeting of the Baboon Control Stakeholders – continued into the next day. Visited an estate in Penhalonga to check the baiting sites and traps.

Featherstone:
On the way to a farm in Featherstone, and on the Beatrice Road, I noticed a truck heading towards Harare, packed with animals, firewood, pots, pans, etc. I immediately did a U-turn and stopped the driver – it was like opening a can of worms. The end result came in the form of a mixed letter of thanks (and confession) in the Herald newspaper:

'Editor – Allow me space in your widely read paper to thank the ZNSPCA for the good work they are doing for the nation. On August 30, 2004, I hired a lorry to transport my 18 cattle, four goats and two donkeys from Masvingo to Chinhoyi.

'As we were driving into Harare, on our way we were stopped by ZNSPCA Inspectors who registered their disappointment at the cramped conditions the animals were being transported in. We then discovered that the two donkeys had died in the truck.

'As if that wasn't sad enough, one of the lorry assistants shouted abusive words at ZNSPCA Chief Inspector Ms Meryl Harrison and this indeed displeased her team.

'However, I must say I was highly impressed by the calm and professional manner in which Mrs Harrison handled the issue. She and the other Inspectors asked us to drive the cattle to the CSC (Cold Storage Commission) pens where we off-loaded them. They then accompanied us into town where we left the dead donkeys for incineration.

'In the evening they drove back, together with me, to the CSC pens and injected all my calves, which looked very weak. This they did at their own expense. The following morning they sent one of their officers at the CSC pens to see whether the calves had improved and also to see us off. They continued to phone me all the way to Masvingo just to know whether all the cattle were safe and healthy... Paul Ncube, Harare.'

CHAPTER THIRTY-THREE

Ben and Storm

'I like to think that when she rubs her face against mine,
she is trying to comfort me by saying, in her own way,
But I was free born.'
– Joy Adamson, Born Free, *1960*

Vermont Farm, Karoi, July 2004

Meryl first heard from Karoi farmer Chalkie van Schalkwyk in July 2004 when she was asked if she could help in getting an Animal Movement Permit. Chalkie and his wife Sandie were managing and living on Vermont Farm and land invasions throughout the Karoi area were continuing at an alarming pace. The owner of Vermont Farm had successfully contested the acquisition of the farm but Orbert, an employee of ZBC (Zimbabwe Broadcasting Corporation), arrived on the scene in May 2004 and said that he had been given an offer letter for the property. Orbert was insistent that everyone should vacate Vermont Farm as he intended to move in. The legal owner of Vermont Farm said the 'offer letter' that Orbert had was not valid and should be ignored. Chalkie and Sandie stayed on but they knew some very tough decisions lay ahead because they had a most unusual pair of animals on the farm.

Chalkie and Sandie had hand-reared a pair of orphaned lions and if Vermont Farm was forcibly taken over they wouldn't have a moment to waste and would have to move the lions immediately to prevent a tragedy. Chalkie had identified a new home for the lions and all he needed was the official paperwork which would allow him to move the lions if he needed to. The bureaucracy and delays were frustrating in the extreme and each day was uncertain and anxious. At any time Orbert could arrive and evict the van Schalkwyk's who had been trying for weeks to move the lions.

At first the couple hoped to move the lions to South Africa but the export permit had been refused. It was only during this process that they discovered that they needed a permit to keep the lions in the first place, something the couple said they didn't know about and had never been asked to provide in the three years that they'd been rearing the lions. They immediately set about trying to get the necessary documentation that would allow them to keep the lions, and to move them.

These were impossibly difficult and painful times for Sandie and Chalkie who were devoted to the lions and Sandie explained how they came to have the lions on the Karoi farm in the first place:

> 'We had been asked if we would foster Ben when he was just 10 days old and a little bundle of fur. We agreed and when he was eight months old, we took on Storm (a lioness – who was nine months old) that my sister had been looking after until they were kicked off their farm. At this age the lions were slightly bigger than a grown Labrador, still very easy to handle and we formed an incredible bond with them. Ben and Storm weren't caged – they had the whole of the front garden (which was huge) to roam around in but we had built a small boma [enclosure] about 1/3 ha [hectare] on the side where we used to lock them up when we went away. Ben was vasectomised in May 2004 as we didn't want them to have cubs but they must have had a fling in late April without us noticing as by the end of June we realised that Storm was not fat, as we thought, but pregnant!'

Throughout May and June Chalkie paid repeated visits to the Department of National Parks to try and get the necessary permits for the lions but there was one delay after another as more and more documentation was required. Their fear of being evicted from the Farm was superseded by an arrest which Sandie explained:

> 'The police kept pushing Chalkie for a permit and on 9 July 2004 finally insisted that he report to the police station with a copy of the permit application papers. Chalkie did this and was promptly arrested and kept in jail for the weekend. He was arrested for "keeping dangerous wild animals in an urban area" – even though we lived on a farm 30kms from Karoi and therefore were not living in an urban area by any stretch of the imagination.
> On the Monday morning before Chalkie went to Court he was interviewed by the arresting officer and told that National Parks staff were coming to shoot the lions. I arrived at the police station to go to court with Chalkie and while the arresting officer was out of the room, Chalks quickly whispered to me to get hold of anyone and everyone I could to try and intervene with Parks. Chalkie's Court case was remanded until 27 July and he was allowed home. Someone gave us Meryl's number and Chalks phoned her that evening to tell her the story and ask her to please use any influence she had to get us the permit as soon as possible as that was one of the excuses the police were using to get us and the lions off Vermont.'

Meryl had had many dealings with the Department of National Parks in the past and went immediately to see Patrick at the permits office. Patrick had always been very helpful and he told Meryl that the application to move the lions had been received but that a decision hadn't been made yet. Meryl asked that the permit request to move the lions be treated with urgency because of the ongoing land invasions and the dire implications that would inevitably arise if a confrontation between lions and land invaders were to arise. Patrick said he'd pass on Meryl's request and she had no doubt he would do his best. There wasn't much else that Meryl could do as this was a government department and the wheels of bureaucracy turned slowly, more so now that politics entered every aspect of life in the country.

As she left the offices Meryl's thoughts turned to 1999, just before the farm invasions and when she and Patrick and others in the Department of National Parks had worked very amiably together to give a new life to Buffy, a chimpanzee. Meryl had arranged for the relocation of Buffy from a life of confinement, solitude and captivity in a wildlife park outside Harare, to Chimfunshi – a world renowned Chimpanzee sanctuary in Zambia. There had been copious amounts of paperwork and red tape involved in relocating Buffy and it had taken many months to get everything in order but in the end with the SPCA and National Parks working together they achieved the goal.

They had been arduous months for Meryl but when she looked back on the frustration and stress, she knew it had all been worthwhile – particularly when she heard how the chimp's life had improved so dramatically. Gone were the days of separation from her own kind and being the object of teasing and taunting. Gone were the abuses the chimp had to suffer – having cold drinks cans and cigarette butts thrown at her. Buffy had been on her own for five years when Meryl got involved. Buffy's companion, a male chimp, had been chained all the time after he kept trying to escape over the wall and in the end had been shot, leaving Buffy completely alone. Meryl was thrilled to have heard recently from Sheila Siddle at the Chimp sanctuary in Zambia how dramatically Buffy's life had changed by the time land invasions were ravaging neighbouring Zimbabwe. Sheila and her team had obviously done a fantastic job in rehabilitating the previously traumatised chimp:

'Buffy is the oldest in this group of 15 chimps. Males, females plus three little ones under the age of three years old. This group is in an enclosure of about 150 acres with an electric fence around.

Sadly Buffy has not fallen pregnant but that seems to be due to the fact that she is too busy protecting the younger ones in her group. Often we will see the other childless chimps playing with the younger ones, but never Buffy – maybe she was not cut out to be a mother, we will never know.

'The staff who have worked with Buffy from the day she arrived know a lot of her bad and good habits also when she is in a good mood or not. Buffy has very long fingers and uses them a great deal to point at an item she requires. Buffy will often greet you by covering her mouth with one hand and with the other she pats her stomach. Why she covers her mouth we do not know. When she gets cross she will stand pointing and then, folding her arms up like a chicken, she flaps them – of course we can't help but laugh at her which in turns makes her more mad, but she does look so funny.'

Even though the relocation of Buffy had taken place almost five years before, Meryl could see that nothing had changed as far as the Department of National Parks was concerned. It still took a long time for decisions to be made and action agreed upon. The bureaucratic wheels turned as slowly as ever.

A few days after Meryl's visit to National Parks she got another call from Chalkie to say they'd been told by a friend that the police had visited their farm and Chalkie's name had been seen on a police list. When Meryl asked what this meant, Sandie explained what had become a way of life for farmers at the time:

'Chalkie's name on the police list meant that they planned to visit him with the intention of arresting him again. Every weekend from then on we had to leave the farm as the police loved to arrest farmers on the Friday as there was no chance they would get bail before the Monday. We feel that this ZBC guy [Orbert] was putting pressure on the police to get us off Vermont – the acquisition notice hadn't expired and all the paperwork for the farm was in order.'

Meryl's first question was – what about the lions? – but Chalkie reassured her immediately. Two farm employees were there and would look after the lions. These two men, both garden workers, had been with the lions from the first, helping to rear and care for them and were totally devoted to the animals. Sandie told Meryl that the lions were always locked in the garden boma when the couple were away. This was the safest place for them, they were familiar with it and stayed at the far end of the enclosure which was very difficult to get to from the outside fence.

It sounded to Meryl as if things were under control but she knew how quickly a situation could change from calm and logical to irrational and dangerous when it came to farm invasions! Shortly afterwards officials from National Parks arrived at Vermont Farm and conducted an inspection. They said they were happy that the lions were being well looked after and were amazed that Chalkie was still able to walk with the lions who by then were over two years old and fully grown. The best news of all came when the National Parks officials said that the lions didn't seem to be a threat to anyone and as far as they were concerned, the farm was not considered to be in an urban area. Everyone breathed a sigh of relief! They were, however, premature because just days later everything was turned upside down again as new warnings of police visits and another arrest were passed on by friends.

Chalkie and Sandie again left the farm, spending one night in Harare and another in Concession – they had become masters at the art of living out of a suitcase, constantly on the move at weekends. Then came the call from a friend and neighbour, the call they had been dreading – National Parks had arrived at Vermont Farm, they had cages and had come to take Ben and Storm away. It could not have been at a worse time for the lions. Storm was heavily pregnant and would undoubtedly abort her cubs if she was moved at this time. A frenzy of phone calls went out in all directions.

Being a weekend it was not going to be easy to get official assistance. Meryl needed to know exactly what was happening at Vermont Farm and she spoke to the neighbour who was there. She quickly asked that the phone be handed over to one of the National Parks officials who were trying to confiscate the lions. It was a terse and one-sided conversation:

'I informed him that he was not to move the lions for several reasons: Storm was about to give birth and I knew that their plan would be to take the lions to the National Parks holding bomas at Nyamaneche. We (the SPCA) had visited the place on several occasions and were not at all happy with conditions there. Finally, I told them that the movement permit had already been applied for. I then contacted C, a senior official at Parks. He agreed with my decision and then promptly phoned his officials still waiting at the farm and told them to leave immediately – but without the lions!'

Meryl was again thankful for the good working relationship she had with C and that when it came to the welfare of animals they understood each other. Meryl knew C personally and they had worked together on many occasions in the past. Being able to phone him, and on a Saturday, was indeed a bonus for Meryl. She had a good relationship with the senior members of National Parks even though they came across difficult issues and had disputes on some occasions. Even though the SPCA legally had the ability to prosecute National Parks, if there were grounds, Meryl always tried to resolve problems diplomatically if she could because it was vital that the two organisations worked together in the best interests of the animals. Meryl knew that National Parks worked under increasingly difficult circumstances with severe shortages of funds and continual government interference.

At 6pm that evening Sandie and Chalkie got the news that National Parks had left – without the lions. Storm had a reprieve and everyone dared to hope that she may even be able to have her cubs in peace on Vermont Farm. Sandie and Chalkie were not sure exactly when the cubs were due but thought it would be some time around early August – six weeks away.

First thing on Monday Meryl was again at National Parks offices but there was no sign of the permit. Once again she appealed for priority to be given to the matter and after that there was little else she could do. In the meantime, at the end of July, Chalkie went to Court and the charge of 'keeping dangerous animals' was thrown out. In fact, he was told by the Judge that he should never have been arrested in the first place! Chalkie and Sandie then thought everything had been sorted out.

For no apparent reason, as so often happened in the land invasions, things went quiet for a while. Meryl's work called her to the other side of the country where farm invasions were continuing and other animals needed to be rescued urgently. She told the van Schalkwyk's she was just a phone call away but heard nothing more about the lions for almost four weeks. When news did come, it was worrying. The person who was re-homing the lions phoned Meryl and asked if there was any news on the Animal Movement Permit. Meryl was surprised to hear that the permit still hadn't been approved and she was very concerned. She knew that if the lions were moved without the correct paperwork and necessary permit then the police and National Parks really could confiscate the animals.

On 10 August Meryl received a phone call from Chalkie. It was bad news. Chalkie told Meryl that he and Sandie were in hiding because the police were trying to arrest him as he had still not moved the lions off Vermont Farm. It was Heroes' weekend, a public holiday always charged with political rhetoric and a particularly dangerous time to be a white farmer. Chalkie and Sandie had left the farm and Meryl recorded the situation in her diary:

'The police had left a message at the farm that he was to appear at Karoi Police Station the following morning at 8am. Chalkie said he was worried because Storm had still not had her cubs, the fencing at the farm they were going to had not been completed and DISPOL (Officer in charge of the District Police) were threatening to shoot the lions. The "new owner" of the farm, this man Orbert, said he couldn't move onto the farm while the lions were still there!'

Meryl was dismayed at the latest developments and immensely frustrated that everything was moving so slowly. Her only concern was for the welfare and well-being of the lions and she didn't have answers to any of the questions that filled her head: why had the permit still not come through and why had no one told her or followed it up; why wasn't the fencing ready and what chance did this now heavily pregnant lioness have of birthing and bonding with her cubs and not rejecting them? Meryl's blood pressure was rising, literally, due to the stress involved in trying to facilitate the safe and immediate movement of the two lions.

She arranged an urgent meeting with the Deputy Director of National Parks. This was as high into the bureaucratic system as she could get with almost no notice and Meryl went into the meeting feeling tense and anxious. Some time later she emerged feeling positive and even hopeful and she met Chalkie and Sandie face to face for the first time, in the parking lot outside the National Parks offices. It was strange for all of them to finally be meeting in person after literally dozens of telephone conversations over so many weeks and the talk was only about the lions as Sandie recalled:

'We discussed the injustice of all of this and told Meryl that all we wanted was a permit so that the police would get off our backs and leave us in peace to move the lions safely.

'Our first and only concern at this stage was for the lions' safety, and to prevent Storm being moved until after she had given birth and had bonded with her cubs. It was absolutely imperative that Storm was not moved prior to her pregnancy or for a week after giving birth. By now, Storm was very, very pregnant and was also grumpy! We were expecting her to give birth any day but because we didn't know when they actually mated, we were only guessing on dates.'

The Deputy Director of National Parks had agreed with Meryl that the situation with the movement of the lions from Vermont Farm was urgent and he promised to give it his immediate attention. Meryl was thrilled at the next development.

'Two days later National Parks officials contacted me to say that I could come and collect the permit. This was fantastic news but overshadowed by Chalkie's phone call to me to say that Storm had given birth to two cubs. He was desperately worried that the stress of the move would cause Storm to reject her cubs.'

Just a week before the permits had arrived, Storm had given birth to her cubs. A few days prior to the birth, Chalkie and Sandie were evicted from Vermont Farm and told to remove all their belongings from the house. Sandie explained the situation with the lions at the time of their eviction:

'We were allowed to leave Ben and Storm there as we couldn't move them. We locked them up in the boma and had the gardeners take turns to stay there day and night. We went back two or three times a day to check on the lions although we were very tense as we kept expecting to see a police car pull up to the gate and have someone arrest us for being on the property. On Wednesday, 17 August, Storm gave birth to one cub. Chalkie went and checked on the lions on his way to the farm where he was putting up the new boma and saw that she had had one cub, which she had suckled. We were due to move the lions on Saturday 20 August. On 18 August Storm gave birth to her second cub, but unfortunately then rejected them both.'

On 20 August, after three months of delays and desperate interventions, Meryl and SPCA Inspector Sternford headed out to Karoi in preparation for the movement of the lions. The next morning they were joined by Tim Paulet, an ex-National Parks staffer and very well-known personality in wildlife circles in the country. Tim, a licensed capture expert, was going to dart and tranquillise the lions so that they could be moved.

Meryl was saddened to hear that both of the lion cubs had been rejected by their mother. With so many strangers around, so many changes to the routine and without the safety and familiarity of Chalkie and Sandie around, it seemed inevitable. The cubs were still alive though and so Chalkie took the little spotted balls of fluff away and gave them to another wildlife expert who would try and save them. One cub, the second to be born 24 hours after its sibling, did not have enough strength and died of pneumonia the day Meryl arrived in Karoi to help with moving its parents.

Meryl had not been involved in darting and tranquillising lions before but she'd had dealings with big cats before. Her happiest memory had ironically happened during these horrific years of farm invasions. The Lion and Cheetah Park outside Harare had been invaded and war veterans would only allow Meryl and no one else to go into the Park. Meryl was tasked with collecting a young lion cub called Venda and taking it to a vet for an injection. It might have been young but certainly knew how to scratch and bite and Meryl smiled as she remembered how the cub had spent most of its time trying to chew her earrings off!

The lions she was looking at now were immense in all respects when compared to little Venda and it was hard to imagine that perhaps once Storm and Ben had also chewed at ear rings. At last the proceedings appeared ready to begin and it seemed strange that such a phenomenal undertaking could go ahead without anything sophisticated or intricate being involved. A few people, an ordinary farm truck and a couple of simple cages would completely change the lives of two lions and two people who were dedicated to rearing them.

'Chalkie enticed the two lions into their feeding cages so that Tim was able to administer the tranquilliser. It wasn't long before they were both out for the count and put into their crates so that they could be loaded onto a vehicle. We then drove in convoy through back roads to get to the lions' new farm. The alternative would have been to drive down the main street in Karoi and this was not the time to draw attention to ourselves. Sternford and I travelled directly behind the vehicle carrying them and it was amusing to see the local people's reaction when they realised they were looking at two very large lions! As we travelled behind them, I felt so sad that yet more animals lives were going to be changed for ever and not necessarily for the best. Once they were off-loaded they soon came around. Chalkie hosed both of them down as it was a very hot day and it was not long before Ben and Storm were tucking into a large hunk of meat each – none the worse for their long hot journey.'

When Meryl contacted Sandie three years later, it was to hear that Ben and Storm and their cub had survived the move to another farm in Zimbabwe. The van Schalkwks were living in the UK and had begun the process of making a new life. Sandie was writing a book and compiling a DVD of video footage about those incredible three years they'd spent with their beloved lions. To be called *Ben and Storm,* the book and DVD would forever be a reminder of a great love between people and lions on a farm in a beautiful country ravaged by the evil that only politics can bring. Chalkie was working in a wildlife park in the UK and Sandie wrote that he continued his love of big cats:

'He looks after the tigers, lions, jaguars, cheetahs, snow leopards and they have just acquired some white lions and a white tiger. He has got this incredible bond with the big cats – definitely this is what he was born to do and it took Ben and Storm to show him that.'

Extracts from Meryl's Diary:

> *'What of October, that ambiguous month,*
> *the month of tension, the unendurable month?'*
> *– Doris Lessing*

September 2004

Featherstone:

To the doctor for another blood test, then on to a farm in Featherstone where the farmer had been evicted having to leave his livestock behind. Sheep in a pretty bad way, instructed remaining workers to take them out for longer periods for grazing, uplifted three lambs whose mothers had died and took them back to the Horse Care Unit (Claire Evans is a qualified shepherd).

Harare:

Contacted a Board member of National Parks to ask what they were going to do about the sable incarcerated in the bomas. He replied that Parks did not have the power to 'seize' them, and he requested that ZNSPCA did it. Heard that two more sable had died. Game Management Africa kindly took four bags of game nuts out to the quarantine pens.

Ruwa:

A friend who is a great gardener came out to Ruwa and re-vamped my little garden – when I got home it looked so pretty and took my mind off other things.

Harare:

Gave a talk to a Rotary Club at Chapman Golf Club – as always members very interested in our work, especially the farm rescues. Later had to get my affidavit to the lawyers dealing with the ownership of the sable.

Harare:

To the Magistrates Court for the dog-fighting case. One of the young men involved was shocked to be remanded in custody.

Harare:

10 September. Went to the funeral of Sister Bowker – lovely lady who had worked at St Anne's Hospital for many years. Several months before I had approached her to see if ZNSPCA could have any medicines, syringes, needles, etc. that they were unable to use as they were past their 'sell by date'. She was always only too happy to put stacks of items aside for us including old towels, sheets, etc.

Tengwe:

To Meidon farm in Tengwe area – situation with cattle still on the farm very serious, but the workers wanting to be paid first, before they will let the cattle go. Farmer has no access to funds as all his equipment which in the normal course of events, he would have sold in order to raise the cash, had been taken over by the new 'farmer'.

Harare:
1 September. Another blood test required. Heard that yet another sable had died in the Beatrice bomas.

A very sad day for me – took my much-loved tan Staffordshire Bull Terrier bitch 'Tawny' to Kamfinsa vets to be put to sleep. For several years she had suffered with Irritable Bowel Syndrome, in the last weeks she had deteriorated a lot and the vet and I made the joint decision to end her pain. Although I have been with literally hundreds of dogs when they were being euthanased, it is always so much more upsetting when it is your own dog. Tawny had always been the very gentlest of dogs, always giving unconditional love and asking for nothing in return. No time even to grieve as Sternford and I have to go to Chimanimani again.

Chimanimani:
16 September. Sternford and I head to Charleswood with the horse box again to attempt to try and remove two more of Roy and Heather Bennett's horses.

Kariba road:
18 September. Saw on TV news that many settlers and ex-farm workers on properties bordering the Harare/ Kariba road who had been evicted from farms had had their homes burnt down by the police. The footage showed many of them camped by the side of the road with all their belongings, including livestock, poultry, dogs, etc. On visiting the area we found rabbits stuffed in small plastic boxes (their hutches having been destroyed), litters of puppies tied up with string to prevent them straying onto the main road, one had already been hit by a car and killed. We uplifted a puppy and several rabbits and took them back to Goromonzi with each rabbit labelled with the owner's name, as we had promised to return them once someone had found them somewhere else to live. That night whilst trying to open a bottle of soda water it exploded in my face, cutting my nose quite badly – resulting in my kitchen floor being covered in glass, soda water and blood – the dogs disappeared rapidly out the back door!

Tengwe:
To Tengwe with Sternford to collect cattle from Meidon Farm. Finally, after many weeks of negotiations, the workers have agreed the cattle can go. Eight cattle trucks have been hired and should be en route to the farm. Sternford and I arrived at the Sub-police Station to collect the escort that had been promised – find a very hostile reception. OIC refuses to give us any help. After a lengthy meeting I decide we will go on our own as the cattle trucks will be waiting at the farm. On arrival at the farm my

truck is immediately surrounded by a very large crowd of workers, settlers and war vets. The cattle truck drivers, sensing trouble, ran to their trucks and took off – I don't blame them! Sternford and I get out to the truck and attempt to talk to them but by that time things were out of control.

The crowd started to chant: 'Kill them! Kill them!' and screaming in Shona that they were going to set the ZNSPCA truck on fire. Many were armed with pangas and badzas. Some of them rushed up to Sternford and I, tearing their clothes and screaming that that was the state of their clothes now because they hadn't been paid. It was a very scary time and I knew that if Sternford and I got into the truck then for sure we would be attacked. I told Sternford not to make eye contact with any of them, nor speak to them and instead he and I leant on the bonnet of the truck – trying to chat nonchalantly about anything that came into my head. Eventually they must have realised we weren't going to react and they gradually drifted away. Slowly Sternford and I got back into the truck and very slowly I reversed down the drive – I have never been so glad to leave a farm!

Went straight back to the police station and I stormed into the OIC's office and said that thanks to his lack of support we had been in very real danger. By this time the mob from Meidon had arrived (they must have walked there while Sternford and I were waiting for the crowd to disperse) and as soon as he realised he had an audience, the OIC started shouting at me (as if we had done something wrong). In the midst of all this chaos the phone rang in the police station and it was for me! One of the truck drivers had phoned the owner of the cattle to say that Sternford and I were left behind. It was John Worsley Worswick on the phone – it was good to hear his now familiar deep voice and he was so concerned for our safety. He wanted to know if we were hurt or if we'd been injured or if there was anything he could do for us or anyone that he could contact.

Bromley:
Farmer phones to say that they had had a dairy cow axed and killed the previous night – settlers on the next door invaded farm suspected. They had lead her away with barbed wire round her neck and then slaughtered her with an axe on the boundary fence of the farm.

Harare:
Yet another blood test. National Parks phoned, wanting to see the Court Order on the sable in the Beatrice bomas before issuing a movement permit – at long last it looks as if we might be getting somewhere.

Goromonzi:
Court case concerning an indigenous farmer that we had charged with cruelty for keeping 15 so-called security dogs in very small cages with no protection from the sun.

October 2004

Harare:
3 October. The Horse Care Unit had been invited to take part in The Oddball Olympics being held Gateway School in Harare. Mark had got a team together for 'the games', whilst Claire and I manned the bric-a-brac stall. Many kind folk in the equine world had donated items, aware that the Evans were looking after many abandoned horses and ponies, all funded out of their own pockets – yet they themselves could ill afford it, having lost their income when they were evicted from the farm that Mark had been working on. All proceeds for the Horse Care Unit.

Goromonzi:
With Mark to a farm in Goromonzi to destroy 14 horses, including foals, that had been left behind on the farm when the farmer had been evicted. No one was looking after the horses – with several stallions amongst them, there was continuous fighting and breeding and they were now completely wild. I had contacted the Lion and Cheetah Park the day before and they came out to collect the carcasses.

Beatrice:
Trimming of sable's hooves and all given vitamin injections in preparation for release.

Harare/Ruwa:
On the way home on the Mutare road, to my horror I saw a little duckling dodging the 5 o'clock rush-hour traffic. I got out of my truck and tried to slow the vehicles down – talk about taking one's life into one's hands! – couldn't catch it, but eventually it disappeared into the long grass.

Lowveld:
15 September. Finally – the day dawned for the re-location of the sable after 950 days in quarantine.

CHAPTER THIRTY-FOUR

The Wildlife Conservancy: a story of death and of life
(Part Two: 2004)

Like the body that is made up of different limbs and organs,
all mortal creatures exist depending one upon another.
– Hindu Proverb

Bubiana, October 2004

It had been three and a half years since Meryl had heard first hand from Guy Hilton-Barber about what was happening to the wildlife in the Bubiana Conservancy and she feared that his latest report would tell a very bleak tale. Guy's 2004 report covered the combined effects of four years of invasions on what had been a thriving and internationally renowned Conservancy. Guy had sent the report to the Governors of the Midlands and Masvingo Provinces, the Director of National Parks, the Department of Veterinary Services, various officials in police headquarters and to the Chairmen of several wildlife conservancies. As in 2000, Guy received neither acknowledgement nor reaction from any of the Government departments.

Guy's report told of a tragedy still in progress and it was a damning indictment of what had really been going on under cover of land re-distribution.

Summary of Invasion Effects: Barberton Ranch, Bubiana Conservancy
Animals found dead in snares May 2000 to June 2004

4 Baboon	*60 Eland*
4 Buffalo (2 maimed, 2 snared)	*5 Giraffe*
23 Cattle (11 snared, 7 cyanide, 5 stock theft)	*26 Impala*

300

6 *Klipspringer*   63 *Kudu*
8 *Sable*   27 *Wildebeest*
86 *Warthog*   73 *Zebra*
5 *Waterbuck*

In addition to the 390 animals found dead in snares and left to rot in the burning lowveld sun, Guy estimated a further 117 animals had been poached and removed without discovery. These numbers were estimated from declining numbers in game counts and the visual disappearance of known herds on Barberton alone. Guy suggested that losses in the Bubiana Conservancy as a whole could be calculated from the equation that Barberton represented 10% of the overrun 112,000 hectares of the Conservancy. It was a chilling thought indeed. Guy went on to list some of the other effects directly attributable to the invasion of Barberton Ranch:

49 months of tourism lost
156 trips to police stations
14 Rhino rescued from snares
22 buildings torched, looted or, vandalised
500 plots of land cleared, approx 1,000 pole and mud huts erected using indigenous timber cut on site
46.5 kilometres of snare wire removed
108.25 kilometres of game fencing wire stolen

In conclusion to his report Guy told of the less visible but more damaging effects of the land invasions:

'There has been an obvious disappearance of the smaller creature that constitute the food-chain. Rock rabbits, hares, tortoises, squirrels, mongooses, honey badgers, antbears, otters, waterfowl, guinea fowl, partridges, francolins – the list is endless and affects the predators and raptors, etc. No account can be taken of the degree of horror of animal suffering and the enormous wastage of meat. The destruction of the environment, hundreds of thousands of trees being felled and the cultivation of several thousand hectares of land in this fragile ecosystem will soon result in desert. The rainfall is insufficient to support arable agriculture and already the squatters are experiencing their fourth consecutive season of crop failure. Conservationists watch and weep as 20 years of wildlife resources are decimated within four years. The entire scenario is hugely offensive to any civilised society as the Government's policy of resettling the invaders elsewhere continues in its stagnant state of political paralysis.'

Meryl was appalled at the horrific numbers of animals slaughtered and the environmental destruction that was still going on in the Bubiana Conservancy in 2004. By now similar reports were coming into the public domain about the situation in other wildlife projects.

The Farmer magazine reported on the Save Conservancy, a massive area incorporating 340 thousand hectares of land and the biggest Conservancy not just in Zimbabwe, but in Africa. Two gruesome photographs accompanied the article, one of a wild dog killed from a snare around its neck; the other of a man wearing a T-shirt bearing President Mugabe's face and the legend: 'Vote Zanu PF'. The man was holding a double handful of biltong [strips of salted, dried meat] made from the meat of animals poached in the Save Conservancy. The tragic irony was that these Conservancies were once Zimbabwe's pride and had received the backing and full support of the Zimbabwe government. Politics and the need to retain power, had reduced great environmental visions and revolutionary conservation practices to little more than the dusty village scenario that had decimated Africa.

The Farmer magazine described events in the Save Conservancy after the government announced they were taking it over:

'More than 270 families moved into the Conservancy. This resulted in sizeable parts of the forest being cut down and burnt... Ironically the settlers have received full backing from the government, the same government that once deemed the area as unsuitable for dry land resettlement schemes, the same one that handed it over to the Conservancy and supported the projects undertaken there with the help of the World Wide Fund for nature.'

As settlers moved in and dismantled fences, the wire was used to make snares – and a veritable orgy of meat harvesting began. Some animals strayed into neighbouring communal areas and posed a threat to villagers resulting in elephants having to be shot. Buffalo, carriers of foot-and-mouth disease, wandered around at will and spreading of the disease to livestock became inevitable. The most tragic part of it all was that the farmers involved in the Save Conservancy made repeated appeals for assistance and intervention to Governors and government ministers. Governor Josaya Hungwe said that the government was in fact going to 'delist' the properties in the Save Conservancy but, as in hundreds of other instances around the country, talk had not translated into action and Zimbabwe's wildlife was paying the price of politicians' ineptitude.

Meryl was powerless to do anything about the massive slaughter of wildlife and destruction of Conservancies. It was a tragic situation with what seemed to be a complete lack of control by anyone in authority. As absurd as it all was, there were little islands of stability in amongst the chaos and Meryl found one.

In mid-October 2004, the hottest and driest time of the year, Meryl travelled to one of the two remaining functional properties in the Bubiana Conservancy. Located on the south-east boundary of Barberton, adjoining the Maranda Communal land, the owner had a trading store and grinding mill which was of considerable advantage to the local people; he was in a strategic position geographically to exercise neighbourly good-will and had been persuaded to give half of his land to the government. In hundreds of other cases where similar proportions of land holdings had been handed over to government, the farmers had not in fact been subsequently left alone and had still gone on to lose the balance of their property in invasions. Fortunately this had not happened here and hence Meryl and SPCA Inspector Sternford were on the road to the lowveld. They were following a truck load of sable who were to be set free after being held in captivity for almost three years.

As she drove, Meryl thought about Sternford and how quickly he had become such a respected part of the rescue team. Sternford had only joined the SPCA the year before but soon learnt what the work entailed and how to handle animals. Married with children and in his late 50s, Sternford lived near Meryl and the SPCA base in Goromonzi. He was an ex-policeman of long standing, having served in both the BSAP (British South Africa Police) and the ZRP. He knew many of the serving police officers that Meryl came in contact with at police stations and this often proved a great asset when it came to dealing with uncooperative members of the police force. Sternford was always very punctual, smartly turned out and not at all a clock-watcher. He was meticulous when it came to preparing dockets and dealing with paperwork and accompanied Meryl on most of the farm rescues after Addmore had left.

Their journey passed through distinctly different areas of country, from grassy highveld to dry, scrubby lowveld where thorn bushes and baobab trees prevailed. They travelled along the Masvingo to Beitbridge Road and turned off about 120 kilometres before the border town of Beitbridge. Once off the main road there were still nearly 100 kilometres of dusty gravel road to negotiate before they reached the ranch.

By now darkness had fallen and driving behind the dust of the truck carrying the precious cargo of sable, visibility was just about nil but they finally made it at midnight. The journey was tiring but also immensely satisfying because setting these sable free was bringing conclusion to a long and exhausting saga. As she drove, Meryl thought about the 18 months of meetings, phone calls, visits and finally legal action which had led to this final victory.

Meryl had first become involved early in 2003 when Johnny Rodrigues alerted her to a case of a herd of 160 sable antelope that were being held in bomas for quarantine purposes outside Harare pending relocation and the animals had been there for a considerable period of time. Johnny Rodrigues, an individual passionately concerned about Zimbabwe's wildlife and founder of the Zimbabwe Conservation Task Force, was dedicated to raising awareness about the plight of Zimbabwe's wildlife – particularly during the period of farm and land invasions. Johnny had contacted Meryl to report the case of the sable being held captive under unacceptable conditions and he asked her to investigate the situation.

The sable had come from a Wildlife Conservancy in the Chinhoyi area and were to be exported. When a dispute arose between the commercial farmers who owned the conservancy and the war veterans in the area who were supported by a well-known government supporter and businessman, Kembo, the animals invariably became stuck in the middle. A legal battle began and carried on for several months and the sable, confined to bomas on private land outside Harare, were still being fed by the owners of the Conservancy.

When the Harare High Court ruled against the owners of the Conservancy, the care and feeding of the sable reverted to Kembo. At first the businessman fed the sable correctly but when the money for food apparently ran out, the antelope began to lose condition rapidly. It wasn't long before animals began to die and when Meryl visited the holding pens she found that the sable were in a deplorable state of health and hygiene.

The animals weren't being given a balanced diet, weren't getting enough food and they were undernourished and emaciated. Many of the females that fell pregnant aborted and the calves that were born did not survive.

'As a result of the appalling conditions the sable were being kept in, I began to hold meetings with Kembo to find a way forward. He was extremely difficult and hostile. To begin with he would not see me and we only had meetings with his lawyer who informed me that I was known as an "eco-terrorist". When I told him that didn't bother me, he said: "It is whites who say that."'

Meryl was determined not to give up and persisted in holding meetings with Kembo – each time he promised to improve the feeding and living conditions for the sable but nothing changed. Finally on 7 September 2004 Meryl sought and obtained a Court Order from Harare Magistrate Mr Guvamombe for the ZNSPCA to seize the remaining 57 sable. The others, tragically, had perished as a result of their 950 day confinement.

'This in effect meant that the SPCA now "owned" the sable and were responsible for their feeding. I approached the WWF [World Wildlife Fund] for a donation towards their feeding and the wages for the workers looking after them. They agreed and I so appreciated their generous donation and readiness to help. Vet Chris Foggin came and trimmed their hooves which were very overgrown as the animals had been confined for such a long period and all were given vitamin injections. The hoof trimming took two days to do as each sable had to be tranquillised first. As well as Chris Foggin, we had two other vets and some veterinary students from the University of Zimbabwe helping. Bearing in mind that the sable had been living in the most appalling conditions whilst the battle for their ownership raged between commercial farmer and the war vets and the fact that they had been confined in the very small bomas for nearly three years – I had to make a decision on what to do with them. The Court Order had given the ZNSPCA permission to seize the animals, and I had to give them the best possible chance of a decent life – they deserved it. They could not stay on at the bomas and the grant that I obtained from WWF to feed them quickly ran out, so Tim Paulet ended up feeding them out of his own pocket.'

In the five weeks that followed, Meryl negotiated with the original Conservancy owners and it was settled that the sable would go to one of the two remaining functioning ranches in the Bubiana Conservancy. Meryl had done the necessary investigations and was happy with the security arrangements and the quality of the grazing. She thought this was the best option for the sable in view of the chaos all over the country.

Almost three years after the sable had been taken into captivity and nearly two years since she had first become involved, Meryl witnessed freedom at last for the sable. It was a great victory and a credit to everyone who had worked so hard and been committed to returning the sable back into the bush where they belonged. This was one of many encounters that Johnny Rodrigues had had with Meryl and he held her in high regard as he later wrote in tribute:

'I have nothing but respect and admiration for this amazing, courageous lady. She frequently risked her own life to help the animals – domestic or wild – subjecting herself fearlessly to confrontations with rabid war veterans and farm invaders. She went way beyond the call of duty for the animals, even to the detriment of her health. The SPCA was a force to be reckoned with when Meryl was here and she will always be a heroine in my eyes.'

Sable are Zimbabwe's most majestic antelope, deep brown to almost black in colour with a white rump and belly and startling black and white markings on their faces. Their heads are crowned with magnificent, long, elegantly curved horns. Meryl felt privileged to have been able to help them and was delighted to record this last entry concerning the sable:

> *'On 15 October 2004 Sternford and I accompanied the first consignment of 34 Sable to the ranch in the Bubiana Conservancy, followed four days later by the remaining 23. When I watched them the next day racing around in the sunshine, head-butting bushes, grazing on legumes – the first green vegetation they had seen for over a year – I realised that at least we had given them a chance to be sables again. Later I learnt that many of the females were pregnant and several healthy calves had been born.'*

57 sable antelope and their new born calves running free and wild on a lowveld property could not replace or repair the tragedy of over 400 animals slaughtered and poached on Barberton Ranch but with life comes hope. Meryl knew this was just one small victory for the Bubiana Conservancy and the dream that had inspired its creation.

Extracts from Meryl's Diary:

> *'Most people sell their souls,*
> *and live with a good conscience on the proceeds.'*
> – Logan Pearsall Smith, 1931

October 2004
Tiny Farm, Nyazura:
22 October. Went with Claire from Horse Rescue Unit to Nyazura after receiving a report of several horses in the area that were running wild – all from abandoned farms. We collected police from Rusape Rural and Nyazura as we were expecting trouble. Found out that 'new farmer' had wanted to take possession of some other horses that had been left behind on a farm at Halfway House. He knew they would be difficult to drive on their own, so got his workers to take the horses left behind on 'his farm' (Tiny Farm), walk them back to Halfway House, pick up the new horses, and then drive them all back through the bush to Nyazura – it was a round trip of 120 kilometres.

At one stage one of the horses must have panicked and run straight into a barbed wire fence which got wrapped round his legs and chest. Claire and I caught up with them just as they were walking down the driveway of the farm – they were so exhausted after walking 120 kilometres that they could hardly stand. It was utterly shocking – they rocked like they could fall over at any minute. And to think the little filly was blind – what must she have gone through?

Things were very hostile on the farm and we feared for the horses' safety, so Claire and I drove back to Goromonzi to collect the horsebox. By the time we got back to the farm it was too late to load so we left the horsebox and one of Claire's grooms to water and feed the horses after their ordeal. Thankfully the trouble-makers had drifted off and we believed the horses would be safe for the night. Mark was worried sick about our safety because we finally only got back to their place after 9.30pm. (Mark was furious that he (or anyone else) had no means of getting hold of us – no cell phone signal where we were and no radio to use in an emergency.)

The next day we returned and loaded all the horses and took them to Claire and Mark's Horse Rescue unit. In total we rescued two ponies ex-Morestar Farm, two greys and one Palamino.

Harare:
25 October. Chairman of Hre SPCA Rose Nurse asked me to take her beloved old Labrador to be put to sleep at the vets – just couldn't face doing it herself. With her track record in animal welfare I was only too happy to help.

Harare:
Another blood test. In the evening went to a farewell party at the Harare Kennel Club for two very good friends of mine – shall miss them so much. So many people leaving now.

28 October. Tim's birthday.

Harare:
30 October. Fete at Dandaro. The Evans' and I had a stall using the masses of bric-a-brac which was being donated by the horsey fraternity; they had all been so supportive. We did very well and all proceeds were for the Horse Care Unit which it so desperately needed – a great deal of interest in the work being done with horses that had been abandoned on farms. Mark and Claire had produced some excellent enlarged photos depicting the condition of the horses before they came to them and how they looked after a few months of TLC.

Later, at a board meeting I was told that I should never have allowed Mark and Claire to keep the funds from this event. This generous couple were now funding the Horse Care Unit entirely out of their rapidly dwindling savings, having lost the farm they were working on like so many other folk in the area.

November 2004
Chinhoyi:
Attended a meeting to discuss the on-going problem at Meidon Farm, at the meeting

were a Deputy Commissioner, Propol and the local District Commissioner – very little progress made. Still not able to move cattle off.

Nyazura:
To a farm at Inyazura with Sternford to rescue a much-loved ginger cat 'Sylvester' who had got left behind when farmers were violently evicted. This often happened with cats: in the mayhem of eviction, they often took off in panic for several days. Border Gezi youths and the 'new manager' of the farm gave us a very hostile reception. Later, a joyous reunion took place in the car park at Sam Levy's Village, as we reunited Sylvester with his owners.

Harare:
3 October. Invited to speak to the Harare Women's International Society at the invitation of their Chairlady Mrs Berens. The very first question at the end of my talk was from a lady sitting at the front whom I did not know. She said that many of the people present had seen the board up in the grounds of a house on the Enterprise Road, declaring that it was the new headquarters of the ZNSPCA. She said that they wanted to know whether the house had been donated or purchased? I had to tell her the truth and replied that it had been purchased.

There was an immediate reaction in the room, with many questions such as: where had the money come from? How much had the house cost? What was the purpose of it? Had the Executive tried to get premises donated?

I had to be honest about it and gave them the facts as best I could – after all it was public funds that had been used for the purchase of the house.

A member of the Harare SPCA Committee who was present, asked me if my Executive realised there was 'such a groundswell of opinion against the purchase of the house'? Several people present were keen to know what I felt about the house? – I told them that maybe 10 yrs ago or 10 yrs hence it might have been a good purchase, but that I thought this was not the time.

An hour after I left the meeting and was on a farm checking some cattle, I received a phone call from a board member, furious with me for revealing details of the house to the Harare Women's International Society. I was amazed – the house after all, had been purchased with money donated by the public.

5 October. Worked all day in the office at Goromonzi preparing material for the coming Inspector's course. In the evening Mark and Claire Evans took me to an Art Exhibition in Harare of Debbie Hart's paintings – So nice to be doing something so different for a change – her paintings of Zim's wildlife, especially the big cats are brilliant.

Goromonzi:
On the way back to Goromonzi from Rusape I stop and issue a warning to driver of a cattle truck. He had stopped in the boiling sun whilst he and his mate had their lunch, disregarding how hot the loaded cattle were getting.

Harare:
Sunday 14 October. Friends invited me to lunch at the Art Cafe in Avondale – had a lovely meal – as I was driving back to Ruwa they phoned to say that there were three horses loose on the Golden Stairs/Mazowe road. Turned round and with the help of a member of the public managed to get them back onto the property where they had come from.

Harare:
Friday 19 November: four members of the Executive are present at a meeting I've been summoned to. I am told that I am 'self-serving, egotistical, interested in self-aggrandisement, am not a team person and that that no one was bigger than the organisation or the job'. One board member told me: 'The Inspectors don't like working with you.'

The Executive Director of NSPCA (South Africa) was also present and told me that I had been extremely disloyal and had I worked for them in South Africa I would have been fired.

Then followed a barrage of complaints about my demeanour and behaviour. I felt torn to shreds which of course was their intention – in their eyes I had crossed the line by voicing my opinion about the purchase of the house.

When they had finished, I told them that obviously, they wouldn't want someone of such poor quality working for them anymore, and that I was giving them my resignation – leaving at the end of December. I had never been given a contract since joining the SPCA.

I walked out to my truck feeling totally numb. I had no idea that that was what they thought of me – animal welfare has been my life.

Harare:
22 November. Invited to the Horse Society annual dinner at a restaurant in Borrowdale – taken there by Mark and Claire. A lovely evening made all the nicer by the fact that I won the raffle!

Ruwa:
Inspector's Training course began – it is the last one I will run. Participants from several SPCA centres attended – held once again at Ruwa Country Club. Several very heavy

rain storms result in buckets being placed at strategic places in the boardroom where rain was dripping through the thatch!

Bromley:
29 November. Two stray stallions to be shot at a stud farm in the Bromley area – they had been causing havoc for many months. The farmer who had once owned them agreed to their destruction.

December 2004
Goromonzi:
1 December. Took my dogs to boarding kennels and arrange to collect Roy Bennett's workers early the next day to go down to Charleswood for the last time to deal with the remaining horses there.

Harare:
Received a beautiful arrangement of flowers anonymously – the card just said – 'From those who cannot speak – to show our appreciation'.

Chimanimani:
2 December. Left for Chimanimani – picked up a dog in Macheke that had been hit by a car and dropped it off at Mutare SPCA.

CHAPTER THIRTY-FIVE

Bokkie

*'You only have power over people so long as
you don't take everything away from them.
But when you've robbed a man of everything,
he's no longer in your power.'*
– Alexander Solzenhitsyn

Charleswood Estate, Chimanimani, December 2004
On 2 December 2004 Meryl set out for Charleswood Estate in Chimanimani
for the last time. She had lost count of how many times she had travelled this
road and been to this farm in the last two years. Thinking backing on it all she
could hardly believe everything that had happened on this one property – it was
barbaric, like a medieval horror film. Meryl's involvement had started in April
2003. By then Meryl had been onto hundreds of seized farms, rescued more
dogs, cats, pigs, cattle, sheep and horses than she could count and had come
face to face with all manner of people undertaking land invasions. Charleswood, however, was going to be different, Meryl knew it and no amount of
past experience could have prepared her for these rescues. On this property
more abuses against people and animals had taken place and for a longer time,
than on any other farm in the country. Here people had been murdered; rape
and torture had taken place; and all but a handful of the farm workers had
been evicted from the property. Eight hundred cattle were on the farm, several
had been axed, others had been slaughtered and the estate was over-run with
government supporters, police, soldiers and members of the CIO.

Charleswood Estate was owned by Roy and Heather Bennett who had
bought and operated the property since the early 1990s as a private company.
Charleswood stood apart from many other commercial farms because Roy had
gone out of his way to make sure that he and his family and their venture
were welcome in the area. He approached local leaders in the district before
purchasing the farm and only when he had their approval did he start opening
up Charleswood Estate. Local people soon named Roy 'Pachedu' – which means

'one of us' and an extremely close relationship between the farmer and the local community grew up over the years. When the Bennetts were overwhelmed with work on the farm, local people would just arrive and help – no payment was asked, expected or given. Likewise the Bennetts worked to help the local people and uplift the community. After Cyclone Eline in early 2000, Roy used his own capital to help rebuild roads, bridges and schools which had been damaged.

Charleswood developed into a highly productive farm with 310 hectares planted to coffee, a beef herd of 880 cattle and a prime tourist lodge – Mawenje – was established on the estate. Charleswood soon became classified as an EPZ (Export Processing Zone) because of the strategic importance of its coffee processing and exports.

Everything that Charleswood had become and everyone involved in the venture came under attack in May 2000 when Roy was approached and agreed to stand as the opposition MP for Chimanimani. Within weeks Charleswood was invaded and there followed a litany of horror which was to continue for the next five years.

When Meryl was first called on to help the animals on Charleswood in April 2003 she reviewed the events so as to be as informed as possible about what she might encounter. It was a grim and frightening account:

May 2000. Heather had a miscarriage after being held hostage when she tried to stop invaders from beating a farm worker.

June 2000. Roy was elected as the opposition MDC MP for Chimanimani.

May 2001. The High Court issued a provisional order banning the State from acquiring Charleswood.

July 2001. A senior government Minister, an Air Vice Marshall, senior army officers and war veterans tour Charleswood.

July 2001. A police officer and settlers move onto Charleswood. DDF begin ploughing.

Over the next month one farm worker is shot and killed, one is shot and wounded, two girls are raped and there are 90 incidents of stock theft, stock slaughter, poaching and theft of farm equipment.

October 2001. Army and police officers acquire and remove 97 tons of maize from Charleswood and physically assault Roy.

August 2002. Army personnel arrive on Charleswood, assault workers and 13 are taken to the police station, beaten and detained for several days.

October 2002. Roy and two associates are assaulted and detained at Chimanimani Police Station, accused of taking photographs within 100 metres of a polling station. Charges are later withdrawn when no evidence can be produced.

Jan 2003. The High Court confirms that Charleswood is protected from state acquisition because of its status as an EPZ. Charleswood is now financially crippled due to being over run with invaders but law enforcement personnel are unable to enforce Court Orders due to political interference.

With all this in mind Meryl had set out for Charleswood Estate. She'd received an urgent phone call from Roy Bennett who asked if Meryl and the SPCA team could go to Charleswood to treat many of his cattle which had been axed by settlers. It was a good five hour drive from Harare to Chimanimani and Meryl left home at 4.30 in the morning in order to get to Charleswood by lunch time. Meryl was accompanied by trainee Inspector Jimmy and a Vet Assistant. Meryl hadn't met Roy but on his advice she didn't have a police escort; Roy said the police were definitely not impartial when it came to Charleswood. Once on the farm Meryl wanted to work fast and thankfully everyone with her was in agreement. Most of the farm workers had by then been evicted from the property by militant invaders but a few had managed to hang on. Roy's Cattle Manager, Simbi, was still there and he immediately went into action. Together with seven or eight of the remaining farm workers and the SPCA team, the cattle were rounded up and work started.

'We inspected the herd and then separated the injured cows and calves and drove them towards a crush. Many were limping badly. Most of the axe wounds appeared to be on their legs and one weaner had had its tail hacked off, another had a deep wound in the shoulder, its mother had also received an axe wound to the head. I informed the Vet Assistant, that we had to work quickly as I felt it would not be long before someone tipped off the police and CIO that we were there. To his credit he worked swiftly and professionally. It was too late for the wounds to be sutured and so they were thoroughly cleaned and irrigated with antiseptic solution and each animal was injected with long-acting antibiotics.

'The majority of the injured were calves and weaners – probably because they were easier to catch. All appeared to be in a great deal of pain. Simbi then took us up to the workshop and barns area where there were two more cattle that had been badly beaten. One, a brown weaner, had a very swollen back and was unable to stand up. We found her crawling across the ground. The Vet Asst. gave her an anti-inflamma-

tory injection and we gave instructions that she must be destroyed.'

As the gruesome work continued Meryl noticed that they had attracted attention and were being watched. Two soldiers, in camouflage and armed with AK 47s, had come to within about 200 yards and were just standing staring at Meryl and the others. They lived in the army base that had been set up on the farm and the soldiers stood and watched for some minutes – to Meryl it felt like hours. She had goose bumps on her arms and felt very anxious but tried to act casually and as if she wasn't concerned by their presence. Once all the animals had been treated Meryl wanted to leave as soon as possible. She left Simbi with wound spray and instructions to treat the cattle daily to prevent screw worm. Simbi said he would and Meryl didn't doubt him for a moment: the man was clearly dedicated to his job and seemed utterly loyal to the Bennett family.

'Zimbabweans are all suffering too much now,' Simbi said to Meryl as they prepared to leave.

'Yes,' she responded, 'many people are now saying that God is on holiday.'

An hour and a half after Meryl had left Charleswood, all hell broke loose as she later recorded:

'The OIC at Chimanimani Police Station, Inspector C, CIO Operative J. M. and one of their thugs had arrived and severely beaten Moses and five other workers. Moses, Roy's Security Manager, had been rushed through to hospital in Mutare where I visited him the next day. His face and hands were swollen horribly and lacerated. He said it was possible the beating was in retaliation for the ZNSPCA's visit. In spite of the obvious beating he had suffered, he appeared unbowed and was wanting to get back to the farm.'

Four days later Meryl got a phone call from Simbi. He told her a cow had been killed the night before, axed to death in one of the paddocks but her calf, luckily old enough to survive on its own, had escaped the slaughter. At the end of the conversation Meryl's eyes shone with a mixture of laughter and tears at the parting comments:

'Take care, Simbi,' she said.

'I will,' he replied, 'and don't forget God's on leave!'

Ten months later, in February 2004, Meryl had been called back to Charleswood again. A new Governor had been appointed for the Manicaland province and in a speech had called on Zanu PF supporters to drive the Bennett family from Chimanimani altogether. A new frenzy over Charleswood erupted and cows and calves were slashed with pangas and axed by settlers. Meryl was appalled at the barbarity:

'Cattle were axed and maimed not for meat or food but to harass Roy into moving his cattle off the land which would give the invaders more land to occupy and plough.'

Local Government Vets in the area were not prepared to go out to Charleswood to attend to the horrific wounds on the cattle. They feared they'd be accused of siding with Roy Bennett and then become targeted by militants themselves. Again the SPCA were the only hope and had arrived late in the afternoon and spent the night at the Chimanimani Hotel. Meryl soaked up the surroundings making the most of peace and the beauty. It gave her strength to face what she knew would be the horrors of the next day:

'The hotel was not quite as smart as I remembered it in the past but the glorious views and scenery made up for everything (even the fact that the toilet in my room was a bit dodgy and I had to constantly fill the cistern with water from the bath – thank goodness for plastic waste paper baskets!).

'I had obviously requested a single room but to my surprise was given a suite – a huge old-fashioned room with a passageway that led to a lounge with a fireplace and a desk. Had dinner with Sternford and Addmore, the service and food was excellent.

'Later in the evening in my room I looked out from the un-burglar-barred window at the breathtaking scenery, the huge craggy hills silhouetted against the dark African sky, studded with bright stars. In the distance a dog barked and it was all so peaceful. It was hard to believe that less than 10 kilometres away down in the valley, murder, rape and brutal assault on the livestock had taken place.

'The next morning at breakfast we met the representative from the International Red Cross who was also in Chimanimani because of the problems at Charleswood. He for the people and us for the animals.'

That was the last normal and peaceful entry Meryl made in her diary. Again she had gone to Charleswood without a police escort, starting out early in the morning and driving straight to the cattle pen. Simbi was expecting the SPCA team and the wounded animals had been rounded up and were waiting to be attended to. As before everyone had worked quickly, not knowing if they would be stopped or chased off.

'Knowing the sorts of injuries we could expect to see after our last visit, it still didn't prepare me for the horror of the cattles' wounds. Innocent and uncomprehending, they stood there obviously in great pain with many flies crawling all over their gaping wounds – especially those that had been axed on their ears, these were still dripping with blood, even though the attack had been four days before. Most of those attacked had again been calves and weaners – because they are easy targets. The youngest calf had a crudely- made arrow protruding from its side – this had been made from a fencing dropper. We gently eased the piece of metal out and treated the deep penetrating wound – the calf never made a sound though it must have been in great pain.

'Some of the weaners could barely walk as they been axed on two legs and had to limp along as best they could. Our last job was to destroy the calf whose leg had been almost severed – this we did with our humane killer and then cut its throat.

'At one stage I could not take it any longer and walked some distance away, tears welling in my eyes. I stood looking at the beautiful scenery of Charleswood Estate and wondered whether Roy and Heather Bennett, their staff and animals would one day be left in peace to get on with their lives. Charleswood is set in the most beautiful surroundings in a green valley with towering blue hills as far as the eye can see. Down the road from where we are is the beautiful Mawenji Safari Lodge, set next to a sparkling stream. This was now silent and deserted – unlikely to ever host tourists and visitors again.'

Meryl's visit to Charleswood on that occasion had ended with a cry for help for 'Bokkie', a dog who had been given to Security Manager Moses by Roy. Bokkie was a medium-sized black dog with a broad head and Meryl thought he may have had a bit of Staffordshire Bull Terrier in him. Bokkie was starting to go a bit grey around his muzzle and had a distinct twinkle in his brown eyes. Meryl was immediately taken with the dog and was told of his bravery because just the night before Bokkie had saved lives.

'A mob of settlers had come and burnt down Moses' house just as the family were sitting down to supper. Bokkie had barked furiously, alerting them. Moses said Bokkie's barking warned them enough to run out the door just as the house burst into flames. Their house was burnt to the ground and the family fled with just the clothes they were wearing. When Moses returned the next day to see what was left of his house, he found Bokkie sitting next to the burnt shell of his former home. Moses found to his horror that Bokkie had been savagely beaten by the mob and his hind leg appeared to be broken. Sadly the family cat had not managed to escape and had burnt to death in the house.'

Moses' car had been set on fire and rolled and was a write off. His house and all the contents had been reduced to ash. Meryl couldn't see anything in the soot and debris that was recognisable. There was no doubt that if it hadn't been for Bokkie, Moses and his family would have perished in the inferno. Meryl guessed that Bokkie's femur was broken and told Moses that a vet was definitely needed. Moses looked away: even a vet had become a luxury he couldn't afford. Meryl's heart was lost to the obvious love between the man and his dog.

'We loaded Bokkie into the back of my truck, Moses waved good bye to him through the window and we headed for the vet in Mutare, arriving there as his surgery was about to close. He confirmed that it was a very bad break at the top of the femur and that the leg would need operating on to insert a pin.'

Meryl guaranteed that all the costs would be met by the ZNSPCA and there and then X-rays were taken. Meryl left Bokkie in expert hands. The vets had worked until 1am; sharp edges of broken bone had penetrated muscle and it was a delicate procedure. Bokkie was going to be in a cage for six weeks but would make a full recovery. When Meryl phoned and told him the good news, Moses' normally deep voice quavered with emotion:
'Thank you. Thank you, that is wonderful.'

Barely two months later Meryl headed out to Chimanimani again. On this occasion she did go to the police station and ask for an escort. After a protracted and heated discussion, a Constable had finally been assigned to accompany Meryl and Sternford. The situation on Charleswood had deteriorated even further. The managers of Mawenje Safari Lodge had been given 30 minutes to pack and leave the property and the remaining farm workers had also been evicted. Meryl had been told that these latest evictions had been carried out by police and army personnel. The evictions had been violent and chaotic and in the mayhem several of the workers' dogs had been left behind and were now stranded without food, water or anyone to care for them.

University of Zimbabwe Law lecturer Derek Matyzak described a situation on Charleswood in April 2004 that beggared belief:

'The army maintains a blockade around the farm, in violation of the Court Orders issued in Bennett's favour. ARDA [Agricultural Rural Development Authority] has moved onto the farm. Taking advantage of Bennett's absence, ARDA has exported 107 tonnes of the farm coffee for its own benefit.'

The notes in Meryl's diary did not refer to the theft of coffee but she described her preparations for the visit and was clearly expecting the worst. Meryl's arrangements that April day, unknown by the vast majority of ordinary Zimbabweans, were chilling – they would have frightened off the bravest of men:

> 'News bulletins reported that Charleswood Estate had been invaded by the army (three battalions) and Support Unit in the early hours of the morning. All farm managerial staff had been forced off the farm.
>
> 'It was with great trepidation that I drove down the twisty roads to Charleswood. I felt very nervous; we just did not know what awaited us. The army were now in control, we knew that several people had been beaten up by them. They were said to be very suspicious of any visitors and had been hostile – confiscating cell phones, etc.
>
> 'Before we left the hotel Sternford and I had stripped my truck of anything that the army might view with suspicion such as the humane killer, bolt cutters, our large knife, the camera, etc. I noticed as we approached the boom that the army had put across the road, that my hands were gripping the steering wheel very tightly.'

Looking at the retreating image of the Chimanimani Hotel in her rear view window, Meryl had driven towards Charleswood, wondering who was watching her and which phones were already ringing. The hotel had become both a sanctuary and a place of anxiety for Meryl.

> 'I was always the only woman and certainly the only white person staying there – which all added to the tension. Whilst this was far from being a wonderful upmarket hotel, the staff were always extremely kind and polite to us. After I wrote to their head office and requested a discount on our bill because we stayed there so often, the manager always knocked a bit off. I was still always very nervous staying there, because we knew members of CIO often stayed there too and of course my truck would be quite obvious in the car park – they knew quite well what we were doing in Chimanimani.'

Once inside Charleswood there were army tents erected at the side of the road and as Meryl had driven along, armed men leapt out to stop and interrogate her and Sternford and the police Constable escorting them. SPCA certificates and letters from the police were shown and after a while they had been allowed to proceed. Meryl wondered what it was that they were guarding here on this coffee and beef farm and why it warranted armed soldiers. Like everyone else, Meryl knew this was just dirty politics. Charleswood had become like a war zone. A little further on, near the implements sheds, Meryl was stopped and questioned again. Certificates were produced once more and just when it seemed they would be allowed to go and treat the cattle, Meryl had seen a soldier running down the hill behind her, shouting as he ran. Again there were questions: who was she, what was the purpose of her visit, who gave her permission to be here? Meryl was ordered to drive back to the sheds and once there the interrogation continued. It had taken an hour but at last Meryl was able to go and treat the four cattle that had axe wounds and to try and find the stranded dogs. The cattle kraal was ankle deep in red mud as there had been recent rain on Charleswood. Even surrounded by such pain and evil, Meryl looked for beauty – and found it:

'There was always a lovely blue haze in the surrounding hills and I could see smoke drifting down from the hillside fires of the many settlers who were encamped on the farm.'

The dogs were very nervous but they managed to catch two which would be taken to the Mutare SPCA until their owners could reclaim them. A third dog could not be caught and so Meryl left food for it – it was all she could do.

Each time Meryl visited Chimanimani, the situation on Charles-wood had deteriorated further, the atmosphere was more tense and military personnel were more in control. When she had visited in May 2004 it was winter, bitterly cold and a year since her first visit. The Chimanimani government Animal Health Inspector had contacted Meryl to say that the cattle were dying on Charleswood and had appealed for her help and intervention. Meryl and Sternford went with the Local Animal Health Inspector to a very tense meeting with the Officer in Charge of Chimanimani Police Station. They had just been given permission to go to Charleswood to check the condition of the cattle when suddenly they were stopped by three men.

'As we walked from the police station to my truck we were intercepted by three men, not in uniform, who asked us to accompany them down an embankment to an office some distance from the charge office. We had no idea who they were or what it was all about but later learnt they were from Army Intelligence and the CIO.'

They were detained and interrogated for three and a half hours and Meryl's patience had been pushed to the limit. As the interrogation continued, more and more excuses were made as to why she could not go to the farm, despite the fact that the police had already given their consent to the visit. In her diaries Meryl recorded what finally became her long overdue breaking point, but she didn't go quietly and was not intimidated, even to the last!

'At times he [the interrogator] was quite friendly saying he would take us out to lunch whilst we waited but the next minute was asking me some very personal questions. It was obvious that he had absolutely no intention of allowing us onto Charleswood. It was now freezing cold in the office and we still had to get back to Harare. I stood up and said we were leaving Chimanimani – goodbye!

'As I started up the ZNSPCA truck our three interrogators opened the back and started to get in – they wanted a lift to Chimanimani. I said, "You have got to be joking – you didn't even ask!" All looked totally taken aback at my response and promptly got into the back of a ZESA truck that was heading towards the village.

'As we left the police station we could see a large white helicopter circling over the small town – by the time we got closer it had landed in the centre of the village with many soldiers in camouflage jumping out. Apparently it was the Presidential helicopter. Roy phoned on my cell phone and suggested that we leave the area straight away.'

A week after she had been interrogated in Chamanimani, Meryl heard in the media that the Zimbabwe Defence Industries (ZDI) had taken over the management of Charleswood. Wanting to get in on the ground floor, Meryl had immediately made contact with the ZDI and went to meet the General Manager, a retired Colonel:

'The retired Colonel immediately said, "Oh, it's you!" – not quite sure where he knew me from but it gets us off to a good start. I explained that the ZNSPCA would like to be able to continue monitoring the welfare of the livestock at Charleswood. He was very understanding and immediately instructed his Secretary to draft and type a letter giving me and my team authority to "treat affected animals at the Estate".'

As was so often the case, the courtesies extended in Harare and the assurances and guarantees that were given were utterly useless out on the farms. On her next visit to Charleswood just a week later, Meryl had a frightening encounter. Approaching the boom across the road at Charleswood, Meryl wasn't too worried when she saw armed soldiers – their presence had become familiar, almost normal.

Stopping her truck Meryl had been surprised when suddenly a young and angry-looking Corporal came over to her and demanded that Meryl move the vehicle to a spot barely a foot away. Meryl ignored him, thinking he was just grandstanding in front of the crowd, showing that he was in control. Meryl's lack of response infuriated the youngster. He shouted and ranted and waved his

AK-47 around and in the end Meryl had moved her truck to the designated spot and waited again for someone to give her permission to go and treat a few animals.

'Two more soldiers approached and I showed them the rtd Col.'s letter. They made me wait for someone they called "The Lieutenant". When the "Lieutenant" arrived I saw that he was holding a pistol which he pointed in our direction. [Later I learnt that this was a CZ pistol.] When I showed him the letter he became hostile and said the army DOES NOT take orders from the ZDI and that THEY were in charge. I could not believe it and was so angry that I just exploded and I told him that it was common knowledge that the animals on Charleswood were suffering, that we are appointed by Government to prevent suffering and that if the ZNSPCA is prevented from doing its job then we could proceed with prosecution.'

The soldier had met his match with Meryl and had no answer to the threat of prosecution or the fact that the local Animal Health Inspector agreed the cattle were dying from tick-borne diseases or worm infestations. Finally the soldier had backed off but the confrontations were not over for Meryl:

'He gave us a Sergeant to accompany us to the school where the only remaining phone on the farm was. As we drove towards the school a 4x4 came up the hill and stopped next to us. It was the Major who was in control of the army at Charleswood. He was polite and knew me and said that a certain Major at 3 Brigade in Harare should be phoned. I lent the Sergeant my cell phone and after a short conversation with "the Major" he passed the phone to me. The Major was very pleasant and told me that the army is only in control of "security" of Charleswood and that ZDI is managing the place and I must make myself known to a Mr Ayub whom ARDA had put in charge.'

Meryl had been shunted from pillar to post in a manner that was so typical of Zimbabwean bureaucracy. Everyone seemed to be the person in charge, or liked to think they were the person in charge but in reality were just little tin Gods. There was always someone else higher up who had the final say. Meryl went to what had been Roy Bennett's old office. It had been taken over and occupied by ARDA personnel and before she could even get in the door, Mr Ayub came storming out – he had obviously just had a phone call and was seething.

'Ayub came charging out, raving and ranting at me – he shouted that he didn't want to speak to me. He was very "suspicious" of me because he saw from my card that I lived in Ruwa and so – he said – does Roy Bennett (he doesn't), that the Lt. had told

him that I was threatening to "sue" Arda etc. Eventually I managed to persuade him that it would be better if we talked in "his office" instead of in front of a now-large crowd of army, Support Unit and Arda personnel.'

Having made himself feel more important by blasting Meryl in public, Ayub had begun to wind down and took Meryl into 'his' office. Meryl had realised that she was not going to be allowed to see the cattle – they were far away, Ayub said, and it would take several hours to round them up. Meryl knew that had been an excuse and that she was getting nowhere. It was already late in the afternoon and she offered to leave the 20 litres of de-wormer and 20 litres of dip with Ayub so that he and his staff could treat the cattle. That offer had finally heralded the point when Ayub obviously felt in control again:

'At last Ayub agreed to something. I asked him if we could treat "our calf" that had been speared and that we had been treating over the weeks. He sullenly agreed that we could. It was still in the garden of Roy's house. This little calf was an orphan, which is why it was being kept near the house so that it could be bottle-fed. Whenever I asked Sibanda if it was getting milk – he said not much, because the soldiers were drinking it all. I tackled the Lieutenant about it, but he assured me they were "giving it some". We walked in, accompanied by the Sgt. and Ayub – Support Unit appeared to have moved out of the premises but there were several soldiers around. Through the open kitchen door I could see silver wine goblets in use on the kitchen table. (I later confirmed with Roy that these were his.)

'The calf was a lot stronger than on our last visit but it was disappointing to find that the wounds on her back, both entry and exit, were infected and full of pus. Her movement was also very uncoordinated as if the spine was affected but we had come this far with her and we weren't going to give up now.'

After Meryl had given Ayub injectable long-acting antibiotics, Savlon, cotton wool and wound spray to continue treating the calf, he had softened even more and asked Meryl to go and look at some weaners in a nearby paddock. There were still a couple of Roy's workers left on Charleswood and Meryl had a rare chance to speak to them and find out how they were.

'At last we were on our own with Roy's workers and able to talk freely with them and find out what was going on. Sibanda came in the front of the truck with us and told us that many weaners were dying because of lack of grazing – most of the paddocks had been ploughed up by settlers and the army. Sibanda said the workers were uncertain whether to stay on or to leave for good. I assured him that Bennett was doing everything he possibly could to get back on the farm and that he had not forgotten them. We drove down to the stream where we found 191 weaners – many of them in a

very poor state, thin and emaciated. Apart from the green grass on the banks of the stream there was virtually no grazing for them.'

Meryl had left Charleswood more concerned than ever about the welfare of the animals stranded there, at the mercy of the 'officials', the army, the settlers and anyone else who wanted a piece of the once-superb coffee and beef farm. By then it was nearing the end of May and there was almost no grass left for the cattle to eat. The animals were getting thinner and weaker and were not being dipped or de-wormed at all. Meryl was at her wits end as to how best to help improve conditions for the animals, apart from de-stocking, which Roy was reluctant to do, but he was as helpless and desperate as she was about the welfare of his cattle. By that time the High Court had ruled six times in favour of Roy Bennett and had done so with consent (ie the Zimbabwe Government had approved of the verdict).

The rulings, however, meant nothing because no one in authority was prepared to enforce them and so nothing changed. Meryl had enquired at neighbouring farms to try and find some extra grazing for the cattle but there was none. A few days later the matter had quickly slipped out of Meryl's control completely when she was tipped off that ARDA were planning to move Roy Bennett's cattle off Charleswood Estate and onto one of their own properties – a large farm south of Harare. Meryl knew this would be simple and blatant stock theft: the cattle belonged to Roy Bennett and had his brand-mark on them but there was no one to stop ARDA. The very best Meryl could do was to ensure the welfare and safety of the animals as they were transported. It looked more and more unlikely that Roy Bennett would be able to return to Charleswood for some time. In an incident in Parliament Roy had pushed Justice Minister Chinamasa to the floor and was going to be penalised for his action.

By late June 2004, the cattle on Charleswood were very thin and many were too weak to be able to withstand a long truck journey. Experienced livestock carriers were reluctant to undertake the job – knowing that they would be moving stolen animals and could face charges of stock theft. In the end it was a small company from Marondera who took on the job but they were inexperienced in the transportation of cattle and had a mammoth task ahead. The journey was daunting as the road was very steep and had dozens of very dangerous bends making ordinary travel slow and painstaking but far worse for heavy trucks carrying live animals.

On 1 July Meryl had waited on Charleswood Estate for the trucks to arrive so that she could monitor the loading and ensure the cattle were treated as gently as possible. It had been far from satisfactory as she later recorded:

'I was disappointed to see how small the trucks were – it would take many, many trips to move over 300 head. Some of the settlers came to help load the cattle but were very rough in the handling – whacking them with sticks and there was lots of shouting. I stopped the whole proceeding and gave everyone a warning. The settlers soon lost interest and drifted off.

'The trucks were not in good mechanical condition, with bald tyres, and one driver seemed to have trouble with the gears. As we drove out of Chimanimani we saw a police road block. Even though I knew they would not be on our side, I decided to take a chance. A young Sergeant came to the window and I showed him my ID and then informed him that the cattle in the two trucks in front of us had been stolen and that they belonged to Mr Roy Bennett. (Stock theft is viewed very seriously and carries very stiff penalties.) The Sergeant just glared at me and shrugged his shoulders: of course he knew where the cattle had come from. Other policemen at the road block moved the cattle trucks on, came to us, ordered Sternford and I out of our truck and started to search it.'

Once past the road block Meryl had soon caught up with the two trucks and knew this was going to be a long and very slow journey:

'They were making heavy going of the very steep hills and the one truck kept coming to a complete stop on steep hills every time he wanted to change gear.'

Meryl had passed the trucks, detoured to Chipinge to collect an abandoned security dog and headed back to Harare for the night. She and Sternford were concerned that they did not meet the cattle truck on the way and guessed that the driver thought he would take a short cut. Inevitably it would have been on a dirt road and the driver would have made much slower progress than if he'd stuck to the main road.

'I hardly slept that night and first thing next morning Sternford and I headed for the ARDA farm. Finally at about midday we could see the trucks lurching down the dusty road. To our disappointment nothing was prepared for them – no water in the troughs or hay put out in the kraals. Sternford and I immediately put out hay and water for them. The cattle looked exhausted – they had been in the trucks for 18 hours. We stopped the cattle that were "down" when the trucks arrived, from being dragged off by the workers until they were up on their feet and feeling stronger.'

Over the next few weeks the decrepit haulage trucks ploughed backwards and forwards on the winding, mountainous roads, gradually removing all of Roy Bennett's herd from Chimanimani. Meryl managed to find the only balance between right and wrong that was possible in this situation and wrote about it in her diary:

> 'Whilst this was theft on a grand scale, ZNSPCA must only be involved with the welfare of the cattle. We continued to monitor the loading, the journey and the off-loading. Approximately 38 cattle were moved each time, divided between two trucks. In all, 190 head were moved and it took weeks with quite a few fatalities found on arrival. Their condition was certainly not good enough to be transported and once they arrived at the ARDA Farm they were all re-branded, with ARDA's brand being burnt on top of Roy's.'

In the dwindling days of her involvement with Charleswood, Meryl managed to remove some of Roy and Heather's horses – two Welsh pony stallions named 'Suspicious' and 'Mauritius' and later 'Jethro', 'Banquelet,' 'Rosie' and her foal and two other mares. On her last visit on 3 December 2004, Meryl finally expressed the feelings she had managed to control throughout this long and heart-breaking saga:

> 'On my last trip to Charleswood I felt a huge sense of sadness over all that had happened there. Bennett's workers had now all been forced off, the school that he had built for their children was empty and silent. The rows of coffee bushes were overgrown with weeds and grass. The rich green pastures had been ploughed up, the livestock was gone. Would this once vibrant, productive commercial farm ever be the same again?'

There were some happy endings to the story, at least for the ponies and for Bokkie. The two Welsh ponies who were mother and daughter were able to go together to a better place and a better life. The mare was called Rosie but no one seemed to know the name of the foal. Using a stand at a school fete to highlight the animal rescues and to raise money for Mark and Claire Evans' Horse Rescue Unit, Claire called for suggestions for a name for the foal. This was particularly appropriate because not only were Mark and Claire helping so many horses that had been stranded due to the farm seizures, but they had also been looking after Rosie and her foal since their rescue from Charleswood.

Under a beautiful blue Zimbabwean sky and as if nothing untoward was happening in the country, there was a huge turnout of people to the fete. Photos of many of the horses that had been rescued were on display and scores of names were suggested for Rosie's foal. 'Holly' was the favourite name and it wasn't long before Rosie and Holly went to a new home in Malawi where they are much loved and Rosie is often ridden by the children in the family.

Bokkie made a full recovery and was reunited with his devoted owner Moses and his family. They were not able to return to their home on Charleswood but were happy – and safe – in a house in the suburbs of Harare. Thanks to Meryl's nomination, Bokkie went on to win the American North Shore Animal League, Elisabeth Lewyt Award for bravery. The citation read:

'This award has been presented to Bokkie to honour his exceptional bravery and loyalty to his owner and his family and his courageous action that saved their lives.

Exceptional courage and bravery – these words were true of Bokkie, of the Bennett family and of all the men and women who worked for and with them. They were also true of Meryl Harrison who did not stop, until the very last day, to stand up for the welfare of the animals on Charleswood.

Extracts from Meryl's Diary:

*'Our lives begin to end the day we
become silent about things that matter.'*
– Dr Martin Luther King

December 2004
Mvurwi:
6 December. To Mvurwi in preparation for moving the leopard at Nyamaneche the next day – stayed with Phillipa & John Fletcher – lovely couple who I had not met before. Viv Wilson and his son Kevin joined us in the evening as they were going to do the darting the next day. Needless to say the evening was spent chatting about the demise of the country's wildlife.

7 December. 6am – darting of the leopard went well and Viv and Kevin were soon on their way back to Chipangali (in Bulawayo) with their precious cargo. The leopard was later collared and released into Hwange Nat Park. Later I drove back to Harare, collected Sternford and drove to Chinhoyi; on the way informed the settlers from Little England still camped at the side of the Kariba road that they would one day get their animals back.

Tengwe:
8 December. With Sternford to Tengwe and Meidon Farm – another meeting with the workers. Delivered dip that the farmer had given us for the cattle. Also went to Tengwe Estate to inform the resident war vet and settlers that we would be collecting the horses in the next week. Received the usual hostile reception. Went on

to Richard Farm in Tengwe – had received reports of horses running around there. Two had apparently already died. Saw a very good-looking bay stallion but couldn't get anywhere near him – had been left behind by the farmer when he was evicted.

Goromonzi:
9 December. Worked in Goromonzi in the morning, started to pack things up in my office. In the afternoon left for Bulawayo as the Chairman and Committee of Byo SPCA had invited me to their 50 years Celebrations. Unfortunately, on the way, just outside Kadoma, one of my front wheels came off and went spinning down the road. I managed to pull to the side of the road and stop. Had to stay the night in Kadoma which turned out to be great as I was able to stay with very good friends and attend the town's excellent pantomime.

Whilst in Bulawayo, to my surprise I was given a beautiful crystal horse together with a very supportive letter from one of the ZNSPCA Board members:

'Dear Meryl, You once told me that you may not always be there for people but that you would always be there for the animals. You are one of those rare people that live up to their beliefs and carry them out. You have given your all for the animals of Zimbabwe and for that I thank you most sincerely and with deep appreciation. You have fought long and hard, never losing sight of your overwhelming desire to protect animals. I will miss your strength and courage, The animals of Zimbabwe if they had a voice, would thank you for always being there for us. I wish you the best for your future – please don't lose contact.'

Harare:
14 December. Had a meeting with old friend Bornwell Chakaodza, Editor of The Standard *newspaper, as he wanted his reporters to do a piece on ZNSPCA looking after the animals belonging to the settlers still camped at the side of the Kariba road – many of them of course ex-farm workers.*

Christon Bank:
18 Sunday December. Had been invited by friends who lived at Christon Bank to a lunch party, but the previous evening there had been problems with the surrounding farm settlers so lunch party cancelled – but I drove out there and brought some of their furniture into town for safekeeping.

Harare:
20 December. Morning in the office in and afternoon went with Sternford to check on the Municipal security dogs at the Warren Park Headquarters.

Harare:
Went to see Stuart Hargreaves to say goodbye and ask if he would write a reference

as we've worked together over many years. I still don't have any idea what I'm going to do after I leave the ZNSPCA but think it wise to be prepared. I realise that as there is no other animal welfare organisation in Zimbabwe apart from the SPCA, it is highly unlikely that I will be able to continue living and working in Zimbabwe. Animal welfare had become my life, but there seems little hope of me being able to afford to stay on.

The Chairman of ZNSPCA told a concerned member of the public that there is nothing to stop me from starting up my own SPCA centre, but that I would have to do all the fund-raising for it myself. Two members of the Harare SPCA Council approached me, asking me to return to run Harare SPCA again – but I declined. With a very heavy heart – I have made the decision to return to the UK.

Meryl later received a highly complimentary reference from the man who was a household name in the country and who held the most senior position of Principal Director of Livestock and Veterinary Services in Zimbabwe's Ministry of Agriculture. Dr Stuart Hargreaves had known Meryl for over 20 years and described her as 'fearless and resolute'. He said that regardless of the circumstances Meryl 'always put the welfare of the animals first and in so doing put her own life at risk'. Hargreaves said that Meryl had been the driving force behind animal welfare in Zimbabwe and the leading figure in the ZNSPCA. In his reference, Dr Stuart Hargreaves wrote:

'Meryl has worked in often very difficult environments but has remained steadfast to her high principles which have protected the wellbeing of animals. She has interacted with all levels of society, and has attained a high level of respect from veterinarians, farmers and members of the public. Meryl is honest and hardworking and her departure from Zimbabwe will be an enormous loss to our country as a whole, but in particular to the animals she worked so hard to protect.'

21 December. Unity Day – Public Holiday. Tim arrived from Bulawayo on the Blue Arrow bus – so great to see him and have his company.

Norton:
23 December. Routine check on animals at the Lion and Cheetah Park. Delighted to see that one of the female baboons that we had moved from UZ [University of Zimbabwe] had had a baby and was being extremely maternal towards it.

Goromonzi:
24 December. Christmas Eve – Dealt with chicken vendors on the side of the Mutare road – visited the abattoir in Bromley and went back to check our cat traps at the farm in Goromonzi.

25 December. Christmas Day. Tim and I spent the day with very good friends – had a lovely day.

Enterprise:
28 December. Tim back to Bulawayo on the coach then I went out to Enterprise where I'd been invited to a meeting by the CEO of one of the largest security outfits in the country. We had been carrying out routine checks on the many dogs there for some months and had implemented several changes to improve the welfare of their security dogs. He had heard that I was leaving, and was concerned about continuing liaison with ZNSPCA.

Goromonzi:
29 December. Spend most of the day sorting out paperwork. I have no idea who is going to take over from me and so a proper handover is not going to be possible. Wanted to try and make sure that they found everything filed in the right place and under the right headings.

Darwendale:
30 December. To Maryland Farm in Darwendale to check on cattle. The owner had been evicted and was now living in Harare but staff had told him that his workers were being prevented from dipping the cattle. Vital that cattle be dipped regularly because at this time of the year the risk of tick-borne diseases is very great. Things there appeared to have returned to normal. Also checked on the sheep, they were out grazing again, having earlier been confined to the garden of an old house on the property for many days – they had eaten the place bare.

31 December 2004
My last day with ZNSPCA and my last day working officially with animals in Zimbabwe. The day began with a member of the Executive phoning my friend Pippa to find out where the truck was. Pippa pointed out that my tenure with ZNSPCA did not actually finish until the end of that day. I had already been asked to return my badges and uniforms.

I drove out to the Goromonzi office for the last time, packed up all my personal belongings: the animal ornaments and pictures that had always moved with me from office to office over the years. I gave goodbye hugs to all the much-loved dogs that we had at the office – little 'Duiker' that I had rescued as a puppy from a beer hall at Marirangwe – full of mange and putzie maggots, now a beautiful whippet-like dog. 'Bully', a delightful Rottie X bitch that we had rescued from a farm in Rusape – she had been left behind by a farmer together with his two Staffies. Neighbours informed me that she was very aggressive with people and should be destroyed. I decided to give her a chance and found that she did not have a nasty bone in her body and was the most gentle of dogs.

Later I carried out a stock-take, with Justine and Sternford, of all the drugs and equipment that I had, and then we took the drug cupboard together with all the drugs to hand them over to Kamfinsa vets – they too made a copy of the list and it was all double-checked again.

I drove to meet Pippa who was to hand over the truck for me – it was 4pm on 31 December 2004. The children from the farm village near our headquarters heard the vehicle and ran to the edge of the road to wave to me as I went past – it was a familiar ritual that broke their routine and ended my day. I saw their bare feet and mud-stained clothes and their innocent little smiling faces. Their shrill, giggling voices called out the usual, 'How are you! How are you!' but I just couldn't wave back or answer. That picture and those sounds would remain frozen in my mind. I drove down the bumpy drive with its familiar potholes – my eyes were blinded with tears, I felt as if someone was tearing my heart out – taking away my very reason to exist.

Afterword

'Exile is a country of shifting borders, hard to quit, yet hard to endure,
no matter your wide shoulders, no matter your toughened heart.'
– Leif Enger, 2001

August 2007

Three years after Meryl had left her position as Chief Inspector of the Zimbabwe National SPCA, she was living in a small bed-sit in Norfolk, England, her rent paid for by the local Council. Her quiet flat, at the end of the corridor on the first floor and with neither garden nor pets, was a far cry from the hot and dusty farms of Zimbabwe and the life and friends she had left behind. Meryl had arrived in England virtually destitute and with just two suitcases. The Zimbabwe Farmers Trust and its Chairman, George Campbell-Johnston, came to her aid almost immediately, helping Meryl with the basics that she needed to start again. The Zimbabwe Farmers Trust, established specifically to help dispossessed farmers and their families, knew Meryl hadn't been a farmer but here was a way to acknowledge and assist the woman who had done so much to help the animals on Zimbabwe's farms.

Contrary to the rumours, gossip and speculation, Meryl had not resigned from her position at the ZNSPCA and left the country because of her health, her age or from the stress of farm rescues. She had left because of her principles. John Worsley Worswick (Chairman of JAG) wrote a tribute to the woman he'd worked closely with and who had been such a beacon of light in Zimbabwe's years of darkness and turmoil:

> *'To say that Meryl and her team of dedicated rescue staff were at the forefront of the battle ground protecting "Animal Welfare" is an understatement. Meryl's professionalism, bravery, dedicated commitment and leadership qualities, which extended way beyond the call of duty, were and still are a role model to us all. This was amply displayed by the high success rate of her rescue teams, to the extent that she garnered respect and even co-operation, at times, from the perpetrators on the ground.*

'Meryl's own "eviction" from the Society as a direct result of her professionalism and unimpeachable integrity in taking a principled stand, again for "Animal Welfare", was a shattering blow to the farming community. She was, without doubt, the lynch pin in the "Farm Rescue" initiative, which all-but collapsed with her early and unwarranted retirement.

'The Farming Community owe Meryl and her teams a huge debt of gratitude that will probably never be repaid, but forgotten she is certainly not.'

Adjusting to living outside Africa, away from her beloved Zimbabwe and without the animals that were her life, was excruciating for Meryl and so she turned her attention, for the first time, onto her past and began investigating who she really was. Having spent all her life believing her mother had died in childbirth, Meryl was shocked to discover that her biological mother, Gwendoline Bates, had not died giving birth to twins in 1939 but had lived until 1996. Meryl discovered that she and her twin brother Colin were illegitimate and that their real names were Avril and Douglas Bates.

Even more dramatic was the revelation that Meryl's biological father, Laurence Stagg, had not in fact been killed in the war (as the twins had been told), but was married and his wife was having a baby in the same Kensington hospital at the same time as Gwendoline Bates was giving birth to her twins. Meryl did not find out anything else about Laurence Stagg but in 2006, for the first time in her life, she had a real birth certificate just like everyone else. She later came to realise that she would never know any more about her father aside from his name. When she met the first relation she found out that she had, Meryl was told that when her mother died, a black-and-white photograph of twin babies had been found in her wallet.

At the time of writing, and because she has neither pension nor savings, Meryl is surviving on State Benefits and working on a voluntary basis for a local animal charity, Feline Care, in Norfolk, where she runs their charity shop. She is also a volunteer for The Cinnamon Trust whose mission statement reads: 'Peace of mind and practical help for people – love, care and safety for their pets.' It is a fitting description of the very ideals Meryl has strived most of her life to achieve.

Whenever she can, Meryl walks dogs for their owners who are too elderly or too ill to able to do it themselves and this is her only hands-on contact with animals. Her anguish at not being directly involved with animal welfare and not being able to 'make a difference' is raw and palpable. Meryl's 10 years of service, first with the SPCA and then the ZNSPCA , the last five of which had been spent in situations of grave danger rescuing animals from invaded farms, seem like a dream to her now, almost as if they never happened. Because Meryl had stood up for her principles, and for the welfare of the animals, she did not leave the ZNSPCA with happy memories but felt as if she had failed.

Meryl was wrong. What she did, with Addmore and a handful of Inspectors from April 2000 to December 2004 was a huge success. It was very real and enormously appreciated – by farmers whose livestock was stranded; by children whose pets were abandoned and terrified; by victims of political violence whose animals were stuck in the middle; by men and women who had been rendered helpless and impotent by ugly politics. At the end of five years there had been only three farms where Meryl and her team had been unable to rescue the animals – despite repeated attempts.

Meryl's work for Zimbabwe's animals, before and during the farm rescues, were an example to all and a great legacy for a country in such disarray in 2007. Wildlife Vet Chris Foggin undoubtedly speaks for most Zimbabweans when he says:

'Whenever I think of Meryl, who I sincerely hope to see permanently back in Zimbabwe one day, three words come to mind – courage, commitment and care. Her work in trying to do the very best for the neglected and abused domestic and wild animals of Zimbabwe, at such a difficult time in our history, will never cease to draw my deepest admiration and respect. I miss her presence now because she is still so needed in this country.'

At the end of five years it was impossible to know exactly how many animals Meryl and her small team had rescued. Certainly the numbers were in multiple thousands but Meryl had never kept count. Meryl hadn't done it for statistics or for fame or fortune. She had done it for a lick, a wag, a contented purr. She had done it for Nandi, a lost and tortured dog, for Tigga, a cat in the rafters, for a little piglet abandoned in the mud and for all the animals: the innocent victims.

Catherine Buckle
Zimbabwe
October 2008

Bibliography

Newspapers and Websites

Blue Cross, website www.bluecross.co.zw

Canada Free Press, website 2003 www.canadafreepress.com/2003 quoting: *The Herald,* 9 January 2003

C.F.U. website www.cfu.co.zw/TertiaGeldenhuys

Daily Mail, UK. October 2002.

Daily Mirror, Harare, Zimbabwe. 7 May 2003.

Daily News, Harare, Zimbabwe. 9 July 2001; 13 September 2001; 9 January 2002; 19 March 2002; 13 January 2003; 24 February 2003.

The Daily Telegraph, UK. 19 August 2002.

Dog World, 'Breed notes', UK. 9 March 2007.

The Financial Gazette, Harare, Zimbabwe. 15 August 2002; 22 August 2002.

The Financial Times, UK. 2 August 2003.

The Guardian, UK. 8 August 2002; 10 August 2002.

The Herald, Harare, Zimbabwe. 10 April 2003.

The Independent, UK. 9 January 2002.

The Mail & Guardian, South Africa. 12 August 2002.

The Sunday Mail, Harare, Zimbabwe. 14 August 1988.

New Zimbabwe website quoting Foster Niumata writing in *Rugby Times*, USA. www.newzimbabwe.com

News 24 (South Africa) website. www.news24.com. 1 April 2002; 18 March 2002; 21 April 2002.

The Star, South Africa, 27 March 2002; 16 August 2002.

The Sunday Independent, South Africa. 29 June 2003.

The Sunday Telegraph, UK. 12 May 2007.

Sunday Times, UK. 28 April 2002.

The Times, UK. 13 August 2002.

Zimbabwe Independent, Harare, Zimbabwe. 9 November 2001.

ZWNEWS (website) www.zwnews.com 4 February 2002; 8 August 2002; 9 August 2002; 10 August 2002; 12 August 2002; 13 August 2002; 15 August 2002; 16 August 2002; 20 August 2002; 30 September 2002; 29 May 2003.

Books, articles, reports and magazines

All About Dogs (magazine), Cherry Grobler, Publisher. South Africa. July/Aug 2003; Sept/Oct 2003.

C.F.U. (Zimbabwe) 2002. 'Situation reports', Jenni Williams, 13 April 2002; 21 April 2002; 5 May 2002; 7 May 2002; 29 May 2003

Cherer Smith, R, *Avondale to Zimbabwe*, Mardon Printers, Salisbury, Rhodesia. (no publication date)

Crawford, Juanita, *Stafford World,* South Africa. Juanita Crawford (publisher), 2002.

The Farmer (magazine), Harare, Zimbabwe. July 17 2001; August 7 2001; August 28 2001; 26 March 2002.

House, J & M; Salt, B, (Comp). *Zimbabwe – a handbook*, Mercury Press, Harare, Zimbabwe, 1983.

Maclean, G.L. *Roberts Birds of Southern Africa*, South Africa, John Voelcker Bird Book Fund, 1985.

Matyszak, Derek, *Political Persecution in Zimbabwe. The Case of Roy Bennett.* Lecturer in Procedural Law, University of Zimbabwe, 2004.

Meadows, Keith, *Rupert Fothergill. Bridging a Conservation Era,* Bulawayo, Zimbabwe, Thorntree Press, 1996.

N.A.D.A. – The Southern Rhodesia Native Affairs Department Annual. 1925. Books of Rhodesia, Bulawayo, 1972.

Sayce, Katherine (Ed.), *Tabex: Encyclopedia Zimbabwe*. Quest Publishing, Harare, Zimbabwe, 1987.

Shearer, Elizabeth (Ed.), *A Harvest of Memories. The Story of the Bromley,*

Goromonzi, Melfort and Ruwa Districts. The History Book Association in association with Munn Publishing, Harare, Zimbabwe, 1987.

Sinclair, I and Hockey, P. *Larger Illustrated Guide to Birds of Southern Africa.* Struik, South Africa, 1997.

Smithers, R.H.N. *The Mammals of the Southern African Subregion.* University of Pretoria, South Africa, 1983.

The Spectator (magazine), U.K. April 2002.

Stuart, Chris and Tilde. *Field Guide to the Mammals of Southern Africa.* Struik, Cape Town, South Africa, 1988.

Donations

If any reader has been moved by the plight of the animals caught up in the land redistribution programme and wishes to make a donation, please contact Meryl Harrison on ndirande@btinternet.com and she will provide up-to-date details of her recommended Zimbabwean animal welfare charities.

Also published by Merlin Unwin Books
www.merlinunwin.co.uk

And Miles to Go Before I Sleep
A BRITISH VET IN AFRICA
Hugh Cran

'In early December 1966, while Britain lay blanketed in snow and darkness, I boarded an East African Airways jet and was flown, in moderate discomfort, from London to Nairobi.

I had never flown before and perhaps it was fortunate that I hadn't, as the novelty of the experience had the concentrating effect of preventing me from brooding on whether I was really doing the right thing. Most people back in Scotland thought I was mad to be going off to the land of the Mau Mau, to a country hissing with man-eating lions, gin-swilling colonials and machete-swinging natives, abandoning a solid, safe career in solid, safe Scotland.

I told people that I was only going for a trial period, perhaps a year at most, just to test the waters. They laughed. They were right to laugh. I remain a vet in Kenya over 40 years later, and I love every minute of it.'

This is a page-turning account of working as a vet at the sharp end.

With razor sharp observation and incisive wit Hugh Cran effectively dispels the myth that life in the tropics, for this white man at least, is all beer and skittles. As he grapples with the realities of post-colonial Kenya, life isn't easy. But he perseveres and after a few inconveniences such as a fractured leg, malaria and the mysterious disappearance of his employer, he is soon travelling far and wide on diabolical roads dealing with everything from cattle and thoroughbred racehorses to zebra, lightning strikes and snake bites, never knowing what to expect next.

But the colourful people who frequent Hugh's Nakuru practice, the sheer vitality of the Kenyan scene and the rewarding nature of the grinding task in hand, keep him answering that persistent phone, day and night, and heading off into the unknown.

£8.99 paperback